Sales Force Design for Strategic Advantage

Sales Force Design for Strategic Advantage

Andris A. Zoltners

Prabhakant Sinha

and Sally E. Lorimer

palgrave macmillan

First published 2004 by
PALGRAVE MACMILLAN
Houndmills, Basingstoke, Hampshire RG21 6XS and
175 Fifth Avenue, New York, N.Y. 10010
Companies and representatives throughout the world

PALGRAVE MACMILLAN is the global academic imprint of the Palgrave Macmillan division of St. Martin's Press, LLC and of Palgrave Macmillan Ltd. Macmillan® is a registered trademark in the United States, United Kingdom and other countries. Palgrave is a registered trademark in the European Union and other countries.

ISBN 1–4039–0305–0

This book is printed on paper suitable for recycling and made from fully managed and sustained forest sources.

A catalogue record for this book is available from the British Library.

A catalog record for this book is available from the Library of Congress.

10 9 8 7 6 5 4 3 2 1
13 12 11 10 09 08 07 06 05 04

Printed and bound in Great Britain by
Creative Print & Design (Wales), Ebbw Vale

To Aurelia and Pat for their support and friendship — AZ

To Anita, Pria, and Meera for our journeys of discovery — PS

To Al, Jamie, and Jack for their love and support — SL

CONTENTS

Figures

TABLES

Sales Force Design for Strategic Advantage focuses on strategic aspects of sales force management. Until now, business executives and managers facing sales force design challenges have had few good options when seeking a reference book. Sales force management books tend to be broad and general, or they focus on topics such as sales force compensation and training. In fact, we could not find a book (before this one) that focused specifically on sales force design. All general sales management textbooks have chapters that address sales force design issues, but they tend to cover the issue superficially and lack practical insights. Alternatively, several consultants have written books on marketing and channel strategies which include sales forces, but while interesting and useful, these books lack the depth of experience, theory, insight, and detail that a sales executive facing a significant sales force design challenge requires.

Three years ago, we wrote *The Complete Guide to Accelerating Sales Force Performance*, a comprehensive sourcebook for sales executives, managers, businesspeople, and students of sales management. Our purpose was to provide a reference of innovative, yet practical ideas for improving sales force productivity in all areas of sales management, including sales force assessment, sizing, structuring, territory design, recruiting, training, first-line management, motivation, compensation, goal setting, precision selling, customer relationship management, performance management, and culture. This book, *Sales Force Design for Strategic Advantage,* explores in greater detail a subset of these topics. Specifically, the issues of sales strategy, go-to-market strategy, sales force structure and roles, sales force size, sales territory alignment, and sales force assessment and implementation are explored in detail, using logical frameworks, practical approaches, and numerous real world best practice examples.

Sales Force Design for Strategic Advantage is a sourcebook for every sales executive or manager with responsibility for strategic sales force planning and management. It can help you define the best role for the sales force in today's rapidly evolving business environment. It can help you successfully face significant sales force design challenges such as sales force creation, expansion, downsizing, mergers, and restructures. It can help you assess your current sales force design, and establish systems and processes that ensure that all the pieces of that design stay aligned as your customers, competitors, environment, and company strategies and goals evolve.

HOW THE BOOK IS ORGANIZED

Sales Force Design for Strategic Advantage is organized around three major themes. The first theme deals with the role of the sales force in today's changing world. This is the focus of the first chapter of the book. The second theme is the heart of the book: how to design a sales force for strategic advantage. Chapters 2 through 8 provide practical frameworks and analytical tools, along with numerous examples of approaches that firms can use to create world-class sales force designs. The final theme of the book deals with how to maintain sales force performance and implement change effectively. This is the focus of the final two chapters. A summary of each chapter is provided below.

Chapter 1 – Designing and Redesigning the Sales Force in Today's Changing World

This chapter provides a perspective on the importance of sales force design in the modern business environment. Sales forces find themselves needing to re-evaluate their size and structure more frequently than ever before as companies face external challenges such as industry consolidation, rapid technological innovation and aggressive competition, and internal challenges such as prolific new product development and intense pressure from shareholders to improve financial results.

Chapter 2 – A Process for Designing the Sales Force for Strategic Advantage

This chapter provides an overview of a structured process that companies can use to ensure good sales force design. The process starts with the development of a sales strategy and a go-to-market strategy that defines the role that the sales force will play in connecting with customers. Once this role is defined, decisions about sales force size, structure, and territory alignment can be made. Chapters 3 through 8 explore each of these major decisions in greater detail.

Chapter 3 – Sales Strategy

Sales strategy defines who a firm sells to, what the customer offering is, and how the selling is done. This chapter describes how a firm can develop a successful sales strategy for delivering the right products and services to the right customers through efficient, yet effective sales processes. The chapter explores issues such as effective market segmentation, creating customer value through the product-service offering, and innovative sales process design. Good sales strategy is a critical first step for developing the best go-to-market and sales force design strategies.

Chapter 4 – Go-To-Market Strategy

This chapter provides a framework for determining which marketing channels can execute the firm's sales strategy most efficiently and effectively. The best go-to-market strategies often include a mix of channels, from both inside and outside the company. Direct sales forces, business partners, the Internet, call centers, direct marketing, and other channel options can all play an important role in connecting a company with its customers and prospects.

Chapter 5 – Designing the Sales Force Structure

Sales force structure answers two central questions: how to divide up all the sales activities among different types of salespeople, and how to coordinate and control their activities to meet the firm's goals. This chapter presents an innovative, new framework for determining the best way to structure the direct sales effort. A properly structured sales force allows the appropriate selling process to be implemented for every targeted market segment. It ensures that the selling and maintenance effort is effective while utilizing selling resources efficiently. It directs selling effort to the right products, markets, and selling activities.

Chapter 6 – Sales Roles

This chapter describes the many different sales roles that exist today. Roles such as product specialist, technical specialist, strategic account manager, telechannel salesperson, and sales assistant allow companies to meet the diverse and complex needs of their customers, and at the same time, can help to reduce selling costs. The chapter also explores the role of sales managers in today's selling environment.

Chapter 7 – Sizing the Selling Organization

This chapter shows how to determine the right size for a sales force. A properly sized selling organization assures that customers and prospects receive appropriate coverage, company products get proper representation, the sales force is stretched but not overworked, and the company makes an appropriate investment in its sales resource. The chapter outlines several market-based sales force sizing approaches and suggests specific tests that companies can use to validate the sizing decision from the perspective of key stakeholders.

Chapter 8 – Sales Territory Alignment

This chapter discusses sales territory alignment, or the assignment of customers to salespeople. Good sales territory alignment is important, as it enhances customer coverage, increases sales, fosters fair performance evaluation and reward systems, and lowers travel costs.

Chapter 9 – Sustaining the Successful Selling Organization

Best-in-class companies continuously seek ways to improve their selling organizations. This chapter presents a sales force productivity framework that companies can use to identify and address ongoing sales force issues, concerns, challenges, and opportunities. Successful companies develop systems and processes to help ensure that all aspects of the sales system are aligned and stay aligned as their markets and product-lines evolve.

Chapter 10 – Managing Change

Successful implementation of a major sales force design change is often challenging. This chapter describes a framework for understanding sales force change, and provides insight on how to successfully implement change in response to major events, such as sales force creation, expansion, downsizing, mergers, and corporate restructuring.

ACKNOWLEDGMENTS

As academic researchers and consultants, we have worked personally with executives, sales managers, and salespeople at hundreds of companies all over the world. Our thanks go to all the people at these fine companies who have helped us to discover and develop the material presented in this book. Because of confidentiality, many of the people and companies must remain nameless, but we owe a great deal of gratitude to all the clients who have worked with us to improve the productivity of their sales forces.

We would like to thank Northwestern University's Kellogg Graduate School of Management for providing a fertile environment for ideas to flourish. Thanks go to our many MBA students, whose lively classroom discussions have contributed tremendously to the material in the book. We also owe our gratitude to thousands of executive and mid-level managers who have participated in the Executive Education Program at Kellogg. Our classroom interactions with these individuals have been invaluable for transforming our theories and frameworks into practical sales force management tools. Thank you to our two research assistants, Agustina Fernandez Moya and Tulika Khunnah, whose work uncovered many of the examples used throughout the book. We are grateful to all our colleagues at Northwestern and elsewhere who have supported us academically and as friends.

We would also like to thank the people of ZS Associates, the consulting firm that we founded in 1983. ZS Associates today has grown to more than 550 employees with offices in seven countries. ZS employs some of the finest consultants and businesspeople in the world, and those people have contributed to the book immensely through their creativity as well as through their evaluation of our concepts. Special contributions came from Özden Gür Ali, Jaideep Bajaj, John Bienko, Matt Brukwicki, Jeff Foland, April Huang, Mathew Isaac, Tobi Laczkowski, Amy Marta, Pete Masloski, Kathryn McKay, Eduardo Meynet, Kanishka Misra, Mike Moorman, Chris Morgan, Marissa Paine, Arshad Rahman, Steve Redden, Samantha Rittenhouse, Tony Russo, Brad Scheidhauer, Brad Seitz, Brian Silverstein, Nancy Smith, Marshall Solem, Craig Stinebaugh, Joe Terino, Kelly Tousi, Frank Walters, and Chris Wright.

We owe very special thanks to two research and editorial assistants at ZS Associates, Mary Henske and Linda Kluver. Mary Henske carefully reviewed every chapter for clarity and content, suggesting revisions based on her extensive sales force knowledge and expertise. She also researched and organized many of the examples that support the book's ideas and theories. Linda Kluver developed many of the book's illustrations. She applied her careful attention to detail by reviewing every figure for consistency and suggesting changes. Both of these individuals improved the quality of the book substantially. Thank you also to Greg Zoltners, a co-author of our earlier book. His extensive sales force research and content development for our previous book provided a strong foundation upon which to build the ideas for this book. Without the help of these fine collaborators, this book would not be in your hands today.

CHAPTER 1

Designing and Redesigning the Sales Force in Today's Changing World

THE ROLE OF THE SALES FORCE

The success of any company depends on its ability to acquire and retain customers. Sales forces are particularly good at helping a company accomplish this in many ways. For example, salespeople sell complex products and solutions into large key accounts with a high degree of control over the sales process. Salespeople provide two-way communication and social interaction with customers; they listen, assess needs, provide solutions, reduce complexity, handle objections, create value, and provide long-term continuing service. Salespeople are flexible; they can customize the product offering and message to a specific customer's needs and buying process, they can smooth out rocky relationships, work cooperatively with other selling partners, and engender customer loyalty. Because of their close, personal relationship with customers, salespeople are an important information gathering resource for the firm.

In 2003, there were over 15 million full-time salespeople in the United States. Field and retail salespeople together represent about 11 percent of the entire full-time work force with their wages and benefits costing the economy over a trillion dollars per year. Table 1.1 shows the size of the largest sales forces in selected industries in 2003. The high impact of a selling organization also comes with a high cost. While companies in some industries spend as little as 1 percent of sales on their sales force, the average company spends 10 percent and some industries spend as much as 22 percent, as shown in Table 1.2. We have seen sustained sales force costs in some companies that are as high as 50 percent of sales.

The sales force is typically the most empowered organization in a company. Usually working alone and unsupervised, salespeople are entrusted with a company's most important asset – its customers. The most important connection the customer has with a company could be the salesperson; for many customers, the salesperson *is* the company.

TABLE 1.1 Total salespeople for the 10 largest US sales forces in selected industries

Industry	Approximate number of salespeople for the 10 largest US sales forces in this industry
Computer and office equipment	102,300
Consumables (food, drink, and tobacco)	82,500
Medical products (pharmaceuticals)	64,900
Insurance	606,400
Communications	66,100
Financial	311,200
Direct to consumer (such as Avon and Amway)	12,400,000

Source: "America's 500 Largest Sales Forces," *Selling Power*, October 2003, pp. 59 and 76

TABLE 1.2 Cost of the sales force in selected industries

Industry	Sales force cost as a percent of total sales*
Banking	0.9
Business services	10.5
Chemicals	3.4
Communications	9.9
Construction	7.1
Educational services	12.7
Electronics	12.6
Electronic components	4.9
Fabricated metals	7.2
Food products	2.7
Health services	13.4
Hotels and other lodging	1.9
Instruments	14.8
Machinery	11.3
Manufacturing	6.6
Office equipment	2.4
Paper and allied products	8.2
Pharmaceuticals	5.6
Printing and publishing	22.2
Real estate	2.8
Retail	15.3
Rubber and plastics	3.6
Transportation equipment	6.2
Wholesale consumer goods	11.2
Overall	**10.0**

* Includes cost of sales compensation, benefits, and field expenses. Does not include cost of sales management or overhead.

Source: reprinted with permission from *Dartnell's 30th Sales Force Compensation Survey: 1998–1999*, copyright 1999 by Dartnell Corporation. All rights reserved. http://www.dartnellcorp.com

Companies take a keen interest in the sales force because of its direct link to sales, its high cost, and therefore its impact on company profitability. The sales force is a major expense. At the same time, the sales force generates revenues; salespeople are the dollar producers. A larger sales force creates more sales than a smaller sales force. A motivated sales force creates more sales than an unmotivated one. A well-trained, well-coached sales force creates more sales than its undisciplined counterpart.

A sales force is a powerful *force*. There is not a sales force anywhere that could not seriously hurt its company's performance. Likewise, there is not a sales force anywhere that could not significantly improve its company's position.

This selling force is truly a powerful asset for successful companies. But the source of its very power is also the reason it is difficult to control, direct, and manage. The sales force consists of people, each with their own capabilities, motivators, and values. People bring creativity, flexibility, and the ability to listen to a customer interaction. They also bring egos and the need for security and meaning. Unlike advertising, they cannot be turned on and off, and unlike a web site, they cannot be expanded and upgraded overnight.

The field sales force is not alone in helping companies find, acquire, and keep customers. A telesales person may be better and cheaper at handling repeat orders, the Internet may be better at letting customers search for the right component or configure a product, and advertising may be better at creating awareness. A salesperson may need help from a product specialist to design a customer application, a finance person to configure a complex financial arrangement, or a customer support person to set up and manage a product demonstration.

The best sales forces are dynamic. Companies change their selling organizations as products and markets evolve. New selling roles are defined. Old selling functions are scrapped. To enter a new market and enhance customer coverage, a sales force is expanded. To reduce costs, some roles are moved from field sales to telesales. To deal effectively with increasing product and customer complexity, sales forces are specialized. To reduce costs in a shrinking market, sales forces are contracted or merged.

This chapter presents a framework for understanding the forces that drive sales force change. Numerous examples of the various external and internal change pressures that sales forces face are provided. The chapter concludes with a case study of sales force redesigns at Xerox.

THE FORCES THAT DRIVE SALES FORCE CHANGE

Constant change is both a threat and an opportunity for sales forces. Selling processes become dated as customers evolve their buying approaches, competitors become more aggressive, new technologies appear, and salespeople's skills and knowledge plateau. On the other hand, new customers emerge, new helpful technologies appear, competitors go out of business, or there is innovation in the sales process and channel itself.

Most sales forces are used to change and are routinely faced with new products, new tools, and internal reorganizations. In recent times, however, the pace of change has increased. New technologies are emerging with increased speed, impacting both the innovation in products and services, and the sales process itself. Cell phones connect salespeople with their customers the moment they step off a plane or get into their cars. The Internet makes information available more quickly, universally, and cheaply than before, and creates an instant connection between businesses and their customers and partners all over the world. Transactions can take place seamlessly between customers and sellers without requiring face-to-face intervention, bridging gaps in distance and shrinking cycle times for numerous tasks.

Change affects the sales force at Medtronic MiniMed

Medtronic MiniMed makes insulin pumps that help diabetic patients maintain insulin levels. These insulin pumps, which are about the size of a beeper, deliver fast-acting insulin continuously to the body through a small tube that is inserted just under the skin. The pump has many advantages over traditional insulin injections. It helps diabetic patients gain better, more consistent control of their blood glucose level. It eliminates the need for injections and rigid meal scheduling, and allows patients to lead a more normal life.

MiniMed's sales had been growing at over 45 percent per year for five years. Then a pharmaceutical company launched a new, long-acting insulin product, and MiniMed's growth rate slowed dramatically. In addition, the launch of new insulin pumps from well-funded competitors was expected in approximately two years. MiniMed was challenged to develop new sales and marketing strategies that would effectively convince physicians and diabetic patients that their product continued to be the best solution for maintaining diabetic insulin levels.

But what should those strategies be? Did the company just need to change its selling message? Was a larger sales force needed to combat the competitive noise level in the marketplace? Was the sales force structured in the best way to ensure continued growth? Was additional sales force training needed to ensure salespeople could sell effectively? Could sales force efficiency be improved by having inside sales and customer support take over the paperwork required to prove medical necessity and secure insurance coverage for patients? Finding the right answers to these important questions would require significant time, analysis, and resources. It was clear, however, that the selling strategies that had driven MiniMed's phenomenal growth in the past could no longer assure the company's success in the future.

The pace of change is also accelerated by the rapid diffusion of the latest business techniques, research, and processes, coupled with a company's inherent desire to be successful. Universities are graduating hundreds of thousands of business majors every year. Executive courses are being offered everywhere. Business books are bestsellers. Successful strategies and tactics from within the firm and outside diffuse through organizations at a rapid pace. Well-educated, experienced, and ambitious people run companies with a strong desire to be "the best." Being "the best" requires rapid adaptation to changing business conditions. Companies are quicker to redesign their selling organizations than at any time before.

Figure 1.1 and Table 1.3 present a framework for understanding the forces that challenge selling organizations in a continually changing world.

These forces fall into two major categories: external and internal. External forces include the environment, the customer, and the competitors. For example, increased competition in MiniMed's market is an external force requiring the sales force to respond or perish at the hands of a more nimble competitor. Internal forces originate within the company itself, and can be traced to a change in strategy or a quest for enhanced performance.

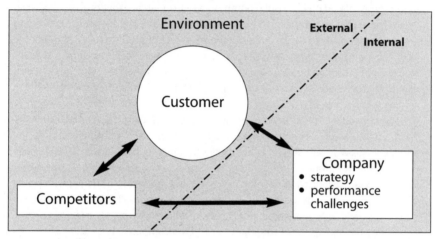

FIGURE 1.1 A framework for understanding the forces that drive sales force change

External forces can originate with customers, competitors, or the environment. Examples of external change forces include:

- Customers are consolidating and the current selling model is no longer effective.
- Competitors have increased their sales force investment and are attacking the firm's most profitable market segments.
- Global competitors with low manufacturing costs are attacking markets with severe price competition.
- New regulations on telesales have put severe limits on a firm's process for lead generation.

TABLE 1.3a External forces that drive sales force change

Customers	Competitors	Environment
• Globally coordinated purchasing	• Product innovation	• Economic changes
• Seeking lowest cost of supplier's product in use	• Channel innovation	• Deregulation
• Emergence of new industries	• Aggressive investment	• Communication technology
• Customer consolidation	• Price competition	• Labor market shifts
	• Bankruptcy	
	• Merger	

TABLE 1.3b Internal forces that drive sales force change

Company strategy	Performance challenges
• New product launch	• High cost to sales ratio
• Merger	• Not enough new customer acquisition
• Selling process redesign	• Complacency
• Become more consultative, less	• Lack of accountability
transactional	• High turnover
• New channel strategy	• Not able to handle customer diversity
• Entry into new markets	• Not able to handle product diversity
• Value-added services	

Change forces can also originate within the company. Managers are constantly looking for better strategies. Shareholders are pushing for sustained growth. Examples of forces rooted in strategic shifts include:

- How does a firm build a sales force for a new product line?
- How will the sales forces of two merged companies be integrated?
- How will the role of the sales force change now that customers have tools to place orders using a company's web site?

Performance challenges also create change pressure from within a company. Successful companies are always looking for ways to get better. Sometimes, sales organizations gradually atrophy. There are many indicators of decline such as:

- The best salespeople are leaving the company.
- Sales and marketing are fighting again.
- Customer focus is waning – salespeople are spending too much time in non-selling activities.
- Customer satisfaction ratings have dropped.
- Salespeople are calling on friends and family too much.
- The sales force has not made its goals for several quarters.

Two case study analyses, one in the packaging industry and one in the pharmaceutical industry, are shown in the inset boxes. In both cases, there are significant opportunities to improve sales force performance.

Typically, if a company's performance is declining gradually, an immediate and urgent response is not sought. However, companies who ignore gradual change pressures often face bigger problems down the road. The best sales force leaders look constantly for improvement opportunities as they participate in an ongoing productivity hunt.

Example from the packaging industry illustrating the opportunity for sales force performance enhancement

A packaging company developed an index of market potential for each sales territory, based on account-specific estimates provided by salespeople as well as business demographic data. Figure 1.2 shows territory sales plotted against the index of market potential. Each dot represents a different sales territory and is labeled with a territory number.

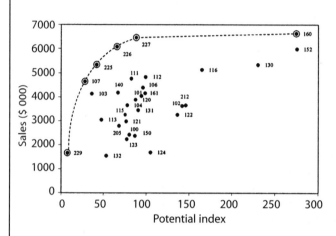

FIGURE 1.2 Sales versus sales potential index

When the scatter of territories is examined, it appears that sales and potential are correlated – territories with lower potential tend to have lower sales and those with higher potential tend to have higher sales. However, there is a great deal of variation in territory performance. The best performing territories are those that have the highest sales, given their market potential. The dotted line arcing across the top of the graph joins these top-performing territories. This line, called the *performance frontier*, represents the best performance that has been attained by members of this sales force for every level of territory potential. The performance frontier demonstrates the sales that are possible for every level of territory potential. These levels of sales are possible because someone in the field force has demonstrated their attainability. Territories that fall below the performance frontier are under-performing other sales territories with comparable potential.

There can be several reasons for so many territories to fall below the performance frontier. Some of the reasons are not within the firm's control. For example, a competitor may be especially strong or the market may be totally underdeveloped in a particular territory. However, there are many explanations that *are* within the firm's control, and insight into these explanations provides ideas for productivity enhancement. For example:

- the customers in a territory require more specialized knowledge or skills than a generalist salesperson can provide

- the salesperson in a territory lacks the right skills to be effective or is not calling on the right kinds of accounts
- a territory is too large to be covered effectively.

By studying territories that fall along the performance frontier, managers can learn what factors drive success in a sales force. For example, if the best-performing sales-people all have similar backgrounds, levels of experience, or personal characteristics, this information can be used to improve the recruiting process. If the best perform-ers utilize other sales resources such as specialist salespeople or sales assistants espe-cially effectively, this "best practice" can be shared with the rest of the sales force.

Performance-maximizing sales forces will take action to bring all territories closer to the performance frontier. The sales for this packaging company would increase by almost 55 percent if each salesperson performed at the performance frontier.

Example from the pharmaceutical industry demonstrating the opportunity for sales force performance enhancement

A pharmaceutical company analyzed data to determine the impact of sales force performance enhancement on company results. Figure 1.3 shows the relative performance of two different products for pharmaceutical sales territories. The rela-tive performance measure in this example was the territory's market share, with each share indexed so that the average territory equals 100 percent. The sales territories have been ranked twice: from highest to lowest relative performance on each of the two products. The two product curves show how relative performance varies, from high to low, across different salespeople.

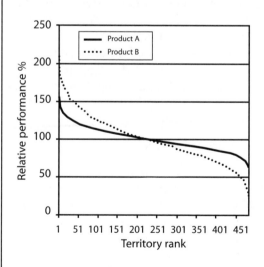

FIGURE 1.3 Relative performance by territory

As Figure 1.3 shows, there is a large range in perform-ance for these two prod-ucts. Relative performance of Product A varies from 152 percent of average in the highest performing territory down to 63 percent in the lowest performing territory. The variance on Product B is even larger – from a high of 209 percent of average down to a low of 27 percent.

The large variance in performance for these

products suggests opportunity for this sales force. For example, how does one salesperson attain 209 percent of average performance on Product B, while another gets only 27 percent? As in the packaging industry example, some of the variance may be due to factors outside the firm's control. Often, however, companies find that analyses like this reveal powerful insights as to how productivity can be improved within their own sales force. Large performance variances can reveal productivity enhancing opportunities in many different sales management areas, including hiring, training, sales force size and structure, territory alignment, motivation, compensation, and information systems.

Graphs like this can also provide insight regarding sales force time allocation. Each individual salesperson has a relative performance ranking for each product. Salespeople that rank high on both products are truly the best performers, while those that rank low on both are clearly weak. However, some salespeople do well on one product, but not the other. It is interesting to study how these salespeople spend their time. Often, they are allocating an above average proportion of their time to their better performing product, and a below average proportion to their weaker product. This demonstrates the value of sales force effort: more effort on a product equals higher performance. If the incremental profits generated by the greater effort exceed the cost of that effort, then a case can be made to add salespeople.

HOW SALES FORCES RESPOND TO EXTERNAL CHANGE PRESSURES

Customer needs, the environment, and competitors are always changing. To succeed in the long term, sales forces must re-evaluate their sales force design on a regular basis and adapt the size, structure, and deployment of their sales organizations in response to external forces. This section includes examples of how companies have responded to three major external change pressures: evolving customer needs, a changing environment, and changing competition.

Responding to Evolving Customer Needs

Customer needs change continuously and markets evolve. Customers often increase in their level of sophistication and expect new or additional services from their suppliers. They change their buying processes and may become more price-sensitive. These types of changes often lead customers to redefine their relationships with suppliers. The following examples show how changes in customer needs inspired Procter & Gamble, Charles Schwab, and Citibank to redesign their sales forces.

Procter & Gamble responds to consolidation of retail customers

In the early 1990s, P&G faced considerable consolidation of its retail customers. Many small, independent stores went out of business, as large national mass merchandisers such as Wal-Mart, and large regional chains such as Kroger and Safeway, began to dominate the industry. P&G wanted to solidify its relationship with the large and growing national and regional chains, while at the same time maintaining widespread product distribution and awareness.

Historically, P&G sales teams were organized by product category. Thus, multiple P&G salespeople covered most retail stores. For example, a single retailer might be assigned to a health and beauty aids salesperson, a food salesperson, a paper salesperson, and a soap salesperson. At the same time, each salesperson covered all types of outlets where their product lines were sold. For example, a soap salesperson might be assigned to cover a mix of grocery, mass merchandise, club, drug, and convenience stores. There was only moderate differentiation in the type of store-level support that each account received. In addition to the product-oriented sales teams, there was a separate group of salespeople assigned to key accounts. Key account salespeople were responsible for calling on the headquarter locations of major accounts to implement product-oriented promotional programs and negotiate price discounts on large orders.

With industry consolidation, account needs were becoming more diverse. Many large national and regional retailers wanted partnerships with their suppliers. Through these partnerships, retailers and suppliers would work together to streamline distribution logistics, improve marketing and sales analysis systems, and make better marketing decisions. Smaller customers did not require such partnerships.

P&G restructured its entire selling organization around the new and evolving needs of its customers. Instead of its historically product-based structure, P&G moved the sales force from a product-based structure to a customer-based structure. The four independent product teams that covered all types of retail outlets were replaced with customer-focused teams. Customers would receive different types of sales force coverage depending on a number of factors, including the type, size, degree of headquarters control, and geographic location of each account. For example, a dedicated vertical team of P&G salespeople might cover a large account with multiple stores in a metropolitan area. This team consisted of a team leader and a mix of category specialists (health and beauty aids, food, soap, paper) and store-level merchandisers. Salespeople on the team were 100 percent dedicated to serving the needs of the account, by performing duties at the retailer's headquarters, stores and distribution points. On the other hand, a small, independent, rural store did not warrant dedicated coverage. With less workload and higher travel requirements, this account was covered by a salesperson who sold the full P&G product line in a geographically aligned sales territory.

Ultimately, this restructuring enhanced P&G's relationships with its most important customers. Responsiveness to all customers increased because each account received sales support from a team of field personnel custom-designed to match the needs of that account. This targeted selling approach also reduced sales force costs. Some of the cost reduction was due to a 25 percent decrease in salesperson drive-time. This restructuring was one of the first of its kind, and has been a model for several other major sales force restructures in the consumer packaged goods industry.

Charles Schwab responds to increased customer sophistication

When customers become more sophisticated, sales force design often needs to change. In the case of financial services firm Charles Schwab, an end in fixed-rate commission regulations in 1975, coupled with an increase in customer sophistication, enabled Schwab to redefine the role of a salesperson in the financial services industry. Prior to this time, financial services salespeople were typically stockbrokers who executed stock market trades and investment purchases for individual investors. These stockbrokers were full-service and expensive.

During the 1980s, the general public's interest in the financial markets grew dramatically as access to financial information increased. Magazines like *Business Week*, *Fortune*, and *The Economist* saw their circulations grow. CNN, MSNBC, and other news networks provided around the clock television coverage. This trend was complemented by the emergence of the Internet in the 1990s. Online services like America Online (AOL) and CompuServe provided instant access to company and industry information that had previously been difficult for average investors to obtain.

As a result of the improved access to information, individual investors became more savvy and confident about their investing abilities. Many investors realized that they no longer needed to pay for the services of a full-scale broker. Charles Schwab responded to this shift in consumer dynamics by creating a system that empowered customers to make their own investments. Without a network of expensive stockbrokers and financial advisors, essentially an expensive sales force, Schwab was able to operate with a much lower cost structure than traditional brokerage houses. Schwab also did not need to provide equity research or promotional sales aids because their customers were self-educated about their investments. These savings were passed on to consumers in the form of lower commissions.

Update: Charles Schwab in the 2000s

Today, Charles Schwab is the widely recognized market leader within the discount brokerage segment. However, the company has faced some recent challenges. With the rapid decline of the high-technology stock market in 2000, online trading fell sharply, cutting deeply into Schwab's revenues and profits. In response, Schwab has added services so that now, in addition to offering its traditional discount brokerage services, Schwab offers a customized service for more affluent clients with at least $500,000 to invest. Interestingly, part of this strategy involves establishing a sales force. For a fee, Schwab customers can now meet face-to-face with a personal advisor who provides investment ideas and planning services. One of the biggest hurdles for Schwab is finding the right people to fill the personal advisor positions. Historically, the Schwab employees who interacted with customers were primarily order-takers, and not qualified to be personal financial advisors. Thus, Schwab is recruiting heavily from outside the company. By mid-2002, 150 qualified advisors were in place, with plans to add 150 more by year-end.

Schwab also recently announced a plan to provide advisory services to smaller clients with under $100,000 to invest. For a fee of $250, the firm provides a one-hour telephone-based consultation with an experienced investment consultant who will review the client's portfolio and recommend changes. Schwab also provides a free service on its web site called "Portfolio Checkup," which is useful to smaller clients for ongoing portfolio maintenance.

Citibank responds to globalization of its customers

Many companies are expanding globally, which creates new opportunities and challenges for their suppliers. Citibank, the banking division of Citigroup, one of the world's largest financial services companies, is a good example. Many of Citibank's strategically important corporate banking customers had expanded their operations around the globe. As a result, they began to require more globally integrated product and service solutions. For example, a global customer's corporate treasurer might want Citibank to offer a standardized set of products and banking services to every geographic market in which the customer operated. Citibank recognized that by changing the design of its sales organization, it could better meet the needs of global customers and thereby gain a competitive advantage.

For many years, Citibank has had a multi-dimensional, or matrix, sales organization in its corporate banking business. The organization has three basic dimensions: geographies, products, and customers. Country managers are responsible for sales in a particular geographic area, product managers are responsible for sales of a particular financial product or service, and customer managers are responsible for selling to a particular major customer. Prior to 1996, geography was considered the dominant organizational dimension. Country managers drove most business decisions and controlled the allocation of resources. Product and customer managers also existed, but they were not considered as important as the country managers.

The customer managers that existed prior to 1996 served the needs of approximately 200 multinational corporate customers. Each of these customers was assigned a Citibank parent account manager (PAM) who covered the parent corporation of the customer. Each PAM coordinated and communicated closely with several subsidiary account managers (SAMs) who served the needs of that customer's subsidiaries in other countries. Since the customer organization was not the dominant reporting structure, the PAMs did not command their own resources. PAMs had to lobby country managers if they needed, for example, a loan specialist to help structure a deal for their customer. This structure did not facilitate the delivery of the globally integrated offering that customers desired.

In order to better serve the needs of its most important customers, Citibank officially launched its global account management initiative in 1996. This initiative elevated the importance of the customer-oriented network of PAMs and SAMs and decreased the importance of the country managers. The PAM–SAM reporting structure became the dominant organizational structure and was expanded to serve the needs of approximately 1400 corporations with a global presence and a high demand for financial services. The PAMs function as value-added gateways to these strategically important accounts, leveraging teams of regional and product specialists, in conjunction with the SAMs, to deliver value to their customers. The PAM's job is to pull together the best team that will deliver the right solution for a customer.

In addition to the structural change, Citibank revamped its sales force incentive system, placing greater emphasis on an individual's contribution to corporate and business unit performance. Performance measures were reformulated to emphasize strength of customer relationship in addition to profitability. One indication of the increased importance of customer, and the de-emphasis on geography, was the way top management tracked performance. Before the reorganization, top management emphasized performance tracking by country: for example, earnings in France. After the reorganization, the emphasis changed to tracking of results by customer: for example, earnings from French companies including their operations not only in France but in other countries as well.

Citibank viewed its global account management program as a significant source of competitive advantage. The program allowed it to leverage its global product platform and relationship network. Citibank could effectively tailor unique, client-specific, global solutions for worldwide customers, while competitors could not.

Responding to a Changing Environment

Environmental forces are a second major source of external change pressure. These include changes in the technological, regulatory, and economic climate affecting a firm. The following examples show how environmental change brought about the need to redesign sales forces at Dell, Avon, and Shell Energy.

Changing technology has affected all sales forces dramatically in recent years. Advances such as cell phones, laptop computers, PDAs, email, and the Internet have transformed the way many salespeople do their jobs. Until recently, salespeople were not able to:

- check their voicemail messages from a cell phone while waiting at the airport
- communicate with customers, partners, and others within their own company via email
- know who was on the telephone from caller ID
- get directions to their next sales call using the car's GPS computer system
- submit expense and other routine reports to headquarters electronically
- check the Internet for the latest news or stock price of an important customer
- deliver a high-tech multimedia sales presentation to a room full of decision makers
- establish prices and delivery schedules while meeting with a prospective customer
- make adjustments and print a revised proposal for a prospective customer on site in minutes.

The Internet along with the worldwide web is certainly one of the most significant technological advancements in recent years, and has affected the selling process of practically every business. The Internet's role in selling varies greatly across companies. At one end of the spectrum, a company may have a simple web page that provides product and service information to prospective customers, along with instructions for contacting the company via telephone or email. At the other end of the range, a company can implement a full-blown e-commerce web site that includes a full online catalog, customer service, order placement and tracking, payment, and automated reorder capabilities.

Dell responds to advancing technology

Dell was an innovator in using the Internet, in tandem with a call center, to reach both consumers and business customers. The innovation in how it sold, and how it integrated its sales process with efficient manufacturing and distribution, has made Dell a market leader. The major innovation was not in the products Dell sells. At one time, the role of Dell's large direct sales force was to sell computer hardware to businesses. Today, however, most business customers place standard hardware orders for Dell products through the web site and/or Dell's call center. Dell even provides software to many of its business customers that helps them track their computer hardware inventory and streamlines the process of placing new orders with Dell. This not only significantly reduces Dell's costs, but it also frees up salespeople to participate in activities with greater expected return. Dell salespeople now partner with their largest customers – selling high value-added products, recommending changes and enhancements, and selling storage services.

Hybrid selling channels can help firms improve efficiency

Many companies are following Dell's lead by building hybrid channels. As their product portfolio proliferates, they recognize that the sales force adds the most value by selling the newer, more complex, and high-value products to the largest, most multi-faceted and strategically important accounts. Smaller accounts and older, less expensive commodity products are sold primarily through alternative, less expensive channels, such as catalogs, direct mail, the Internet, or telemarketing. Hybrid channels can also cooperate in performing complementary sales functions for the same customer. For example, telesales plays a role in prospecting, salespeople bring solutions to the customer and negotiate the sale, and the Internet is used to process the order.

Avon responds to the emergence of the Internet as a new sales channel

The emergence of the Internet as a new sales channel has forced all companies to rethink the processes that link them with their customers and suppliers. Avon, the world's largest direct seller of beauty products, has incorporated the Internet into its sales model. With the vast majority of women in the United States in the workforce and not at home, Avon's traditional door-to-door sales approach is outdated. In 1997, the company launched its first Internet venture, Avon.com, which allowed customers to purchase selected products online. The web site, however, angered many Avon salespeople who saw it as competition for their customers. With 98 percent of Avon revenues coming from its direct salespeople, the company needed to devise a plan that exploited the web, but at the same time did not alienate the sales force.

In 2000, Avon launched a new e-sales program designed to supplement, but not cannibalize, the efforts of its salespeople. Avon salespeople were given access to an easy-to-use web-design tool that allows them to create personalized web sites that link to the Avon.com site. Salespeople provide their customers with access to their Avon web site. Customers can save time by ordering Avon products through their sales representative online. Salespeople earn the same commission if they deliver an online order to a customer as they would for an in-person order. They earn less commission if a third party, such as UPS, delivers the order. Salespeople are also encouraged to submit their own orders online. Avon.com still allows customers to place orders directly through the company, but the site now encourages them to search for an Avon "e Representative" in their area.

Shell Energy responds to government deregulation

Another type of environmental change that can affect sales forces is government regulation. For example, deregulation of the US utility industry in the 1990s had dramatic implications for the industry's sales forces. Prior to deregulation, utility companies were regulated monopolies. Their customers were captive. Utility sales forces were comprised largely of salaried engineers on a two-year rotation before their next promotion. Deregulation brought change and competition. Large accounts now needed to be sold because their energy needs could be met by multiple suppliers. A pre-deregulation sales force that was activity-oriented, risk-averse, reactive, and analytical had to transform into a post-deregulation sales force that was flexible, risk-taking, proactive, and sales-oriented. In addition, more salespeople were needed to establish important customer relationships quickly, before competitors became entrenched.

The Atlanta office of Shell Energy faced these challenges in 1998, when the state of Georgia deregulated its natural gas industry. Shell, which had been providing natural gas to Georgia since 1950, was one of 18 natural gas companies contending for commercial customers. Shell decided that rather than establish its own in-house sales force, it would outsource the selling duties. This made sense for several reasons. First, the state had set a deadline for signing up customers, so moving quickly to establish a strong initial customer base was critical. An outsourcing firm would be able to recruit qualified salespeople more quickly than Shell could. In addition, the fixed cost of establishing an in-house sales force was prohibitively high. Finally, outsourcing allowed Shell to mitigate risk since it was not sure how profitable the new business would be.

The process of acquiring customers in the newly deregulated market was truly a joint effort between Shell Energy and its outsourcing partner. Shell retained responsibility for setting marketing strategy and determining what to sell. Shell also had an inside sales force of lead generators who worked closely with the outside sales team. The outsourcing partner was responsible for recruiting the 26 outside salespeople and two managers, segmenting and prioritizing customers, determining the sales process, providing sales and cost reports, and designing the sales compensation package. Shell and the partner worked together to provide sales training and participate in monthly sales meetings. Shell continued its relationship with the outsourcing firm even after the initial state deadline for signing up customers had passed. After the deadline, salespeople concentrated on renewals and up-sells, as well as attracting new, large customers. Eventually, it may make sense for Shell to consider bringing these activities in-house, once the profitability of the new business and the ongoing sales force needs become more certain.

Tight labor markets can affect sales force design

Economic changes, such as shifts in labor markets, can affect sales force design. For example, in a strong economy many companies are trying to hire more salespeople. As demand increases, the supply of qualified people in the labor pool decreases. Thus, the average quality of applicants for sales positions goes down. Sales forces face a dilemma: they can either relax hiring standards or hire fewer salespeople.

With either choice, sales force design is affected. If the sales force lowers its hiring standards, new salespeople may not be qualified to take on the same job responsibilities as existing salespeople. As a result, new salespeople may require specialized assignments that do not require the same breadth of product knowledge, customer knowledge, or selling skills. Alternatively, if the company chooses to hire fewer salespeople, existing salespeople will have too much work to do. The company must find a way to cover this excess workload, possibly by reassigning some of it to alternative channels, such as telemarketing, the Internet, sales assistants, or an indirect selling partner.

Responding to Changing Competition

Changes in the competitive intensity of an industry represent a third major source of external change pressure. The sales force must respond whenever competitors become more numerous, larger, wealthier, smarter, more aggressive, or more global. Additionally, if a competitor is distracted in a merger or collapses due to product problems or ethical lapses, a sales force response can help a company capitalize on this opportunity. The following examples show how changing competition brought about the need to redesign sales forces at Apple Computer and in a specialty chemical company.

Apple Computer responds to intensifying competition

When the competition changes in an industry, companies should reexamine the design of their sales forces. In a competitive market, sales can depend on a company's share of voice with customers. Thus, if a company's major competitors are leaving the market or are downsizing their sales forces, competitors will be spending less time with customers. In this case the company can also reduce its sales force without losing share of voice. On the other hand, if competitors are hiring more salespeople or new competitors are entering the market, the company will need to increase its sales force in order to maintain share of voice.

Companies who sell indirectly (through selling partners) sometimes bring their sales force in-house when competition intensifies. For example, throughout the 1980s and 1990s Apple Computer dominated the education market for computers. As the turn of the century approached, competition was increasing. When in 2000 Dell outsold Apple for the second consecutive year in the education segment, Apple management took action. For years, the company had relied on a loose affiliation of third-party resellers to reach education customers. In an attempt to tighten its hold on the market, Apple severed its relationship with the resellers and established its own in-house sales team.

Dropping resellers is a big decision. It is usually painful and fraught with risk. Apple's resellers knew they would be let go just before the summer peak buying time for schools, and thus had no incentive to build a pipeline of demand for the new academic year. As a result, the new sales team got off to a rocky start. Nevertheless, Apple management remained committed to the concept of using in-house salespeople in order to maintain better control of its most important market in the face of intensifying competition.

Catalyst manufacturers respond to rapid product commoditization

In the 1990s, suppliers of specialty chemicals (catalysts) witnessed their product lines undergo commoditization. Catalysts are used to increase the rate of chemical reactions in certain manufacturing processes, such as petroleum refinement and chemical and polymer production. Major companies such as Engelhard, Akzo-Nobel, Grace Davison, and Royal Dutch/Shell compete in a global market for catalysts of about $10 billion annually.

Commoditization of catalysts occurred as the pace of technological change in the industry slowed. Product improvements got incrementally less significant and price became the major differentiator. In order to maintain profits and differentiate themselves from competitors, catalyst companies began to bundle value-added services with their products. These services included manufacturing process troubleshooting and expertise, cradle-to-grave product stewardship, analytical measurement and detection systems, and creative catalyst purchasing arrangements, such as leasing.

This change in focus required a new sales approach. Historically, each catalyst salesperson had a geographically defined sales territory and called on accounts from many different industries. The sales message focused primarily on product features and advantages, and only limited knowledge of industry needs and manufacturing processes was required. Now, effective selling of value-added services required a much deeper understanding of the customer's needs. The successful salesperson was a solutions provider who understood the details of the customer's manufacturing process and knew how to leverage the full range of capabilities within the catalyst supplier organization.

To encourage salespeople to become customer and process experts, rather than product experts, many industry sales forces were restructured. Sales territories were redefined by market, rather than geography. This market focus made it possible for salespeople to be more effective at selling to customers in their assigned industry of expertise. Though some efficiency would be lost because salespeople had to travel further to reach their customers, this loss would be more than offset by the increased effectiveness gained through specialization.

HOW SALES FORCES RESPOND TO INTERNAL CHANGE PRESSURES

The examples discussed so far illustrate external change forces – customers changing, the environment shifting, or competition intensifying. All sales forces must respond to these events if they want to succeed. The best organizations not only adapt quickly and effectively to external events, they also implement new customer strategies, launch new products, innovate in the sales process, and seek constant and consistent improvement in their performance on an ongoing basis. These internal change forces fall into two linked categories which are described in this section: shifts in company strategy, and the hunt for greater productivity through the management of performance challenges.

Responding to Shifts in Company Strategy

When companies make significant changes to their company and marketing strategies, sales force design is often affected. Strategy changes can include the launch of new products, the entry into new markets, mergers and acquisitions, and changes to go-to-market strategies and selling processes. The following examples show how strategic change brought about the need to redesign sales forces at AstraZeneca, SonoSite, United Parcel Service, Kinko's, and CIBA Vision.

Two pharmaceutical giants – Astra and Zeneca – merge their sales forces

Sales force redesign can be challenging in merger situations – especially when two sales forces of equal size and strength are brought together. During a merger the sales force is usually under tremendous time and cost pressure. Speed is of the essence to minimize customer and organizational uncertainty and limbo. Customer relationships and key company personnel are at risk, especially if the merger involves downsizing and when communication channels are weak. If not done right, the resulting selling organization can become weaker than either of its pre-merger partners. It is common to see a drop in the short-term joint performance of merger partners.

Pharmaceutical giants Astra and Zeneca avoided many of the merger mistakes that most sales forces make when they combined their worldwide selling organizations in 1999. By using a well-defined, structured process, they were able to move quickly, but at the same time complete all the basic steps required for designing any new sales organization. The process they used is illustrated in Figure 1.4.

The two keys to the success of the AstraZeneca merger were extensive communication between management and the sales force, and

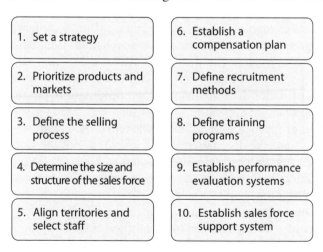

FIGURE 1.4 AstraZeneca sales force merger process

Source: Henry Canaday,"The Amazing 4000-Strong Sales Force," *Selling Power,* May 2001, p. 61

involvement of the sales force in the decision process. Sales leaders from Astra and Zeneca met almost immediately to discuss differences in the two sales organizations and to create a foundation for building a new, unique, merged organization. An "integration advocacy group" composed of people from both companies and all different sales roles represented the sales force viewpoint. The members of this group also became advocates for the merger to their peers. Throughout the merger, there were routine teleconferences, question and answer sessions, and newsletters to keep the sales force informed. The process of merging the sales forces involved more than 300 meetings with over 500 AstraZeneca managers in 40 different countries.

Speed of implementation was critical to the success of the AstraZeneca sales force merger. Just three months after the merger closed and one month after the company began operating as a single legal entity, implementation plans were completed for sales forces in 40 different countries. These implementation plans became fully operational just one to six months later, depending upon the country.

Medical technology company SonoSite implements a new go-to-market strategy

Sales force design is often affected when go-to-market strategies change. Medical technology company SonoSite launched its initial product, the world's first all-digital, hand-carried ultrasound system, in 1999. At that time, SonoSite decided to use a national distributor to sell the product to private physicians, hospitals, imaging centers, and radiologists in the United States. SonoSite felt that the distributor had strong customer relationships and exceptional access to the medical imaging market. Despite the distributor's excellent reputation, however, it was not successful selling SonoSite's product. The distributor was not experienced at selling a new, technologically complex product like the ultrasound system. In addition, the distributor had so many other products to promote that the SonoSite product got very little selling time.

SonoSite dropped the distributor and replaced it with its own direct sales force. Since the distributor's weak knowledge of the technology was a key reason for failure, SonoSite decided to hire only salespeople with strong technical backgrounds, mostly nurses who were trained and experienced users of ultrasound technology. This strategy too was not successful. While the nurses were very knowledgeable about the product, they were not salespeople. Most preferred to spend their time scanning patients and were not aggressive enough to ask customers for their business.

Finally, SonoSite moved to a different salesperson profile, building a team of professional salespeople. This time, SonoSite hired only salespeople who were experienced sellers of capital equipment, such as medical devices or copiers. These salespeople could sell customers on the benefits of the SonoSite product and could successfully close deals. They were trained in the basics of the technology, but needed help when customers required in-depth training or product support. To fill this void, SonoSite retained many of the nurses that were formerly salespeople and assigned them to a new role as clinical application specialists. As such, they performed product demonstrations and provided customer support, allowing salespeople to focus on selling. This final strategy has stood the test of time. In the first year after implementing the strategy with a fully staffed sales force, US revenues were up 79 percent from the previous year. Gross margin improved as well. The company attributed a good deal of this improvement to the efforts of its sales force. Building on this success, the company has expanded its direct sales approach to the European market.

UPS and Kinko's enter new markets

New markets can also drive sales force redesign. This is a combination of external (emergence of a customer need) and internal (new company strategy) forces at work. For example, the rapid growth of dot-com businesses in the late 1990s provided suppliers of many products and services with an opportunity to acquire new customers. Since the needs of this high growth segment were sufficiently different from those of traditional brick-and-mortar companies, many suppliers developed sales processes aimed specifically at the dot-com segment. For example, United Parcel Service created a dedicated e-commerce sales force of about 140 people who were dedicated to serving the needs of dot-com customers, especially the more established companies.

Kinko's, the world's leading provider of document solutions and business services, provides another example of a company that restructured its sales force in order to pursue a new market opportunity. Kinko's operates a major global chain of 24-hour copy and business service centers. Historically, Kinko's customers were very fragmented. Most were business travelers, college students, or small corporate accounts with which Kinko's had a limited relationship. In 1998, Kinko's made a strategic decision to proactively seek out larger, more sophisticated corporate customers. It hoped to establish longer-term, profitable relationships with these large companies by being a business-to-business partner and providing comprehensive printing and copy services.

This evolution in strategy demanded that Kinko's adapt its selling process to keep pace with the transition. Historically, Kinko's salespeople were primarily order takers. They dabbled in signing up small corporate clients, but never landed the large corporate customers. To change this,

Kinko's established a new sales process that would enable salespeople to be effective with the more sophisticated purchasing managers and procurement agents at large corporations. This process, called the Customer Relationship Cycle, consisted of seven steps: assess, plan, propose, close, fulfill, support, and expand. The first four steps led to an initial sale, while the last three focused on follow-up and service to ensure that Kinko's continued to expand business with the customer.

To execute the new selling process, Kinko's created a separate 500-person plus sales force to focus on large corporate customers. To support the new sales organization, numerous new programs were required. This included new goals, a new pay plan, revised marketing materials, and a new intranet site that allowed salespeople to access important product and service information. New training programs were also put in place to help the salespeople learn how to converse in a consultative and meaningful manner with customers to find out what they needed and how Kinko's could fulfill those needs. This training program was based on a best practices model developed by studying top performing salespeople and regions.

CIBA Vision launches new products

New products frequently drive sales force redesign. In some cases, an entirely new sales force is established to sell a new product. Other times, the new product is added to the portfolio of an existing sales force. When this happens, adjustments to the size and structure of the existing sales force may be required to ensure that salespeople have the time and expertise to sell the new product effectively. For example, CIBA Vision had a single sales force selling contact lenses and lens care solutions to eye care practitioners. In 2003 the company launched several new products, including two new solutions and a line of cosmetic lenses. The existing sales force did not have the capacity to manage these new products on top of the numerous existing product lines they were already selling. Thus, the company increased the number of salespeople by more than 30 percent and split the sales force, creating a dedicated medical device sales force for contact lenses and a dedicated lens care sales force for solutions. Now each customer is seen by two CIBA Vision salespeople, one for lenses and one for solutions. The new structure allows salespeople to develop greater expertise so they can better educate customers on the benefits of the products they sell.

Responding to Performance Challenges

Many familiar performance challenges do not require immediate attention, but if left alone, they can escalate into bigger problems. This includes issues such as "turnover of the best salespeople is too high," "sales are not growing fast enough," "we are not developing enough new accounts," or "the sales force is too complacent." Many companies have changed the design of their sales force in response to a variety of symptoms that were diagnosed through their ongoing efforts to hunt down productivity improvements. The following examples show how the desire to improve performance led to sales force redesign at a newspaper company, Procter & Gamble, and a medical device company.

Companies discover that too much time gets spent on non-selling tasks

Often, a first step toward discovering productivity enhancement opportunities is to learn more about how salespeople currently spend their time. A newspaper advertising sales force administered an activity survey to its sales force for this purpose. Table 1.4 summarizes the salespeople's responses. According to the survey, only 34.6 percent of the sales force's time was spent selling. More time was spent servicing existing accounts (40.8 percent) and on administrative tasks (16.8 percent). Based on this discovery, the company developed the role of sales assistant. Sales assistants were able to take over many of the non-selling tasks related to servicing existing accounts, such as checking advertisements, dealing with production problems, handling

TABLE 1.4 How salespeople spend their time – results of a survey of a newspaper sales force

Type of activity		Activity	Percent of time
Selling	34.6%	1. Active selling to advertisers (face-to-face or phone)	22.8
		2. Active selling to non-advertisers (face-to-face or phone)	10.7
		3. Entertaining advertisers and non-advertisers	1.1
Servicing	40.8%	4. Developing presentations and proposals	4.6
		5. Account planning	4.4
		6. Account maintenance and customer service	8.5
		7. Insertion orders	8.4
		8. Creative and layout work	4.9
		9. Dealing with production problems	4.0
		10. Dealing with credit, billing and collection problems	6.0
Administration	16.8%	11. Meetings	3.0
		12. Paperwork and administration	7.6
		13. Training	2.0
		14. Travel (to/from accounts)	4.2
Other	7.8%	15. Other	7.8
Total			**100.0**

billing and collection, and completing paperwork. As a result, salespeople were freed up to spend more time selling. Since the sales assistants were paid less than the salespeople, efficiency improved dramatically. The sales assistant position also created a new career path, as the best sales assistants could be promoted to a sales job.

Sales assistants enhance productivity at International Paper

A number of salespeople in the xpedx distribution division of International Paper use sales assistants. Salespeople at xpedx are paid 100 percent on commission. Many of them have hired their own sales assistants to reduce administrative burden and create more time for selling. The commissions they receive from their incremental sales more than cover the cost of paying a sales assistant's salary.

Procter & Gamble discovers that critical tasks can get overlooked

A sales force activity survey at P&G revealed that salespeople who sold the adult incontinence product Attends to nursing homes were spending a great deal of time hunting new customers at the expense of servicing existing customers. Nursing home personnel at some current accounts were getting frustrated and were considering switching suppliers. In response, the company established a service organization dedicated to providing nursing homes with the services they needed, such as nurse training, inventory management, and reimbursement advice.

A medical device company responds to high selling costs

In an effort to reduce selling costs, a medical devices company wanted to eliminate the redundancies and inefficiencies inherent in its highly specialized sales force structure. The company had multiple sales teams actively promoting products into the same market segments. Thus, several different salespeople from the company frequently called on the same customer contacts, particularly in the purchasing department. This resulted in confusion among customers. Salespeople felt accountable for selling their own products, but no one was accountable for the customer as a whole. In addition, since several salespeople had to drive to the same account, travel costs were high. Also, each sales team had its own regional management structure, hampering coordination and adding significantly to sales costs. The company felt it could gain significant competitive advantage by bringing the full force of the company portfolio to their customers in a unified manner.

To address these issues, the company designed a new corporate sales organization. This organization had fewer sales teams representing all the divisions. The new structure included account managers who could sell customer solutions across the entire product portfolio, and technical specialists who could provide detailed product expertise when needed. The structure allowed clear accountability for sales targets across accounts, segments, and geographies. Finally, although total headcount did not change, the number of non-customer-facing managers (that is, managers whose primary job was to manage salespeople, rather than customers) decreased by 23 percent.

BEING ADAPTIVE IS CHALLENGING

As the above examples show, sales organizations must confront a wide variety of change pressures. Those who are successful in the long run are flexible, adaptive, and implement well. However, the process of adapting and implementing effectively is not always easy. For every success story, there is another story of a change initiative that failed. Consider the case of office equipment maker, Xerox. Xerox has received a great deal of publicity for changing the design of its sales force several times in the last 20 years. The remainder of this chapter explores two major sales force restructures at Xerox.

Xerox in the Mid-1980s – An Example of How a Sales Force Can Participate in a Successful Strategy Implementation

During the mid-1980s, Xerox Corporation's dominant position in the office equipment market was in jeopardy. Japanese firms with good products and lower prices posed a serious competitive threat. At the same time, new electronic workplace technology, such as fax machines, desktop publishing, and workstations threatened to make Xerox's flagship product, the plain-paper copier, obsolete.

In response to these market changes, Xerox management implemented an aggressive strategy aimed at repositioning the company as a leader in office automation. A key element of this strategy was an increase in customer focus. Changes in organizational structure and customer feedback mechanisms encouraged all Xerox employees to be more attuned and responsive to the evolving needs of customers.

At the center of this customer focus strategy was Xerox's 4000-plus member sales force. Historically, Xerox had maintained separate sales forces for each of its major product lines. The largest sales force was dedicated to selling copier-duplicator equipment, and several smaller sales forces sold information processing systems, printing systems, office systems, and sales engineering. As a result of this product-based structure, many customers interacted with several Xerox salespeople representing different sales forces.

In 1985, the separate product-line organizations were merged into a single full-line sales force organized by customer segment and geography. Five market segments were defined, based on customer size, operational needs, and buying procedures. The market segments included custom system users (the largest commercial customers with multiple branch offices and specialized needs), standard commercial accounts (made up of a variety of medium-sized businesses), small businesses, third parties (such as dealers and distributors), and institutional customers (such as government and educational institutions). Under the new organization, salespeople were responsible for selling the full line of Xerox products to the customers in their designated segment, within a geographic area. One benefit of the reorganization was to increase productivity. As Xerox's product line expanded, it became too costly to add an additional specialty sales force for each new product. The primary objective of the reorganization, however, was to improve customer focus. The new structure allowed customers to work with a single Xerox salesperson to meet all of their document processing needs.

Figure 1.5 compares how the Xerox sales force covered various products and market segments before and after the 1985 reorganization.

With the sales force reorganization, numerous new sales force programs were adopted. An extensive multi-year training program was implemented, so that all salespeople could acquire the product and technical knowledge required to fully assess and satisfy customer needs. An internal office information system was installed in district sales offices, providing salespeople with quick access to up-to-date customer, product, and competitive data. The incentive compensation program was revamped to encourage salespeople to engage in activities appropriate to the needs of customers in their designated market segment.

The 1985 reorganization at Xerox was a success. The company experienced steady revenue growth in the years following the reorganization. In 1987 and again in 1989, the Xerox sales force was recognized as one of "America's Best Sales Forces" in a survey conducted by *Sales and Marketing Management* magazine. The company was lauded for its excellent reputation among customers and its ability to retain old accounts.

Xerox in the late 1990s – An Example of How a Poor Sales Force Reorganization can Affect Company Results

Xerox continued to enjoy success throughout the next decade. In May 1999, Xerox stock hit a record high of $64 a share. But despite the long-term record of success, trouble was brewing at the company. The market for high-tech stocks was weakening. Competitors continued to eat away at Xerox's market share. Changes were needed if Xerox was to meet its

Before the 1985 reorganization – sales force specialization by product

Product / Market	Copier–duplicator equipment	Information processing systems	Printing systems	Office systems	Sales engineering
Custom system users (large businesses)	Direct sales person – copier specialist	Direct sales person – information processing specialist	Direct sales person – printing systems specialist	Direct sales person – office systems specialist	Direct sales person – sales engineering specialist
Commercial (mid-sized businesses)					
Small businesses					
Third parties					
Institutional customers					

After the 1985 reorganization – sales force specialization by market segment

Product / Market	Copier–duplicator equipment	Information processing systems	Printing systems	Office systems	Sales engineering
Custom system users (large businesses)	Direct salesperson – custom system user specialist				
Commercial (mid-sized businesses)	Direct salesperson – commercial specialist				
Small businesses	Direct salesperson – small business specialist				
Third parties	Direct salesperson – third party specialist				
Institutional customers	Direct salesperson – institutional customer specialist				

FIGURE 1.5 Before and after comparison of product–market coverage by the Xerox sales force

aggressive revenue growth targets. At the same time, Xerox suffered from increasing discord among its top executives. A series of internal tensions, bad accounting practices, and mismanaged implementations sent the company's share price plummeting.

Despite the troubles, Xerox management persisted in its effort to implement a new, two-part business strategy. One part of the strategy focused on large, global customers and the other part focused on smaller customers. For large customers, Xerox's strategy was to help big companies create new ways to use documents more creatively and efficiently. This meant that Xerox salespeople would sell industry-specific bundled packages of products and services to the largest accounts. The bundled packages included copiers, software, consulting, and outsourcing contracts. For smaller businesses, the Xerox strategy was to broaden the network of indirect channels, such as office superstores, value-added resellers, agents, telemarketing, and the Internet. This would enable Xerox to reach a broader base of customers. It would also reduce costs, because the indirect channels had significantly lower overhead than the direct sales force.

The 4300-member Xerox sales force played a critical role in the implementation of the new strategy. The sales force was realigned twice during 1999. The purpose of both reorganizations was to shift direct selling effort towards the largest, global customers and to create separate industry-specific selling teams. In the first reorganization, four industry sectors were established: financial services and healthcare, manufacturing/industrial, graphic arts, and the public sector. Several months later, two additional sectors were added: professional services and retail/wholesale. Under the new organization, the majority of Xerox salespeople were responsible for selling a bundled document processing solution to large customers in a designated industry segment. These salespeople could provide information on every Xerox product and solution that was important to customers in their assigned industry. In addition, product specialists could be called upon to help close a sale. Many of the medium-sized and small accounts formerly covered by direct salespeople were reassigned to indirect channels.

Figure 1.6 shows how the Xerox sales force covered various products and market segments after the 1999 reorganization. As with the 1985 reorganization (shown in the second half of Figure 1.5), salespeople specialized by market segment. However, in 1999 *industry* was added as an important dimension for defining more precise market segments for large customers. In addition, indirect marketing channels, such as office superstores, value-added resellers, agents, telemarketing, and the Internet, took on increased importance, as they became the primary way that Xerox connected with its smaller customers.

Unlike the 1985 reorganization, the 1999 sales force restructure was not initially successful. The reorganization was pushed down from the highest

Product / Market	Copiers and other hardware	Software	Consulting	Outsourcing	Other products and services
Large financial service and healthcare firms	Direct salesperson – financial service and healthcare specialist				
Large manufacturing firms	Direct salesperson – manufacturing specialist				
Large graphic arts firms	Direct salesperson – graphic arts specialist				
Large public sector firms	Direct salesperson – public sector specialist				
Large professional service firms	Direct salesperson – professional service specialist				
Large retail and wholesale firms	Direct salesperson – retail and wholesale specialist				
Medium- and small-sized firms	Indirect channels: office superstores, value-added resellers, agents, telemarketing, Internet				

FIGURE 1.6 Product–market coverage by the Xerox sales force after the 1999 reorganization – sales force specialization by industry-based market segment

management levels at Xerox and the sales force was not involved in the decision-making process. The resulting organization confused the sales force, took away too much local control, and was not endorsed by the Xerox sales management team. The realignment caused a huge disruption of account–salesperson relationships – almost two-thirds of the customers were covered by a different salesperson after the reorganization. In all the turmoil, performance fell well short of goal and many good Xerox salespeople left the company. There is still debate on the restructuring. Was it the idea or was it the implementation?

By mid-2001, Xerox found itself in serious financial trouble. Nevertheless, new CEO Ann Mulcahy, who began her career as a Xerox salesperson, was optimistic about the company's future. In an interview with *Sales and Marketing Management* magazine, she shared her belief that the turnaround at Xerox would depend largely upon the success of its sales force.

Change is Difficult, but Necessary

As the Xerox story shows, the success of a sales force redesign often lies in the implementation. Well-thought-out implementation processes are essential to support the successful execution of new strategies. In 1985, Xerox backed its sales force redesign with numerous programs supporting the change – training, information systems, and a new sales compensation package. As a result, the sales force was prepared and motivated to carry out its new responsibilities. On the other hand, weak implementation caused confusion and a lack of acceptance by the sales force in 1999. Poor execution impeded the success of what may ultimately prove to be a sound business strategy for the firm. In the words of one former Xerox executive, "There was always a huge gap between the visionary aspirations the company nominally was pursuing and what it actually drove employees to do." Building a bridge to close that gap is what good implementation is all about.

Update: Xerox in 2003

When Xerox CEO Ann Mulcahy reported to shareholders in mid-2003, the company's future looked much brighter. The firm had returned to full-year profitability in 2002. The company's financial health had improved significantly and several actions aimed at reducing costs had been implemented successfully. Many new products had been launched, complemented by an array of solutions and services. The company was focused on continued growth through investment in high growth areas such as color production, digital production, and the document and business service markets.

Changing a sales force is hard work. Sales forces are made up of people, and people naturally resist change. At times, they may feel threatened and try to protect their turf. They may need to develop new skills and knowledge. They may lose familiar account relationships and need to establish new ones. They may be reassigned to a new manager. They may be asked to relocate. All these changes are difficult and are frequently met with resistance.

Resistance to change at a chemical company

A chemical company resisted changing the design of its sales territories for fear it would lose the salesperson that had the highest sales in the company. Analysis revealed that this salesperson had a sales territory with four times the sales potential of the average territory. The salesperson was skimming the cream off the best accounts, earning high commission dollars, and leaving thousands of dollars of opportunity unrealized. The salesperson's success had little to do with his own efforts and was instead due primarily to his lucrative sales territory.

Numerous company systems are affected when sales forces change. Information systems that have been in place for years may no longer be adequate. Hiring practices may need to adapt to new hiring profiles. New training programs may be needed to help salespeople develop the necessary competencies. The way that performance is measured may change. The compensation program may need adjustment.

Change is difficult, but necessary in today's rapidly evolving world. Sales forces that are not adaptive will not survive. The chapters that follow in this book are designed to help answer two questions:

- What is the best sales force design for an organization?
- How does an organization make the transition to the new sales force architecture?

CHAPTER 2

A Process for Designing the Sales Force for Strategic Advantage

WHAT IS SALES FORCE DESIGN?

Sales forces play different roles in connecting companies with their customers. Consider the cosmetics industry. Avon has almost 4 million independent sales representatives selling its wide range of cosmetics, skin care, fragrance, and other personal care products directly to consumers in over 140 countries. Revlon, on the other hand, reaches its customers through partnerships with retail outlets around the world. Revlon's salespeople work with buyers at retail chains on issues such as product mix, logistics, and pricing. Revlon's consultants and merchandisers spend their time in retail outlets demonstrating products, restocking merchandise, rearranging shelves, and setting up displays.

The confectionery industry provides another example of varied sales force design. Two major companies, Hershey Foods and Mars, employ different strategies for using food brokers as intermediaries to reach retail outlets. In late 2001, Hershey transferred all broker network sales responsibilities in the United States to its direct sales force. Mars, on the other hand, added brokers and expanded their responsibilities, leaving its direct sales force responsible for only a few of the top accounts.

Sales force design can also vary between companies that sell directly into the same marketplace. Figure 2.1 compares the direct sales forces of two wine and spirits wholesalers. Both wholesalers sell to liquor stores (off-premise), and restaurants and bars (on-premise). Both have a national accounts sales force to connect with national retail chains. However, their strategies for covering the local independent liquor stores, restaurants, and bars differ. Wholesaler number 1 establishes sales force coverage based on the size of the account. Large accounts are assigned specialist salespeople. These salespeople specialize both by product (wine versus spirits) and by market (off-premise versus on-premise). Smaller accounts are assigned generalist salespeople. These salespeople carry both product lines and sell to both markets. Wholesaler number 2, on the other hand, does not vary sales force coverage based on account size. All Wholesaler number 2 salespeople are product specialists, carrying only one of the two product lines.

Product / Customer	Wholesaler no. 1		Wholesaler no. 2	
	Wine	Spirits	Wine	Spirits
National retail chains	National accounts sales force		National accounts sales force	
Large liquor stores	Off-premise wine specialist	Off-premise spirits specialist	Wine specialist	Spirits specialist
Large restaurants and bars	On-premise wine specialist	On-premise spirits specialist		
Small liquor stores	Generalist			
Small restaurants and bars				

FIGURE 2.1 Comparison of sales force design at two wine and spirits wholesalers

Figure 2.2 shows an alternative sales force design for another company that uses a mix of generalists and specialists. This company sells specialized software to banks. Major banks are covered by generalist salespeople who are responsible for maintaining the ongoing relationship between the company and the bank. These generalists rely on product specialists as needed to provide technical expertise and help close sales. Medium-sized, community banks are covered by product specialists only. Small banks are not assigned to a direct salesperson. Instead, they are covered by the company's telesales division.

Market	Sales force coverage
Major banks	Relationship salespeople backed by product specialists
Community banks	Product specialists
Small banks	Telesales

FIGURE 2.2 Sales force design at a software supplier to banks

A company is faced with many choices when designing its sales force. Some of the key sales force design questions are:

- What is the role of a sales force versus other channels, such as telesales and the Internet?
- Should the company sell directly (using its own sales force) or indirectly (using a partner) or in collaboration with a partner?
- How many salespeople are needed?
- Should salespeople be generalists or should they specialize by product, market, or selling activity?
- Should there be global account teams? Major account teams?
- What are the reporting relationships within the sales organization?
- What are the coordination and control mechanisms?
- At what levels in the organization should various decisions be made?
- Who is responsible for which products and activities for each customer?

The answers to these sales force design questions, and how well a design is executed, affect customer coverage, costs, and company profitability. The right sales force design and its implementation enable a company to maximize the effectiveness of its interaction with customers, while at the same time maintaining efficiency so that costs are kept under control. Good sales force design can mean the difference between lackluster results and extraordinary profitability. In a competitive market, it can mean the difference between surviving and thriving.

This chapter describes a process for designing the sales force. Many companies have used this process effectively. The process follows a series of logical steps that allow a company to define how it will connect with its customers and what role the sales force will play in that connection.

Sales force design questions at a telecommunications company

A large wireless telecommunications company faced several sales force challenges. At large accounts, the company's direct sales force was losing sales to competitors. Salespeople lacked the depth of customer industry knowledge required to compete successfully at these major accounts. In addition, salespeople were ineffective because they did not understand the many different wireless applications available to sell. At small accounts, direct sales force coverage had become too expensive and was not profitable. The need for greater effectiveness with large accounts and greater efficiency with small accounts demanded that the current go-to-market strategy change.

The company realized that an enhanced sales process with more product and market knowledge was required for major accounts. This could be addressed by using a team selling approach, with teams comprised of industry specialists, applications specialists, and corporate account managers. Small accounts needed to be sold through less expensive channels such as telesales and the Internet. Each of these organizations needed to be sized to maximize the company's profitability.

The sales force design process described in this chapter provided the company with a framework for working through these important decisions.

A SALES FORCE DESIGN PROCESS

The forces of change discussed in Chapter 1 – customers, competitors, the environment, corporate strategies, and performance challenges – exert constant pressure on sales forces. Customer needs evolve. Competition intensifies or falters. The economy fluctuates. Technology advances. New products are launched. Growth objectives must be achieved. Every year, companies build new selling organizations or re-evaluate existing go-to-market strategies in order to compete better. How does one begin to redesign a sales force? Which issues are the most important? Which sales force design questions should be addressed first? What is a logical thinking framework that captures the elements of sales force design?

Figure 2.3 presents a tested process for sales force design. The process is organized into three main parts. Step 1 focuses on determining an appropriate sales strategy. This includes making decisions about how to segment customers, what products and services to offer each segment, and what sales process is most appropriate for each segment. Step 2 focuses on defining a go-to-market strategy. This involves selecting the sales and marketing channels that best meet the customer needs in each market

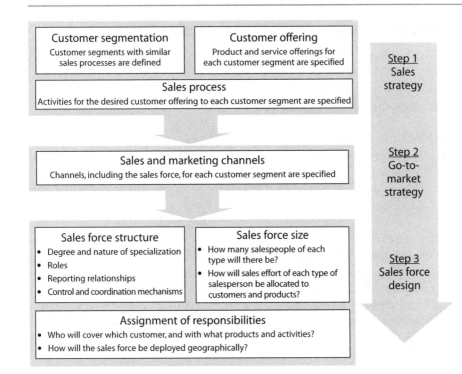

FIGURE 2.3 Sales force design process

segment. The firm has many channel choices including internal options such as advertising, direct mail, telesales, the Internet, and a sales force, as well as options outside the company such as distributors, retailers, value-added resellers, collaborators, and agents. Step 3 addresses the details of sales force design. This includes defining what the sales force structure looks like, what sales roles exist, how many salespeople are needed, what supervisory and coordination roles exist, and how specific customer, product, and activity responsibilities are assigned. This detailed process contains many elements, and in any given situation, a firm may focus on some or all of the elements. For example, if the sales process or the go-to-market approach are not changing, a company would segment its customers and concentrate on sales force design details including structure, size, and deployment. If there are concerns about sales force cost and effectiveness, all elements of this design process may be relevant. In still other situations, companies may seek to streamline their sales process without changing any of the other elements.

The following sections describe each of the three steps of the Sales Force Design Process in more detail.

Sales Force Design Process – Step 1 – Sales Strategy

A world-class sales force is a powerful asset for any company. Yet using a sales force is just one of a whole range of options for finding and keeping customers. Step 1 of the sales force design process takes a step back from the sales force to address three issues.

- What types and groups of customers (market segments) exist?
- What products and services will be valued by and sold to each segment?
- What activities are required to sell the firm's products and services to each segment?

As Figure 2.4 shows, sales strategy defines the sales process for each market segment. Developing this strategy has three components. First, the market must be segmented into meaningful, actionable customer clusters. Second, a customer offering consisting of the right mix of the firm's products and services has to be matched to the needs of each market segment in a way that emphasizes the firm's differential competitive advantage. Finally, the most appropriate sales process must be developed for each market segment. This sales process includes all the essential work that a firm must accomplish in order to attract and retain customers. In some situations, the sales process is explicitly defined, while in very simple, and in very complex and customized environments, the process is defined at a very broad level. Each of the components of a firm's sales strategy is described further below.

Customer segmentation

Customer segmentation involves organizing a diverse group of customers and prospects into meaningful homogeneous segments so that selling

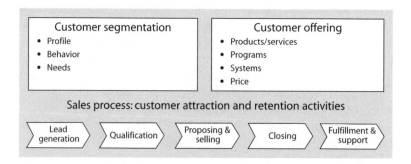

FIGURE 2.4 Sales force design process – Step 1 – Sales strategy

strategies can be prioritized and customized. There are many criteria that are useful for segmenting customers, including customer profile, behavior, and needs. The best segmentation schemes create actionable segments such that similar sales activities are appropriate for customers within the same segment and different sales activities are needed for customers in different segments.

Figure 2.5 shows the market segmentation scheme used by a company that sells a small medical device to physicians for use with their patients. Customers are segmented by usage history (users of the company's product, users of competitive products, and non-users who are new to the type of therapy), as well as by volume.

Usage history / Volume	User (current customer)	Competitive user	New to therapy
High volume			
Medium volume			
Low volume			

FIGURE 2.5 Market segmentation for a medical device company

Different sales activities and varying amounts of selling time are required for customers and prospects in each of the different market segments. Volume determines the amount of selling time that a company may want to invest in the opportunity. Higher volume accounts get more selling time than lower volume accounts. Usage history determines the specific selling activities. With current users, salespeople spend most of their time providing service and support. With competitive users, salespeople focus on demonstrating the advantages of the firm's products over its competitors. With non-users, salespeople educate prospects on the benefits of the therapy method, before selling the firm's product advantages. Because varying levels of effort and different selling tasks are required for each market segment, this segmentation scheme facilitates the development of an effective sales strategy at this medical device firm.

Customer offering

For each market segment, the firm has to determine the mix of products and services that will be valued by that segment. Different product and service alternatives may be offered to different customer segments based upon their needs as well as their economic value. Figure 2.6 shows a simplified version of the matrix that a newspaper syndication service uses to match product offerings with market segments. The company sells four major products (shown in the columns of the matrix) to five different customer segments (shown in the rows of the matrix). Products are matched to customer segments, based on their needs. For example, Sunday TV book ads are sold only to the top 40 US newspapers, since smaller newspapers do not have Sunday TV books. Comics and puzzles are sold in all markets, since all types of newspapers can include these products. A matrix like this is the cornerstone for an effective sales strategy. It helps the firm direct selling resources toward those product-market combinations that offer the best opportunity.

Product / Customer segment	Sunday TV book ads	TV listings	Weather forecasts	Comics & puzzles
Top 40 US newspapers	✓	✓	✓	✓
Other large US newspapers		✓	✓	✓
Small daily US newspapers		✓	✓	✓
College and weekly newspapers				✓
International newspapers				✓

FIGURE 2.6 Matching of product offerings to customer segments at a newspaper syndication service

---

A broader view of the product offering

A company's product offering often extends beyond the product itself. Buyers may place significant value on the services, programs, and systems that surround the product. For example, in addition to providing its core products, the newspaper syndication service described above also offers customers an online delivery system that allows them to download purchased products from a convenient web site. This online delivery system is an important part of the company's product offering and is a significant source of value for many customers.

Sales process

The activities required for a firm to sell its products and services to customers can be organized into a defined sales process for each market segment. Other terms that companies use to describe their sales processes include selling activities, selling motion, and essential work. A sales process is typically comprised of a series of steps that advance the probability of a sale. For example, first the firm must generate and qualify leads. Next, it must sell to the customer and develop a proposal. Following this, it must close the deal. Finally, it must fulfill the customer's order and provide ongoing support.

To determine a sales process, the firm must define all the interactions that need to occur in order to do business with a customer. Important considerations include customer needs, buying processes, and purchase influencers, as well as customer size and opportunity.

Sales Force Design Process – Step 2 – Go-To-Market Strategy

The sales strategy of Step 1 has to be linked to the marketing channels that will be used to accomplish the selling activities. As Figure 2.7 shows, go-to-market strategies often include a mix of channels.

Sales and marketing channels					
Value-added partners	Direct sales force	Tele-channels	E-channels	Agents/ distributors/ retailers	Advertising & promotion

FIGURE 2.7 Sales force design process – Step 2 – Go-to-market strategy

Go-to-market strategies use multiple selling channels that work together to accomplish critical selling activities in an effective, yet efficient manner. For example, Figure 2.8 shows a simplified version of how an office products company sells its product lines to businesses. The company defines its sales process to include five stages: lead generation, qualification, pre-sales, closing, and fulfillment/support. The firm's go-to-market strategy specifies that lead generation and qualification are done by telemarketing, thus increasing the efficiency with which these tasks can be completed. The pre-sales and close of sale activities require face-to-face contact for maximum effectiveness, and are accomplished by a more expensive generalist and specialist sales force. Finally, fulfillment and support are handled by less expensive customer service reps, once again providing efficiency in channel design. By using multiple selling channels, the office products firm enhances overall productivity.

Product \ Task	Lead generation	Qualification	Pre-sales	Close of sale	Fulfillment/support
Office products	Telemarketing		Generalist sales reps		Customer service reps
Furniture	Telemarketing		Generalist and specialist sales reps		Customer service reps
Computer supplies	Telemarketing		Generalist and specialist sales reps		Customer service reps

FIGURE 2.8 How an office products company sells

Sales Force Design Process – Step 3 – Sales Force Design

Sales strategy and go-to-market strategy logically lead to sales force design. As Figure 2.9 shows, sales force design has three components. First, there is the structure of the sales force and the various sales roles that will be needed. Second, is the issue of sales force size. Finally, specific activities and accounts are assigned to individual salespeople and teams. Each of these components is described further below.

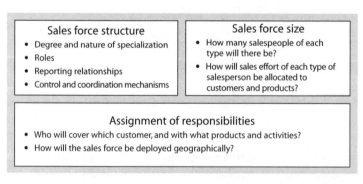

FIGURE 2.9 Sales force design process – Step 3 – Sales force design

Sales force structure

Sales force structure deals with two central questions: how to divide up all the sales activities among different types of salespeople, and how to coordinate and control the activities to meet the firm's goals. Sales force structures are often represented by organization charts with accompanying job descriptions. Structures define the different sales roles, reporting relationships, and team structures that exist to serve the diverse needs of customers. Sales roles at many companies are very focused and specialized. As a result, sales force structures can be quite complicated. Multidimensional matrix organizations, where salespeople are part of multiple groups, are common.

A well-structured sales force is essential for connecting effectively with customers. A good sales force structure allows the appropriate sales process to be implemented for every targeted market segment. It ensures that the selling and maintenance effort is effective while utilizing selling resources efficiently. It directs selling effort to the right products, markets, and selling activities.

A multidimensional matrix organization at Citibank

At Citibank, a single salesperson may report into a customer relationship manager as well as an industry group manager and a geographic group manager. In addition, product specialists also report into product group managers. Multidimensional matrix organizations like this are sometimes so complex that it is difficult to represent their structure on a two-dimensional piece of paper!

Sales force size

The question of sales force structure is linked to the issue of sales force size. How many salespeople are needed? How many generalists? How many specialists? How many managers? What is the size for any structure? The size of the sales force is directly linked to company sales, costs, and profits.

Companies use many different methods to size their sales forces. Occasionally sales forces are sized based on the number of salespeople that the company can afford, given the revenue forecast. Some companies study the sales forces of their major competitors and match their sales force sizes. The best approaches to sales force sizing link the number of salespeople not only to financial ratios and competitive data, but also to customer needs and the ability of sales force effort to generate sales. Customer-based methods recognize the simple fact that the best sales force size depends upon the amount of selling activity required to cover customers in the targeted market segments. Thus, the right number of salespeople is determined by the number and size of customer segments being considered for direct coverage, the selling tasks to be performed, the amount of time it takes to complete those tasks, and the sales and profit expectations from each customer segment.

By linking sales force size to customer needs, a company makes it possible for customers and prospects to receive appropriate coverage. The right sales force size also ensures that company products get proper representation, the sales force is stretched but not overworked, and the company makes an appropriate investment in its sales resource and generates the desired results.

Assignment of responsibilities

For any sales force structure and size, specific accounts and selling responsibilities need to be assigned to each salesperson or selling team. This is the nitty-gritty detail of sales force design. Everyone in the sales force needs a "list" of which accounts, products, and selling activities are his or her responsibility. In a traditional generalist sales force, assignments are typically determined by geography – each salesperson is expected to fully cover all the accounts in a particular region of the country, state, metropolitan area, or set of postal codes. With specialized sales structures, assignments are much more complex. In addition to geography, assignments may be determined by the type of customer, as with the software supplier to banks (see Figure 2.2) that has some salespeople cover major banks and others cover community banks. Alternatively, assignments can be made by product as with wine and spirits Wholesaler number 2 (see Figure 2.1) that has some salespeople sell wine and others sell spirits. Assignments can be determined by selling activity, as with the office products company (see Figure 2.8) that has one person generating leads, another selling, and a third handling ongoing support. Often, assignments are based on a combination of these factors. For example, wine and spirits Wholesaler number 1 (also in Figure 2.1) assigns accounts based on customer type (liquor stores versus restaurants and bars) and product (wine versus spirits).

Assigning accounts to salespeople can be time-consuming and complex

There are many different ways to assign salespeople to accounts, products, and selling tasks. In fact, there are over 1000 ways to assign just ten accounts to two generalist salespeople. Since the problem grows exponentially with additional accounts, salespeople, and specialization, one can imagine the enormity of the task for any reasonably sized sales force. Frequently, the number of possible assignments exceeds the number of atoms in the universe! Fortunately, excellent computer tools exist to find good assignment combinations from the astronomical array of possibilities.

The way a company assigns accounts, products, and selling tasks to salespeople affects customer coverage. If salespeople are given too much to do, some of their accounts, products, or selling activities will be neglected. If salespeople have too little to do, they are likely to spend too much time on low-return accounts, products, or activities. Making good assignments will enable fair performance evaluation, match rewards with individual performance, and reduce travel costs.

Sales Force Design Process – A Holistic View

Figure 2.3 presents the sales force design process as a sequence of orderly steps. A sales strategy is developed first, followed by a go-to-market strategy, and finally a sales force design. Decisions made in the early steps of the process affect choices in the later steps. The selected sales process affects channel choices, and go-to-market strategy affects sales force organization and size. The sequential approach provides a logical organization of the major sales force design decisions. However although the process is organized sequentially, a firm's sales strategy, go-to-market strategy, and sales force design are highly interdependent. Alignment and compatibility across all decisions is essential for success. Any constraints the firm has on downstream decisions in the sales force design process will have an impact on the upstream decisions.

The interdependencies of sales force design choices are best illustrated through examples. If a company has a generalist sales force, it cannot effectively execute a sales process that requires a high degree of specialized product or market expertise. If a company is wed to using distributor organizations or dedicated contract sellers who value their independence, sales strategies that require a high degree of control over the sales process may not succeed. In this case, it may be difficult to implement a sales strategy that seeks to invest heavily in customers for a new product launch or for aggressive new account development. A sales strategy that looks for efficiency by applying lower cost resources such as telesales and the Internet will not succeed if the go-to-market strategy relies on a commission-chasing sales force and does not explicitly assign small accounts to lower cost channels. In addition, a company that uses a direct sales force may find it difficult to successfully introduce new channels that compete directly with the sales force, such as a distributor or the Internet.

In order for a sales force design effort to be successful, the various components of the design must align well with one another. In addition, each component must be compatible with the sales force culture, salespeople's capabilities, and the sales compensation plan.

Most companies re-evaluate at least part of their sales, go-to-market, and sales force design strategy every two to three years. With each re-evaluation, there is a history and momentum that needs to be considered. Usually, the company has a go-to-market approach and sales force design with salespeople already in place. History often constrains sales force design choices. The train is moving. Changes that derail the train will not produce the desired results. Adjustments to sales force design must anticipate and accommodate any organizational constraints to change.

> **Achieving alignment and compatibility of sales force design decisions at Avon**
>
> For many years, Avon has relied on a large direct sales force to sell its beauty care products. When the Internet emerged as an important selling channel, Avon launched a buying site for customers. This angered many Avon salespeople, who saw the site as competition for their customers. Only when Avon allowed the sales force to control the site and get credit for Internet sales did the strategy work.

NINE SALES FORCE DESIGN INSIGHTS

To summarize the sales force design process, here are nine insights that highlight some of the major themes that are discussed in the remaining chapters, and thus provide a roadmap for the rest of the book.

Good Sales Strategy Starts with an Understanding of Customer Needs

Like many good business decisions, the right sales force design choices start with a thorough understanding of customers' needs. Through understanding, the company can tailor its product and service offering appropriately for each customer segment, and can design a sales process that strengthens the buyer–seller connection. Companies with only a few customers can customize their sales process for each individual customer. Most companies, however, have too many possible customers to make it practical to have a customized plan for each. Thus, most companies find it productive to segment customers into groups and then customize their offering and their sales process for each group. Developing a good customer segmentation scheme, establishing a product and service offering for each segment, and designing the most effective sales process for each segment will be discussed further in Chapter 3 (Sales Strategy).

The Best Go-To-Market Strategies Acknowledge that We Live in a Multi-Channel World

Sixty years ago, the decision of how to go to market was easy. Companies either hired their own direct salespeople or sold through a distributor. Today, the list of go-to-market options is mind-boggling. In addition to networks of direct salespeople and distributors, companies sell through telesales, mail order, company-owned retail outlets, brokers, value-added resellers, licensing and joint distributor agreements, dealers, agents, the Internet – the possibilities are almost endless!

The cost of using different selling channels to perform various selling tasks varies greatly. For example, the cost of using telesales to connect with a customer is just a fraction of the cost of making an in-person sales call. At the same time, there is great variance in the effectiveness of different selling channels for different tasks. An in-person sales call is much more likely to result in a sale but may be not as efficient as a telephone call for prospecting. Thus, companies are challenged to develop go-to-market strategies that allow multiple selling channels to work together to deliver the highest possible value to the customer and profitable sales for the firm. Developing a good go-to-market strategy is discussed further in Chapter 4 (Go-To-Market Strategy).

Specialize the Sales Force when Significant Effectiveness Gains are Possible

Generalist sales organizations tend to maximize efficiency. Each salesperson sells all products and performs all selling activities for all of the accounts in a defined geographic territory. With this structure, territories tend to be the most geographically compact, so that travel costs are minimized and the sales force generates high levels of call activity and face-to-face selling time.

While generalist sales organizations are efficient, they are often not very effective. Markets, products, and selling activities can be complex. At the same time, they can be very heterogeneous. For example, selling a large copy machine requires different knowledge and skills from those for selling office supplies. Selling pharmaceuticals to a large hospital system requires different skills and knowledge from those for selling the same drugs to an individual physician. A generalist sales force cannot possibly be effective at selling a broad and complex product line to a diverse set of customers that require many different selling tasks. Sales forces that want to be effective in these situations need to specialize. But in doing so, they give up efficiency. Evaluating the trade-off between efficiency and effectiveness is at the heart of the sales force structure decision. This is the focus of Chapter 5 (Designing the Sales Force Structure).

Consider New Sales Roles

Companies that once served the needs of each customer with a single, generalist salesperson have introduced many new roles: product specialists, technical specialists, strategic account managers, telemarketing reps, and sales assistants, to name a few. These roles help companies meet the diverse and complex needs of their customers, and at the same time become efficient by reducing selling costs. Sales roles are the focus of Chapter 6 (Sales Roles).

Maximize Profits – Don't Contain Costs

Salespeople are an economic investment. They are profitable as long as the incremental gross margin (sales minus product costs) that they generate exceeds their cost (salary, benefits, taxes, bonuses and commissions, car, computer, travel, administrative and field support). Many companies manage their sales force size by specifying that sales force costs should be maintained at a constant percentage of sales. While this approach helps the company contain costs, it does not maximize profits. Usually if a company adds salespeople, its sales force cost to sales ratio will go up. This is because additional salespeople cost the same as existing salespeople. However, due to diminishing returns, additional salespeople cannot typically match the average sales of existing salespeople. This does not mean that the additional salespeople are not profitable. Increased profits may mean a higher sales force cost ratio. A profit-maximizing approach to sales force sizing is discussed in Chapter 7 (Sizing the Selling Organization).

Spend Time with the Right Customers, Products, and Selling Activities

Deploying sales force effort in a smart way has a significant impact on sales and profits. A sales force that allocates its time wisely among different customer segments, products, and selling activities will outperform a larger sales force with average deployment of sales force effort. In other words, it is better to work smarter than to work harder.

The value of good sales force deployment

A study of sales forces at 50 companies sheds light on the value of appropriate effort deployment. The study revealed that, on average, a 3.2 percent improvement in three-year profitability could be achieved through better allocation of sales force time. At the same time, only a 1.3 percent improvement could be achieved by changing sales force size. Another observation that emerged from this study is that focused strategies dominate scattered strategies. Sales potential tends to be concentrated. Therefore, strategies that direct sales force effort to the right customers significantly outperform those that spread this effort across all possible customers.

Sales force time allocation issues will be addressed in Chapter 5 (Designing the Sales Force Structure), Chapter 7 (Sizing the Selling Organization) and Chapter 8 (Sales Territory Alignment).

Create the Right Assignment of Customers and Activities to Salespeople

One way that a company encourages the sales force to spend time on the right markets, products, and selling activities is by assigning customers and activities to individual salespeople in a smart way. If the selling workload is not fairly distributed among salespeople, some customers, products, or activities will be neglected while others will receive more attention than is profitable. Empirical data show that companies often do not pay enough attention to the way they make their sales force assignments.

Developing good assignments that keep all salespeople challenged, but not overworked, is the focus of Chapter 8 (Sales Territory Alignment).

The majority of salespeople do not have the right workload

A study of over 4800 salespeople at 18 companies in four different industries revealed that 56 percent of the salespeople were given assignments that gave them either too much work to do, or not enough work to keep a salesperson fully busy.

Assess Sales Force Performance Continuously

The best companies assess sales force performance on a regular, ongoing basis in search of constant productivity improvements. In successful sales forces, the many decisions, processes, and systems – the sales force drivers – align effectively with the sales force design. Sales force drivers include hiring and training processes, compensation programs, performance management, and information support systems. Frameworks for assessing sales force performance, along with examples of analytic tools that can enhance this process, are discussed in Chapter 9 (Sustaining the Successful Selling Organization).

Pay Attention to Customer and Salesperson Impact when Implementing Design Changes

Many sales force designs that seem excellent on paper fail in the field due to poor execution. Disruption to customer relationships or a sales force that is unhappy with the planned changes can hurt sales significantly. A new design may also need different systems and processes. The issues around sales force design change are discussed in Chapter 10 (Managing Change).

Sales Strategy

How this chapter is organized

INTRODUCTION

Sales strategy defines *who* a firm sells to, *what* the customer offering is, and *how* the selling is done. Successful sales strategies define effective yet efficient sales processes that deliver the right products and services to the right customers.

Developing a sales strategy is the first step in the sales force design process introduced in Chapter 2. Figure 3.1 provides an overview of this step and its three major components. First, the market must be segmented into meaningful, actionable customer clusters. Next, the firm must determine the best product and service offering for each market segment. A successful sales strategy focuses the firm's resources on customers and product/service offerings that have strategic importance and good profit potential. Finally, the most appropriate process for selling the right product/service offering to each market segment must be defined. This process includes all of the activities required to sell, deliver, and service the firm's offerings. In this book, the term *sales process* is used to describe this work. Other terms that capture this concept are selling activity, customer attraction and retention process, essential work, and selling motion.

This chapter describes and provides examples of the three major activities required for sales strategy development:

- Activity 1: Segment markets
- Activity 2: Determine product/service offering
- Activity 3: Design sales process

The chapter concludes with sales strategy insights that can help companies succeed in the long term.

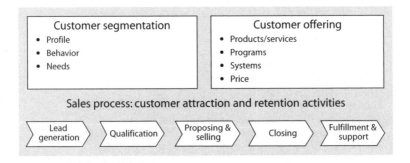

FIGURE 3.1 Sales strategy activities in the sales force design process

SALES STRATEGY DEVELOPMENT ACTIVITY 1: SEGMENT MARKETS

The first step in developing a successful sales strategy is to segment the firm's customers and prospects into meaningful, actionable clusters. The benefits of customer segmentation are discussed below. Following this discussion, ideas on how to segment markets are explored. Next, the importance of sales potential as a market segmentation criterion is discussed. Finally, ideas for sourcing market segmentation data are provided.

Why Segment Markets?

Customer segmentation helps companies meet the needs of diverse customers

Customers differ in many ways. Some are large and some are small. Some want the best price, others the best service. Some are early adopters, eager to try the latest innovation, while others prefer well-tested solutions. Some customers are interested in many of the products and services a company has to offer whereas others want only a select few.

Customers can also have very dissimilar buying processes. Some customers make purchasing decisions centrally, others delegate purchasing to individual departments or locations. Some have a single point of control for purchases and others have many people influencing the buying decision.

Successful sales strategies exploit customer differences to enhance sales impact and efficiency. A large, profitable customer gets more attention than a small, less profitable one. A technically-oriented customer receives different information than a service-oriented customer. A customer who likes to order over the Internet is treated differently from one who prefers to deal exclusively with a salesperson. Table 3.1 summarizes several ways that customer differences can affect sales strategies.

Customer segmentation organizes a large universe of customers and potential customers into groups with common characteristics so that customers can be prioritized, and sales and marketing efforts can be customized. A company that has a limited number of potential customers, such as a tier-one supplier of gaskets to automobile manufacturers, can plan sales strategies for each individual customer. However, when a company has thousands of possible customers with diverse needs, it is more practical to first prioritize and plan at the segment level.

Figure 3.2 illustrates a range of segmentation approaches that vary based on how granular, small, and specific the market segments are.

TABLE 3.1 Impact of customer differences on sales strategy

A difference in:	Can affect:
How much a customer buys How much a customer can buy How profitable a customer is	How much sales and marketing effort a company invests
How loyal a customer is	What mix of sales and marketing activities is used
How a customer makes buying decisions	What the sales process is
Where a customer gets information	What channels are used to provide information
Why a customer buys or would buy	What the sales message is
How eager a customer is to try new products	The point in the product's life cycle that the customer is approached
How price sensitive a customer is How much service and support a customer needs	What products and services are offered, and what the value proposition is for the customer
Where a customer buys	How sales channels are designed

Mass marketing places all customers into the same segment and plans one standard sales strategy for all customers. This is the easiest and most efficient way to approach the market, but it is not usually very effective because customer differences are not acknowledged. At the other extreme, the individual customer approach tailors sales strategies to the needs of individual customers. Each customer is, in fact, its own segment and has its own customized sales process. This sales approach is very effective, but unless the number of customers is small, it is not very efficient. Most companies plan their sales strategies using a level of segment granularity that falls somewhere between these two extremes. Segmented market approaches (where there are a few meaningful, actionable segments) and micro-market approaches (where the segments are further subdivided to the point where each segment has just a few

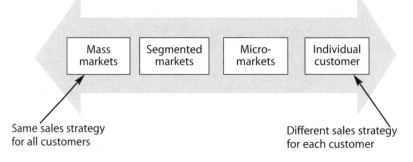

FIGURE 3.2 Range of granularity of customer segmentation approaches

members) are practical alternatives that allow companies to plan effective yet efficient selling strategies for large numbers of diverse customers. For those segments that are covered by a sales force, individual salespeople can then adapt and customize the planned segment strategy for specific customers.

The impact of technology on individual customer marketing

Historically, the sales force was the best way for a company to implement individual customer selling approaches. Customization is a key component of a sales force's impact. A salesperson can treat each individual customer as its own segment by adapting the company's strategy and product/service offering to customer needs and adjusting the sales process even as it is being executed.

Today, advances in data availability and technology make it possible for companies to implement individual customer marketing approaches using delivery channels that are much less expensive than sales forces. Companies know more about their customers today than ever before. At Amazon.com, shoppers are greeted with at friendly "Hello, we have recommendations for you!" along with a list of suggested purchases based on what the customer has purchased in the past. At Google.com, the popular Internet search engine service, constant data mining and thorough prescreening of potential advertisers ensure that the right advertisers get matched with the right pages on Google's web site, enabling the company to achieve click-through rates five times the industry average. Even neighborhood stores are using technology to implement individual customer marketing approaches. A pizza delivery company uses the phone's caller ID feature to link incoming calls to a database of past purchases. The pizza company then knows who is calling and what they are likely to order even before answering the telephone.

Technology can be used to create individual customer marketing approaches and is often significantly less expensive than a sales force. Smart go-to-market strategies often involve sales forces working together with technology solutions to deliver high levels of customization at reasonable cost.

Examples of customer segmentation

Figure 3.3 shows an example of how trade school Universal Technical Institute (UTI) segments its customers. UTI targets non-college bound high school graduates for one- and two-year technician training programs in fields such as automotive, heating and cooling, and marine repair and mechanics. Most leads for potential students (that is, customers) come from high schools. Since there are thousands of high schools, UTI wants to focus its limited sales force resources on those schools with the greatest possible return. Thus, high schools are segmented based on their potential to be a good source of students. The attractiveness of a high school is enhanced if the school is large, the school has industrial arts teachers, and a smaller percentage of the student body is college bound.

Figure 3.4 provides a second example of customer segmentation. This example comes from a pharmaceutical company. This company segmented

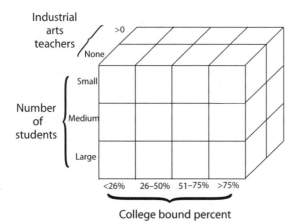

College bound percent

For simplicity, not all segmentation dimensions are shown here

**FIGURE 3.3 Example segmentation of high schools for
Universal Technical Institute**

physician customers based on a combination of the physician's sales
potential (derived from historical prescriptions written for a particular drug
category) and loyalty to the firm's products. The size of each bubble in the
figure reflects the number of customers in the group. This segmentation
helped the salespeople at the firm understand customer differences and
customize the amount of selling effort and the selling message for different customer types.

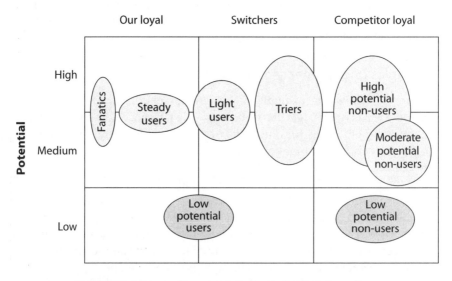

**FIGURE 3.4 Example segmentation of physicians for a
pharmaceutical firm**

A final example of customer segmentation is shown in Figure 3.5. IVAC Medical Systems used this scheme. (IVAC merged with IMED in 1996 to form ALARIS Medical Systems.) IVAC's main products were infusion pumps to deliver fluids and drugs into the body. The useful life of a pump was about five years, and a hospital typically decided to replace the pumps in most or all of the hospital departments at the same time. About 20 percent of pumps in use were replaced in any given year in the market. A hospital would complete a significant amount of planning and evaluation before deciding which product line to purchase. IVAC identified three segmentation dimensions that influenced the appropriate sales process for each hospital: the size of the hospital, the type of hospital, and the status of the hospital. Possible status choices were:

- *Secure* – a current IVAC customer that would *not* be buying new pumps in the next year.
- *Vulnerable* – a current IVAC customer that *would* be buying new pumps in the next year.
- *Opportunity* – a current customer of a *competitor* that *would* be buying new pumps in the next year.
- *Potential* – a current customer of a *competitor* that would *not* be buying new pumps in the next year.

Status information was gathered by the company's sales force.

The customer segmentation used at IVAC drove many sales force design decisions. It helped the company determine which hospitals to target, what sales message to communicate, how to allocate sales force time, how many salespeople to have, and how to design sales territories with manageable workloads.

Status	Teaching hospitals				Community hospitals			
	Very large (>1000 beds)	Large (500–1000 beds)	Medium (200–499 beds)	Small (<200 beds)	Very large (>1000 beds)	Large (500–1000 beds)	Medium (200–499 beds)	Small (<200 beds)
Secure								
Vulnerable								
Opportunity								
Potential								

FIGURE 3.5 Example segmentation of hospitals for IVAC Medical Systems

Customer segmentation provides a framework for action

Companies use dozens of different criteria for segmenting markets, and the same set of customers can be segmented in multiple ways. In order to create segments that are actionable, similar sales processes should be appropriate for customers within the same segment and different sales processes should be needed for customers in different segments.

The UTI segmentation scheme (see Figure 3.3) was actionable because it allowed the company to allocate sales and marketing resources more effectively. A large high school with industrial arts teachers and a high percentage of non-college-bound students gets a high level of effort. A small school without industrial arts teachers and a high percentage of college-bound students gets no effort. Other segments get effort levels that are between these two extremes.

The pharmaceutical company segmentation (see Figure 3.4) was actionable because it enabled the company to create a customized and powerful selling message for each customer segment. An entire vocabulary emerged from this segmentation scheme. Terms such as "fanatics," "triers," and "users" helped the salespeople conceptualize segment differences and deliver the most effective sales message.

The IVAC segmentation (see Figure 3.5) was actionable as it was the key concept behind the redesign of the company's sales force. For each customer segment, a sales force workload requirement was developed, along with an estimate of the likelihood of IVAC's success at winning an account. This analysis helped the company determine which accounts it should target, how many salespeople it needed, and how sales territories should be designed.

In summary, good customer segmentation creates a foundation upon which a company can make sales and marketing decisions and take action. It helps the company understand customers, define the sales process, allocate resources more effectively, and design a sales force of the right structure and size.

How to Segment Markets

Three types of customer segmentation criteria

As illustrated in Figure 3.6, companies can segment their customers based on three different types of criteria: profile, behavior, and needs. These three types are listed in increasing order of data and analytical sophistication, from bottom to top in the figure. First, profile criteria define who a customer is, for example, a customer's industry, geographic location, or size. Next, behavioral criteria define what a customer does, for example,

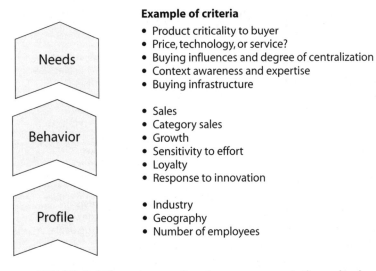

Example of criteria

Needs
- Product criticality to buyer
- Price, technology, or service?
- Buying influences and degree of centralization
- Context awareness and expertise
- Buying infrastructure

Behavior
- Sales
- Category sales
- Growth
- Sensitivity to effort
- Loyalty
- Response to innovation

Profile
- Industry
- Geography
- Number of employees

FIGURE 3.6 Three types of customer segmentation criteria

how much it buys, how fast it is growing, or how loyal it has been to the company in the past. Finally, needs criteria define what a customer requires. This might include information about how a customer buys or what decision criteria are most important to the customer (for example, price versus technology versus service).

Profile criteria. Profile criteria are sometimes called demographics or "firmographics" in business-to-business markets. UTI (see Figure 3.3) used profile criteria such as the number of students, the number of industrial arts teachers, and the percent of college-bound students to segment high schools. Table 3.2 shows another example of a segmentation scheme based on profile data for a company that sells yellow page advertising in Las Vegas. The customer segments are ranked by sales potential.

Profile criteria are important if sales actions vary depending on the value of that characteristic. For example, medical equipment company IVAC (see Figure 3.5) chose size and type of hospital as profile criteria because the values of these variables affect their sales process. Large hospitals require more time to sell. They have more departments and more people involved in the buying decision than small hospitals. The type of hospital also influences sales activities. For example, a teaching hospital is more likely to migrate quickly to a new technology than a community hospital.

Behavioral criteria. Behavioral criteria can be a powerful way to segment customers because they are based on what a customer actually does. The

TABLE 3.2 Example of customer segments based on account profile – Yellow Page advertising in Las Vegas

Rank	Customer segment	Rank	Customer segment
1	Attorneys	24	Schools – business & vocational
2	Physicians & surgeons – M. D.	25	Optometrists, O.D.
3	Insurance	26	Contractors – building, general
4	Dentists	27	Beauty salons
5	Chiropractic physicians	28	Jewelers – retail
6	Restaurants	29	Pest control
7	Entertainers – adult	30	Pawnbrokers
8	Auto repairing & service	31	Janitor service
9	Air conditioning contractors & sys.	32	Travel agencies & bureaus
10	Plumbing contractors	33	Printers
11	Hotels	34	Optometrists
12	Real estate	35	Automobile wrecking
13	Veterinarians	36	Carpet & rug dealers – new
14	Storage – self-service	37	Clinics
15	Swimming pool contrs., dealers, & designers	38	Mortgages
16	Locks & locksmiths	39	Electric contractors
17	Automobile renting & leasing	40	Furniture dealers – new
18	Florists – retail	41	Roofing contractors
19	Carpet, rug & upholstery cleaners	42	Hospitals
20	Transmissions – automobile	43	Pizza
21	Glass – auto, plate, window, etc.	44	Wedding chapels
22	Appliances – major	45	Motels
23	Automobile dealers – new cars		

segmentation scheme used by the pharmaceutical company (see Figure 3.4) is behavioral. It reflects how loyal each physician has been to the company's products and to competitors' products, as well as how many prescriptions each physician has written for a particular drug category in the past (potential). When behavioral segmentation schemes are combined with measures of market potential, as is the case for most pharmaceutical companies, they naturally include the concept of competitive position.

Market segmentation based on customer profile data at Dell

Dell uses customer profile criteria to determine the best sales process. When Dell sells to universities it uses a different sales process than when it sells to corporations. With universities, Dell offers a standardized program. Buyers are encouraged to perform many services themselves, with the university computer store playing a role in processing orders, billing, and installing hardware and software. With corporations, Dell offers a highly variable and customized program based on the buying processes and information technology infrastructure of the customer. With corporations, Dell wants to become an approved supplier and is often willing to provide customized services, such as keeping track of the customer's hardware inventory.

> ## Behavioral segmentation benefits a not-for-profit organization
>
> A not-for-profit organization used behavioral segmentation for prioritizing which companies its salespeople should call on to solicit corporate donations. Companies were first segmented according to their history with the not-for-profit organization – existing donors had made a contribution in the previous year, former donors did not contribute last year but had done so in previous years, and prospective donors had not previously contributed. Additional behavioral criteria helped to further refine the segments. Existing donors were segmented according to last year's contribution level and also by whether or not they were a new donor last year or had renewed a prior year's contribution. Former donors were segmented according to the size of their last donation. Finally, prospective donors were segmented by company size and industry (profile data) and also by the historical success of the not-for-profit organization at soliciting donations from other companies in their industry. This behavioral segmentation scheme helped the not-for-profit organization prioritize selling effort and direct resources toward those market segments with the greatest potential return.

Needs criteria. Customer needs shape opportunity and behavior. To the extent that these needs can be understood in terms of products, services, and buying processes, they are the most powerful and actionable way to segment customers. For example, IVAC Medical Systems (Figure 3.5) based its customer segments, in part, on whether or not a hospital would need to purchase new infusion pumps in the coming year. Approximately 20 percent of all hospitals would have this need in any given year. Thus, using customer needs as a basis for segmentation was a very good way to direct sales force effort to the segments with the greatest expected return.

Customers have product-driven and/or service-driven needs. For example, a product-driven FedEx customer is interested in getting the package to its destination on time. A service-driven customer is also interested in tracking the package and having the FedEx computer allocate shipping costs back to departments or projects. A product-driven Sun Microsystems customer wants a Sun server and Solaris software. A service-driven customer also wants help configuring and maintaining the system, and assistance in getting the system to work with data storage units, data bases, and software systems that come from other suppliers or value-added resellers.

Another framework for using customer-need-based criteria for segmentation is provided in Figure 3.7. The columns capture three common

	Cost	Technology	Relationship
Product-driven			
Service-driven			

FIGURE 3.7 Example of segments based on customer needs

customer needs: cost, technology or product features, and relationship or trust. These needs have different value to different customers, and can be key determinants for developing the appropriate sales process for each customer.

More examples of customer segmentation criteria

As the above examples show, customer segmentation schemes can be based on who a customer is (profile), what a customer does (behaviors), and what a customer requires (needs). The best segmentation schemes are often based on creative combinations of all three of these criteria types. For example, Figure 3.8 illustrates segmentation based on three factors – volume, growth, and the degree of decision-making centralization. This example comes from a firm selling a consumer-industrial product through different types of stores. Volume is based on historical purchases and is therefore behavioral. Growth potential is estimated using a combination of historical growth (behavioral) and future growth potential based on projected customer needs. Together, the volume and growth criteria characterize the attractiveness of the customer. Finally, the degree of centralization specifies the customer's buying preferences. Different types of buying organizations require different types of selling and merchandising activities.

Buying process	High 3-year growth potential (>100%)				Medium 3-year growth potential (50% to 100%)				Low 3-year growth potential (<50%)			
	>$200K volume	$125K–200K	$50K–124K	<$50K volume	>$200K volume	$125K–200K	$50K–124K	<$50K volume	>$200K volume	$125K–200K	$50K–124K	<$50K volume
Centralized												
Shared control												
Decentralized												

FIGURE 3.8 Example of segmentation based on potential, behavior, and needs

To summarize, Table 3.3 provides a synopsis of the wide variety of segmentation criteria used by companies across many industries. Each criterion contains an example that shows how an actual company has applied it. There are many other situations in which each of these criteria may be appropriate; the examples do not provide an exhaustive list of the possibilities.

TABLE 3.3 Customer segmentation criteria – examples from a variety of industries

Segmentation dimension		Example
Profile criteria Segmentation based on who the customer is	Industry	*Networking provider:* segments customers by type of business: government, education, utility, finance, retail, healthcare, or hi-tech
	Type of customer	*Technical school:* segments prospective customers by stage of life: high school student or adult
	Market level	*Industrial product manufacturer:* segments customers by their position in in the distribution chain – distributor, OEM (original equipment manufacturer), or end-user
	Size of customer	*Newspaper syndication service:* segments newspaper customers by size of circulation
	Scope of customer	*Consumer electronics manufacturer:* segments retail dealers into national, local, or independent dealers
	Geography	*Software provider to sawmills:* segments customers geographically because of regional differences in timber products
Behavioral criteria Segmentation based on what the customer does	Sales history	*Office supply company:* segments customers based on last year's purchases of firm's products
	Loyalty	*Telecommunications provider:* segments customers based on the firm's past relationship with the customer – current accounts, new accounts, and lost accounts (ones who have switched to a competitor)
	Customer vs prospect	*Computer manufacturer:* assigns current accounts to "farmer" salespeople and prospects to "hunter" salespeople
	Growth	*Telecommunications provider:* segments customers based on potential for future growth
	Sensitivity to effort	*Pharmaceutical firm:* segments physicians by their degree of response to past promotional efforts
	Response to innovation	*Pharmaceutical firm:* segments physician customers into "early" vs. "late" adopters, based upon each customer's willingness to try new therapies
Needs criteria Segmentation based on what the customer needs	Need for service	*Mutual funds broker:* segments customers by the amount of help they desire – "delegators" vs. "self-directed"
	Preferred sales approach	*Paper products company:* segments customers by those preferring a consultative vs. transactional sales approach
	Need for customi- zation	*Automobile insurance company:* segments customers by those requiring a standard vs. a non-standard plan for risky drivers
	Product's importance to buyer	*Manufacturing supplier:* segments customers according to whether the the firm is the customer's primary supplier, secondary supplier, or tertiary supplier
	Buying influences & degree of centralization	*Consumer products firm:* segments retail chains based on where purchasing decisions are made – at headquarters or at local stores
	Awareness	*Medical device firm:* segments physicians by their familiarity with the company's products and therapy method – past users of company products, past users of competitive products, and non-users of the therapy method
	Customer's desired role in buying	*Computer manufacturer:* segments customers by how they prefer to buy computers – in a retail store, over the telephone, or via the Internet

Two approaches to developing customer segments

There are two approaches to developing customer segments: the a priori approach and the post hoc approach. The a priori (also called ex ante) approach uses a hypothesis about how the marketplace should be divided into segments. This hypothesis is usually developed by a group of managers or other personnel and is based on available data, intuition, and organizational experience. The group uses known criteria that they feel are relevant, such as customer size and industry to create segments. The hypothesis is tested by analyzing these segments and working forward to see if the segments have distinct behaviors or needs, seek different benefits, enable viable product or service differentiation, and/or require different sales processes.

The a priori approach to segmentation has advantages and disadvantages. It is relatively easy and inexpensive to implement and therefore used frequently by companies. In addition, managers and salespeople readily accept the resulting segmentation schemes because sales input is an important part of the process that creates the segments. On the negative side, however, since the a priori approach relies on people to pre-specify market segments rather than deriving segments from data, it may overlook important but hidden dimensions that truly differentiate customers.

The post hoc or "after the fact" approach to segmentation allows analysis of primary customer data to drive the discovery of the relevant segmentation criteria. Analytical techniques are used to identify groups of customers that have similar needs and behaviors, seek the same benefits, and/or require the same sales process. Then the analysis works backwards to see if these groups can be defined in terms of demographic or other standard profile dimensions.

The post hoc approach to segmentation also has advantages and disadvantages. Because it is data-driven, it is objective and often provides new insights into the market. However, it is often not used by companies because it is complex, expensive, and time consuming, and it still requires intuition and insight to characterize the segments. In addition, the post hoc approach can require frequent collection of primary data, which is often an expensive and lengthy process. Occasionally the segments do not lend themselves to identifiable demographics and thus an actionable segment strategy is elusive.

Whichever approach is used, the ultimate objective of market segmentation is to develop a defined list of predictive characteristics that can be used to identify which segment each customer belongs to. These characteristics can include a mix of profile, behavioral, and needs criteria. If profiles, behaviors, and needs are well understood for all customers and prospects, the best approach is to use the behaviors and needs as a basis for segmentation. Typically, however, profiles are well developed, behaviors are partially understood, and needs are known only for a few customers. Thus it is often necessary to link the known needs and behaviors to the profiles of known customers, and then extrapolate this linkage to the accounts with unknown needs and behaviors.

For example, suppose that UTI (see Figure 3.3) decides to open a new school in a geographic market it has not previously served. It wants to contact high schools in the area to provide them with information to be passed on to prospective UTI students. Since UTI has not contacted these high schools before, it does not know how many interested students each will have and therefore how much sales effort will be required. However, if UTI knows the profile of each high school (the number of students, the percentage college-bound, and the number of industrial arts teachers), some assumptions can be made. It is reasonable to expect the unknown needs of a new high school to be similar to the known needs of a high school with a similar profile that has been covered by the sales force in the past.

Customer segments evolve over time

Developing a good segmentation scheme typically requires multiple iterations. The firm's experience grows and its information evolves and improves with time. For example, early segmentation schemes used at IVAC Medical Systems were based on a combination of historical sales, bed counts, and surgical procedure counts at hospitals. This first pass at market segmentation provided a general idea of the relative importance of different hospitals. However, over time, hospital purchasing became more streamlined and centralized, and opportunities for IVAC became lumpy. Since IVAC's equipment had a four to five year useful life, the age of the equipment at each hospital was a major determinant of selling activity. Also, whether the hospital was a current IVAC customer or the customer of a competitor was important. For example, current IVAC customers who were in the market for new equipment were vulnerable – they needed a strong defensive selling approach, focusing on the customer costs of switching to another supplier. Competitive customers who were in the market for new equipment were an opportunity – they needed an offensive approach aimed at convincing the account to convert to IVAC by focusing on the products, and how IVAC planned to ease the transition for the customer. By adding data on the current status of each hospital to the list of segmentation criteria (see Figure 3.5) IVAC was able to create segments that were much more homogeneous in terms of their required selling activities.

In addition to companies getting smarter with the way they segment their customers, customers evolve and move to new segments with time. This is particularly true when segments are based on behavioral criteria. In fact, the whole goal of marketing and sales is to change the behavior of the customer. For example, a "vulnerable" IVAC hospital becomes "secure" once a successful sale is made (see Figure 3.5). In the pharmaceutical company example (see Figure 3.4), successful marketing and sales effort turns a "high-potential non-user" into a "trier," then a "user," and eventually a "fanatic." Re-segmenting customers helps marketers identify important movements between segments, as well as evolutions within segments.

In summary, market segmentation is not a one-time exercise. Companies should be prepared to continually update and refine segmentation schemes as new information becomes available and as customers change.

Sales Potential is an Important Segmentation Criterion

Sales potential is used as a segmentation criterion in many of the examples discussed in this chapter. In the UTI example (see Figure 3.3), high school size, percent of non-college-bound students, and industrial arts teachers are used as surrogate measures of sales potential for high schools. At the pharmaceutical company (see Figure 3.4), historical prescriptions written for every drug are captured for each physician. Each physician's potential is the aggregate of all prescriptions that they have written for drugs in the category. At IVAC (see Figure 3.5), hospital bed numbers are used as a surrogate for the sales potential of hospitals. Sales potential is an important basis for segmentation, and thus the estimation of account sales potential merits further discussion.

Sales potential is an important segmentation criterion for three reasons. First, accounts with larger potential typically warrant greater levels of sales and marketing investment. Second, by combining sales potential data with sales data, it is possible to calculate the level of penetration into an account and to evaluate sales performance. For example, if a high potential account has low sales, there is an opportunity to improve. Third, the extent of penetration can help define the required sales process. For example, a highly penetrated account may need value-added programs to enhance the account's loyalty to the company. Low penetration accounts, on the other hand, need targeted sales and marketing effort to study the account needs and assess competitive vulnerability.

How to estimate the sales potential of an account

In some industries, direct measures of account sales potential are available. For example, in the US pharmaceutical industry, companies can purchase electronic pharmacy records that show how many prescriptions each physician has written for a particular drug category. In most industries, however, the actual sales potential of an account is not known. Thus, companies use surrogate measures and markers to estimate account potential. Surrogate measures capture customer size in terms of number of employees, office space, or overall sales. Markers are categorical, such as a customer's industry or the presence of a centralized buyer.

Surrogates can be found in virtually every industry. Table 3.4 provides some examples of surrogate measures of sales potential that various companies have used.

TABLE 3.4 Surrogate measures of sales potential used by companies in different industries

Industry	Surrogate measure of sales potential
Pharmaceuticals	Historical prescriptions written for a particular drug category in countries where pharmacy records are kept electronically.
	Physician office size, physician specialty, size of patient waiting area, and patient demographics in countries where electronic pharmacy records are not available.
Office equipment	Number of employees, number of white collar workers, industry.
Computer software and peripherals	Installed number of different types of computers, overall company revenue, number of company locations.
Health and beauty aids sold in retail stores	Type of outlet (mass merchandiser, drug store, grocery store, etc.), all commodity store volume.
	Buying Power Index – census track data on income, retail sales, and population.

Salespeople can provide estimates of account potential

Often, companies ask their sales force to provide estimates of account potential. A medical imaging equipment manufacturer asked its salespeople to complete a survey of all the customers and prospects in their territory to determine what medical imaging equipment was currently in use. The survey captured the manufacturer and acquisition date of almost every medical imaging system in the country. This data provided an excellent estimate of the future potential of each account. However, if this input from salespeople is used to set goals, salespeople may develop a pessimistic view of account potential!

Frequently, companies find it useful to translate surrogate potential measures into potential revenue dollars. This makes the sales potential estimate more meaningful and actionable. Heuristic approaches accomplish the translation in a systematic and rational way. Two variations of a useful heuristic approach are described below.

Start by segmenting accounts based on surrogate measures such as industry and the number of employees. Then study the sales to accounts in each segment and develop a rule for estimating the level of sales that should be possible for each account. For example, consider the frequency distribution of sales at accounts in the market segment shown in Figure 3.9. There are 100 accounts in the segment. The height of each bar shows how many of these accounts produce the sales levels identified on the horizontal axis. One approach to estimating sales potential is as follows:

- Determine a certain percentile, for example, the 80th percentile of sales for the segment (i.e. determine the level of sales so that 80 percent of the accounts in the segment have sales below this level). In the example 80 percent of the accounts fall below $50,000 in sales.
- Use this as a proxy for the sales potential of all accounts in the segment whose sales are lower than this level. In the example, any account with less than $50,000 in sales would have a potential of $50,000.

An alternative heuristic for translating surrogate potential data into revenue dollars is:

- For each segment, calculate the maximum sales that any account in the segment has achieved. In the example, maximum sales are $95,000.

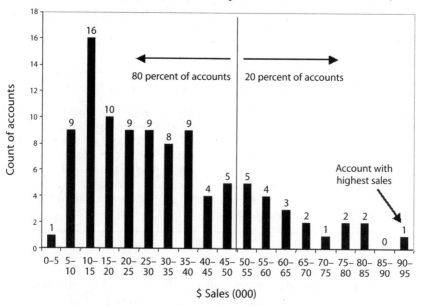

FIGURE 3.9 Frequency distribution of sales to accounts in one market segment

- Define the sales increase possible in the other accounts as the difference between the account's current sales and a certain percentage, such as 50 percent of the gap to the maximum. In the example, if an account has current sales of $30,000, its potential is estimated as $30,000 + .5 * ($95,000 − $30,000) = $62,500.

The appropriate percentile (in the first heuristic) or percentage (in the second heuristic) to use for estimating potential depends on the stage of the product or customer in the life cycle. In the growth stage, a higher percentile or percentage is appropriate. In the mature stage, a lower percentile or percentage is appropriate. Different heuristics may be appropriate for customers and prospects, or for low-penetration and high-penetration accounts. Heuristic approaches are approximate, yet they can be extremely valuable to sales organizations that wish to develop meaningful estimates of account sales potential.

Sources of Data for Market Segmentation

Gathering quality data for market segmentation is crucial. Data can come from sources that are either internal or external to the company. Examples of internal data sources include sales and factory shipment records as well as call or prospect lists from the sales force. Examples of external data sources include industry associations, general guides to business information, data vendors, and government statistics.

When selecting a data source, consider not only accuracy and cost, but also the degree of fit between the data and the problem, particularly if the data have been compiled for other purposes. In addition, consider the future availability of the data, so that segmentation can be updated on an ongoing basis as needed. When choosing an external supplier of data, consider factors such as reputation, technical expertise, experience and reliability of the supplier. Data constraints often impose practical restrictions on how much or at what cost the company can obtain information about its customers.

Some sources of data for market segmentation

Association sources: *Directories in Print* and *Encyclopedia of Associations.*
General business information guide source: *Encyclopedia of Business Information Sources.*
Leading US business data vendors: Dun & Bradstreet, American Business Information, Database America, IMS, Trinet, R. L. Polk, TRW, Infobase, and Equifax.
US Government sources: US Census Bureau, Bureau of Economic Analysis, Bureau of Labor Statistics, www.fedstats.gov

SALES STRATEGY DEVELOPMENT ACTIVITY 2: DETERMINE PRODUCT/SERVICE OFFERING FOR EACH SEGMENT

Once the appropriate market segments have been defined, sales strategy development proceeds with a focus on determining the firm's product and service offering for each segment. Different market segments may value the firm's offering in different ways or for alternative reasons. The firm increases the value of its offering in the eyes of its customers by proposing solutions that are tailored to each market segment's specific needs.

GE Medical Systems offers array of services to hospital customers

GE Medical Systems sells a large array of products to hospitals, including MRI, CT, and X-ray imaging machines. These products are sold outright, financed by GE, or on a shared-risk basis where GE takes an interest in the imaging unit. GE can design the space, train or provide the personnel, or manage the units. GE even provides training to its customers in topics such as Six Sigma quality, and Leadership through its Work-Out™ (a GE trademark) program for problem solving. This array of offerings is tailored to the specific needs of a hospital or healthcare network.

To establish value for each market segment effectively, it is important to understand how customers make their buying decisions.

Why Do Customers Buy?

Firms and their customers have mutual incentives for doing business with one another. A customer will be motivated to buy from a firm if he or she believes that the value of the firm's offering exceeds its price. At the same time, the firm wants to sell at as high a price as possible. The firm's incentive to sell is driven by the extent to which price exceeds cost. The relationship between perceived value, price, and cost, and their impact on incentives of the company and its customers is shown pictorially in Figure 3.10.

As Figure 3.10 shows, firms that want to increase the incentive for customers to purchase can do so by pursuing two different strategies – either a lowest price strategy or a value creation strategy. With a lowest price strategy, the firm reduces its prices, thus widening the gap between perceived value and price and increasing the customer's incentive to purchase. If a firm hopes to pursue this strategy without sacrificing profitably, it must become more efficient and reduce its costs. Alternatively, a firm can choose to pursue a value creation strategy. This involves increasing the perceived value of the firm's offering to customers, thus widening

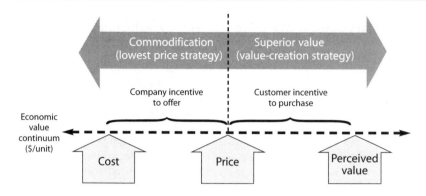

FIGURE 3.10 Impact of cost, price, and perceived value on incentives for companies and their customers

the gap between perceived value and price and increasing the customer's incentive to purchase. By offering customized solutions tailored to the needs of specific market segments, firms increase customer value. Examples of companies that have pursued both lowest price and value creation strategies are provided below.

Companies can pursue value-creation and low-price strategies simultaneously

In the consumer banking industry, automatic teller machines create value for many customers. They are convenient, allowing customers to access their money outside of regular banking hours at a multitude of locations. At the same time, ATMs help banks lower their labor costs because they reduce the need for bank tellers. Thus, an ATM can both create value for customers and allow a bank to charge lower prices for services.

Lowest price and cost reduction strategies

Firms pursuing lowest price strategies must reduce costs if they hope to maintain profitability. Often, firms drive down costs by creating efficiencies in their manufacturing processes or their acquisition of raw materials. Firms in numerous industries have followed this strategy by moving manufacturing to countries such as Taiwan, Korea, and Singapore in the 1960s and 1970s, and to China, Malaysia, and India more recently. Cost advantages can also come through economies of scale or new production technologies. In addition, companies pursuing low price strategies often strive to streamline non-value-added costs, such as administrative and other overhead expenses, by shortening distribution channels, and by using lower cost sales channels.

Wal-Mart pursues low-price strategy by reducing product acquisition costs

Mass merchandiser Wal-Mart is well known for its success in pursuing a low price strategy. Wal-Mart reduces its product acquisition expenses by working closely with its suppliers to streamline costs. For example, P&G and Wal-Mart began a partnership program during the 1990s aimed at cost reduction. Specialists in sales, finance, information technology, and logistics from both companies worked together to make the process of delivering hundreds of P&G products through Wal-Mart and on to consumers more efficient. The partnership has allowed Wal-Mart to achieve major savings in inventory. At the same time, the partnership has helped P&G cut costs and bring value to its customers, Wal-Mart, and itself. Today, 18 percent of P&G sales are to the 100 million people who shop at Wal-Mart's stores each week.

Lowest price strategies can also focus on cost reduction through the sales process itself. Many firms leverage lower cost selling channels such as telesales, direct mail, and the Internet to perform parts of their sales process. In fact, these channels can be better than a sales force at accomplishing some selling tasks, such as lead generation, routine order placement, and customer service. Many firms use lower cost selling channels to reach low potential or remotely located accounts For example, the sales force for the business-to-business manufacturer shown in Figure 3.11 spent 20 percent of its time with low volume accounts that produced only 2 percent of the firm's sales. By shifting coverage of these accounts to the firm's telesales group, the firm reduced sales force costs substantially without risking significant loss in sales volume.

At high potential accounts, many firms pursuing lowest price strategies have worked together with customers to successfully streamline the entire

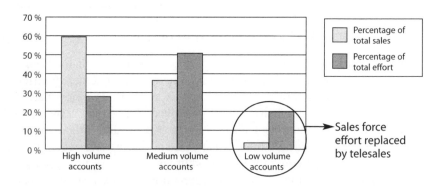

FIGURE 3.11 Comparison of sales and sales force effort for a business-to-business manufacturer

---

American Hospital Supply works with customers to reduce buying and selling costs

American Hospital Supply Corporation (now Cardinal Health Medical Products and Services) revolutionized its industry when during the mid-1980s it radically simplified the ordering and restocking process for its disposable hospital supply products. The company installed computer terminals at the locations of its hospital and medical supply store customers. These terminals connected directly to American Hospital Supply's computer system, so that orders could be placed directly as soon as supplies fell below a certain level. Prior to the computer terminal installation, orders were taken and processed by the sales force. The streamlined ordering process not only reduced logistical costs, but also increased customer loyalty and gave American Hospital Supply a significant advantage over its competitors.

---

process of selling, buying, and distributing products, thus reducing costs for both the firm and its customers.

Value creation strategies

Value creation strategies involve increasing the worth of the firm's offering to customers. Value is conceptualized in Figure 3.10, and is measured by the monetary worth of the benefits a customer expects to receive. One way to assess customer value is to think about it from three different perspectives: functional, economic, and psychological. An offering has functional value if it helps the customer solve a problem or accomplish a goal. An offering has economic value if it helps the customer make money, save money or improve efficiency. Finally, an offering has psychological value if it makes the buyer feel less uncertain, more secure, or more fulfilled. Firms can increase customer value by tailoring their offering to address the diverse functional, economic, and psychological needs of each market segment.

Sources of customer value at Hanna

Children's clothing manufacturer Hanna Andersson offers its customers a program called Hannadowns. The program allows customers to return clothes that their kids outgrow and get a 20 percent discount on their next purchase. Over 10,000 pieces of clothing a month are donated to charity. The Hannadowns program offers customers all three types of value. The program has functional value because it provides a way for customers to dispose of outgrown clothes. It has economic value because it provides customers with a 20 percent discount on their next purchase. Finally, it has psychological value because it highlights the quality of Hanna's clothing and helps customers feel good about donating to charity.

Sources of customer value. Usually the major source of customer value is derived from the product itself, but the selling company can extend value beyond the tangible characteristics of the product. The company can develop an extended product and a value proposition that includes various services, programs, or systems. Several examples of value-added services, programs, and systems are presented in Table 3.5.

TABLE 3.5 Services, programs, and systems that create customer value

Value-enhancing services
- Delivery – customer lead times, variation from promised delivery dates, condition of the product on arrival, just-in-time delivery, willingness to hold inventory for customer
- In-person sales calls
- Installation, after-sales support, and maintenance services
- Customer training
- Assistance with resolution of quality control and production issues
- Assistance with integrating the firm's products with the customer's products
- Ways to get help with troubleshooting - toll-free helplines, user manuals, Internet sites

Value-enhancing programs
- Custom sizes and mix variety
- Long-term contracts that avoid price fluctuations
- Financing options – deals, terms, conditions, rebates, or guarantees
- Partnering – co-design, joint marketing research, or co-promotion
- Programs that provide advice and consulting, specification, process engineering or redesign

Value-enhancing systems
- Ordering systems– computer-to-computer ordering, shared material resource planning, electronic information exchange, order tracking
- Credit, billing, and collection procedures and systems
- Systems that improve responsiveness, such as databases that log complaints or monitor actual delivery dates against promised dates

---

Service enhancements to Butterball's products

Butterball™ (a registered trademark of ConAgra Brands, Inc.) offered its customers a unique service advantage when in 1981 it opened its Turkey Talk-Line. This 24-hour hotline was created to assist struggling chefs with preparing the holiday bird. In 2002, the hotline had a staff of 45 home economists and nutritionists who respond to over 100,000 questions in November and December. In addition, in 1995 Butterball launched butterball.com, one of the first consumer web sites, complete with turkey preparation tips and recipes.

In developing the offering for each customer segment, a firm must implicitly prioritize customers. A sequential thought process for pursuing opportunities can bring discipline in many situations. Such an assessment can be the cornerstone of a sales process. An example sequence follows:

- Is there an opportunity? Is the customer willing and able to buy?
- Are the firm's offerings (product and value-added offering) competitive?
- Can the firm win? What is our firm's sales strengths and nature of relationships with the customer?
- Is it worth winning? What is the value of winning the sales and is it worth the investment?

The detail at which such an assessment is done depends upon the purpose of the assessment. A detailed customer-by-customer or opportunity-by-opportunity assessment is needed during the actual selling to accounts. For planning purposes, a simplified assessment of opportunities is sufficient.

System enhancements at UPS

United Parcel Service offered its customers a unique systems advantage when in 1995 it became the first package delivery company to offer online tracking to customers. Within six months, 100,000 customers a day were logging on to check up on their packages' progress. In 2002, the UPS web site averaged more than 6 million online tracking requests per day.

Program enhancements at SCP Pool

SCP Pool, the nation's largest swimming pool supply company, offered its customers a unique program advantage when the backyard swimming pool business slowed significantly during an economic downturn. SCP's customers were mostly small and local swimming pool contractors and maintenance companies. None of these customers had the resources to launch a large-scale marketing campaign aimed at encouraging people to build backyard pools. SCP's sales force initiated such a campaign. They developed marketing kits for contractors that educated consumers on the benefits of pool ownership. They also developed a web site with an online brochure and a contractor directory. Contractors that participated in the program reported a large increase in good leads and up to 15 percent more business.

Value-creation strategies incorporating the sales process. Customer value can also be delivered through the sales process itself. Anyone dealing with a damaged automobile appreciates the insurance agent who expeditiously processes the claim and quickly authorizes repairs. A software buyer may value the experience and perspective of a salesperson who has dealt with other similar customers in complex environments. A purchasing agent responsible for buying hundreds of different replacement parts may value a computerized inventory management and ordering system that eliminates the need to contact a salesperson for routine purchases.

Dell delivers corporate customers value through electronic ordering system

Successful personal computer manufacturers recognize that business customers, in addition to wanting good prices, value a solid vendor relationship, ease of doing business, and good technical support. These features have become an important part of the value they offer to customers. Dell offers corporate customers free software for tracking computer hardware inventory and placing new orders with Dell. This software fulfills an important need for the customer and at the same time, strengthens the customer's ties to Dell as a supplier.

Cisco's sales force helps resolve channel conflict

Cisco Systems offered its customer US West (a large telephone company) a creative program advantage. In 1998 US West decided to enter the digital subscriber line (DSL) market for high-speed Internet access, and chose Cisco to provide the computer networking infrastructure. Part of Cisco's offering to US West was a program called Jump Start which helps customers build their marketing programs. Joint planning sessions between Cisco's Jump Start group and US West's marketing organization generated a creative idea for selling to US West's customers. US West wanted to sell its DSL service to other Internet service providers (ISPs). But because US West was also an ISP, these businesses were reluctant to purchase from their competitor. Cisco salespeople stepped in to help out, creating a credible buffer and convincing the ISPs that US West was not interested in stealing customers. Cisco salespeople even earned a commission from Cisco every time they signed up a new DSL customer for US West.

SALES STRATEGY DEVELOPMENT ACTIVITY 3: DESIGN SALES PROCESS

In order to provide the right products and services to the right customers, certain activities, tasks, and work must be performed. These activities can be organized into a defined sales process for every market segment. The right sales process is essential for making an effective customer connection. The sales process is also an important way that firms deliver value to their customers.

From the time a customer hears about a product, to the closing of the sale and the servicing of the product, many interactions with the selling company take place. A sales process is an organized flow of all the activities that need to be accomplished so that a company can successfully do business with a customer. Every contact the customer has with a company and its products is a chance for the company's offering to shine. All aspects of the interface between a firm and its customers help to "sell."

This section of the chapter begins with a description of the major components of a firm's sales process and some sales process examples.

A sales process in the health and beauty aids industry

A consumer products firm sells a wide assortment of health and beauty aid products through retail stores. The firm generates demand for its products by advertising to consumers. This is accomplished by working with an advertising agency and various media companies which create and deliver the desired message to a broad audience. In addition to advertising to consumers, the firm must connect with the retailers who sell their products. The firm employs a full-time sales force to call on retail store managers and buyers to show them how they can improve profitability by including a suggested shelf presentation of the firm's hundreds of stock keeping units (SKUs) in their store. These salespeople also meet with retail store managers to demonstrate new product lines, explain the advertising programs that support their products, review and place orders, and discuss upcoming promotions. If a retailer places an order, the firm works with shippers to ensure that products are delivered to the retailer as needed. Upon delivery, the firm's part-time merchandising sales force helps place products on the shelves or in the back room inventory. Then, on an ongoing basis, these part-time merchandisers visit the stores to verify that packages have not expired, clean shelves and fill open slots with products, and count the inventory held in the back of the store. They also reconcile inventory records and record activities at the store on a hand-held computer, and upload this data nightly to the firm's central computer.

Following this, a conceptual framework for defining a sales process is presented. Finally, some factors that affect sales process choices are described and numerous examples are provided.

The Components of the Sales Process

A firm's sales process can be viewed as the way to attract and retain customers. Figure 3.12 shows the five major phases of the sales process. These phases are interest creation, pre-purchase, purchase, immediate post-purchase, and ongoing post-purchase. The large arrows in the figure show the primary flow of selling activity, while the small arrows show secondary flows that are essential for building long-term customer relationships. With a new customer, the process starts with interest creation. However, with an existing customer, the sales process is continuous. Good post-purchase interaction leads to enhanced interest creation and pre-purchase activity, as it supports a continuing business relationship with the customer.

The five major phases of the sales process are described further below, illustrated by the activities performed in each phase by a large newspaper selling advertising space to potential advertisers and advertising agencies.

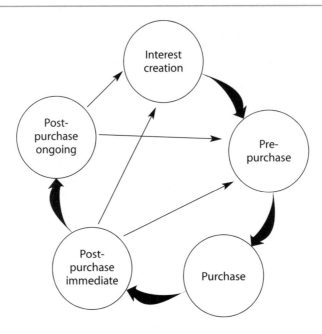

FIGURE 3.12 Phases of the sales process

Sales channels and the sales process at the health and beauty aids firm

Different sales channels can be used to accomplish the work required in different phases of the sales process. The health and beauty aids firm uses advertising to create interest among consumers, while using a full-time sales force is to perform interest creation, pre-purchase, and purchase activities for retailers. A part-time merchandising sales force performs the immediate and ongoing post-purchase work that keeps the firm's products flowing smoothly through the retail stores.

Interest creation

In order to obtain sales, sellers first have to get prospective customers interested in their products and services. Interest creation can include activities such as creating awareness, prospecting or identifying potential customers, generating leads, generating traffic or inbound calls, providing information about the company's products and services to prospective customers, and identifying purchase influencers both internal and external to the customer. Interest creation is often accomplished through trade shows, direct mail, and advertising, but salespeople can prospect as well.

> ### Interest creation activities at the newspaper company
>
> Salespeople follow up on leads generated by the company's marketing department. This frequently involves making cold calls on prospective advertisers.

Pre-purchase

During the pre-purchase phase, customers and prospects are seriously considering making a purchase. Often, they are evaluating competitive product offerings. Pre-purchase activities for sellers include qualifying prospective customers, explaining features and benefits, assessing customer needs, cooperating with the customer in problem solving, demonstrating company and product capabilities, comparing the offering with the competition or substitute offerings, and listening carefully to what customers want.

> ### Pre-purchase activities at the newspaper company
>
> Salespeople make formal presentations and have informal discussions with prospective customers. They tell customers what section of the paper (sports, business) and placement on each page is available at what price. They also provide statistics on reach, coverage, and advertising payback.

Purchase

Purchase is the final flurry of activity culminating in a sales transaction. It is the activity most likely to involve direct salespeople. Purchase activities include bidding, writing proposals and documentation, writing orders, persuading, negotiating, finalizing terms, and closing the sale.

> ### Purchase activities at the newspaper company
>
> Salespeople negotiate with customers about the size, placement, length of run, and price of their advertisement.

Immediate post-purchase

The sales process does not end with a purchase. The product must be delivered and installed. The buyer must be trained and questions must be answered. Bills must be sent and collected. Immediate post-purchase activities include providing credit and finance, checking order status, delivering the product, breaking down bulk quantities, installing the product, handling returns, training users, processing ownership, and collecting initial payment.

Immediate post-purchase activities at the newspaper company

Salespeople provide art assistance to small customers who do not generate their own artwork. For larger customers, the salespeople coordinate with the customer or the advertising agency that is providing the artwork.

Ongoing post-purchase

The sales process is continuous. After the immediate post-purchase activities are completed, the seller's focus shifts from the "attraction" part of the sales process to the "retention" part of the process. Work focuses on nurturing a continuing business relationship with the customer. This can include activities such as introducing new products and technologies, performing customer market analysis, developing joint customer marketing programs, monitoring inventory, providing customer service, handling complaints, staying in touch, placing reorders, collecting ongoing payments for credit purchases, and providing ongoing training.

Ongoing post-purchase activities at the newspaper company

Salespeople make adjustments to advertisements for subsequent print runs. They also keep in touch with their customers, seeking new opportunities for future business.

Table 3.6 summarizes the varied activities that can comprise a firm's sales process.

Sales processes depend on customer needs, product and market characteristics, and a variety of environmental factors. Figure 3.13 shows an example of the steps of a sales process, and for each step, specifies the activities, the participants, and the data and tools used.

A Framework for Defining a Sales Process

Good sales strategies define an appropriate sales process for each major customer or customer segment. Figure 3.14 provides a conceptual framework for how a company can vary its sales process based on the size and information needs of its customers. Large customers that have a high need for information and solutions get a lot of hand-holding. The sales process includes consulting, customization, and problem solving. When a smaller

TABLE 3.6 Activities that comprise a sales process

Interest creation	Pre-purchase	Purchase	Immediate post-purchase	Ongoing post-purchase
• Prospecting and identifying potential customers • Generating leads • Generating traffic (inbound calls) • Identifying purchase influencers, both internal and external to the customer • Creating awareness of the product, the need for the product, and the company • Providing information about the company's products and services • Identifying potential selling partners and informing them of the company's capabilities	• Explaining features and benefits • Qualifying customers and prospects • Assessing customer and prospect needs • Cooperating in problem solving • Demonstrating company and product capabilities • Comparing the company's product offering with competitive or substitute offerings • Listening	• Persuading, negotiating, and finalizing terms • Bidding • Writing proposals and documentation • Closing (asking for the business) • Writing orders and reorders	• Checking order status • Delivery • Installation • Training • Handling complaints and returns • Providing financing • Collecting payments	• Monitoring inventory • Developing joint customer marketing programs • Performing customer market analysis • Introducing new products and technologies

customer has a high need for information and solutions, however, it is often not economically feasible to provide such customized service. With these customers, the sales process consists of performing a quick needs assessment and solution, and then targeting those customers and prospects that are economically viable. When customers have low need for information and solutions, the sales process also varies based on customer size. For large customers with low information needs, the sales process focuses on enhancing the relationship by providing high-quality service, automatic re-buys, and prompt delivery. For small customers with low information needs, the sales process is very cost effective, frequently encouraging customers to place their own orders through the company's call center or web site.

Step	Develop opportunity and customer insight	Customize offering and value proposition	Develop proposal and terms	Negotiate and close	Implement solution	Maximize long-term value
Activities	• Analyze opportunity and penetration • Identify targets • Define customer situation and needs • Get customer agreement on need • Map decision-making process and influences	• Develop solutions in close partnership with selected client personnel • Socialize concept with decision makers and influencers • Finalize offering • Anticipate source of value for each stakeholder	• Develop proposal • Develop terms	• Present proposal • Identify concerns • Identify unanticipated benefits • Revise offering and proposal • Close	• Meet to plan implementation • Assess impact on existing processes • Develop implementation plan with milestones • Implement • Follow up	• Assess satisfaction • Assess business impact • Provide ongoing support
Participants	• Market analyst • Industry specialist • Account executive	• Account executive • Industry specialist • Finance	• Account executive • Industry specialist • Finance • Sales manager	• Account executive • Others, as needed	• Account executive • Implementation team	• Account executive • Account service specialist • Others, as needed
Data and tools	• Sales data • Market intelligence • Customer influence map	• Customer ROI • Value proposition templates	• Proposal templates • Configuration and pricing tool		• Account executive • Implementation team	• Follow-up templates

FIGURE 3.13 An example of a sales process

Figure 3.15 shows how this framework for defining a sales process is used by a seller of mutual funds. The sales process varies based on the amount of money a customer has to invest. Investors with under $100,000 are assigned to the company's call center. The telesales brokers who respond to these calls answer questions, execute transactions, and try to upgrade customers to a higher investment level. For investors with over $100,000, the sales process varies based on their desire for information and help. "Delegator" investors want a consulta-

Customer size and opportunity		
Large	**Account maintenance** Continue high-quality service Automatic re-buy (EDI) Prompt delivery Enhance value proposition Relationships Friendship	**Effectiveness selling** Solve and consult Cooperation Customization Integration Partnership
Small	**Efficiency selling** Take orders and assure distribution Consider self-ordering (lower price)	**Targeted selling** Quick needs assessment and solution Explain features and benefits Economic evaluation
Buying process	Low information, low solution needs	High information, high solution needs

FIGURE 3.14 A framework for defining a sales process

tive relationship with their broker. Brokers who deal with delegator investors make investment recommendations and provide ongoing portfolio management services. "Self-directed" investors, on the other hand, just want their investment transactions executed. Thus, the selling activities of brokers who deal with self-directed investors are limited to answering questions and executing transactions. Self-directed investors are also encouraged to use the company's call center.

Investment level		
Over $100K "Gold" customers	**Account maintenance** Handle incoming calls Provide investment information, including priority notice about new products Execute investment transactions	**Effectiveness selling** Handle incoming calls from assigned clients Provide investment information, including priority notice about new products Execute investment transactions Provide portfolio recommendations Provide ongoing portfolio management services
Under $100K	**Efficiency selling** **Targeted selling** Handle incoming calls Provide investment information Execute investment transactions Try to upgrade clients to >$100K level	
Investor profile	"Self-directed" investors	"Delegator" investors

FIGURE 3.15 Major selling activities for a seller of mutual funds

Another useful way to categorize sales processes is to think in terms of transactional, consultative, and enterprise selling. *Transactional selling* is targeted to a buyer who understands the product and is interested in an inexpensive and painless transaction. *Consultative selling* matches the needs of buyers who want and are willing to pay for total value of the product in use. These customers are interested in the seller consulting with them to enhance the value of the product by, for example, helping streamline the supply chain, or providing insights on how the product can be integrated with other products to further enhance its value. *Enterprise selling* refers to the situation when a supplier and customer collaborate extensively and deeply to create value for each other. Intel engages in "enterprise selling" with Microsoft, and P&G with Wal-Mart. Figure 3.16 shows a generic sales process and how the stages are treated differently in transactional selling and consultative selling. The transactional selling process focuses on the purchase itself. The consultative selling process adds value throughout the process. Problems arise when customers want the service of a consultative process, and want to pay the prices of a transactional process. The challenge with such value-draining customers is for the seller to match the opportunity with the sales investment.

Factors that Influence the Sales Process

The appropriate sales process is predicated on defining the essential work that needs to be accomplished to meet customer segment needs

	Recognition of needs	Evaluation of options	Resolution of concerns	Purchase	Implement
Transactional selling	Customer has fully defined needs & problems	Customer is aware of options & relevant decision criteria	Customer has few issues or concerns	Seller can help make purchase cheap & painless	Customer knows how to use product
Opportunity to add value	Low	Low	Low	High	Low
Consultative selling	Help define customer needs	Design customized solutions & help make informed choices	Counsel customers & help resolve concerns	Help make purchase easy & painless	Advise & problem solve rollout issues
Opportunity to add value	High	High	High	High	High

FIGURE 3.16 Transactional and consultative sales processes

economically. Several factors can contribute to the development of the final sales process. These factors are listed and described in Table 3.7. The impact of each of the six factors on sales process design is described further below.

TABLE 3.7 Six major factors affecting sales process design

Factor	Description
Customer needs	• Customer's perceived value for the product • Centralized or decentralized buying • Customer's product evaluation process and composition of the decision-making unit • Negotiation
Market characteristics	• Buyer concentration • Diversity of usage • Existence of collaborators and co-suppliers • Seller's competitive position • Competitors' strategies
Product characteristics	• Physical product characteristics • Complexity/degree of customization/need for user education • Life cycle/maturity • Risk to customer • Seasonality
Economic factors	• Market segment potential • Contribution margin • Distribution costs
Company environment	• Product line breadth • Company goals and resources • Corporate culture
Country and industry environment	• The economy • Technology, communications, and transportation • Regulatory framework

Customer needs

To design the best sales process, a company must start by understanding what their customers and prospects want and need during the buying process, and how they buy. These needs usually vary across customers or customer segments. Figure 3.17 shows an example of how the selling process could be matched to a customer's buying process.

Several aspects of customer needs affect sales processes. First, the perceived value of a purchase and the product's importance to the customer are important considerations. A customer who views a product as very important and expensive may demand a lot of personal attention, training, support, or customization. Another customer for whom the

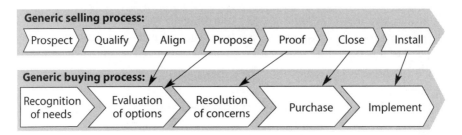

FIGURE 3.17 Linking the selling process steps to a customer's buying process

product has less risk or importance may instead value efficient ordering and delivery. A company's sales process also depends upon how customers buy. A customer with many branch offices will need one sales process if purchase decisions are made centrally at headquarters and another if purchase decisions are made locally in the branch offices. A customer's product evaluation process and composition of the

---

Different customer needs require different sales processes

Two different customers want to buy computer hardware and software for their business. The first customer is a small business owner who knows very little about computers. Thus, he needs a lot of advice and support. He needs consulting about what products to buy, training on how to use them, and ongoing access to help and support services. The second customer is a computer specialist at a large company. This buyer has consulted with experts within her company and knows what she wants to buy. She needs minimal ongoing advice and support – these services are provided by others at the company. What is most important to this buyer is that she gets a good price and an efficient buying process, with all the needed products bundled conveniently together.

Selling to Schlumberger

Companies that want to sell successfully to oilfield and information services company Schlumberger must consider the innovative buying processes in place at the company. Schlumberger has its own intranet shopping site designed specifically for its employees with buying responsibility. Buyers at Schumberger use the site to purchase equipment and supplies for the company, ranging from computer hardware and software to office supplies to products for maintaining and repairing equipment and facilities. Only products from preferred suppliers are included on the intranet shopping site. To become a preferred supplier, a seller must offer high value and good pricing and must work with Schlumberger to create links between Schlumberger's internal intranet buying site and the seller's own Internet ordering site. Only suppliers that can integrate these activities successfully into their sales processes will be successful at selling to Schlumberger.

> ### Selling to Sam's Club and Costco
>
> A packaged food and beverage company that sells to warehouse stores organizes its sales process differently for two of its major customers: Sam's Club and Costco. Sam's Club conducts all buying at its headquarters in Bentonville, Arkansas. The sales process requires the Sam's Club sales team to be located in Bentonville to best serve the customer's ongoing needs. Costco, on the other hand, has eight regional buying offices. The food and beverage company divides its Costco sales team among these eight locations in order to implement a sales process that is responsive to the buying needs of each region.

purchasing decision-making unit are also important considerations. An account with a single decision maker requires a different selling approach than one where a committee decides. Finally, the desire of customers to negotiate with the seller can determine how the sales process should progress.

When selling to complex organizations with many decision and influence points, it is useful to map the customer organization along various dimensions:

- *Buying roles:* is the person a user, an evaluator, a decision maker, or approver? Some people can wear multiple hats. Some roles can be formal, and others can be informal.
- *Buying orientation:* is the person technical, financial, relationship, or solution oriented?
- *Level of support:* is the person an advocate, a supporter, neutral, or antagonistic?

The selling process consists of developing a map and a sales strategy that addresses the various needs of the decision influencers.

> ### Sales processes must address the needs of different purchase influencers
>
> A company wants to purchase a new CRM system for the sales force. A task force comprised of individuals from several different departments has been asked to make the decision which system to purchase. The salespeople and sales managers on the task force want to know, "How will it work for me?" The computer services group wants to know, "Does it meet specifications?" The finance director wants to know, "What is the ROI?" Finally, the individual in charge of the task force wants to know, "How can we make this happen?" The sales process must cater to the diverse needs of these different purchase influencers.

Negotiation in consumer automobile purchases

Traditional car dealerships plan for negotiation as part of their sales process. As a result, educated and informed buyers who are willing to negotiate generally pay less for a car than unaware buyers who accept the first price offered. Recently, "no haggle" car dealerships have become popular. These dealerships promise the same price for a given vehicle to all buyers, thus catering to consumers who do not like to negotiate.

Market characteristics

Market characteristics also play a role in determining the best sales process. The degree to which buyers are concentrated is an important consideration. An original equipment manufacturer of automobile components can have a highly customized sales process that involves a lot of sales and engineering design interaction with each customer, since the company sells to a limited number of large automakers. On the other hand, this highly customized, personal approach would not be practical or affordable for a company selling inexpensive products such as office supplies to millions of potential customers.

The firm's competitive position also influences the sales process. If a firm has a strong relationship with a customer already, the sales process may focus on offering value-added programs that enhance loyalty. When the firm sells to a different customer that has a strong relationship with a competitor, the sales process focuses instead on understanding the customer's needs and identifying competitive vulnerability. Additional market characteristics that influence the sales process include the diversity of ways that a product is used and the strategies of the firm's major competitors.

A military analogy is useful in thinking about competitive strategy. If one is attacking an entrenched competitor, one has to decide whether the sales process is one of frontal attack, flanking, or fragmentation. Frontal attack is appropriate if you have the power and strength to do it, a strategy often recommended for the number two firm in a market. For smaller players, the best strategy usually is to make a flanking move: that is, a move in an uncontested area. With no uncontested areas, the best strategy is to attack along a narrow front that is not defensible, for example, where the defender does not have the best offering. In the 1970s, when IBM dominated the data centers and the "back office" of most large companies, DEC (Digital Equipment Corporation) frequently did a flanking attack in other departments such as R&D.

Defensive strategies are for incumbents, and the best defense is to attack oneself. For example, if the coverage of a customer segment is weak because of a weak partner, a company can create other partnerships which also target

---

Diversity of product usage affects sales processes in chemicals

A chemical producer sells the same chemical to customers in more than 30 different industries, and the various industries use the product in very different ways. For example, one customer uses the chemical as an industrial lubricant, while another uses it as an additive in personal care products. Due to the extreme fragmentation and diversity of the product's usage, it is not possible for the company's salespeople to understand every possible product application. Thus the company's sales process focuses on educating customers about the physical properties of the chemicals.

Strategies of major competitors affect sales processes

The goals and strategies, market segment focus, and distribution methods of a firm's competitors play an important role in determining a company's sales process. A company may need to offer certain sales process features just to achieve competitive parity. For example, if a major competitor has a 24-7 toll free customer service number, the company may need to offer this service as well or risk losing sales. In other cases, competitive advantage is the goal. For example, UPS achieved a significant competitive advantage when it became the first package delivery company to offer online package tracking to customers.

---

the same segment. The leader has to also defend against any strong offense by a smaller competitor. Today's nuisance can become tomorrow's headache. Sales processes have much to learn from the military!

Product characteristics

Product characteristics also help to determine the right sales process. The complexity of a product, the degree to which it needs to be customized, and the need for user education, are all key considerations. Complex products often require customization and extensive training and support, both during and after the sale. Straightforward products are typically sold with less face-to-face interaction. The maturity of a product is

---

Physical product size can affect the sales process

In 2002 the top three companies that sold to consumers directly in their homes were Amway (homecare, nutritional, and personal care products), Avon (cosmetics, decorative products, and jewelry) and Tupperware (house wares and kitchenware). All of these companies sell products that are relatively small in size and light in weight, making it possible for a salesperson to carry samples door-to-door. A seller of very large and heavy items, such as automobiles or large appliances, could not sell in this way. Customers who want to see these items before making a purchase decision must visit a retail show room.

Risk affects how a pharmaceutical company sells

A biotechnology company sells an expensive drug that is administered as an injection at the pediatrician's office to infants at risk of serious respiratory infection. Because of the drug's high cost and the fact that insurance reimbursement takes a long time, doctors do not like to hold large amounts of the drug in inventory. Thus, the company's salespeople must visit physicians frequently, taking many small orders. In addition, they must spend a great deal of time educating the doctors' office staff on the logistics and reimbursement requirements for the drug.

Seasonality affects the sales process

The selling activities required for sellers of toys, books, and other popular gift items change significantly as retailers prepare for the holiday gift-giving season. The selling activities of one pharmaceutical manufacturer varied so greatly by season that it established two different sales territory alignments for the sales force. Each salesperson had one territory assignment for the cold and flu season and another assignment for the allergy season.

another important consideration. Customers will need more information when they buy a new product than when they buy a mature product. Finally, a product's physical characteristics, the risk associated with purchasing it, and seasonality can all play a role in determining the best sales process.

Economic factors

Economic factors also play a role in determining the best sales process. A product's contribution margin is an important consideration – a high margin product should get more selling resources than a low margin product, if the top line impact of additional selling effort is the same. In addition, all the costs related to distribution of the product need to be considered. This includes the cost of customer communications, transportation and storage, order receipt and processing, as well as financial risk.

Office products supplier varies selling channels by account size

An office products supplier varies its sales process and selling channel options for different sized accounts. All accounts can place orders via the company's catalog and web site. In addition, medium volume accounts also have the option of placing orders via an assigned telesales person, large-volume accounts via a generalist face-to-face salesperson, and the largest accounts via a specialist face-to-face salesperson. Thus the more important the account, the more attention it receives from the seller and the more channel options it has available.

A company's selling approach should also acknowledge economic differences between customer segments. Successful companies dedicate more selling resources to protecting and growing their largest, most profitable, strategically important market segments, while reducing their expenditure against low value accounts. The more important the account, the more attention the customer receives during the sales process. Often, the most important customers are also given more channel options.

Company environment

The company environment is also a factor in determining the best sales process. A company with a broad product line may have a different sales process from a company that sells just one or two products. Corporate goals and resources also help to determine what sales process options are feasible. Finally, the corporate culture influences the sales process. A company with a culture of teamwork and collaboration will often use a different sales process than a company with a more aggressive and competitive culture.

Corporate culture helps to define how UPS sells

United Parcel Service (UPS) has a strong culture of teamwork and customer focus. As a result, every UPS salesperson is asked to communicate regularly with the drivers in his/her area. This encourages the sales and delivery people to work together as a team to resolve customer problems and respond to customer feedback.

Country and industry environment

Finally, the country and industry environment helps determine the right sales process. Often when the economy is strong and business is booming, sales processes become reactive to customer needs. When the economy weakens, sales processes must transform to be more aggressive and proactive. The state of technology, transportation, and communication

---

Laird Plastics adjusts selling approach in weak economy

In early 2001 after a ten-year boom, the US economy began to weaken. The recession hit many companies hard and affected the way they sold to customers. Laird Plastics, a distributor of semi-finished plastic materials to a wide range of businesses, had to adopt a much more aggressive sales approach. When the economy was strong, Laird's customers called with orders. During the recession, the phones stopped ringing. Salespeople had to become much more proactive, calling on customers, creating new applications, asking for the order, and offering better deals.

Government deregulation affects sales processes for utilities

Deregulation of the utility industry in the late 1990s brought about dramatic changes in how utility companies sell. Prior to deregulation, utility companies were monopolists. Their customers were captive, so there was no real need to sell. In many cases utility sales forces were made up of engineers on a two-year rotation before their next promotion. With deregulation came competition, and utility companies had to adopt a much more proactive selling approach. In many cases, utility companies had to hire entirely new sales forces, made up of people who were aggressive, risk-taking, and flexible – a completely different profile from that of their pre-deregulation salespeople.

---

infrastructure in a market also plays a role in determining the best sales process. Finally, the regulatory framework in a country or industry can affect how a company should sell. Anti-trust laws, consumer protection legislation, or equal employment opportunity laws can all affect the work that is required for a seller to connect effectively with customers.

SEVEN SALES STRATEGY INSIGHTS

A firm's sales strategy defines the sales processes needed to connect the right customers with the right products and services. Below are some insights that can help you develop sales strategies that are consistent with long-term success.

Look Beyond the Product to Create Superior Value for Customers

A customer buys a product either to consume it, to integrate it into its own offerings, or to resell it. In each case, understanding how the customer benefits from the product can help a supplier create enhanced value for that customer. Understanding the total cost of the product to the buyer can also unearth opportunities. For example, in addition to product costs, what are the ordering costs, inventory costs, and service costs? By working with the customer to reduce these added costs, a firm can create considerable value for the customer and can achieve significant competitive advantage. Recall the example where P&G partnered with Wal-Mart to wring out channel costs and increase profitability at both firms.

The Sales Process can be a Source of Customer Value

If salespeople do little more than recite information from product brochures, the customer will not be willing to pay a higher price to cover the cost of an expensive sales force for very long. The sales role will be replaced by channels that are much more efficient, such as the Internet and direct mail catalogs. In order for a direct sales force to have longevity, the salesperson and the sales process must be a source of customer value. For example, a salesperson for a leading-edge communication product helps customers use the new technology to enhance their business. A salesperson for an office supply company helps customers streamline purchasing, reduce total acquisition costs, manage inventory, and allocate costs to departments. Successful sales forces deliver value through personal interaction with customers that could not be delivered using other, less expensive sales channels.

Understanding Customer Potential Leads to Better Sales Strategies

Understanding customer potential is critical to the development of good sales strategies. When customer potential is known, the firm can allocate effort more effectively and can set realistic expectations for performance management. Firms that do not understand customer potential often spend too much time defending small amounts of existing business, and scatter their effort too broadly against opportunities. The investment in even an approximate understanding of customer potential usually pays for itself quickly.

Focused Sales Strategies Dominate Scattered Sales Strategies

For most companies, profit-maximizing sales strategies focus the firm's resources on targeted products and customers. Salespeople do not naturally or instinctively allocate their effort in the firm's or in their own best long-term interest. Many salespeople tend to spend too much time with "friends and family" or current customers, and the effort against prospects or new customers tends to be too diffuse to have sufficient impact. The familiar 80–20 rule, though seldom literally true, reflects the accurate belief that sales potential and sales are concentrated. A variation of this rule, the 80–20–30 rule, reveals a powerful truth – that the typically high investment that most companies make in the bottom 30 percent of customers can cut the firm's profits in half.

New Markets and New Products Typically Require Significant Investment

Launching new products and expanding into new markets is exciting and often essential for future revenue growth. In the short term, however, these activities will likely hurt a firm's profitability. Companies that want to launch new products and/or reach new markets must be willing to invest significant resources if they want to succeed.

First, consider new product introductions. The cost to sell new products is often higher than the cost to sell existing products. The sales force must be trained, the customer must be educated, the sales cycle will be longer, and customers will need higher levels of support. A typical new product launch can consume 50 to 60 percent of a sales force's time.

Reaching new markets also requires a significant investment of resources. The cost of acquiring a new customer is typically three to six times that of retaining an existing one. An office products firm, for example, that spends $200 in selling time to close a sale in an existing account might spend $1000 or more to sell the same products to an entirely new customer. New customers must be located, contacted, educated in the firm's products, and convinced of the benefits of doing business with the firm. All of this costs money.

Protect Strengths

When selling new products or selling to new markets, consider the opportunity cost. Significant investment of resources in new product and market areas often drastically reduces the time and money available to support existing products and markets. Assuming that existing products will retain their sales in the absence of selling effort is dangerous. Sales may be maintained due to carryover for a short period, but will suffer in the long run even for strong products. Many existing products fail to make their sales targets when companies launch new products or enter new markets and divert effort away from the existing products.

When a company chooses to launch a new product or go after a new market, it should launch hard, yet at the same time protect the products and markets that are currently strengths. The only way to do this is to expand the firm's marketing investment. This might mean adding salespeople, forming new alliances or partnerships with distributors, adding telemarketing capacity, and/or expanding Internet-selling capabilities. All of these responses have inherent risks, and each must be evaluated in comparison to the expected value it will bring.

Look to the Future

Successful sales strategies are forward looking. For each major customer segment, companies need a "vision." Two aspects of any customer or customer segment need to be considered. First, how will the opportunity in a segment evolve? Second, how will the buying process in a segment evolve? For example, which customer segments does the company's business come from now and where is it expected to come from in the future? Does the company expect to grow sales as the market segment grows or by taking market share from competitors? Will the account become more centralized in its decision making? Will the customer rationalize the number of suppliers?

Segment growth projections are an important consideration when determining investment levels. If the number of customers in a segment that currently generates high sales is declining, then the company may need to invest in other, higher growth segments if it wants to maintain or grow sales and profits. By projecting future revenues for each customer segment, companies can allocate their selling resources better. Some firms look at the lifetime value of customers to help with investment and sales strategies.

Go-To-Market Strategy

INTRODUCTION

Chapter 3 presented a framework for determining a firm's sales strategy, including the right product and service offering and sales process for each type of customer. Next, the firm must decide which sales and marketing channels are best suited to deliver this sales strategy. This is the firm's go-to-market strategy, as illustrated in Figure 4.1.

Go-to-market broadly refers to how a firm serves its customers with a combination of sales, financing, logistics, and service. In this book and chapter we take a narrower view, focusing on how different parts of the firm's sales process such as prospecting, qualification, and closing are performed. Successful firms make go-to-market choices that enable efficient yet effective connections with their customers and prospects. Many

Sales and marketing channels					
Value-added partners	Direct sales force	Tele-channels	E-channels	Agents/ distributors/ retailers	Advertising & promotion

FIGURE 4.1 Go-to-market activities in the sales force design framework

industries have evolved from viewing the sales channel as consisting of a talking tape recorder (the salesperson) and a delivery truck, and now view the sales channel as a way to add customer value to the firm's products and services.

Go-to-market strategies use resources from both inside and outside the company. Inside resources include a company's direct sales force, product specialists, service specialists, telesales personnel, and e-channels. Outside resources include collaborators, co-suppliers, partners, wholesalers, distributors, independent agents, value-added resellers, and retail outlets. Companies creatively combine the use of internal and external resources to execute their sales strategy in order to reduce the cost of connecting with customers and, at the same time, to enhance customer impact. Sales forces, whether company-owned (direct) or independent (indirect), often play an important role in this connection.

Examples of How Sellers Connect with their Customers

The following three examples illustrate different ways that companies go to market.

Figure 4.2 shows how a networking equipment manufacturer goes to market. This company sells a very technical, complex, and customized product that has high value and high risk for the customer. Thus, a highly specialized sales force is used to serve the customers. Salespeople specialize both by market and by task.

Figure 4.3 illustrates how an office products supplier goes to market. Compared with the products of the networking equipment manufacturer, this company's products are simpler, low risk, and do not require customization. Thus, it is not necessary for a highly specialized sales force to be involved in every step of the selling process. The office products supplier uses a direct mail catalog and telemarketing to generate and qualify leads. Both of these selling channels are much less expensive than a direct sales force. Generalist salespeople participate in selling to qualified leads and in closing sales. Product specialists are used only to sell the

Task / Market	Selling	Technical assistance
Major carriers and service providers	Major carrier specialists	
Other carriers and service providers	Other carrier specialists (some hunters, some farmers)	
Enterprise accounts – government, education, utilities	G/E/U enterprise specialists	Sales engineers
Enterprise accounts – finance and retail	F/R enterprise specialists	
Enterprise accounts – healthcare and high-tech	H/H enterprise specialists	

FIGURE 4.2 Go-to-market strategy for a networking equipment manufacturer

Task / Product	Lead generation	Qualification	Pre-sales	Close of sale	Fulfillment/ support
Office products	Direct mail catalog and telemarketing sales force	Tele-marketing sales force		Generalist sales reps	Customer service reps
Furniture				Furniture and computer supply specialist sales reps for large accounts	
Computer supplies				Generalist sales reps for small accounts	

FIGURE 4.3 Go-to-market strategy for an office products supplier

Task / Market	Interest creation	Pre-purchase	Purchase	Post-purchase
Professional salons	Trade shows Direct sales Distributors Independent reps Web site Direct mail	Direct sales Distributors Independent reps	Direct sales Distributors Independent reps Web site for small orders	Direct sales Distributors Independent reps
Retail accounts	Co-op advertising Television Billboards Distributors Independent reps	Direct sales Independent reps	Direct sales Independent reps Web site for small orders	Direct sales Independent reps

FIGURE 4.4 Go-to-market strategy for a hair care products supplier

furniture and computer supply product lines to the largest accounts. Customer service representatives assist with order fulfillment and ongoing customer support.

Figure 4.4 shows how a hair care products supplier goes to market. Again, this company offers simple, low-risk products. Because this company has many potential customers, it sells through many different channels. In addition to using a direct sales force, the company uses advertising, direct mail, trade shows, the web, and outside distributors and independent sales representatives to connect with customers at various stages of the selling process.

DEVELOPING A SUCCESSFUL GO-TO-MARKET STRATEGY

A firm's go-to-market strategy defines the selling channel or combination of channels that can best execute the firm's sales strategy. A wide array of selling channels exists today. Sixty years ago, choosing the right selling channel was much simpler. Sellers typically sold through a single channel, either their own direct sales organization or a distributor. Today, selecting the right selling channels is much more complicated. Companies reach customers not only through direct sales and distributors, but also through telesales, brokers, licensing arrangements, joint distributor agreements, dealers, agents, new retail formats (such as club stores), the Internet – the list is very large. Complicating the matter further, today most companies sell through multiple channels. For example, a company might have a direct sales force organized into a matrix of multiple teams and specialists that call on large, important accounts. The company might sell to smaller customers through a network of distributors. The effort of both the direct sales force and the distributors might be further supported and enhanced by a telesales group and a corporate web site. Channels are not always clearly divided by customer – sometimes the same customer has several channel choices for acquiring a company's products. For example, many types of computer hardware are available both through the manufacturer and from value-added resellers.

Types of Selling Channels

As shown in Table 4.1, selling channels can either be totally owned by the selling company, totally independent of the selling company, or somewhere in between.

Company-owned resources include a company's direct sales force, as well as other selling resources that the seller owns and controls.

At the other extreme, selling channels can be completely independent of

Table 4.1 Selling channel options

Company-owned	Company-connected	Independent partners	Independent
Direct sales force	Agents	Co-sellers	Wholesalers
Company tele-channels	Brokers	Collaborators	Distributors
Company web site	Exclusive distributors	Systems integrators	Dealers
Company-owned retail stores	Franchises		Independent agents
Company catalog	Dealerships		Value-added partners
	Manufacturer's reps		Independent retailers
	Joint ventures/co-marketing		Direct mail companies
			Independent catalogs
			Internet intermediaries

the selling company. An independent market intermediary, such as a distributor or wholesaler, buys goods from a seller and then resells them at a higher price to the ultimate consumer or to another market participant, such as a retailer.

Lands' End offers consumers a choice of company-owned selling channels

For years, Lands' End clothing manufacturer has relied solely on company-owned selling channels, including a catalog, a company web site, and a large telesales organization that handles inbound calls. In addition, clothes are sold through a handful of company-owned retail outlets in selected states. In 2002, retail giant Sears acquired Lands' End and began to sell its merchandise through all full-line Sears' retail stores, offering consumers yet another channel option.

P&G relies on independent selling channels

Procter and Gamble sells its line of consumer products through independent retail outlets. Grocery stores, drug stores, and mass merchandisers buy products from P&G in bulk, and then resell them to individual consumers.

Independent channels can take still another form, where two or more independent partners collaborate to provide a solution to a customer.

Finally, company-connected selling channels include organizations that have an exclusive relationship with the seller. For example, automobile dealerships and fast food franchises are independently owned yet obligated to sell the parent company's products exclusively and follow specific guidelines. Company-connected resources also include organizations that represent a company without taking title to goods.

> ### Siebel uses alliances to deliver e-business solutions to customers
>
> Siebel Systems, a leading supplier of Customer Relationship Management and e-Business products, uses a network of over 750 partners specializing by industry, product, and service, to provide the systems implementation, software integration, and infrastructure deployment needs of its customers. Customers typically acquire the software from Siebel, and use one or more specialist partner firms to perform the systems integration and deployment.

Manufacturer's reps, brokers, independent contract salespeople, and agents do not buy the products they sell. Instead, they earn a commission from the manufacturer when they make a sale on their behalf.

Selecting the Right Selling Channels

The critical go-to-market activity is selecting the right channels to deliver the sales strategy. In other words, the company must determine the channel or mix of channels that can best execute the selling process for every targeted market segment. Channel selection is driven by customer needs and preferences, along with an evaluation of the efficiency and effectiveness of the various channel choices.

Customer needs and preferences influence channel selection

Customers have preferences for how they buy. A successful go-to-market strategy acknowledges which channels customers and prospects prefer to buy from. Customers who value the convenience of placing orders on their own schedule are more inclined to use a catalog or the Internet. A business-to-business buyer might be more inclined to buy from a supplier or distributor with a proven record of on-time delivery or from one that provides product availability at a moment's notice. A facility manager might prefer to deal with a few distributors that carry the hundreds of maintenance products he or she needs, as opposed to working directly with the manufacturers of each product. A customer that values relationships ("I know who to call to make things to happen") may prefer to buy directly from a salesperson, rather than over the telephone. A selling channel is most effective when it is well suited to executing the selling process that addresses a customer's needs and carries out the firm's strategy.

All channels do not have the same capacity or capability to perform each activity within the sales process. Table 4.2 gives an example of how one company evaluated the ability of different sales channels to accomplish important aspects of its sales process.

TABLE 4.2 An example of how well different channels perform various sales activities

Channel → Activity ↓	Strategic account teams	Direct field force	Value-added resellers	Resellers	Retail	Tele-channels	Direct mail	E-channels
Needs assessment	4	3	4	2	1	3	1	1
Complex communication	4	4	4	2	3	3	1	2
Total solutions	4	3	4	3	1	2	0	1
Self-service	2	2	2	2	4	3	4	4
On-site installation	4	3	4	3	2	0	0	0
24-7 availability	2	2	3	2	1	4	0	4
Fast local support	3	3	4	3	3	0	0	0
Quick access to information	2	3	3	3	3	4	0	4
Relationship	4	4	4	3	2	3	0	1
Low price	1	2	3	3	3	4	4	4

(4=Excellent, 3=Good, 2=Fair, 1=Poor, 0=Very poor)

IBM uses multiple channels to reach customers

IBM uses a variety of direct and indirect channels to reach customers. For large enterprises such as Boeing, IBM has dedicated teams. IBM serves small and medium businesses directly with a sales organization that handles its wide product portfolio. But IBM also uses wholesalers to distribute its line of laptop computers. In addition, IBM has a large network of partners who add software or services to IBM products, integrate IBM products with products from other firms, and sell in specific markets such as Legal and Financial Services. IBM in fact tries to steer small customers to its partners.

Customer preferences drive channel choice at Bourns

At electronics maker Bourns, the percentage of total sales going through distributor channels, as opposed to direct channels, doubled between 1994 and 2001. This shift was primarily due to customer demand. Bourns' customers liked the way that distributors could help lower their costs by offering programs such as design, logistics, and supply chain management.

The efficiency–effectiveness trade-off

In addition to customer needs, the concepts of efficiency and effectiveness are central to the channel selection decision. Some channel options, such as advertising, direct mail, and the Internet, reach a large group of customers and prospects very cheaply. These channel options are very efficient. Other channel options reach fewer customers and prospects but provide an opportunity for an active two-way interaction. These channel options are very effective. Personal selling falls within this category. A framework for defining the concepts of channel efficiency and channel effectiveness appears in Figure 4.5.

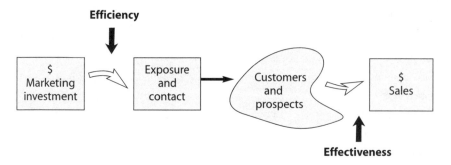

FIGURE 4.5 Channel efficiency and effectiveness

A firm invests money in marketing its products and services to customers and prospects. This money may be spent on a variety of marketing channels. The firm can use its money to buy advertising space in trade publications, create promotional web sites, send direct mail to customers and prospects, exhibit at trade shows, pay distribution partners, employ telemarketers, or employ field salespeople to call on customers and prospects. The money the firm spends generates marketing exposure or contacts with customers and prospects who respond by buying the firm's products and services. Efficiency reflects the rate at which the marketing channel converts its monetary investment into exposure or contacts. A highly efficient marketing channel has a high level of exposure or contact for its investment. Table 4.3 contrasts the cost per contact for a variety of channel options.

TABLE 4.3 Average cost per contact to reach business markets

Specialized business publication	$ 0.45
Internet	$1.25
Direct mail	$2.50
Business letter	$14.75
Telemarketing	$35.00
Trade show	$210.00
Industrial sales call	$300.00

Source: *Marketing Tools* magazine, Penton Media, Inc. 2003. All numbers in USD, available at www.e-marketinggroup.com/the_costs_content.htm

Effectiveness represents the buyer's response to the exposure or contact created by the marketing channel. Highly effective marketing channels have high impact and high conversion to sales rate per exposure or contact. Channel effectiveness is much harder to measure than channel efficiency. Chapter 7 covers some methods to measure the effectiveness of the personal selling resource.

Ideally, companies would like to use selling channels that are both efficient and effective. Typically, however, there is a trade-off between efficiency and effectiveness. Channels that are highly effective tend not to be very efficient. Likewise, channels that are highly efficient tend not to be very effective. For example, compare the effectiveness of a personal sales call with that of several low-cost channel options. For the cost of one in-person sales call a company could instead reach 667 prospects with a specialized business magazine advertisement, send a direct mail piece to 120 prospects, or reach eight or nine prospects via the telephone. Yet a personal call is much more effective. A personal call has a higher likelihood of resulting in a sale. In addition, the dollar amount of the sale is likely to be much higher with a personal call. So while advertising, direct mail, and telesales are more efficient, they are also less effective. Companies must evaluate this trade-off when selecting selling channels or deciding how to use a mixture of channels to assist with the various steps of a selling process.

In general, the bestselling channel executes the selling process effectively in the most cost-efficient way. Before moving a selling activity to a more expensive channel, such as from telesales to in-person sales, the key question to ask is: Does the more expensive channel deliver enough of an increase in effectiveness to justify a decrease in efficiency? Before moving a selling activity to a less expensive channel, such as from telesales to the Internet, the key question to ask is: Does the gain in efficiency offset the loss in effectiveness?

Airlines restructure sales forces after September 11, 2001

Many airline industry sales forces restructured after the dramatic decline in demand for services following September 11, 2001. In an effort to streamline sales operations, many major carriers cut back on face-to-face visits with smaller clients such as travel agencies and began servicing these accounts through telesales. Field sales effort was refocused on major corporate accounts. The major carriers also eliminated sales management positions and centralized more of their sales operations. Delta eliminated the district sales manager layer and centralized the handling of contracts and corporate requests for proposals at its Atlanta headquarters. Northwest decreased the number of sales regions and correspondingly cut the number of district sales managers. Continental consolidated sales management into two divisions and identified many mid-market accounts that could be turned over to telesales, while increasing the number of national corporate salespeople focusing on their most important accounts.

Figure 4.6 compares several selling channels in terms of their effectiveness and efficiency. As the figure shows, sales forces are generally the least efficient (highest cost per exposure) but most effective (highest sales per exposure) way to connect with customers.

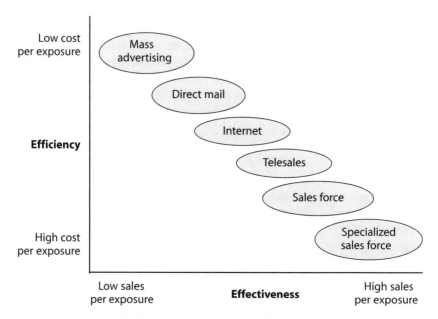

FIGURE 4.6 Efficiency and effectiveness of alternative selling channels

Should a high-touch or a low-touch channel be used to execute the sales strategy?

Channels on the lower right-hand corner of Figure 4.6, such as sales forces, are considered high-touch channels. These channels involve a lot of personal, often face-to-face interaction between buyers and sellers. High-touch channels are typically highly effective, but not very efficient. Thus, selling activities conducive to high-touch channels are those that benefit significantly from personal interaction and discussion between the buyer and seller. This includes explaining and demonstrating the company's products and services, understanding the decision-making process of a customer organization, educating the customer, customizing the offering, listening, solving customer problems, and negotiating contracts. Complex products and complex customer buying processes lend themselves well to high-touch channels. For example, professional services such as consulting, accounting or law require creative, personal design to meet customer needs and therefore are usually sold through high-touch channels.

Channels on the upper left-hand corner of Figure 4.6, such as mass advertising and direct mail, are considered low-touch channels. These channels do not involve personal interaction between buyers and sellers. Low-touch channels are typically highly efficient, but are often not very effective. Selling activities conducive to low-touch channels are routine tasks that include creating awareness, training that can be done effectively via the Internet or a user's manual, placing orders and reorders, and billing and collecting payments. Low-touch channels are efficient at selling non-differentiated, well-understood products like office supplies and standard replacement parts. In addition, older products that are well known and understood by customers are often sold through low-touch channels. Low-touch channels can also enhance the efficiency of selected channel functions such as configuration and ordering of complex products. In addition, firms with sales that are widely dispersed across a large customer base and geography often use low-touch channels, since reaching every customer with a high-touch channel is not cost-effective.

Companies often achieve the right balance of efficiency and effectiveness by employing a combination of high-touch and low-touch channels to execute their selling process for different market segments. Figure 4.7 shows how a company that provides an Internet service for buying and selling recycled auto parts balances efficiency and effectiveness by combining selling channels. A direct sales force is used to perform the activities that require the most creativity and personal

The size of the customer pool influences channel choices

The hair care products company (see Figure 4.4) has millions of potential customers. Using a direct sales force to call on each customer is not practical. Thus, in order to achieve wide penetration at reasonable cost, the company sells its products through professional salons and retail outlets, and uses a wide variety of selling channels to reach both the salons and outlets and the product's end-users, including trade shows, direct sales, distributors, a web site, direct mail, and various forms of advertising. The salons and retail outlets are able to combine products from multiple manufacturers and provide an assortment of products to the buyer.

Selling channels can change over the product life cycle

Watlow Electric Manufacturing Company sells industrial heaters, sensors, and controls through a mix of distributors, resellers, and OEMs, in addition to its own direct sales force and telesales group. Watlow frequently changes the distribution channel for a product as the product matures. With new products, customers need a company salesperson to answer technical questions. Later, after customers have been using the product for a while, they want a convenient way to purchase it and do not need as much face-to-face contact. At that point, the product is turned over to a less expensive, lower-touch channel such as a distributor or the company's telesales group.

Market \ Task	Lead generation	Qualification	Pre-sales	Close of sale	Fulfillment/ support
Salvage yard	Internet and call center	Direct sales force			Internet and call center
Auto repair shops					
Paint shops	Indirect sales force				

FIGURE 4.7 How an internet market for recycled auto parts combines high- and low-touch selling channels

interaction and can therefore benefit most from a high-touch approach – qualifying leads, pre-selling, and closing sales. Lower-touch channels perform routine activities such as lead generation, order fulfillment, and product support. An indirect sales force sells to a distinct market segment – paint shops. Once the indirect partner closes a paint shop sale, the company's Internet site and call center take over to fulfill the order and support the customer.

Companies often assign their highly effective, but expensive, high-touch channels, like a direct sales force, to protecting and growing their largest, most profitable, strategically important accounts. Figure 4.8 shows how one firm tailored its go-to-market strategy based on the size and potential of different customer segments and products. Dedicated, expensive, and effective global account teams meet the needs of the largest and most strategically important global accounts. Small accounts, on the other hand, get field force coverage for one product (Product B), telesales and Internet coverage for another product (Product A), and no coverage at all for a third product (Product C).

Account type	Sales channel		
Global accounts	Global account teams		
Key accounts	Strategic account managers/teams		
Regional accounts	Field sales force		
Small accounts	Telesales/ Internet		No sales coverage
	Product A	**Product B**	**Product C**

FIGURE 4.8 Product–market coverage example

Managing "Hybrid" Channels

Most companies use multiple selling channels to serve their customers. There are several hybrid channel models.

- Different customers can be served with different channels; for example, when a company deals directly with key accounts, and uses resellers to service other customers.
- The same customer can be served by a combination of channels that perform complementary functions; for example, when an account manager and technical experts collaborate to sell and the customer uses the company web site to place and track orders.
- The same customer has channel choices; for example, when the customer can buy directly from the manufacturer or buy through a value-added reseller.

While these hybrid go-to-market strategies have many benefits, they can be challenging to manage. When different elements of the sales process are done by different entities, coordination can be difficult. For example, the auto parts recycling company in Figure 4.7 provides role clarity by dividing selling channel responsibilities by market segment. One channel serves paint shops and another serves salvage yards and auto repair shops. The company also provides role clarity by assigning particular sales process work steps to different channels. One set of channels does lead generation and fulfillment/support and another does qualification, pre-sales, and closing. All the channels are encouraged to work together to provide the best possible customer experience, but they need to coordinate activities so that customers are not lost in the hand-offs.

Firms that allow customers to choose their preferred sales channel typically do so in order to expand market coverage. This can be an effective way to reach more customers, but at the same time if the channels compete with one another, channel conflicts can arise. The firm does not benefit when several channels offer the exact same product to the same customers. The customer is confused. Additional channels do not increase sales; they just shift sales from one channel to another. Selling costs increase and margins decrease. Channel participants fight over incentive pay, resulting in high channel turnover.

Firms can encourage healthy tension between competing channel members, without destructive conflict, by using complementary channels that satisfy different needs or customer types. For example, a software provider may use several different systems integrators as channel partners, each with expertise in a particular industry or situation. Because each channel partner has unique strengths, customers are steered towards the appropriate partner based upon their particular needs, and channel conflict is minimized.

The Role of the Sales Force in Connecting with Customers

Sales forces play a valuable role in connecting companies with customers. Sales forces have many advantages over other selling channels. Only a sales force can sell complex products and solutions into large key accounts with a high degree of control over the sales process. Salespeople provide personal two-way interaction: they listen, assess needs, provide solutions, reduce complexity, handle objections, create value, and provide long-term continuing service. Salespeople can be very flexible and effective. They are the "putty that fills all holes." They can work cooperatively with go-to-market partners. They create "sticky" relationships that engender customer loyalty. As one sales manager put it, "If I tell 100 salespeople to turn left at the next light, about 25 will go right, and wouldn't you know it? One of them will find the gold about half the time." The magic of sales forces is their initiative and creativity. They also listen, and bring insights back to the company.

Should the Company use a Direct or an Indirect Sales Force?

If a company decides to use a personal selling model to connect with customers, it must decide whether to have a direct or indirect selling organization. These two types differ in who bears the risk associated with the sales investment and how the sales force resources will be managed and controlled.

With a direct sales force, salespeople are employees of the company. They dedicate their complete selling effort to their employer, who has the ability to control their activities. The company hires and fires direct salespeople and pays their salary, commissions, and bonuses.

With an indirect sales force, the company contracts with an independent sales organization to sell the company's products and services to customers. This independent organization may sell the products and services of other companies as well. There are many types of independent selling organizations. They include agents, brokers, distributors, manufacturer's reps, independent contract salespeople, wholesalers, dealers, retailers, stocking representatives, non-stocking distributors, value-added resellers (VARs), and system integrators. Different industries use different intermediaries.

The various independent selling organizations can be classified into two major types, depending upon whether or not they take title to the product. The first type of independent selling organization earns a commission on sales without ever taking title to the product. Title passes directly from the manufacturer to the purchaser when a sale is made. Common examples are independent sales reps, agents, and brokers. The second type of independent selling organization purchases products from a manufacturer and resells the products to customers. These organizations typically inventory the product and may add value to it before selling it. Their compensation is the difference between their purchase price plus associated expenses and their selling price. Common examples are distributors, wholesalers, and retailers.

Companies frequently use a mix of direct and indirect selling approaches

Often, the type of selling organization varies by market segment:

- Xerox uses direct salespeople to call on large, strategically important customers but relies on indirect selling channels such as office superstores, value-added resellers, and agents to reach smaller customers.
- A confectionery manufacturer calls directly on club stores, drug stores, and mass merchandisers, but uses food brokers to reach grocery stores, convenience stores, and other retail outlets.
- A dental supply company sells directly in major metropolitan areas, but in rural areas, it sells through local distributors.

When to use an indirect sales force

Several aspects of a company's situation determine whether it is best to use a direct or an indirect sales force. The following conditions make it attractive for a company to sell indirectly.

An indirect partner has capabilities that would be very hard for the company to replicate. A partner may have already established relationships with key customer decision makers or may have expertise with customers or products that would take significant time and effort for the manufacturer to develop. Many companies use indirect partners to establish an initial presence in a new market, and move to a direct sales model after they gain some experience and build their own internal resources.

Varco International uses outside salespeople to connect with customers in China

Varco International, a seller of equipment for oil rigs, contacts out to intermediary partners when it sells in China. Chinese oil companies are government controlled, so it is difficult for in-house sellers to gain access unless they know the right people. Not many people have these connections, and those that do will not usually work for a foreign company. Thus, Varco contracts with outside salespeople who can make the right introductions and broker a deal between the two companies.

Corporate resources and experience drive go-to-market strategy for Takeda

Japanese drug company Takeda did not always have the resources and experience needed to field its own sales force in the United States. Thus for many years, Takeda sold its products in the United States through a partnership with US-based Abbott Laboratories. Then in 1995, Takeda set a corporate goal to become an "R&D-driven global company" and accelerated its efforts to expand outside of Japan. Fueled by the blockbuster financial potential of a new drug, Takeda established its own US-based sales organization in 1998. This 500 strong sales force, along with an entire support infrastructure, was established in less than a year, and doubled in size just a year and a half later.

There is a need to gain rapid entry into a market. An indirect selling partner can help a company get into a market more quickly than it could on its own. Indirect selling partners can also help companies in situations where tight labor markets make it difficult to recruit qualified salespeople.

Outside selling partner helps Shell Energy speed up market entry

When Shell Energy faced deregulation of the natural gas industry in the state of Georgia there was a very high need for speed. The state had set a deadline for signing up customers, so moving quickly to establish a strong initial customer base was critical. Shell partnered with an outside selling partner who was able to recruit and train new salespeople much more quickly than Shell could on its own.

The company's products have synergies with other products that an indirect partner sells. Sometimes a selling partner has products and/or services that complement a company's offering. An indirect partner can add value to customers by bundling together the product lines of several different manufacturers. Often companies with a limited number of products sell through outside partners, so that selling costs can be shared across the partner's product assortment. Then as the company's product line broadens and selling costs can be allocated across multiple products, it becomes economically feasible to hire a direct sales force.

Indirect selling provides 3M's customers with convenient one-stop shopping

3M sells its line of industrial products such as scrubbing pads, metal sealants, respirator filters, carpet treatments, lens covers, and floor finishes through wholesaler W. W. Grainger. Grainger, the largest industrial distributor of products to keep facilities and equipment running, offers the broadest selection in the industry. Grainger distributes the products of over 1200 suppliers. There are nearly 600 Grainger branch stores throughout North America. Customers can also order through a catalog, direct mail, telesales, the Internet, and a direct sales force. Many customers value the convenience of purchasing a complete assortment of industrial products from a single company.

Selling through indirect partners can also help companies manage product positioning conflicts.

Indirect selling helps NewStar Media manage product positioning conflicts

NewStar Media sells books on tape that appeal to a broad and diverse set of customers. Audio books that appeal to scholarly types (for example, an unabridged version of a Shakespeare play) might sell for $20 or more at a bookstore. Lower-priced audio books that appeal to a broader audience are sold through mass retailers and are typically priced under $10.

An indirect selling partner makes it possible to achieve efficiency gains. A partner can provide a company with efficient access to thousands of potential customers that it otherwise would not reach. Sometimes a partner can help a company gain geographic coverage efficiency by allocating the cost of travel between accounts across multiple product lines. An indirect partner can also give a company the economic ability to call on smaller accounts.

Indirect selling allows insurance company to reach smaller employers

An insurance company uses direct salespeople to call on large employers with 1000 employees or more. These direct salespeople also call on insurance brokers and consultants, who in turn sell the company's products to smaller employers.

There is a need to limit risk exposure. A direct sales force is an expensive investment in human capital. In the event of failure, the decision to have a direct sales force is not easily reversed. As any salesperson who has experienced a downsizing or layoffs knows, eliminating a sales force is a painful process. Avoidance of loss is a criterion companies use in judging management performance. For this reason, companies who are risk-averse and want protection on the downside should consider selling indirectly.

Costs are controlled with indirect selling. With many indirect selling arrangements, sales expenses are directly related to sales volume. Thus, if the product doesn't sell, the firm's selling expenses are minimal. Typically, for products with low sales, total selling costs are less with indirect selling. For products with high sales, however, total costs are less with direct selling.

Advantages of selling directly

While indirect selling makes sense in many situations, there are also many situations that favor a direct selling model.

The firm can better control selling activity. A company ensures that all selling effort is devoted to its own products with a direct sales force. Additionally, the company can directly control how sales activity should be allocated across products, activities, and customers. The company also has flexibility to quickly redirect sales force effort as needed.

A direct sales force helps SonoSite control selling effort

Medical equipment maker SonoSite initially tried to sell its new hand-carried ultrasound system through distributors. Since the system was technologically complex and the distributors had so many other products to sell, SonoSite's product did not get the necessary quantity or quality of effort, and the product launch failed. SonoSite decided to drop the distributor and hire its own salespeople instead so that the company could control the amount and quality of selling time dedicated to its product. The direct approach was extremely successful, and SonoSite (2003 revenues ~$80 million) has about 60 percent market share in the portable ultrasound market against a formidable competitor, GE Medial Systems (2003 revenues ~$13 billion).

Pepperidge Farm considers buying out indirect selling partners

Pepperidge Farm used several hundred indirect selling partners to sell and deliver its cookie and cracker product line to retailers. Partners were independent contractors with their own delivery trucks. Each was given a defined geographic territory to cover and was compensated by earning a percentage commission on sales. Since this business was quite lucrative, over time a market developed for the territories. A contractor leaving the business was free to sell his/her territory to anyone who wanted it.

Pepperidge Farm's sales and distribution system worked well until Pepperidge Farm wanted to pursue a business relationship with Wal-Mart. Since Wal-Mart conducts all buying at its headquarters in Bentonville, Arkansas, it demands a centrally coordinated effort from its suppliers. Pepperidge Farm had difficulty meeting this demand because it had to work through hundreds of independent contractors. Thus, it considered buying out the contractors and replacing them with a more controllable resource – its own direct sales force. Unfortunately for Pepperidge Farm, the market had driven the cost to buy out the contractors to an unreasonably high level. Pepperidge Farm could not possibly afford to buy out hundreds of contractors at the market price for their territories. As a result, Pepperidge Farm missed out on an opportunity to gain distribution with an important customer. Today, Pepperidge Farm products are sold in Wal-Mart, and the company continues to work with its network of independent distributors.

The firm has ownership of salesperson quality. With a direct sales force, the company controls the hiring profile, the recruitment process, and the training and coaching of salespeople. Thus, the company can ensure that only people with the right profile sell its products.

General Mills controls sales force quality through a direct selling model

Minneapolis-based consumer foods giant General Mills puts a lot of stock into having a high-quality sales force. The company invests heavily in its recruitment process. New hires go through a series of interviews, as well as a battery of tests that gauge selling ability, personality, and social skills.

Sales activities can be coordinated with other company functions. Having a direct sales force allows personnel in other company departments, such as marketing, customer service, and operations, to have greater access to the salespeople who interact with customers on a daily basis. This enables personnel throughout the company to be better informed about customer needs and competitor's capabilities.

Teradyne engineers and salespeople work together to meet customer needs

Boston-based Teradyne, a provider of automated test equipment for the semiconductor, telecommunications, and computer industries, relies on close communication between personnel in many departments when designing new products. Teradyne's engineers interact and communicate closely with the sales force (in addition to operations, marketing, and finance), to ensure that customer needs are being met. This interaction would not be possible if Teradyne did not have its own sales force.

The firm wants full customer ownership. Having a direct sales force allows a company to own the customer relationship and control the total customer experience. The company can identify who its customers are, develop an understanding of their current and evolving needs, and build a product/service offering that meets these needs. Having this ownership can be a significant source of competitive advantage.

> ### Customer relationships drive success at Northwestern Mutual Insurance
>
> *Sales and Marketing Management* magazine chose the sales force at Northwestern Mutual Life Insurance Company as one of the top sales forces in America for the fourth time in five years. (Northwestern Mutual tied with Cisco Systems for top honors in 2000.) While many companies at that time were rushing to incorporate the latest technological wizardry into their sales processes, Northwestern Mutual remained committed to a tried-and-true sales strategy that had characterized the company for decades – a delivery system of 7500 sales agents who focused on developing long-term relationships with customers. The depth of these relationships was critical to Northwestern Mutual's ability to gain market share, boost sales, retain its salespeople, and lead the industry in ordinary life insurance sales.

Closeness to the customer encourages core capabilities development. Finally, developing sales competency can be a source of strategic advantage for a company. A sales force with an intimate understanding of its customers' needs and the ability to use the company's products and services to meet those needs, has a distinct advantage over competitors without such knowledge.

> ### A medical company's salespeople attend surgeries
>
> A company that sells orthopedic implant devices for mending bone fractures and replacing joints developed strategic advantage through its sales force's close relationships with surgeons. The company's salespeople would frequently be present during surgery to observe how the products were being used, and on some occasions, to even provide pointers on product application.

SIX GO-TO-MARKET STRATEGY INSIGHTS

Selecting the right selling channels for each market segment is an important decision. Below are some insights that can help you develop go-to-market strategies that are consistent with long-term success.

Your Go-To-Market Strategy can be a Source of Competitive Advantage

Innovative selling approaches can allow companies to gain significant competitive advantage. Dell has rapidly become one of the top personal computer manufacturers. Dell has achieved a dramatically lower cost structure than its competitors through innovation in the collection of customer orders, and through efficient management of its supply chain to almost eliminate its ownership of inventory. Dell bypassed the traditional retail and distributor channels for personal computers, first by using an inbound telesales center, and now by having customers configure their own systems and place orders through a call center or its web site. The Dell web site currently handles 400,000 transactions a month. Companies like Dell that develop innovative ways to sell, make, and deliver their products often enjoy a sustainable competitive advantage.

We Live in a Multi-Channel World

A "one size fits all" approach to channel selection rarely succeeds in today's selling environment. The best go-to-market strategies typically involve multiple selling channels working together to deliver customer value. Hybrid go-to-market strategies often help firms reach more customers and prospects profitably. The company in Figure 4.9 uses variety of selling channels to balance the need for efficiency and effectiveness during the various stages of the sales process.

	Lead generation	Quality	Account plans	Develop opportunity	Tailor value proposition	Prove solution	Develop terms	Negotiate & close	Implement solution	Maximize value
Tele-prospecting	◇	◇								
Strategic account manager			◇	◇	◇	◇	◇	◇	◇	◇
Field sales force			◇						◇	
Telesales										◇
Tele-customer service									◇	
Tele-tech support									◇	
Internet	◇	◇							◇	

FIGURE 4.9 Using multiple channels for various sales process steps

Whereas Figure 4.9 shows a sales process where multiple channels collaborate to serve a single customer, hybrid channels can also be designed to divide customers based on the sales opportunity and the relative cost of using different channels.

Bracco Diagnostics benefits from a multi-channel selling approach

Bracco Diagnostics, a leading provider of contrast agents for medical imaging, faced challenges during the 1990s as slow market growth and price erosion hurt the company's sales. Bracco had traditionally relied on its direct sales force to serve the needs of all its customers and prospects, including physicians, nurses, and administrators in hospitals and freestanding image centers. But in the new, less-favorable selling environment, the cost of calling on many customers with the direct sales force had become greater than the expected value of those customers. At many small accounts, the company was essentially losing money on every sales call.

Rather than continuing to make unprofitable sales calls or dropping small customers, Bracco management decided to create an alternative, lower-cost selling channel. The company established a telesales organization to call on low-value customers and prospects. The new approach had immediate positive results. The cost savings were significant: operating costs decreased 20 percent, bringing the company's cost structure in line with industry benchmarks. The largest savings came through reductions in the size of the direct sales force. At the same time, Bracco's sales increased by nearly 10 percent and market share increased by 1.4 percent. Customer satisfaction and retention improved as well. The direct sales force could focus on serving the needs of the firm's most important customers without distraction from smaller customers. The needs of smaller customers were better served as well because the telesales organization could focus on meeting their needs. Many small customers said they actually preferred telephone contact to face-to-face coverage, since it was less intrusive and more time-efficient.

The Role of the Sales Force is Changing

The sales force's role in a firm's go-to-market strategy is evolving as information becomes more widely and easily available to customers. Once, the primary mission of the sales force was to communicate the features and benefits of the firm's offering to customers and prospects. Today, however, customers are much better informed than in the past. With easy access to information via the Internet and other industry resources, customers can research a firm's products and services long before meeting with a salesperson. More and more, customers are unwilling to pay higher product prices to cover the cost of an expensive sales force if the salespeople are only repeating information that is easily obtained from a promotional brochure or the firm's web site.

In order to be successful in today's selling environment, sales forces must create value for their customers. A web site can provide a list of product features and benefits, but a salesperson can work creatively with a customer to determine exactly how those features and benefits apply to the specific situation. A web site can provide general answers to frequently asked questions, but a salesperson can be flexible and respond specifically to a customer's concerns. A telesales support rep can talk a customer through a series of troubleshooting steps, but a live salesperson can fix the problem more quickly on site. Successful sales forces create value while leveraging other sales channels to perform tasks that those channels can do better.

A Sales Strategy Change may be Necessary if Star Performers are Holding the Company Hostage

In some industries, the salesperson has a great deal of power with the customer. In these cases, top-performing salespeople sometimes hold their company hostage, making demands that are not in the best interest of the company. For example, a company wants to expand its sales force to capitalize on market opportunity, but existing salespeople have so much customer power that they fight the change successfully. If this is a persistent problem, the company may want to revise its sales strategy so that customers have more than one connection to the company. That way, no single channel member (the salesperson, for example) has too much power. Product specialists, telesales, finance, and R&D may all play a role in meeting customer needs. This broadening of customer contact, however, cannot solely be driven by the company's need to reduce the power of the sales force. Customers will not be willing to use the new connections unless they add significant value to the sales process.

Technology is Changing the Channel Structure

Changing technology has affected all companies dramatically in recent years. Advances such as cell phones, laptop computers, email, and particularly the Internet have transformed the way that many people do their jobs. These developments have changed the channel structure as well. Before the mid-1990s, the Internet did not exist as a selling channel. Yet, according to research company eMarketer, by 2004 worldwide business-to-business e-commerce revenues will exceed $1 trillion. Despite the fact that nearly 1000 Internet companies have folded, the web continues to thrive as a strong and viable selling channel.

Technology advances have made it possible to deliver some products electronically. The Internet can also help deliver product training and customer service in an efficient and effective manner.

During the height of the Internet boom in the late 1990s, many businesses were launched with the promise of "disintermediation," or the ability to shorten the channel between manufacturers and their customers through the use of computer and communication technology. Businesses were launched in industries as varied as furniture, medical supplies,

<table>
<tr><td>

Ecast delivers games and music to bars, restaurants, and hotels

Ecast delivers games and music to juke boxes and video game machines over a broadband network. It plans to expand its offerings to include other digital products such as movies. Whether Ecast succeeds in the market or not, it is clear that technology will be the dominant way to deliver digital products in the future when high speed connections are ubiquitous.

</td><td>

Cisco satisfies 70 percent of customer service inquiries online

Cisco Systems does a vast majority of its software upgrades online, receives over 75 percent of its orders online, and satisfies 70 percent of customer service inquiries online. Savings generated by having customers serve themselves online are estimated at about $400 million a year.

</td></tr>
</table>

groceries, chemicals, and auto parts. As many of these businesses have died, the mainstream manufacturing firms themselves have begun to use the same ideas to streamline their channel structures. The role of technology and the sales force in connecting a firm with its customers depends upon the value that each channel can create for the customer. Figure 4.10 provides a framework for determining how technology can replace or enhance the efforts of a sales force in a firm's go-to-market strategy.

Today even salespeople, the traditionally low-tech selling channel, must be technology literate to succeed. Most salespeople use a laptop computer to manage their accounts, perform routine administrative tasks, and get access to product, pricing, customer, competitor, and environmental information. In addition, technology can help a salesperson

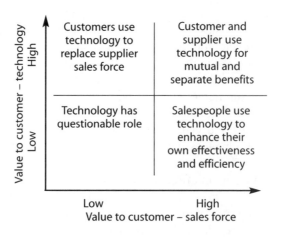

FIGURE 4.10 A framework for assessing the value of technology and the sales force in a firm's go-to-market strategy

---

High-tech presentations are more effective

A study at Portland State University revealed that buyers retain 78 percent more information when a presentation is delivered in multimedia through a laptop and digital projector than when they receive the same information from overhead transparencies.

---

deliver a more effective sales presentation or can provide live product configuration assistance.

Go-To-Market Strategy should be Reassessed at Least Every Two Years

Constant attention to the firm's go-to-market strategy will keep the strategy fresh. A company's go-to-market strategy should be constantly challenged as the five forces of change discussed in Chapter 1 – customer needs, competitors, the environment, corporate strategies, and performance challenges – exert pressure on the firm.

Entering a New Market Can Require a New Go-To-Market Strategy

For many years furniture maker Herman Miller sold office furniture to large corporate clients through a network of independent dealers. These dealers received big contracts for hundreds of pieces of furniture to outfit corporate headquarters. In the mid-1990s, an explosion in the number of small and home offices created a new demand for the company's products. Many small business owners wanted to purchase individual pieces of furniture. Unfortunately, this rapidly growing market was not profitable for Herman Miller's existing dealers. Thus, Herman Miller found new distribution partners – retail stores – that could help them serve the exploding small-business market segment. In 1994, they introduced Herman Miller for the Home, a product line that allowed individual furniture pieces to be purchased through retail stores such as Crate and Barrel and Office Depot.

Successful companies seek constant and consistent improvement in their selling channel performance. Go-to-market strategies should be reassessed at least every two years, and in some cases more frequently.

Designing the Sales Force Structure

INTRODUCTION

Sales force structure answers two central questions: how to divide up all the sales activities among different types of salespeople, and how to coordinate and control the activities to meet the firm's goals. Sales force structures are often represented by organization charts with accompanying job descriptions for the various roles.

The Elements of Sales Force Structure

Sales force structure defines how the sales force will execute the sales strategy. As shown in Figure 5.1, there are several sales force structure decisions. At the core level, salesperson roles and specialization define the types of customers each salesperson will call on, the product or service portfolio that each salesperson will sell, and the activities that each salesperson will perform. The sales force structure also includes the reporting relationships that exist within the sales force. The reporting structure helps to define the coordination and control mechanisms that direct the activities of salespeople, influence the flow of information, and synchronize activities and information flows within the organization.

How Sales Force Structure Fits into the Sales Force Design Process

Before we discuss the various sales force structure options, it is useful to review how the firm's sales force structure fits into the overall sales force design process. This also provides a good opportunity to outline the organization of the remaining chapters of the book.

Chapters 3 and 4 presented an approach for developing a firm's sales strategy and go-to-market strategy. Sales strategy specified targeted

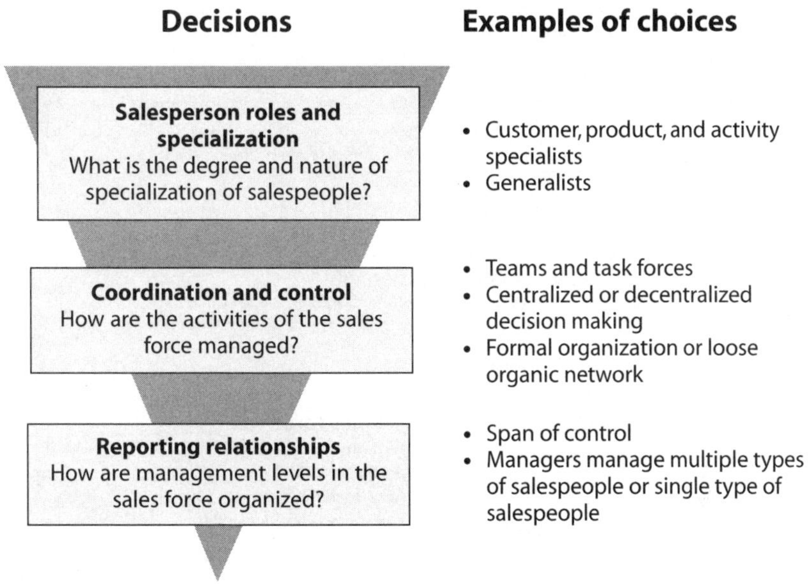

Decisions   **Examples of choices**

Salesperson roles and specialization	
Salesperson roles and specialization What is the degree and nature of specialization of salespeople?	• Customer, product, and activity specialists • Generalists

Coordination and control How are the activities of the sales force managed?	• Teams and task forces • Centralized or decentralized decision making • Formal organization or loose organic network

Reporting relationships How are management levels in the sales force organized?	• Span of control • Managers manage multiple types of salespeople or single type of salespeople

FIGURE 5.1 Sales force structure decisions

customer segments, the product offering to each customer segment, and the resulting sales process. Go-to-market strategy identified the sales channels and sales resources that are best suited to carry out this sales process.

The remaining chapters in this book focus on the use of a direct sales force as a key part of the firm's sales strategy and go-to-market strategy. As shown in Figure 5.2, designing the sales force involves three major components:

- *Sales force structure:* This consists of specifying various roles, the nature and degree of specialization, and the coordination and control mechanisms including the reporting relationships for the sales organization. Sales force structure is the focus of this chapter. A more detailed treatment of sales roles is included in Chapter 6.
- *Sales force size:* For any sales structure, the number of salespeople in each role needs to be determined. Sales force size is the focus of Chapter 7.
- *Sales force deployment:* For any sales force structure and size, specific accounts and activities need to be assigned to each sales territory or salesperson. Sales force deployment is covered in Chapter 8.

The last two chapters of the book provide insights on how to make any sales force design work and how to make the transition from one sales force design to another.

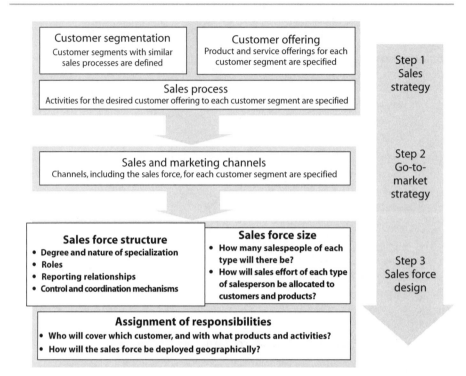

FIGURE 5.2 Sales force structure in the sales force design process

Why Sales Force Structure is Important

Sales force structure has a direct impact on customers and on company results. From a customer perspective, structure decisions determine how many different salespeople the customer sees, how knowledgeable salespeople are about their products and customers, and therefore how responsive salespeople can be to the customer's needs. From a company perspective, structure influences how effectively the sales force generates revenues, how efficiently it manages costs, how adaptable it is to evolving situations, and whether or not it has the flexibility to change quickly.

Sales force structure affects every member of the sales force. It specifies the responsibilities or roles of different salespeople by defining how the sales force will execute the sales strategy. This includes identifying the type of customers each salesperson will target, the product or service portfolio that each salesperson will sell, and the activities that each salesperson will perform.

Sales force structure also defines how sales activity is coordinated and controlled. It identifies how different sales roles will interface, the sales manager's role, and the reporting relationships. Sales force organization charts range from very simple structures where each salesperson reports to a single manager, to very complex matrix structures, where each salesperson is linked to several parts of the organization that focus on specific products, customers, selling activities, and/or geography.

Sales force structure shapes many other sales force decisions. Since the structure determines sales job descriptions, it affects the hiring profile for sales and sales management positions. It influences sales force training needs, performance evaluation systems, career paths, and the compensation plan. It affects sales territory alignment, reporting relationships, and the need for communication and coordination between different salespeople. The sales force structure also has a major impact on sales information and support systems.

DRIVERS OF SALES FORCE SPECIALIZATION

Companies have many choices of how to specialize the roles within their sales organizations. When a company sells a narrow or uncomplicated product line to market segments that are similar, salespeople are typically generalists. Each salesperson sells the company's full product line to all customer types. Generalist sales roles promote efficiency because sales force travel and coordination needs are minimized.

Avon salespeople are generalists

Beauty company Avon has over 3.5 million independent sales representatives who sell not only the company's extensive line of beauty and related products, but also sell fashion jewelry and accessories, apparel, gifts, and collectibles. There are no defined sales territories; an Avon salesperson can sell to any customer he or she develops a relationship with. This structure works for Avon because, although the product line is broad, Avon's products are not complex and can be easily understood by a salesperson with the aid of company catalogs. The structure also gives each Avon salesperson freedom to decide how to spend his or her time, encouraging independence and entrepreneurship. Insurance, investment products, and office supply companies have similar sales force structures.

Companies with diverse and complex product lines may enhance sales force effectiveness by designing sales roles that are specialized by product.

Roche Diagnostics salespeople specialize by product

Roche Diagnostics, a leading supplier of medical diagnostics products, has a broad, complex product portfolio that includes research equipment and reagents, analyzers and reagents, glucose meters and strips, and diagnostic tests. The product line is too large to be handled effectively by a single sales team. To further complicate the situation, sales of some products cannot be tracked at the customer level. The company's sales force is organized into four separate product-based teams. These teams share hospitals as major customers.

Companies that sell to customers with diverse and complex needs often design sales roles that are specialized by market or customer. Market and customer specialization increases effectiveness because salespeople can become experts on the particular industry or types of customers they target. Market and customer specialization can also help companies become more efficient by varying the amount and type of coverage to accounts with different sales potential.

Nextel salespeople are industry specialists

Many of the salespeople that sell to large corporate customers at Nextel, a wireless telecommunications company, specialize by industry. Salespeople sell to customers in one of several industry segments, such as construction, financial services, healthcare, manufacturing, and government.

Market specialization can match sales effort with opportunity

Many companies have sales roles that specialize by customer opportunity. For example, accounts may be classified as large, mid-market, and small. At most companies, sales are very concentrated. Thus, a small number of large accounts have significant strategic importance to the firm. These accounts typically get special sales force attention, such as a dedicated global or strategic account team. The mid-market account segment is usually quite large. While no single account has critical importance to the firm, in the aggregate these accounts contribute a great deal of business. Typically, a company's traditional sales force spends the greatest amount of time with mid-market accounts. Finally, the small accounts segment usually has a very large number of accounts, many of which are not likely to generate enough sales to pay for the cost of in-person sales effort. Efficiency strategies are usually employed at small accounts. These accounts are often covered by less-expensive selling channels, such as telesales, the Internet, or direct mail.

When the selling activities required are diverse and complex, companies sometimes design sales roles that are specialized around those activities. Activity specialization can enhance both sales force effectiveness and efficiency.

Activity specialization enhances effectiveness in the computer industry

Many firms in the computer industry organize their sales forces into a hunter/farmer structure. "Hunter" salespeople specialize in finding business at new accounts. Once a sale is made, a "farmer" salesperson takes over the account to cultivate and grow the relationship and generate repeat business. Having two sales roles allows companies to better match salespeople with the right personality and skills to the right job, thus increasing overall effectiveness.

Activity specialization improves efficiency for Grainger

Grainger, a maintenance, repair, and operational supply (MRO) company, achieved efficiency gains by reassigning routine, administrative selling tasks from an expensive salesperson to a cheaper resource. Once a sale is made, the sales force turns many accounts over to an inside telesales group that handles post-sales support, such as order placement and delivery.

Companies that sell several different product lines to a diverse set of customers often have selling processes that require salespeople to perform many dissimilar and complex activities. Companies in this situation often have generalist salespeople, as well as a mix of product, market, and/or activity specialists.

A hybrid selling model at ABC

Television network ABC uses a hybrid selling model. ABC has client specialists that focus on selling advertising time to a particular advertising agency or directly to a major client. In addition, there are "product" specialists called daypart specialists that focus on selling ads in a particular time slot, such as daytime, primetime, or late-night. A client specialist is responsible for developing a partnership, executing buying and planning goals, and finalizing deals with a particular major client or agency. The client specialist calls in daypart specialists to help with pricing and specific details of the deal for the various dayparts.

A Framework for Determining Sales Force Specialization

Figure 5.3 provides a framework for thinking about the factors that determine the degree and type of sales force specialization that is appropriate for a company. Should salespeople be generalists, selling all products and performing all selling tasks for all types of customers? Or, should the sales force employ specialists, focusing on a particular product, market, and/or selling activity? This decision is driven largely by the firm's sales strategy. The need for sales force specialization depends upon the complexity and diversity of the selling process, as compared with a salesperson's bandwidth, skills, or capacity to perform that process. In addition to the selling process, the firm's strategy, culture, and need for flexibility can influence the sales force specialization decision.

This section of the chapter begins by exploring the linkage between the firm's sales strategy and sales force specialization. Following this, the influence of company objectives and strategy on sales force specialization and structure is discussed.

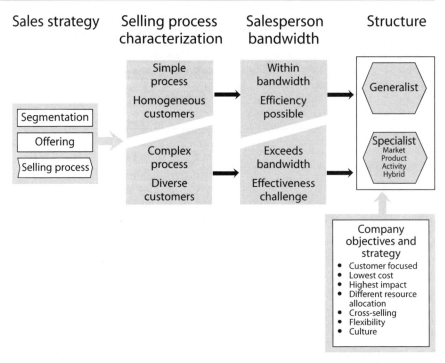

FIGURE 5.3 A framework for determining sales force specialization

How the Sales Strategy Affects Sales Force Specialization Decisions

A single generalist sales force is almost always the most efficient way to reach customers. Salespeople will have smaller sales territories, less travel time, and more face time with customers. Table 5.1 illustrates this efficiency.

TABLE 5.1 A comparison of efficiency for generalist versus specialized sales roles

	Scenario 1	Scenario II
Sales force organization	A single geographic team	Two specialty teams
Number of salespeople	100	70 and 30
Sales territory description	Each sales territory has roughly 1% of the country	Overlapping territories: the 70-person team has territories that are on average 43% larger in size than the geographic team. The 30-person team has territories that are on average 3.3 times as large as those in the geographic team.

However, while a generalist sales force is most efficient, it may not be very effective. One salesperson may not be able to acquire the skills and knowledge required to effectively sell a large, complex, or hard to sell product and service portfolio. Similarly, one salesperson may not be able to sell effectively to several different customer segments that have complex and diverse needs.

Salesperson bandwidth: a primary determinant of sales force specialization

In the world of telecommunications, bandwidth refers to the amount of information that can be carried through a communication channel such as a phone line, cable, fiber, or a satellite connection. This concept of bandwidth can also be applied to salespeople. There is a limit to how much an individual salesperson can understand and be effective at selling. At some point, a salesperson who is responsible for selling multiple products and performing many different selling tasks for a large range of customer types becomes overwhelmed by the job. The job exceeds the salesperson's bandwidth.

When a sales job exceeds their bandwidth, salespeople are likely to drop the customers, products, or selling activities that are most difficult or unpleasant for them. Unfortunately many of these customers, products, and activities may have strategic importance or large profit consequences to the company. Thus, a salesperson attempting to do a job that exceeds his or her bandwidth will no longer be able to produce the results the company desires.

Companies that sell many complex products to many diverse markets require a sales bandwidth that is much greater than the capacity of a single salesperson. For example, IBM sells hundreds of different hardware and software products, as well as professional services. It sells to customers of all sizes, ranging from huge multinational corporations to individual home computer users. It sells to numerous different industries in over 80 different countries. Table 5.2 lists the major categories of products, services, and markets sold by IBM in 2003, according to the company's web site. The bandwidth required for a salesperson to understand all of these products, services, and markets is virtually impossible to imagine. A single salesperson, no matter how intelligent or hardworking, could never do this job.

Of course, IBM's sales force of over 35,000 people is organized into many different divisions with many different types of sales specialists. In addition, the company relies on thousands of business partners, including distributors, value-added resellers, and software vendors, to sell many of its products in many markets. Complex structures like this frequently evolve as salesperson bandwidth is challenged by product line growth and market expansion.

Table 5.2 Sales bandwidth required for IBM

Services sold	Products sold	Markets sold to
Application hosting	Personal computing	*By size*
Application management	• Notebooks	• Multi-national
Application portfolio	• Desktops	corporations
services	• Workstations	• Large business
Business continuity and	• Monitors	• Medium-sized business
recovery	• Handhelds	• Small business
Business exchange	Upgrades, accessories and	• Home and home office
Business intelligence	parts	*By industry*
Business transformation	Micro-electronics	• Aerospace and defense
outsourcing	Networking	• Automotive
Buy and supply solutions	Printing systems	• Banking
Content distribution	Point-of-sale systems and	• Chemicals & petroleum
Custom application services	kiosks	• Consumer packaged
Customer relationship management	Servers	goods
(CRM)	• Blades	• Education
e-business hosting	• Mainframe	• Electronics
e-business integration solutions	• Intel processor-based	• Energy and utilities
e-business training	• Midrange	• Engineering
e-commerce	• UNIX	• Financial markets
e-learning	• Clusters	• Government
Enterprise applications (ERP)	Storage	• Healthcare
e-procurement	• Disk systems	• IBM business partners
e-workplaces	• Hard disk drives	• Industrial machinery
Facilities hosting	• Micro-drives	• Insurance
Financial management solutions	• Tape systems	• Life sciences
Human capital solutions	• SAN, NAS, and iSCSI	• Media and
Information technology outsourcing	IBM certified used	entertain ment
Infrastructure & systems management	equipment	• Pharmaceuticals
Integrated technology services	Software	• Retail
IT certifications	• Application and web	• Shipbuilding
Maintenance services	development tools	• Telecommunications
Managed hosting	• Applications – desktop	• Travel and
Managed storage	and enterprise	transportation
Mobile and wireless services	• Application servers	• Wholesale
Network integration and deployment	• Business integration	• Wireless
Network management	• Collaboration and	*By geography*
Networking training	knowledge	• Africa
On demand workplace	• Database and data	• Asia
Package application services	management	• Australia
Performance management	• e-learning software	• Europe
Portals, knowledge and content	• Enterprise messaging	• North America
management	• Host transaction	• South America
Procurement services	processing	• 80+ countries
Product life cycle management	• Networking	• 28+ languages
Security and privacy services	• Operating systems	
Security training	• Portals – commerce –	
Storage services	personalization	
Storage training	• Security	
Strategic change solutions	• Storage management	
Strategic outsourcing	• Systems management	
Supply chain and operations solutions	• Wireless – voice –	
Technical support services	pervasive	
Transformational outsourcing		
Wireless e-business solutions		
Wireless security services		
Wireless training		

IBM's sales force restructures in 2001

IBM completed a major restructuring of its sales force in 2001 to address bandwidth concerns. Before the restructure, many of IBM's customers felt that IBM's salespeople knew a little about a wide variety of topics, but lacked the depth of industry knowledge that customers needed. IBM responded by restructuring the sales force into teams based on customer size and industry. That way, salespeople could be trained as industry experts, and were thus able to respond to customer needs more quickly. Because the salespeople were structured in teams, they could offer IBM's entire portfolio of products and services without going through red tape to find the appropriate internal help.

The number of different products and markets that one salesperson can handle varies greatly, depending upon the situation. If products and markets are not complex, the products are similar, the target markets are homogeneous, or the sales process is transactional in nature, then the number of products and markets a salesperson can handle increases.

Amway salespeople are generalists

An Amway salesperson is able to effectively sell over 450 Amway nutrition and wellness, personal care, home care, home tech, commercial products, a variety of services and educational products, plus thousands of brand-name products from a catalog.

If products or markets are complex and require extensive knowledge, or are very different from one another, then the number of products or markets a salesperson can handle decreases. Most sales forces that sell highly technical products ask each salesperson to sell just a few products or services. Alternatively, they complement their generalist salespeople with focused product specialists. Similarly, most sales forces that sell products or services requiring extensive customer knowledge have each salesperson specialize in selling to just a few customer segments.

How to recognize bandwidth problems

Signals that the existing sales force is facing bandwidth constraints often come from customers. Customers might complain that their needs are not being met because salespeople do not understand their business or their product and service needs. Customers may demand salespeople who are more knowledgeable about their industry or who have in-depth, technical expertise. These signals should be addressed immediately; it may be too late if a company waits until new deals are lost or customers stop buying.

Bandwidth constraints and customer relationships

A decision to split a sales job that has grown too great for a salesperson's bandwidth is easier when different products are sold to different customers or to different decision makers within each account. For example, a computer manufacturer's sales team that sells two complex products – one to the aircraft industry for computer-aided design, and one to the movie industry for realistic animation – can be split cleanly along product and market lines. The decision to split the sales force is more difficult when multiple products are sold to the same customers or decision makers. Splitting a sales force in this case means that more than one salesperson will need to call on the same customer. This can lead to customer confusion, and requires coordination on the part of the company.

Signals that bandwidth problems exist can also come from salespeople. Salespeople may complain that they are overloaded, overwhelmed, or lack critical knowledge or competencies necessary for success. Too many of them may be missing their sales goals. Companies frequently misdiagnose this as a training problem, but it is often a sign that the bandwidth required for the sales job has grown too large. Sales forces in this situation are typically unmotivated and often experience high salesperson and manager turnover.

Clues that the sales job has grown beyond the available salesperson bandwidth can also come from examining how salespeople spend their time. The sales force will begin to sell very selectively. The unfamiliar, less glamorous or harder to sell products and customers will be ignored in favor of the comfortable, fun, or easy products and customers.

Three factors that introduce complexity into the sales strategy: markets, products, and activities

The concept of "sales strategy" consisting of customer segmentation, customer offerings (referred to in this chapter more generically as

---

Product line expansion drives new sales roles at Hollister

Healthcare products manufacturer Hollister broadened its product line over many years through a mix of new product development and acquisition. By 2000, Hollister's single generalist sales team was selling five different product lines. Each product line had its own set of customers and decision makers, with very little overlap. The products were at very different points in their life cycles. Each product line had a very distinct value proposition and faced a different set of competitors, requiring the sales force to master several different positioning messages. In order to increase the effectiveness of the salespeople and drive revenue growth, Hollister split the product portfolio between two separate sales roles. That way, each salesperson could be more knowledgeable selling a smaller number of products to a more focused audience.

"products"), and the sales process was introduced in Chapter 2 and developed in Chapter 3. Excessive complexity or diversity in any of the three parts of a firm's sales strategy – customers, products, or selling process activities – can challenge salesperson bandwidth. Complex products or vast product lines can quickly exhaust a salesperson's capabilities. Diverse market segments with multiple buying points are equally challenging. Varied activities, such as prospecting, selling, and servicing, that suit salespeople with very different personalities and skills can also lead to bandwidth problems.

Sales forces deal with bandwidth concerns by establishing specialists that focus on a subset of their products, markets, or selling activities. Specialization is a "divide and conquer" strategy. A sales strategy that is difficult for a single generalist salesperson to accomplish is partitioned into pieces, and each piece is accomplished by a different person. If this is done, the customer contact becomes more effective. Sales calls have higher impact because salespeople can develop deeper knowledge and a higher level of skill through focus. As a result, they have more credibility with customers, are better problem solvers, and can be more persuasive in their sales approach. But specialization is not free. The increase in effectiveness frequently comes at the expense of efficiency. Accountability and coordination problems can also arise when specialization results in multiple salespeople working together for a sale. If the roles are not clearly articulated, the customer may be confused and not know which salesperson is responsible for what.

Figure 5.4 illustrates the three dimensions of complexity that can challenge sales force bandwidth and the various types of specialization that emerge to deal with that complexity. The types of specialization shown in the figure – product, customer, activity, and hybrids combining two or three of these dimensions – will be discussed later in this chapter.

How Company Objectives and Strategy Affect Sales Force Specialization and Structure Decisions

Analysis of the sales strategy provides a good starting point for determining possible types of sales force specialization. Salesperson bandwidth can create the need for specialization to achieve greater effectiveness with customers. However, companies sometimes create specialized sales roles beyond the level demanded by salesperson bandwidth constraints. Sales force specialization is also an important way that firms reinforce company strategies and facilitate the accomplishment of key objectives. For example, specialized sales roles can help a firm improve focus on important customers, create competitive advantage through product or industry expertise, or achieve operating efficiencies. Table

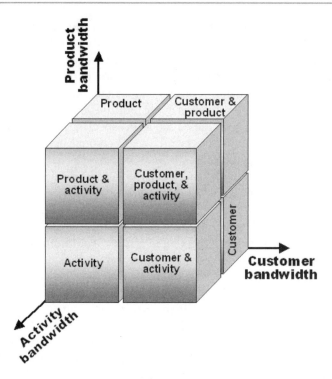

FIGURE 5.4 Market–product–activity framework for determining sales force specialization

5.3 provides some examples of how specialization can help implement a company's objectives and strategy.

The following examples show how companies have used a variety of sales force specialization and structure solutions to achieve customer focus, increase customer impact, reduce costs, manage resource

---

The link between company objectives and sales force structure in the software industry

The link between company objectives, strategies, and sales force structure was evident in the software industry in 2002–3. Several major software companies, such as Microsoft, SAP, and America Online, restructured their sales organizations during that time. While company goals at Microsoft focused primarily on revenue growth, those at SAP and America Online focused primarily on cost reduction. These different strategies led to different sales force structure solutions.

At Microsoft, revenues and income had been growing consistently, despite a challenging economic climate. The company's sales force strategy was to increase emphasis on selling solutions to customers, not just software. Solution selling required a greater depth of industry expertise. Thus, Microsoft expanded its sales

TABLE 5.3 Company objectives and strategy drive sales force specialization

Company objectives and strategy	Implications for sales force structure
• Make it easy for customers to do business with the firm • Cross-sell across product lines • Provide bundled offerings (one-stop shopping for customers)	• Single point-of-contact for decision makers (a single salesperson per account or an account manager who coordinates the activities of multiple product or activity specialists)
• Take better care of customers • Offer superior value-added service • Drive revenue growth	• Product and/or market specialists for maximum effectiveness
• Have the highest operational efficiency/ lowest selling costs	• Organize selling responsibilities geographically to reduce travel costs • Shift non-critical selling activities to lower-cost resources such as telesales or the Internet
• Launch a new product successfully while protecting existing product lines	• Establish a launch team, keep remaining salespeople focused on key existing product lines
• Protect business with key customers • Adapt to rapidly changing customer needs	• Establish customer-based selling teams for key accounts that can evolve with customer needs
• Develop more new customers	• Establish a hunter sales force dedicated to new account development

force by 20 percent and established seven new industry vertical selling teams to serve the needs of large customers in the retail, healthcare, automotive manufacturing, high-tech manufacturing, oil and gas, media and entertainment, and professional service industries. These industry vertical teams were added to five vertical teams that had been established two years earlier in financial services, telecommunications, state and local government, federal government, and education. The teams included sales, service and support, partner engagement, and marketing functions. The purpose of these vertical teams was to allow Microsoft to get closer to the business challenges faced by its customers, enabling it to sell more complete solutions addressing specific business needs. In short, the new structure encouraged Microsoft salespeople to be more effective sellers and thus helped the company drive revenue growth.

At SAP, one of the world's largest providers of business software, bleak economic conditions led to sharp revenue declines. In order to improve profitability, the company's strategies naturally focused on cost reduction. The company began 2003 by eliminating 132 sales positions in the US, a 3 percent reduction in its total sales force. Along with the reduction in headcount, the sales force was restructured. Instead of each salesperson specializing in a particular industry, sales territories were reorganized geographically. Thus, each salesperson sold a wider array of products to a more local group of customers.

Online service provider America Online (AOL) implemented a similar sales force change when faced with plummeting advertising revenues in late 2002. The company implemented a 20 percent reduction in ad-sales staff, and reorganized sales assignments by region. Like the SAP sales force, the AOL ad-sales group had previously been organized vertically by industry. The new geographic sales territories at SAP and AOL allowed salespeople to be more efficient in covering their customers and thus helped the companies reduce costs.

allocation, and implement cross-selling initiatives. Sales force structure is also an important way that firms reinforce their culture and maintain needed flexibility.

Achieving customer focus through sales force specialization

Customers want to work with salespeople who are knowledgeable about the products they sell and competent at performing all the necessary selling tasks. In selling situations with high bandwidth, this frequently suggests that multiple salespeople should call on each customer. Yet too much specialization can be undesirable to customers. Customers that see too many different salespeople from the same company may demand a more coordinated effort or less sales force pressure.

Customers of a medical systems company want to see fewer salespeople

A medical systems company sold a broad line of products to hospitals and other medical facilities. The products ranged from large capital equipment and software systems to smaller equipment and reagent chemicals. Because the company's products were diverse and technically complex, the company had assigned several specialist salespeople to each customer. This allowed salespeople to maintain a depth of technical expertise. Most customers saw five to seven different salespeople. Feedback from customers, however, indicated that they preferred to deal with just one or two company salespeople. Perhaps a sales force redesign is needed.

Increasing customer impact through sales force specialization

Customers prefer to buy from suppliers who know the customer's business and industry well. Specialization by industry is very effective. Consequently, companies like Microsoft, IBM, and Nextel have established industry vertical selling teams in an effort to increase the effectiveness of their salespeople with customers and drive customer value and revenue growth.

IBM reorganizes the sales force of its $13 billion software business

In 2004, IBM reorganized its sales and support staff of 13,000 people in its software business around 12 vertical industry segments including financial services, retail, and manufacturing. The change is designed to focus IBM salespeople and its third-party partners so that products and services can be tailored more specifically to the needs of customers. The change, it is hoped, will refocus IBM salespeople on industry solutions and not just software. IBM already had customer teams and industry verticals in an organization that cuts across its product lines. In this case, a product line (software) sales force was also aligned around industries.

Reducing selling costs through sales force specialization

Sales force specialization can help a firm reduce selling costs. This is achieved in two ways. One way is to match the expertise of a high-cost solution-oriented salesperson to the needs of a strategic, high-value customer, while providing a less expensive salesperson for moderate-value customers. The second way is to lower costs by turning over selling tasks formerly done by field salespeople to less expensive substitutes such as telesales.

HP establishes new sales support role for increased efficiency

When Hewlett Packard management undertook a major initiative during the 1990s to increase sales force productivity, it discovered that salespeople spent between 30 and 50 percent of their time configuring and quoting systems for customers. To alleviate the burden, HP established two teams of configuration-support specialists, one on each coast. This allowed a salesperson to make one 15-minute phone call to a configuration specialist who would construct a package, make sure it worked, and check to see that it could be ordered and built. A quote could be faxed to a salesperson or the customer, often in a matter of minutes. This resulted in a significant increase in the time salespeople could spend meeting with customers and selling.

Managing resource allocation through sales force specialization

Sales force specialization influences the level of attention that different products, customers, and selling activities receive. The best way to ensure that a product, customer, or activity obtains a specific level of selling effort is to set up a dedicated sales force to sell that product or to focus on that customer or activity. Managerial directives, training, coaching, and incentive compensation plans can influence the allocation of selling effort, but their success is not guaranteed. A specialized structure can ensure that an intensive level of sales force and management attention is directed towards strategically important products, customers, and activities.

Sales force structure at P&G encourages key customer focus

When Procter & Gamble wanted to solidify relationships with its most important national and regional chain customers in the United States, it established vertical selling teams dedicated to serving the needs of these customers. These teams are organized around individual accounts or types of accounts. For example, P&G has approximately 300 people dedicated to serving the needs of its largest customer Wal-Mart at its headquarters in Bentonville, Arkansas. The P&G Wal-Mart team consists of people from sales, marketing, distribution, supply-chain management, IT, and finance. Their goal is to enhance Wal-Mart profitability with P&G products while increasing revenues and profits for P&G.

Implementing cross-selling programs through sales force structure

Corporate strategies that focus on exploiting cross-selling opportunities with other company divisions can lead to sales force structure changes.

FleetBoston Financial reorganizes for more effective cross-selling

FleetBoston Financial is a global, diversified financial services firm with customer offerings that include consumer banking, corporate banking, brokerage services, mortgage services, and wealth management. Each of these business areas has its own sales force. The inter-relationships between these areas create many potential cross-selling opportunities.

In 2002, Fleet created a Wealth Strategies sales force to encourage cross-selling between its Private Client Group (PCG) and its Quick & Reilly brokerage subsidiary. The Wealth Strategies salespeople are experts in estate and tax planning, charitable giving, retirement strategies, and business succession plans. These salespeople work closely with Private Client Group account managers to make sure PCG clients are aware of Fleet's wide range of brokerage services available through Quick & Reilly, and to help structure solutions that include these services. For example, a Wealth Strategies salesperson might help create a charitable foundation with the majority of assets being held in growth and income stocks. Initially, the Wealth Strategies group was centrally located at Fleet's Boston headquarters. In 2003, Fleet decided to expand and decentralize this sales force to better service customers across the country.

More change is in store for FleetBoston Financial. In October of 2003, Bank of America announced that it will acquire FleetBoston, creating one of the largest financial companies in the world.

Reinforcing company culture through sales force structure

Good sales force structures reinforce the company's culture. Structure can affect whether the sales organization will be internally competitive versus cooperative, or empowering versus controlling.

> ## Sales force structure supports company culture at W. L. Gore
>
> Consider the unique culture at industrial products company W. L. Gore, the maker of Gore-Tex lining for weatherproof jackets. Gore has a culture built around innovation, empowerment, and teamwork. The company's sales force structure is designed to encourage this culture. The sales force is organized into what Gore calls a lattice structure in which there are no titles and no official lines of reporting. Every salesperson has a sponsor who functions as a mentor, not a boss. Sales leaders function like coaches. Salespeople work together on teams to meet the needs of their customers. This structure helps to perpetuate the entrepreneurial culture of the company.

Achieving organizational flexibility through sales force structure

A sales force structure affects how quickly and painlessly a sales force can reorganize and adapt in response to change. Customer needs evolve, competitors get smarter, and the selling environment changes over time. In addition, corporate strategies evolve and the sales force may get pressure from management to improve sales performance. Good sales force structures can adapt to these change pressures. They allow the company to react quickly by adjusting its selling approach without a major structural overhaul, or by changing the structure itself without major organizational trauma.

Frequently, organizations are reluctant or difficult to change. There are several ways that sales force structures can become inflexible, thus hindering adaptation and renewal. First, when a fragmented sales force has several totally independent sales forces that do not interact with one another, power structures that resist change can emerge. Managers in these types of organizations often defend their turf and strongly resist interference by other managers. There is very little flexibility to shift resources as needed at the local level unless the shift is forced by top management. Second, structures that have several sales forces with strong interdependence, including many coordination mechanisms and overlapping responsibilities, can find it hard to change one part of the structure without redesigning the whole organization. Finally, structures that are highly specialized give salespeople very specific knowledge and skills. If the specific knowledge and skills become obsolete, it can take a lot of effort to retrain salespeople for other jobs. This leads to organizational inflexibility.

SALES FORCE SPECIALIZATION CHOICES

There are four basic models of sales force specialization: generalist, market-based, product-based, and activity-based. A fifth choice – hybrid specialization – combines elements of two or more of the basic models. The following section describes key characteristics, advantages, and disadvantages of the various sales force specialization choices. Examples are also provided.

Generalist Sales Roles – Without Customer, Product, or Activity Specialization

Some companies have only generalist sales roles. Each salesperson performs all the sales activities required to sell the company's full product-line to all customer types.

Generalists in the bottled water industry

A firm that sells bottled water to residential and commercial accounts uses general-ist salespeople to sell water coolers and bottled water delivery contracts. The sales-people are also responsible for installing the coolers and making bottled water deliveries on a regular basis. Territories are determined by geography, so that every salesperson covers both the residential and commercial accounts that fall within a contiguous and compact geographic area.

Generalist sales roles are most effective when a straightforward selling process can be used across products and customers. Many start-up companies launch their first products using generalist salespeople. Generalists are efficient, and create no duplication of effort since just one salesperson calls on each customer. Salespeople can live close to their accounts so that travel time and costs are minimized, and there is more face-to-face selling effort.

Sales force structures that include generalist sales roles are usually simple and easy to understand. They frequently have low administrative overhead because salespeople do not need to coordinate selling activities since each account is covered by just one salesperson. There is no confusion regarding who is responsible and accountable for each customer, and the customer always knows who to talk to.

The primary disadvantage of generalist sales roles is that generalists are typically not as effective as specialists in situations that require high sales-person bandwidth. This is because while a generalist may have basic knowledge of many products, markets, and selling tasks, he or she may lack the depth and expertise required to win at competitive accounts.

Another disadvantage of generalists is that they have to do everything. This can be difficult for a single individual. A generalist's work can have a high administrative component that consumes time that could be spent selling. Alternative roles such as sales assistant and telesales can off-load some of this administrative burden.

Controlling sales force effort allocation with generalist salespeople

Generalist sales roles encourage entrepreneurship among salespeople because each salesperson "owns" his or her own customers and has freedom to make decisions about how to spend his or her time. However, controlling the allocation of sales force effort can be a challenge for the firm. Generalists who sell many products to many customers often chose to work inside their comfort zone, potentially ignoring some products, customers, or selling activities that may be of strategic importance to the company. Management can attempt to redirect sales efforts through coaching and incentives, but these mechanisms are not always successful.

Market-Based Specialization: Customer Segmentation as a Determinant of Sales Force Responsibility

With market-based specialization, each salesperson is responsible for selling the firm's entire product line to a particular market segment or customer. Market-based specialization is good for companies that sell to customers with diverse and complex needs. Industry and customer opportunity-based specialization models are the most commonly used. Figure 5.5 shows how a networking equipment manufacturer uses both specializations. Each salesperson in the enterprise account group (the group that covers the firm's largest, most strategically important accounts) specializes in selling to a particular industry. One salesperson calls on carriers and service providers (such as AT&T and Sprint), another calls on government, education, and utility accounts, a third calls on finance and retail accounts, and a fourth calls on healthcare and hi-tech accounts. Customers that the large account and geographic account teams call on are not sufficiently large to require specialization by industry.

If customer needs, product mix, and the sales process vary substantially across industries, market-based specialization allows a sales force to be more knowledgeable and effective with customers within its specific industry. Market-based specialization helps companies direct intensive selling effort towards strategically important customers or market segments.

Market focus enhances sales force effectiveness

A company that sells airport parking services targets two separate markets – travel agents who influence leisure travelers and corporations who influence business travelers. Even though salespeople have enough bandwidth to cover both markets, the company's sales force is specialized by market. This increases the effectiveness of sales calls. Each salesperson becomes more focused on the needs of his or her assigned market segment (either travel agents or corporations), making the sales force more knowledgeable and valuable to customers and thus generating higher sales.

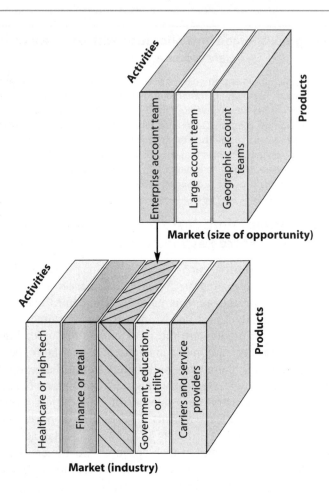

FIGURE 5.5 Industry-based and size-based market specialization

Market-based specialization can also help companies be more efficient, by varying coverage based upon the size and potential of the customer.

Sales force structures with market-based sales roles can be highly adaptive and respond quickly to changes in customer needs and buying processes. Knowing an industry or customer gives the salesperson an amazing advantage. Customers feel comfortable and are pleased that they don't need to educate salespeople who already understand their requirements and needs. The sales force can be trained and kept informed about the issues and trends affecting its particular industry or customer. Market-based specialization also encourages consultative selling. Salespeople are more likely to discover new ideas for products and marketing approaches that will appeal specifically to their customers. This depth of customer knowledge can give a firm significant competitive advantage, particularly in commodity markets.

> ### Market specialization enhances efficiency of a chemical sales force
>
> Sales force coverage of the customers of a chemicals producer is determined by customer size. Large customers are assigned to an outside field salesperson. Small customers and prospects, who are not likely to generate enough sales to make an in-person sales call profitable, are assigned to an inside telesales salesperson. Telesales also assists occasionally with larger accounts, if the work to be done does not require an in-person visit.

Market-based specialization makes it easy for management to control the effort allocation to each customer or market. However, this flexibility can be limiting when the business from a particular market segment or customer is depleted. For instance, if a vertical selling team is established to serve the needs of a major account and that account decides to switch to a competitor, the team is left with nothing to do. Entire industry vertical teams can be at risk as well if industry growth changes dramatically.

> ### Telecommunications industry slump leaves vertical selling teams with too little work
>
> There was tremendous growth in the telecommunications industry between 1996 and mid-2000. Many companies who sold to this industry created specialized telecommunications selling teams. When the industry took a dramatic downturn beginning in mid-2000, many telecommunications sales specialists were left with too little to do. For example, by the end of 2003, Lucent Technologies had approximately 20 percent of the 155,000 employees it had in 1999. Numerous key account teams of suppliers to Lucent were disbanded or downsized.

Market-based specialization works well at firms with products that have strong brand identity. For a firm with weaker brands, market-based specialization strengthens customer relationships, but at the same time it may weaken the brands because management's attention is focused on the performance of markets or customers, rather than on specific product or brand results.

> ### Achieving both customer and brand focus at P&G
>
> When Procter & Gamble restructured from product-based to market-based specialization of its sales organization during the early 1990s, sales force responsiveness to the needs of major customers increased. However, the restructure took some of the focus off individual brand performance. During 2001 P&G restructured again, in an effort to restore the strength of its brands. Major accounts were still serviced by account teams, but the salespeople on those teams became even more specialized. More team members focused on particular product lines, such as laundry detergent, cosmetics, or diapers.

Product-Based Specialization: Customer Offering as a Determinant of Sales Force Responsibility

With product-based specialization, each salesperson is responsible for selling a particular product or set of products to customers. More than one salesperson may call on customers, with each salesperson representing a different product line. Figure 5.6 shows a product-based division of responsibilities for an orthopedic device firm. The firm targets two separate markets – office-based orthopedic surgeons and hospitals. The company's salespeople specialize by product. Some salespeople sell implant devices which include total replacements for hips, knees, shoulders, and other joints. Other salespeople sell trauma devices which include plates, rods, and screws used for mending bone fractures. Each salesperson sells his/her assigned products to all office-based orthopedic surgeons and hospitals that fall within a defined geographic region. Every office-based surgeon and hospital is seen by two separate salespeople – one for implants and one for trauma devices.

Product-based specialization increases sales force effectiveness at companies that have a broad or complex product line. Product-based strategies also help companies intensify their sales force effort for strategically important products. By dedicating a sales force to a key product line, the company guarantees that significant sales force effort will be placed against that product line.

Sales structures with product specialists are often the easiest to manage from a corporate perspective. Many companies have product business units. Having product-based sales roles makes it easier to track financial data by product and create product-level profit and loss statements. Product-based specialization can also lead to closer relationships between sales and other product-based departments such as

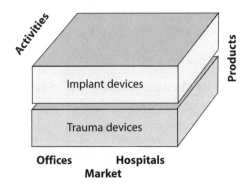

FIGURE 5.6 Product-based specialization

Cruise line splits selling responsibilities in order to strengthen brand identity

Royal Caribbean International and Celebrity Cruises created product-based specialization to strengthen the identity of its two cruise brands. Royal Caribbean International offers a family-oriented, active lifestyle cruise, while Celebrity offers cruises with white-glove service and gourmet dining. Two single-branded salespeople who know their products intimately call on travel agents, and so the travel agents become more knowledgeable about each brand's distinctive characteristics and target market, and can make the right recommendation for their travelers. In addition, each salesperson can focus on those travel agents that have clients who are likely to enjoy their particular cruise. Royal Caribbean salespeople focus on developing relationships with travel agents that cater to families, while Celebrity salespeople focus on the agents with a more upscale clientele.

---

production, research and development, and marketing. Another advantage of product-based specialization is that it makes it easy for management to control the effort allocation to each product line. If a product line needs more attention, management can simply increase the number of specialists assigned to sell the product line. Likewise, if the sales effort allocated to a product line is too high, management can decrease the number of specialists to guarantee that less time will be spent on the product line.

The disadvantages of product-based specialization are the duplication of effort, a possible lack of customer focus, and increased coordination requirements. Different salespeople may travel to the same customer. This duplication of effort can lead to frustration among customers because they may have to repeat the same information for multiple salespeople from the same company. Customers can also become confused about which salesperson is responsible for which products. The company may need to expend more sales management time in order to

---

Should competing products of a company be sold by different salespeople?

Companies sometimes place products that compete with one another into separate selling organizations. For example, when Royal Caribbean International and Celebrity Cruises were sold by a single salesperson, the salesperson's goal was to help travel agents select the cruise that best fit the needs of each customer. However, with different salespeople selling each cruise line's products, the salesperson's goal is to convince travel agents that his or her cruise line is the best. The company expects better overall performance with its two sales forces. But, to the extent that the two cruises compete for some of the same customers, this approach focuses more on making a sale and less on matching the right product to the right customer. This dilemma highlights the tension between company and customer interests.

---

provide adequate coordination at the customer level, adding to overhead. In addition, salespeople are responsible for extra documentation and communication with the other salespeople that call on the shared customer. Figure 5.7 captures the tension of a product-based organization dealing with a customer that wants to buy the entire product portfolio as a bundle.

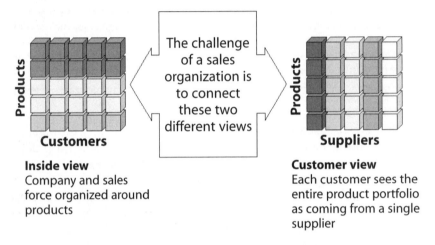

Inside view
Company and sales
force organized around
products

Customer view
Each customer sees the
entire product portfolio
as coming from a single
supplier

FIGURE 5.7 Product-based specialization

Duplication of effort with product-based sales forces

Salespeople who work for companies with multiple product-based sales forces often report chatting with colleagues from their company's other product divisions while waiting to see customers.

Structures based on product specialization can be inflexible if a product gets pulled from the market or becomes dominated by competitors.

Product-based specialization sometimes limits flexibility for pharmaceutical firms

Some pharmaceutical companies have set up specialty sales forces for products that have subsequently been withdrawn from the market for safety reasons. When this happens, the sales force is left with nothing to do.

Activity-Based Specialization: Sales Process as a Determinant of Sales Force Responsibility

With activity-based specialization, each salesperson is responsible for performing different parts of the company's sales process. For example, Figure 5.8 shows how a seller of electric motors created specialized sales roles by splitting the sales process at each account into two parts. Sales process activities requiring salesmanship such as lead generation and qualification, and closing are done by an account manager. Sales process activities requiring technical expertise, such as prototyping and pricing, and fulfillment and support are done by an application engineer.

Activity specialization can increase sales force effectiveness. A task that is technically complex or requires in-depth specialized knowledge can be performed more effectively by a salesperson who is specifically trained and experienced at performing that task. Companies also use activity specialization to increase sales force focus on critical selling activities, such as developing new business or providing customer service and ongoing maintenance.

Activity specialization can also increase efficiency by lowering the cost of the sales process. Routine or administrative tasks can be assigned to cheaper selling resources. Consumer products firms often hire merchandisers to manage displays, shelf placement, and inventory in retail stores.

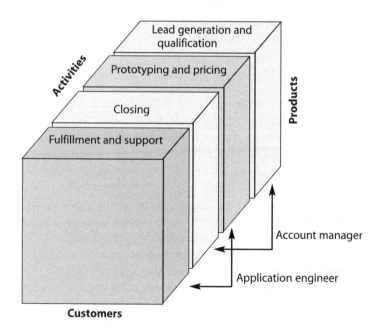

FIGURE 5.8 Activity-based specialization

This frees up time for higher paid salespeople to work with buyers to plan longer-term strategies, sell in special promotions, or discuss new products. Many sales forces use sales assistants to do routine or administrative work, thus freeing up salespeople to spend more productive time with customers. Companies also use non-sales force channels, such as telesales or the Internet, to reduce administrative selling costs.

Sales assistants enhance productivity at International Paper A number of salespeople in the xpedx distribution division of International Paper hire their own sales assistants to help with administrative tasks. This creates more time for selling. The commissions they receive from their incremental sales more than cover the cost of paying a sales assistant's salary.	**Field and telesales teams improve efficiency at Oracle** At Oracle, an inside and outside salesperson are matched one-to-one and work together as a team to meet customer needs and achieve a territory sales goal.

Hybrid Specialization: Customer Segmentation, Customer Offering, and Sales Process as Joint Determinants of Salesperson Responsibility

Companies that sell several different product lines to a diverse set of customers often have selling processes that require salespeople to perform many dissimilar and complex activities. Companies in this situation often have hybrid sales force specialization. Their sales force structures may include a mix of generalist, as well as product, market, and/or activity specialist sales roles.

Hybrid specialization often involves teams of salespeople working together to serve the needs of each customer. For example, Figure 5.9 shows how a seller of software to banks meets the needs of its customers through a mix of different sales roles. The firm sells three major software products to different sizes of banks. At major banks, account managers represent the company's full product line. These account managers rely on product specialists to help close sales of specific products. The account manager has to understand the full spectrum of needs at the account and acts as a single point-of-contact for the customer, coordinating the activities of product specialists as needed. Community banks do not generate enough business to justify dedicated account managers. Thus at community banks, product specialists make independent sales calls where they discuss the features and benefits of their particular software product. Finally, small banks do not generate enough volume to justify any in-person selling effort. Telesales contacts these banks via telephone representing the firm's full product line.

Product \ Market	Product 1	Product 2	Product 3
Major banks	Account manager		
Community banks	Product specialist	Product specialist	Product specialist
Small banks	Telesales		

FIGURE 5.9 Seller of software to banks: an example of hybrid specialization

Figure 5.10 shows how a tire manufacturer meets the diverse needs of its customers with a hybrid specialization that includes a mix of sales roles. The firm sells several brands of tires for consumer and commercial vehicles. The firm sells to two major markets with very different needs. The first market is original equipment manufacturers (OEMs), who use the tires on new vehicles. OEMs include automobile and truck makers and farm equipment manufacturers. The second market is mass merchandisers, retailers, automobile repair chains, and small tire retailers who sell replacement tires. In the original equipment market, each tire is custom designed for a particular vehicle. Thus, the sales force that covers that market is highly specialized. For every OEM account, each type and brand of tire has an account team, consisting of sales, engineering/R&D, and customer service personnel. Team members collaborate to create products that best fit the customer's needs and provide adequate returns to the company. There is virtually no product customization in the replacement market. Salespeople specialize in selling either consumer

Product \ Market	Consumer market tires						Commercial market tires	
	Car tires		Light truck tires		High performance tires		Commercial truck tires	Farm equipment tires
	Brand 1	Brand 2	Brand 1	Brand 2	Brand 1	Brand 2		
Original equipment manufacturers (Ford, GM etc.)	OEM Consumer account teams	OEM Consumer account teams	OEM Consumer account teams	OEM Consumer account teams	OEM Consumer account teams	OEM Consumer account teams	OEM Commercial account teams	OEM Commercial account teams
Replacement tire retailers – major accounts (Wal-Mart, Sears, etc.)	Consumer replacement major account vertical teams						Commercial replacement major account vertical teams	
Replacement tire retailers – small accounts	Consumer replacement salespeople with geographic sales territories						Commercial replacement salespeople with geographic sales territories	

FIGURE 5.10 Tire manufacturer: an example of hybrid specialization

market or commercial market tires, but they do not specialize further by type of tire or brand. Major accounts like Wal-Mart, Sears, and national auto part chains, are covered by dedicated vertical teams of salespeople. Smaller accounts like independent auto part chains and small retailers are covered by individual salespeople with geographic sales territory assignments. Hybrid sales roles enable the company to be both effective and efficient at selling its broad product line to customers with very diverse needs.

Another example of hybrid sales force specialization is the "hub and spoke" design. One account manager "owns" each account and acts as the primary contact for the customer. The account manager coordinates the activity of multiple sales specialists as needed by the customer. Specialists are called upon to provide detailed product or technical information or to help close sales. Figure 5.11 shows the structure used by a large healthcare manufacturer. Each hospital is assigned to a generalist account manager who is the "quarterback" for the hospital. The account manager coordinates the effort of several sector managers, each of whom specializes in one of the major product categories the firm sells. Sector managers coordinate the effort of product sales specialists, who are experts on a particular product within the sector. Each customer can be seen by an account manager, several sector managers and many more product specialists. The account manager's job is to ensure that all of this selling activity is coordinated appropriately across all of the influencers and buyers at the account level.

Hybrid sales force specialization allows sales forces that face diversity and complexity on several dimensions – products, markets, and/or selling activities – to deliver value to customers more effectively. It is possible to design sales roles around all combinations of the three dimensions of specialization: market and product, product and activity, market and activity, and market, product, and activity.

Industry verticals at Microsoft

Industry vertical selling teams have helped Microsoft better meet the needs of larger customers. Microsoft has verticals in a number of industries including government, finance, education, healthcare, retail, and manufacturing. Vertical selling teams range in size from 90 to 300 people and are led by general managers. Team members have specialized industry expertise and thus are well prepared to understand the problems faced by customers and to guide the development of industry-specific solutions. Teams are often located near the headquarters of key customers. For example, Microsoft's oil and gas industry vertical is located in Houston, Texas. Salespeople on this team can effectively sell highly specialized and integrated geological and geophysical applications as part of the total Microsoft solution.

FIGURE 5.11 "Hub and spoke" hybrid specialization

The customer intimacy that hybrid specialization can create for a firm can be a significant source of competitive advantage.

The major disadvantage of hybrid specialization is that the resulting sales force structures are often very complex and challenging to implement successfully. These structures can require a high degree of internal coordination, which means more sales managers or more time spent by the salespeople coordinating their activities. Individual accountability is diminished since several people create the sale in each transaction. When things go well, people naturally tend to feel a heightened sense of personal contribution, and when things go badly, they tend to feel that others are not pulling their weight.

> ### Hybrid specialization can limit organizational flexibility
>
> When a sales force structure with many different hybrid roles has too many interdependencies and overlapping responsibilities, it can be difficult to change any part of the structure without redesigning the whole organization. In addition, hybrid sales roles create salespeople who are highly specialized. It can take a lot of effort to retrain them for other jobs.

COORDINATION AND CONTROL IN SALES FORCE STRUCTURES

Much of this chapter has focused on the division of work among different types of salespeople. When only one salesperson touches each customer, the primary management responsibilities are to ensure that salespeople are hired, trained, coached, and that they perform with maximum impact to meet the company's goals. As a sales organization gets more specialized, coordination and control of sales force activities becomes more important and challenging. This section discusses coordination and control approaches, reporting relationships, and sales manager span of control issues.

Coordination and Control Approaches

Several approaches are possible for controlling a sales organization, and many methods can be used to coordinate the activities of people whose work jointly determines an outcome. Table 5.4 summarizes a spectrum of coordination and control approaches. At one end of the spectrum is a top-down command-and-control approach with highly standardized work processes for salespeople. At the other end is a decentralized loose organic network that encourages salespeople to be very creative and adaptive in their sales approach. In the middle are integrated approaches such as teams, task forces, and matrix organizations that seek to create forums for collaboration or channels of communication. The choice of the best approach depends on several factors, which are discussed below.

Command and control approach

A command and control approach is characterized by a management style that is centralized, with strong one-way downward directive communication. Upward communication focuses on compliance with the downward directives. The command and control approach emphasizes standardization of work processes. The sales process tends to be simple, but the organization to control it tends to be large and complex. The command and control approach promotes efficiency. This approach can work well in stable environments, provided the firm has salespeople and

TABLE 5.4 Spectrum of coordination and control approaches

	Command and control approach	Integrated approaches	Organic network approach
Description	Standardized work processes One-way downward directive communication Control culture	Mix of work processes and communication channels: • Teams and task forces • Matrix organizations • Synced organizations • CRM systems	Creative and adaptive work processes Highly decentralized, flat organization Empowerment culture
Primary benefit	Promotes efficiency	Balances need for efficiency and flexibility	Promotes flexibility
When it works best	Stable environment Straightforward sales process Company knows the bestselling process for each customer segment	Mixed environment and sales process	Dynamic environment Complex sales process Salespeople know the bestselling process for each customer

sales managers with a compatible personality and style. In dynamic environments, however, a command and control approach is likely to fail. Standardized processes quickly become obsolete in changing environments and will not have the customer impact needed for success.

Organic network approach

At the other end of the spectrum, organic structures are highly decentralized and have very little standardization of work processes. They emphasize creativity and adaptability of salespeople. They empower the salesperson to implement the bestselling process for each customer. The sales process tends to be varied and complex, whereas the organizational structure to control the people tends to be flat. Organic structures work well in dynamic environments, where the sales organization needs the flexibility to adapt quickly to changing market needs. However if the environment is fairly stable or the organization is large, a highly organic approach will create unnecessary inefficiencies within the sales force.

Integrated approaches

Integrated approaches to sales force coordination and control are a compromise between the extremes of command and control and organic

---

A key challenge for growing sales organizations

Organizations that use an organic approach successfully when they are small, often find that as they get larger, they do not seem to function as well. Frequently, this is because they have increased specialization without a corresponding increase in the level of integration and coordination. As a sales organization gets larger and more diverse, it becomes necessary to standardize sales processes, hiring profiles, training programs, and other sales force productivity drivers. This formalization helps the firm take advantage of economies of scale, and quite often, is necessary just to keep the organization running effectively. While formalization enhances performance on routine tasks, it inhibits performance on new challenges. Thus growing companies in dynamic environments frequently struggle to achieve the appropriate balance between the efficiency of standardization and the flexibility of organic systems and processes.

---

network styles. Integrated approaches create some formal channels for coordination and control within the sales force, while at the same time allowing flexibility as needed to meet customer needs. Coordination and control mechanisms can take many different forms within an integrated approach. Sales managers and major account managers can act as liaisons between salespeople who share the same customers. Cross-functional teams can be created, keeping team members informed, and providing a forum for developing strategies and tactics, as well as for planning and adapting them. Customer relationship management (CRM) systems can keep people informed across multiple customer contact points. Matrix organizations can be created, so that communication and accountability channels cut across simple vertical boundaries. Mirrored or synced sales organizations can be created that encourage cooperation between the salespeople who share customers.

Coordination is important when product-based teams collaborate

Many pharmaceutical companies have multiple product-based sales teams that promote drugs to physicians. Each team sells its own product portfolio, but major products are often promoted by more than one team. This co-promotion enables the company to achieve greater frequency of contacts for important products to high-potential physicians.

There is a significant need for coordination among salespeople who co-promote products to the same customers. Timing is important – a physician who is visited in the morning by a pharmaceutical salesperson selling a particular product is not likely to welcome a visit from a different salesperson selling that same product in the afternoon. In addition, coordination is necessary if the company hopes to achieve the optimal call frequency to important physicians.

Reporting Relationships

The sales force structure specifies the hierarchy of reporting relationships that exist within the sales force. In its simplest form, similar salespeople report to a first-level sales manager, and groups of first-level sales managers report to a second-level sales manager, and so on. Reporting structures and the coordination between various sales roles can get complex when multiple types of specialized salespeople touch the same customer with varying product and activity responsibilities. Simple geographical reporting, separate reporting, matrix reporting, integrated reporting, and synced sales organizations are discussed in this section.

Simple geographical reporting

Figure 5.12 shows an organization chart for a sales force with a geographical reporting structure. All salespeople have generalist sales roles. Reporting relationships are determined by geography, with each salesperson reporting to a district sales manager who reports to a regional sales director who reports to the vice president of sales.

With a geographical structure, there is clear accountability for customers and the sales process. For salespeople, the lines of communication are unambiguous and the career path is straightforward. The challenging part of geographical structures for very large organizations is the possible divide between sales and marketing. If the marketing organization

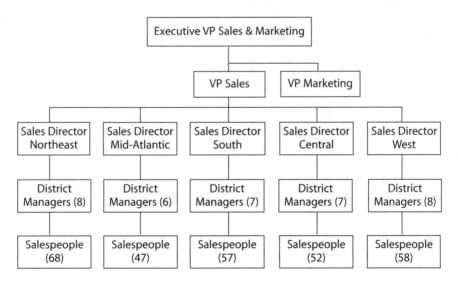

FIGURE 5.12 Organization chart for a sales force with a geographical structure

is large with multiple product managers, the coordination between sales and marketing can become more complicated.

Separate reporting

Several sales forces within a company, organized around markets, products, and customers, can each have their own separate, simple reporting structure similar to the one shown in Figure 5.13. Figure 5.13 gives an example of such a structure for a company organized around two separate product-based business units.

Like the simple geographic structure, this structure has clear accountability and lines of communication. In addition, by having a separate organization for each product line, excellent product focus and control exists up and down the organization. However, separate reporting structures have some disadvantages. A separate reporting structure makes it difficult to achieve coordination at the customer level if the separate organizations share customers and those customers desire a unified offering. Customers can receive calls from two salespeople from two independent company business units. In order to synchronize this effort, each salesperson may have to coordinate with several salespeople from the other business unit, and each sales manager may have to coordinate with several managers in the other unit as well. Many industries face this challenge. Before

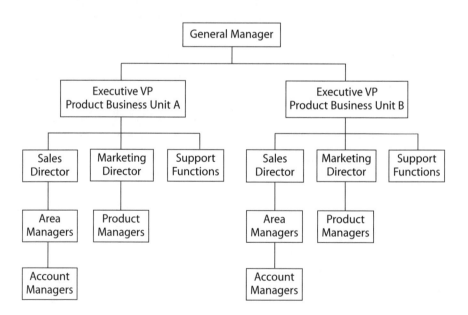

FIGURE 5.13 Organization chart for a sales force organized in product business units

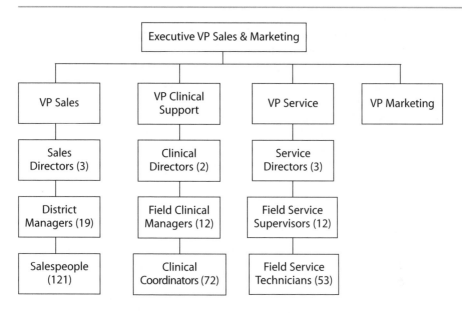

FIGURE 5.14 Organization chart for a sales force specialized by activities

organizing around customers, IBM had seven divisional sales forces potentially calling on the same customers in an uncoordinated way, sometimes with competing products.

The reporting structure for the medical device company in Figure 5.14 provides another example of separate reporting. It splits the activities of the sales process among different types of salespeople – sales, clinical support, and service. Each role has its own management structure.

The company in this example kept the sales, support, and service reporting relationships separate for several reasons. First, the skills required for the three roles are very different, and it was felt that a single manager could not manage and coach all three types of people. In addition, if the company had to choose a manager for all three types, it would likely select someone with a sales background, and not a clinical or service background. As a result, the clinical coordinators and service people would feel that their career path was limited, since their managers would not have a background similar to their own. A challenge for this separate reporting structure is that every sale requires tight coordination among the three types of people. Some firms use a matrix structure to enable better coordination.

Matrix reporting

Matrix reporting defines a hierarchical organization with a superimposed horizontal structure that creates multiple lines of communication and control across the organization. Matrix reporting is needed when a simple hierarchy cannot capture the necessary channels of collaboration within a company. For example, if a company is organized in product business units, and the sales force is organized by market, a "dotted line" relationship, or secondary reporting relationship, may be needed between the salespeople and the product organization. Geographic scope of a customer can also lead to the need for matrix reporting. For example, a salesperson handling the Opel account in Germany (a division of General Motors) might need to collaborate with an account manager who is responsible for

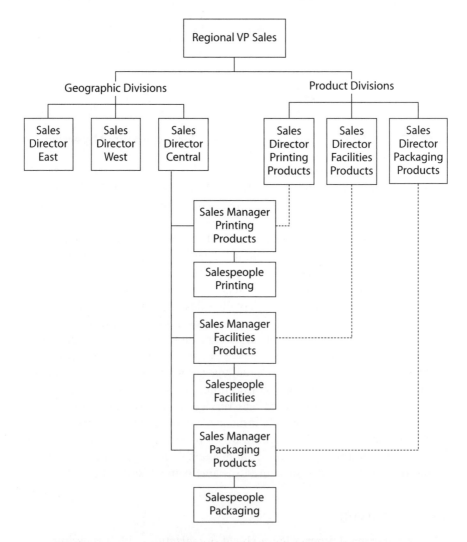

FIGURE 5.15 Organization chart for a maintenance, repair, and operational supply (MRO) company

General Motors in Detroit. In some cases, a salesperson might report to one manager, and have "dotted line" to another. In other cases, a salesperson might actually report to two people.

Figure 5.15 shows an organization chart with matrix reporting for one region of a maintenance, repair, and operational supply (MRO) sales force that sells three product lines. This sales force is organized into four levels: regional vice president, sales director, sales manager, and salesperson. The regional vice president has overall responsibility for sales of all products in the region. The six sales directors are organized into both geographic and product-line divisions. Three sales directors have geographic responsibility – each of them oversees sales of all product lines in one geographic sales area that comprises approximately one-third of the region. The other three sales directors have product-line responsibility – each of them oversees sales of one product line across the entire region. The sales managers and the salespeople who report to them specialize by product-line but are allocated geographically. Every sales manager reports to two different sales directors; directly to the geographic director and indirectly to the product-line director.

Sales force structures that are organized around multiple dimensions, such as market, product, and activity, can be even more complex. Hybrid sales organizations require complex matrix reporting relationships. Primary and secondary reporting relationships need to be thought out in advance of a design implementation. A good rule is that the primary reporting structure (whether it is geography, product, activity, or customer) should be determined by the dimension that requires the most control, collaboration, and communication. Other dimensions can form the "dotted line" reporting relationships. The market dimension has emerged as the most important structure dimension in many recent sales force organization structures. Whatever the dominant reporting dimension is, the other dimensions still have to be managed to ensure a smooth working system.

Integrated reporting

Integrated reporting is another possibility for specialized sales forces. Specialist salespeople report to a common manager at a very low level in the sales organization in an integrated structure. Figure 5.16 shows an example of a sales force with integrated reporting.

Integrated structures can work well when specialty teams share customers and coordination is required at the account level. They are also flexible because resources can be shared as needed at the local level, without requiring approval from higher-level managers. On the other hand, integrated structures require sales managers at a low level in the organization to manage a more diverse group of people. First-level managers may need to understand a broader product line, more types of customers, or many dissimilar selling tasks. If this requirement exceeds the manager's bandwidth, then the teams have to be kept separate. For example, the MRO company in Figure 5.15 keeps product specialists independent at the first management level, but integrates them at the second level. Managers of integrated structures can find it difficult to run sales meetings, because of the diverse needs and perspectives of the different salespeople who report to them.

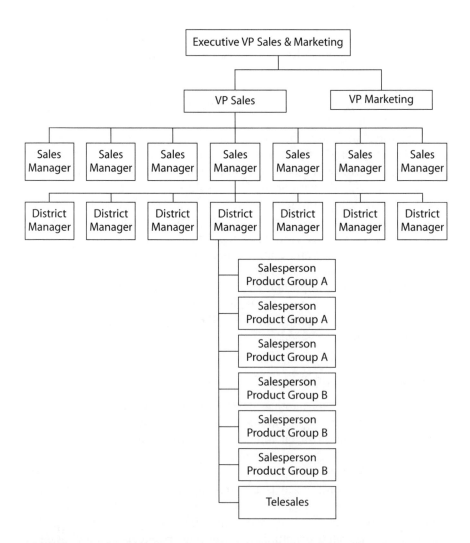

FIGURE 5.16 Organization chart for specialists with integrated reporting

Synced sales organizations

When multiple sales specialists from a single company call on the same customers, there is always potential for customer confusion. Account teams often minimize this confusion by designating someone to be "in charge of" the customer. For example, an account manager would be responsible for achieving a coordinated effort across multiple sales specialists at the customer level. But what if the company does not want to assign a particular person to play the role of coordinator? Many companies have used synced or mirrored territory alignments to encourage teams of equals to work together to provide a coordinated customer effort in the absence of a specified account manager.

In a synced or mirrored alignment, sales territories for two or more sales roles are geographically identical or in sync with one another. There can be a one-to-one relationship or a many-to-one relationship between sales territories for different sales roles. Figure 5.17 shows an example of a synced alignment from a sales force with account managers, technical specialists and telesales personnel. The seven account manager territories are labeled with numbers. Account manager territories 1, 2, and 3 are synced with Technical Specialist A's territory. Account manager territories 4, 5, 6, and 7 are synced with Technical Specialist B's territory. All seven account manager territories and both Technical Specialist territories are synced with a single telesales territory.

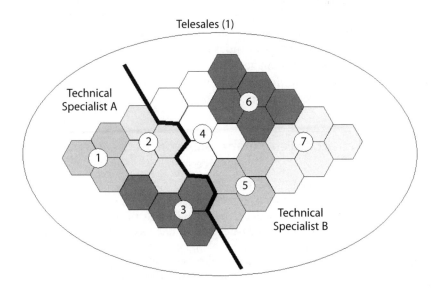

FIGURE 5.17 Synced sales organization with seven salespeople, two technical specialists, and one telesalesperson

---

Mirrored territories facilitate co-promotion in the pharmaceutical industry

A pharmaceutical sales force has three product-based sales teams that co-promote or cross-sell important products. This co-promotion allows increased access and higher frequency of calls to key customers, and strengthens the firm's relationship with its most important customers. The sales force has one set of mirrored geographic sales territories, and each territory is assigned to three different salespeople – one from each product-based team. The three salespeople work together, collaborating to ensure that their efforts are coordinated at the customer level, particularly when products are co-promoted to the same customers by two or three of the salespeople.

Synced or mirrored alignments have many advantages. Because they encourage teamwork in the field, customers receive more integrated and coordinated effort. This facilitates co-promotion and cross-selling and provides flexibility. Synced alignments also foster a culture of internal cooperation and encourage salespeople that call on the same customers to develop and share insights. They can positively affect results through peer influence. Synced alignments can also help to minimize the impact of salesperson turnover. When one salesperson leaves the company, a synced partner that already has a relationship with that salesperson's customers can cover the required responsibilities until a replacement is hired. All of these benefits are especially evident when synced partners report to a common manager who can facilitate and encourage teamwork within each synced group.

A downside of having a synced or mirrored alignment is that the flexibility to realign sales territories quickly is limited. A change proposed by a single salesperson or manager affects all layers of the overlay. Thus, many people need to be involved in evaluating and approving a change, slowing down the process. Synced and mirrored arrangements work best

---

Synced territories encourage teamwork between sales and service

A firm's sales force and telephone service organization have territories that overlay one another in a three- or four-to-one ratio. Each telephone customer service rep provides support for all the customers covered by exactly three or four salespeople, allowing each salesperson to coordinate with just one service rep and each service rep to coordinate with just three or four salespeople. The synced territories encourage teamwork between the sales and service organizations, providing salespeople with a greater awareness of customer support issues. This enhances the credibility of the sales force with customers, and enables them to better manage customer expectations and sell in ways that reduce demands on customer service.

when there is substantial overlap in the customer base that each team sells to. This helps to ensure that each common territory has the right workload and potential for each of the individual salespeople in the different sales roles. A final downside of synced alignments is that free-riders can emerge. One or more salespeople in a synced team can coast, relying on other team members to drive results. The free-rider problem needs to be addressed through good management or teamwork-based incentives.

Sales Management Span of Control

One of the most frequently asked organizational questions is, "What is the proper span of control for my sales force?" In other words, how many direct reports should each sales manager have? In sales, the range of span of control is quite large across companies – sales managers can oversee as few as 3 to as many as 30 salespeople, with 7 to 12 being the most common range. Another question that is frequently asked is, "How many different levels of management are appropriate?" This question is related to span of control. For a given number of salespeople, more levels tend to mean that there will be more managers and each manager will have fewer direct reports, while fewer levels means that each manager will have more direct reports and the organization will be flatter.

The issues of the number of management levels and span of control are important because they directly affect sales force costs and revenues. There are trade-offs that firms must make when determining their sales span of control. Flat sales organizations with higher span of control have lower costs. Vertical communication is faster and has less opportunity for distortion. Sales managers have less time to "interfere" in the sales process and selling time is greater. On the other hand, multi-level organizations with lower spans of control provide higher quality and quantity of management time. Managers have more time for coaching, planning, organizing, and coordinating, and more time to assist with sales. When these activities are done effectively and with the appropriate frequency, the result is increased sales force effectiveness and higher productivity.

In any situation, there is an optimal span of control. Figure 5.18 illustrates the impact of having too small or too large a span of control.

There are several approaches to determine the proper span of control. Some industries collect survey data and develop a benchmark for the industry. Then each company can decide how its span of control will compare to industry norms. Many managers reflect on their personal experience to come up with estimates based on what worked for them. Companies also examine sales force costs to determine how many levels and managers the company can afford and still keep costs in line with the sales budget.

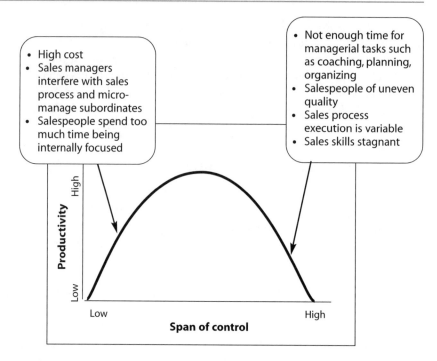

FiGURE 5.18 Span of control optimality

In general, fewer levels with higher span of control are appropriate when the managerial task is not time-consuming. Lower span of control is appropriate when the managerial task is time-consuming. The factors that increase the time a manager needs to spend are:

- dissimilarity of work across salespeople (more overhead to manage different types of people)
- geographic dispersion of salespeople (more travel time)
- many inexperienced salespeople (may need more coaching)
- need to closely control sales force activity (more management direction)
- extensive coordination required across salespeople or with others in the organization
- significant customer time required from managers, either to perform parts or all of some sales activities
- significant administrative time required for tasks such as planning and expense management.

A workload build-up approach can be used to determine the best span of control. This approach begins by specifying the activities that an effective sales manager should perform for each of his or her salespeople, and then proceeds with the estimation of the average amount of time that these activities require. To determine how much time the manager has available for people management, the time required for administration tasks, selling and other activities is subtracted from the total work time. The span of control is determined by dividing the manager's time capacity for people management by the average time required to manage each salesperson. The data required to implement this approach are based upon both field input and external benchmarks. A simplified illustration of this approach is shown in Figure 5.19.

Companies that create a sales force from scratch, or those that plan to gradually expand a sales organization, sometimes begin with a lower span of control and plan to increase it over time. This allows more sales management time for recruiting and training new salespeople while the organization is growing. As the team gets larger and more experienced, the

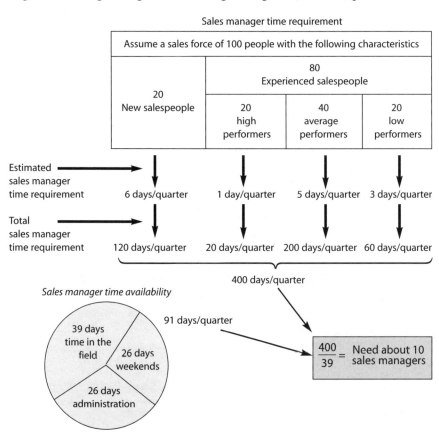

FIGURE 5.19 Span of control workload buildup illustration: sales manager time requirement

proportion of newly hired salespeople naturally declines and the span of control can increase.

A FIVE-STEP PROCESS FOR DETERMINING SALES FORCE STRUCTURE

Sales force structuring requires experience and wisdom. Mathematical formulas and algorithms for finding good structures do not exist. The detailed five-step process discussed below can help organizations when they need to restructure.

Major changes to sales force structures are never taken lightly, for good reason. A primary threat of a significant sales force structure change is that salespeople will not execute the sales strategy effectively or will leave the company because they are unwilling to give up accounts, take on different roles and responsibilities, relocate, or put their current income level at risk. The disruption of a restructure can also jeopardize customer relationships or hinder the achievement of a revenue goal. Companies are sometimes unwilling to restructure and be the first mover in an industry because they are reluctant to deviate from an established industry-wide sales force structuring paradigm.

Successful companies are not afraid to change outdated sales force structures in order to keep pace with market shifts. Successful restructuring requires that a company devote significant effort to designing the structure they need and to creating an implementation process that will result in the new structure. A five-step process to determine the right structure for a sales organization is shown in Figure 5.20. Each of the five major steps of this process is described further in this section.

Steps 1 to 4 of the five-step process for developing a good sales force structure describe a logical way to create structure alternatives, while Step 5 describes a way to evaluate these alternatives. Frequently sales leaders construct their own intuitive structures. These structures need to be evaluated regardless of how they have been constructed. Thus, Step 5 of this process is useful to all companies that want to evaluate and compare structure alternatives, even if the alternatives have not been generated using the methods described in Steps 1 to 4.

Step 1	Step 2	Step 3	Step 4	Step 5
Assess the need for product, market, and activity specialization	Develop coverage matrix	Generate specialization alternatives	Generate reporting, and coordination and control choices	Evaluate structures alternatives; select structure

FIGURE 5.20 Five-step process for developing a sales force structure

Step 1: Assess the Need for Product, Market, and Activity Specialization

The bandwidth required to perform all the selling activities for all the firm's products to all the desired markets influences whether a company's salespeople should be generalists, product specialists, market specialists, activity specialists, or a combination of these. The first step in determining the right sales force structure is to study the products, markets, and selling activities to determine what type of specialization might be required. To complete this assessment, the company should consider several questions about its products, markets, and selling activities.

First, product-focused questions determine the salesperson's product bandwidth. Some important questions to be answered are:

- Can one person master and sell all the products and/or services the firm offers?
- Are special skills and/or experiences required to understand, describe, and service the company's product portfolio?
- Can significant effectiveness gains be obtained through product or service delivery specialization?
- Will important products or services get ignored if a generalist salesperson sells them?

Next, market-focused questions determine the salesperson's market bandwidth. Some critical questions include:

- Can the market be segmented so that customers and prospects in each segment have similar buying processes?
- Are there significant selling process and/or industry expertise differences across customer segments?
- Do the customer segments have significant market potential?
- Can significant effectiveness gains be obtained by specializing for these segments?
- Will important markets be ignored if a generalist salesperson sells to all market segments?

Finally, selling activity-focused questions determine the salesperson's activity bandwidth. Some important questions are:

- How critical is each activity?
- Are some critical activities complex, requiring a specialist to perform them effectively? How much value would be added if these activities were done by a specialist?

- Can some activities be performed more efficiently by a lower cost resource, such as a telesales-person or a sales assistant?
- Do some activities distract from the most critical selling activities? Should these activities be assigned to a specialist to increase sales force focus on the most critical activities?

The answers to these questions help establish the opportunity for product, market, and activity specialization.

Step 2: Develop Coverage Matrix

A coverage matrix is a two- or three- dimensional grid that displays the products the company sells, the markets to be covered, and/or the selling activities that need to be performed. Each cell in the matrix requires some sales force coverage. The matrix provides a picture of what the sales force needs to accomplish. Thus, the matrix provides a good framework for creating sales force specialization alternatives.

Companies that choose to specialize along all three dimensions – products, markets, and selling activities – may want to create a coverage matrix in three dimensions. Figure 5.21 shows an example of such a matrix.

While a three-dimensional matrix is the most complete way to illustrate sales force coverage needs, in most situations it is only necessary to draw the coverage matrix in two dimensions, selecting the two dimensions that offer the greatest opportunity for specialization. For example, Figure 5.22 shows a coverage matrix for a pharmaceutical company. Products and markets were selected as the rows and columns of the matrix respectively, since these dimensions, and not selling activities, were considered to be the most important dimensions for possible specialization.

Figure 5.23 shows a coverage matrix for major corporate accounts at a wireless telecommunications provider. In this case, markets and selling tasks were selected as the rows and columns of the matrix.

Finally, Figure 5.24 shows a coverage matrix for a computer hardware and software company. In this case, products and selling tasks were selected as the rows and columns of the matrix.

Step 3: Generate Specialization Alternatives

Once the matrix is designed, alternative sales force structures can be generated. Each cell in the matrix requires sales force coverage. Groupings or clusters of cells can represent the responsibilities of separate specialty sales forces. Good clusters would have similar selling processes within cluster members and different selling processes between clusters. For example, the matrices shown in Figure 5.25

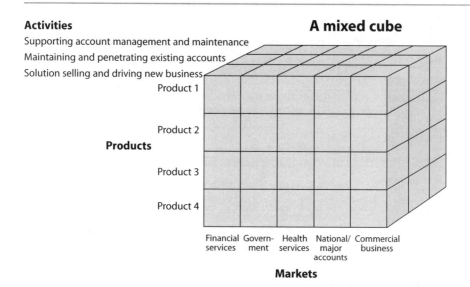

Activities

Supporting account management and maintenance

Maintaining and penetrating existing accounts

Solution selling and driving new business

A mixed cube

Products

Product 1

Product 2

Product 3

Product 4

Financial services   Government   Health services   National/ major accounts   Commercial business

Markets

FIGURE 5.21 Example of a three-dimensional coverage matrix

	Markets					
Products	Generalist	Allergist	Pediatrician	Psychiatrist	Cardiologist	Hospital
Antibiotic – Oral 1						
ACE						
Antidepressant						
Antibiotic – Oral 2						
Antihistamine						
Antibiotic – Inj						

FIGURE 5.22 Coverage matrix for a pharmaceutical sales force, by product and market

demonstrate several alternative organizational structures for a sales force that sells wine and spirits to liquor stores (off-premise) and restaurants and bars (on-premise). This sales force selected markets (off-premise and on-premise) and products (wine and spirits) as the rows and columns in its coverage matrix. Markets were further divided into large and small accounts.

Alternative A in Figure 5.25 clusters all matrix cells into a single partition. Generalist salespeople sell both products to all markets with this alternative. Alternative B clusters cells into two partitions by product.

Markets	Selling tasks				
	Lead generation	Qualification	Pre-sales	Close of sale	Fulfillment/ support
Banking and financial services					
Government					
Education					
Building and construction					
Healthcare and medical					
Manufacturing					
Communications and cable					
Real estate					
Transportation					
Utilities					

FIGURE 5.23 Coverage matrix for major accounts at a wireless telecommunications provider, by market and selling task

Products	Selling tasks						
	Understand customer's needs	Develop plan	Communicate plan to customer	Articulate value	Develop solution	Close	Monitor
Services							
Servers							
Storage							
Software							

FIGURE 5.24   Coverage matrix for a computer hardware and software company, by product and selling task

Thus, there are two types of product specialists with this alternative – spirits salespeople and wine salespeople who sell to all markets. Alternative C clusters cells into two partitions by market. There are two types of market specialists with this alternative – salespeople who sell both products to off-premise accounts and salespeople who sell both products to on-premise accounts. Finally, alternative D clusters the cells of the matrix into five different clusters. For large accounts, each product-market cell is its own cluster. Thus in large accounts, salespeople specialize by both product and by market. For small accounts, all matrix cells are clustered together. Thus, all small accounts are covered by generalist salespeople.

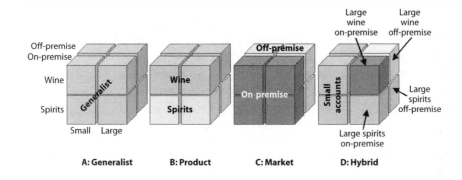

FIGURE 5.25 Alternative sales force coverage plans for a wine and spirits distributor

As this example shows, there are many different ways to partition a coverage matrix. The best ways take into account salesperson bandwidth as well as effectiveness and efficiency. These dimensions were assessed through the questions in Step 1 of the five-step process for developing a good sales force structure. In addition, the following tests can help a company determine the appropriateness of a particular partitioning of its coverage matrix.

1. *Within cluster homogeneity:* Are cells that have similar selling process requirements clustered together in the same partition? For example, if selling spirits is very similar to selling wine, then these two products should be clustered together, as in alternatives A and C. If selling to on-premise accounts is very similar to selling to off-premise accounts, then these two markets should be clustered together, as in alternatives A and B.

2. *Between cluster heterogeneity:* Are selling requirements different across the various partitions or clusters? For example, if selling spirits is very different from selling wine, then the two products should be clustered into different partitions, as in alternative B. If selling to off-premise accounts is very different from selling to on-premise accounts, then the two markets should be clustered into different partitions, as in alternative C.

3. *Communication and coordination needs:* Are cell combinations that require communication and coordination clustered together in the same partition? Suppose for example that it is important for the salesperson who sells spirits to an off-premise account to know about the wine purchase needs of that account. Then the company should consider clustering spirit sales and wine sales to off-premise accounts together, as in alternatives A and C.

4. *Cluster size:* Clusters need to be large enough in sales potential to support a separate sales team. For example, alternative D recognizes that the individual cells for small accounts may not have enough sales potential to economically justify a separate team. Thus, all small account cells are clustered together and are covered by generalist salespeople.

Figure 5.26 is an example of an assessment tool used by one company to compare selling process similarity across different product lines and thus determine how to structure the sales force. In this situation, the company had three major product lines. One product line consisted of several non-differentiated, commodity products, while the other two product lines were newer and had distinct advantages over competitors' products. As the figure shows, the company used a selling process consisting of four primary activities. First, decision makers must be identified. Next, the sales force must influence the behavior of these decision makers. Following this, salespeople must negotiate and close deals. Finally, ongoing customer service must be provided.

The different activities in the selling process vary in importance for each of the product lines. The size of each bar on the chart shows the relative importance of each activity. For example, selling commodity products requires a salesperson to focus on negotiating and closing and

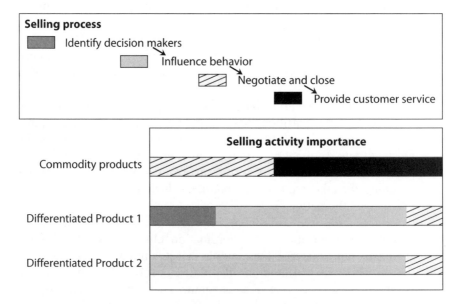

FIGURE 5.26 Sales force structure assessment: selling activities required for different product lines

providing customer service. Selling Differentiated Product 1 requires the salesperson to identify decision makers and influence their behavior before negotiating and closing a deal. Differentiated Product 2 requires two primary selling activities: influencing behavior and closing sales. The comparison of the importance of different selling activities for each of the product lines helped the company determine that they should have two product-based sales forces: one to sell commodity products and another to sell differentiated products.

This type of assessment tool can also be used to compare the selling processes across various market clusters, such as on-premise and off-premise in the wine and spirit distributor example. A selling activity importance chart can be created for all potential market segments. By looking at the similarities or lack of similarities, a decision can be reached regarding the creation of market-based sales organizations.

Step 4: Generate Reporting, and Coordination and Control Choices

Under each alternative for specialization, reporting relationships, team structures, and span of control choices have to be developed. Earlier sections of this chapter describe some of the factors that need to be considered in making these decisions.

Step 5: Evaluate Structures Alternatives; Select Structure

Once developed, the various sales force structure alternatives must be evaluated on key success criteria. A good framework for evaluating structures examines the desirability of different alternatives from the standpoint of three major stakeholders at the firm: the shareholders, the customers, and the employees. A good sales force structure meets the needs of each of the three stakeholders. It allows the company to meets its sales and growth objectives, it allows the sales force to meet customer needs, and provides salespeople with rewarding and challenging work.

Figure 5.27 summarizes the success criteria that can be used for evaluating sales force structure alternatives from the perspective of the firm's shareholders. Shareholders want the firm to meet or exceed its revenue and profit goals. Specifically, shareholders desire a sales force structure that delivers the firm's *sales strategy*; selling the right products to the right customer segments through the right sales process. At the same time, they want to link customer offerings with targeted customers through a selling process that has high impact (*effective*) and low cost (*efficient*). They want a sales force structure that is manageable in that the sales force energy is coordinated and controlled, and the organization learns and changes as

FIGURE 5.27 Sales force structure success criteria that are important to shareholders

customer needs and the markets evolve. Finally, shareholders want a sales force structure that can be implemented and has the flexibility to evolve as the market shifts and the firm's product line or selling process changes.

Figure 5.28 shows how each of the four basic types of sales force specialization – a pure generalist model, as well as structures that are designed around product, market, and activity specialization – are likely to profile in terms of the success criteria important to shareholders. This same framework can be used to evaluate various types of hybrid structures as well. The number of arrows in each cell shows the degree to which each sales force structure choice facilitates the accomplishment of the corresponding goal.

In addition to the shareholder perspective, sales force structure alternatives should be evaluated from the perspective of customers and salespeople. As shown in Figure 5.29, customers may value the firm's ability to provide solutions to their business needs, to provide trustworthy salespeople, and to provide a single point of accountability or contact for the company. Salespeople may value their independence, the chance to develop competency and expertise, and having a manageable bandwidth requirement. Each of the four basic types of specialization has varying ability to achieve each of these customer and salesperson objectives, as shown by the number of arrows in the corresponding cell of the figure.

Ease of implementation is important to evaluating sales force structure alternatives

Some sales force restructures create so much chaos and disruption for customers and salespeople that the benefits of a theoretically sound design are rendered worthless because there is no practical way to make the transition from the current design to the new design. For example, many sales forces have been unable to successfully manage the shift from product-based specialization to market-based specialization because of transition difficulties.

		Generalist	Market	Product	Activity
Sales strategy	Product line effort control	↑	↑	↑↑↑	↑
	Customer effort control	↑	↑↑↑	↑	↑
	Activity effort control	↑	↑	↑	↑↑↑
Effectiveness	Product knowledge when product complexity and diversity is high	–	↑	↑↑↑	–
	Customer knowledge when customer complexity and diversity is high	–	↑↑↑	↑	↑
	Activity knowledge when activity complexity and diversity is high	–	–	–	↑↑↑
Efficiency	Travel efficiency	↑↑↑	–	–	↑
	Matching sales process and effort to account opportunity	↑	↑↑↑	–	–
	Matching cost of selling resource to task difficulty	↑	↑	–	↑↑↑
Manageability	Accountability for results	↑↑↑	↑↑↑	↑↑↑	–
	Simplicity of internal processes and systems	↑↑↑	–	–	–
	Ease of customer coordination	↑↑↑	↑↑↑	–	–
	Compatibility with internal product business unit organization	–	–	↑↑↑	–
	Adaptability to customer needs	↑	↑↑↑	–	↑↑
Ease of implementation and flexibility	Ease of implementation	Depends on current state			
	Ability to react to large market shifts	↑↑↑	–	–	–
	Ability to change organizational structure	↑↑↑	–	–	↑

FIGURE 5.28 Dimensions for evaluating sales force specialization from the standpoint of the company's shareholders

		Generalist	Market	Product	Activity
Customer	Ability to provide customers with valuable solutions to business needs	↑	↑↑↑	↑↑	↑↑
	Enduring trusted relationship	↑↑	↑↑↑	↑	↑
	Single point of accountability	↑↑↑	↑↑↑	–	–
Salespeople	Independence	↑↑↑	↑↑↑	–	–
	Development of competency and expertise	↑	↑↑	↑↑	↑↑
	Manageable bandwidth requirement	–	↑↑	↑↑	↑↑

FIGURE 5.29 Evaluating structures from customer and salesperson perspectives

The final list of criteria for evaluating sales force structure alternatives is typically customized to reflect the company's current situation. Figure 5.30 shows an example of the success criteria used by one company to evaluate its sales force structure alternatives. The structure choices at this firm were narrowed down to two "finalist" structures that were evaluated on the criteria the company considered to be the most important. The length of the arrow shows how well each alternative met the specified

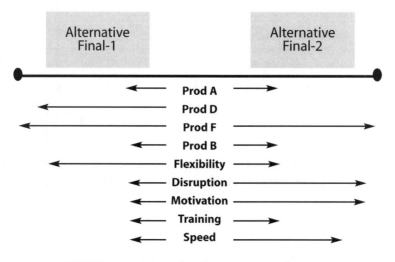

FIGURE 5.30 Example of structure evaluation

criterion. Alternative Final-1 dominates on its ability to make Product D successful and providing flexibility, whereas Final-2 was better in terms of minimizing disruption to customer relationships, improving the motivation of the current sales team, and implementation speed. The firm evaluated these tradeoffs and decided which alternative was better.

No structure should be finalized without a risk assessment. When evaluating a sales force structure, management should look ahead and consider the likelihood and impact of possible environmental, customer, competitive, and company strategy changes that could occur. The final sales force structure should be adaptive to the change pressures the firm is most likely to face.

Sales Roles

INTRODUCTION

Every sales force structure specifies roles for the selling organization. Some structures consist primarily of generalist sales roles, in which each salesperson performs all selling activities for all products and all customer types. Companies that have homogeneous customers, few product lines, and simple selling processes find the use of generalists easy and efficient. As diversity and complexity along these dimensions increases, companies migrate to multiple specialized sales force roles. Many companies have several different specialists performing separate sales roles. In almost every organization the Pareto Principle applies, meaning that a large percentage of the company's sales come from a small percentage of the company's accounts. For example, many consumer goods firms see 20 percent or more of their business come from a single account – Wal-Mart. This concentration of opportunity suggests that large accounts need to be treated differently from small accounts by the selling organization. Major accounts deserve a dedicated resource with an appropriate role – the major account manager.

Sales force structure and sales force role decisions are intertwined. The structure decisions discussed in Chapter 5 are made with roles in mind. Role definitions emerge almost spontaneously as the company makes its sales force structure choices.

Recall that a sales strategy defines who the firm sells to, what the customer offering is, and how the selling is done. Successful sales strategies define effective yet efficient sales processes that deliver the right products and services to the right customers. Role definition is the assignment of individuals to sections of the sales strategy. Stated another way, the three dimensions of sales strategy – markets (who the firms sells to), products (the customer offering), and activities (the sales process) – get divided into pieces that are assigned to various types of individuals (roles) within the selling organization.

Once defined, the company's sales strategy needs to be implemented. Some customers, products, and activities require highly skilled selling and add significant value, while others provide lower value and are routine. In the simplest case, a generalist salesperson can do everything. Alternatively, some sections of the sales strategy can be partitioned and assigned to people in different sales roles. For example, pieces of the firm's sales process that require highly skilled selling and add significant customer value can be executed most effectively by a focused, specialized salesperson. Figure 6.1 shows how a seller of electric motors assigns various sales process activities to the individuals in different sales roles who can execute those activities most effectively.

Quite often a lower-cost selling resource can be dedicated to selected aspects of the firm's sales strategy. This is a powerful way to gain efficiency. It is a work replacement strategy. Are there steps of the selling process that can be accomplished by a selling resource that is cheaper than a salesperson with equal or greater effectiveness? Can low-value customers be reached less expensively? Can certain types of products be

Lead generation	Qualification	Pre-sales	Close of sale	Fulfillment/support
Sales manager		Sales manager and application engineer	Sales manager	Application engineer

FIGURE 6.1 Sales roles for a seller of electric motors

sold more economically? Sales assistant, merchandiser, telesales, and part-timer are roles companies frequently use to execute their sales strategy more efficiently. These roles free up salespeople to focus on the high-value customers, products, and sales process activities. Figure 6.2 shows how a seller of office products assigns different customer types to individuals in different sales roles. This enables the firm to match selling investment appropriately with opportunity.

Large businesses 100+ workers			
Urban markets	Rural markets	Medium-sized businesses 20–100 workers	Small businesses <20 workers
Specialist salespeople for office supplies, technology, furniture, and paper product lines	Generalist salespeople	Telemarketing	Direct mail catalog with inbound call center

FIGURE 6.2 Sales roles for a seller of office products

BENEFITS OF SPECIALIZED SALES ROLES

Specialized sales roles can benefit customers, salespeople, and the firm. These benefits are illustrated through the two examples already given – the electric motor company and the office products company. The seller of electric motors to original equipment manufacturers (OEMs) defines two sales roles: sales manager and application engineer. Each role has responsibility for different stages of the sales process, as shown in Figure 6.1. Sales managers generate and qualify leads, perform non-technical pre-sales activities, and close sales. Application engineers assist sales managers with technical pre-sales activities such as providing detailed product presentations, demos, prototypes, and quotes, then assume primary responsibility for customer fulfillment and support after the sale is closed.

Specialized sales roles have many benefits for the electric motor firm, its customers, and its salespeople. From a firm standpoint, since the skills required to sell electric motors to OEMs are diverse and complex, it is diffi-cult to find salespeople that possess all the skills necessary to execute the complete selling process. By defining two sales roles, the firm has a wider pool of job candidates to choose from. Engineers with excellent technical skills and weaker selling skills are good candidates for application engineer positions. Salespeople with exceptional selling skills but weaker technical skills are good candidates for sales manager positions. Through specializa-tion of expertise, overall sales force effectiveness increases, and the sales force generates higher sales. In addition, more people touch the customer, thereby reducing risk for the company in case of sales force turnover. From a customer standpoint, customers have two points of contact with the seller. Since each point of contact has a specific expertise, this makes it easier to do business and allows for quicker response to their inquiries. Finally from a sales force standpoint, salespeople find work more meaningful because their skills and interests match well with the requirements of their role and their areas of weakness are covered by the other sales role.

In the second example shown in Figure 6.2, a seller of office products to businesses assigns sales roles by the size and location of its business customers. Large businesses in urban markets are seen by multiple prod-uct-line specialists. In rural markets where travel requirements are greater, each large business is covered by a single generalist salesperson. Medium-sized businesses in all locations are covered by telemarketing. Finally, the sales force does not cover small businesses at all – instead, these busi-nesses receive the company's direct mail catalog and can call in orders over the telephone.

The specialization of sales roles has many benefits for the office prod-ucts firm, its customers, and its salespeople. From a firm standpoint, differ-ent sales roles allow the firm to match spending appropriately with opportunity. The most effective and expensive selling resources – product specialists – focus solely on the largest, most important customers in urban areas where travel time and costs are reasonable. In rural areas, a single generalist salesperson serves the needs of each large customer, thus help-ing to control travel costs. Since medium and small-sized customers are not likely to generate enough sales to justify face-to-face coverage, their needs are met with less expensive sales channels – telemarketing and direct mail. By matching sales resource investment appropriately with opportunity, overall sales force efficiency increases and sales force costs are kept in line. From a customer standpoint, customers get a level of atten-tion appropriate to their level of need. Costs are managed so prices are lower. Finally from a sales force standpoint, the variety of sales roles offers career path options. Telesalespeople with the right acumen and aspirations can become generalists, while the best generalist salespeople can be promoted to become product specialists.

DOES YOUR SALES FORCE NEED TO REDEFINE SALES ROLES?

Since sales force structure and role decisions are intertwined, any sales force reorganization will require role redefinition. The need to reorganize comes about as the forces of change – customers, competitors, the environment, corporate strategies, and performance challenges – exert pressure on the sales force.

Roles may also need to change if the current sales strategy is not being executed effectively or efficiently. Sales force roles often become more specialized as the company's product line broadens, and customer sophistication and diversity increase. This is an effectiveness improvement strategy. New roles also are created when firms seeking to enhance productivity discover that some work performed by a salesperson can be performed equally effectively by a lower-cost resource such as a sales assistant or a telesales representative. This is an efficiency enhancement strategy.

Sometimes role evolution is very subtle. For example, a salesperson may need to take back some work from a sales assistant if effectiveness has declined significantly without compensatory efficiency gains, or a salesperson may take back some account segments if customers have rejected the company's telesales organization.

Table 6.1 shows some common circumstances that companies have remedied successfully by creating new sales roles. More detail about each of these sales roles will be provided later in the chapter.

SALES ROLE CHOICES

Sales roles are created by partitioning the sales strategy into components and assigning each component to a salesperson or channel that can execute that component either more efficiently or more effectively. Efficiency-focused sales roles typically lower the firm's selling costs by assigning some elements of the sales strategy to lower-cost individuals or channels. Effectiveness-focused sales roles typically increase the firm's revenues by assigning selected elements of the sales strategy to focused specialists. Examples of the various sales roles currently used by many companies appear in Table 6.2.

How Sales Roles Can Reduce Costs through Improved Efficiency

Sales roles that focus on cost reduction target efficiency improvement. For example, a telemarketing salesperson averages 25 to 30 completed calls per day, while a face-to-face salesperson averages just 5 to 6 calls per day.

Table 6.1 Examples of circumstances that suggest a need for new sales roles

Sales force symptom	New sales role that might be needed
• Customers complain that salespeople don't have sufficient product or technical knowledge • Salespeople focus on easy-to-understand products and ignore complex ones • Salespeople aren't getting access to technical decision makers	Product specialist Technical specialist Application engineer
• Industry knowledge is required to sell effectively	Market specialist
• Large accounts need special attention; small accounts may be getting too much attention; mid-market has a huge number of accounts	Major account managers Mid-market salespeople Telesales
• Customer retention is poor – insufficient business comes from existing customers each year	Service consultant Customer service rep Retention specialist
• Many customers have switched to competitors	Win-back specialist
• There are too few new customers • Salespeople spend so much time servicing existing customers that they have little time to spend generating new business	New customer acquisition Specialist or hunter
• There are not enough qualified leads	Lead generation Telemarketer
• Salespeople spend too much time doing administrative tasks	Sales assistant
• Salespeople spend too much time providing information that is accessible from the company's web site, product brochures, or other internal systems • Salespeople spend too much time with low opportunity accounts • Travel costs are excessive	Telesales
• A new product launch requires intensive sales force effort for a short period of time	Launch strike force

Telesales is a more efficient way to reach customers because it generates a higher level of call activity for a lower level of investment. Efficient sales roles leverage the use of less expensive resources, allowing the work of the selling organization to be completed at lower cost. Examples of efficient sales roles include generalist salespeople, sales assistants, customer service people, telesales, and part-time and independent salespeople.

There are several ways that sales roles can bring about sales force efficiency. Small, compact sales territories, that are typical of generalist sales forces, will have less travel time than large, dispersed territories.

TABLE 6.2 Examples of efficient and effective sales roles

Efficiency-focused sales roles	Effectiveness-focused sales roles
Sales assistant	Product specialist
Service consultant	Technical specialist
Customer service specialist	Market specialist
Telechannels	Account manager
Part-time salespeople	Strategic account manager
Independent salespeople	Global account manager
Generalists	Hunter
	Farmer
	Strike force
	Launch force
	Win-back specialist
	End-user specialist
	Marketing liaison
	Job sharing

Therefore, sales forces made up of generalist salespeople tend to have more face-to-face time with customers than sales forces comprised of multiple specialist sales teams.

"Too much time spent on non-selling tasks" is a common complaint heard from salespeople. Frequently, cheaper sales resources can accomplish this work without any loss in efficiency. Efficient sales roles are very useful during the stages of the selling process where the value added by a highly paid field salesperson is low. Typically this includes the earliest stages of the selling process such as lead generation and qualification, and the latter stages that occur after a sale is closed, such as order fulfillment and ongoing support.

Many companies segment their accounts into opportunity tiers. For example, they may classify accounts as large, mid-market, and small. An efficiency strategy is usually employed at small accounts. Rural accounts also present coverage challenges. Telesales, email, web sites, and direct mail are common ways to communicate with these segments.

Product portfolios can exceed the bandwidth of a selling organization. Older products, products with low sales, or products with low margins will get overlooked by a sales force carrying a broad product line. Alternatives such as telesales, part-timers, or independent sales agents can improve the economics of selling these products.

Salespeople hire sales assistants

Some salespeople do not wait for their company to restructure. Salespeople for some office supply companies use part of their own commission payment to hire sales assistants that perform administrative work so that they can free themselves to sell more. Many real estate agents hire sales assistants to help with paperwork and office tasks, giving them more time to focus on high-value tasks such as listings and closings.

How Sales Roles Can Increase Revenues through Improved Effectiveness

Sales roles that focus on revenue growth target effectiveness improvement. Effectiveness reflects the rate at which the sales force generates sales for its effort investment. For example, according to a survey of business-to-business marketers conducted by Cahners Research, a telemarketing salesperson eventually closes a sale averaging $17,894 with 57 percent of customers contacted. A face-to-face salesperson eventually closes a sale averaging $82,721 with 62 percent of customers contacted. Face-to-face selling is more effective than telesales because it results in higher revenues. Effective sales roles use specialized expertise and a focused strategy to increase the value that the sales force brings to customers, thus resulting in higher sales. Examples of effective sales roles include product, market, and activity specialists, and account managers that coordinate the activities of multiple specialists.

While effective sales roles are likely to generate higher revenues, they can also increase the firm's costs. Compensation is typically higher for specialized sales representatives than for general sales representatives. Often, these effective sales roles involve greater travel and management overhead, especially when multiple specialists are assigned to the same customer. Because of this loss in efficiency, effective sales roles are best used only to serve the customers, sell the products, and perform the selling activities that are of primary importance to the firm. For example, effective sales roles often cover large, strategically important customers and sell high-volume or high-margin products and services. Additionally, effective sales roles are often best used during the stages of the selling process where the value added by a highly skilled and highly paid field salesperson is greatest. Typically, this includes the stages at the heart of the sales process, such as pre-sales and closing.

Figure 6.3 summarizes the efficiency/effectiveness emphasis for sales role definition. Efficiency strategies are likely to be most appropriate for easy-to-understand products, small accounts, and activities of moderate complexity and value. Effectiveness strategies are most appropriate for strategic products, large accounts, and high-value-added, more difficult activities. The challenge for many companies is where to draw the line. Perhaps a good heuristic is to pursue efficiency strategies as long as the incremental return from an effective strategy such as specialized personal selling does not recover the cost of that effective strategy effort. Similarly a firm should pursue effectiveness strategies as long as the incremental value obtained from those strategies exceeds the cost of the additional personal selling effort. In this way, role definition needs to balance efficiency and effectiveness.

Most sales roles are designed with one primary goal in mind – either efficiency improvement (cost reduction) or effectiveness gain (sales

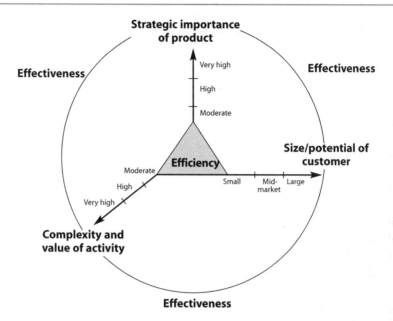

FIGURE 6.3   Efficiency/effectiveness balance can reduce costs and increase revenues

increase). Yet sometimes a sales role enhances both the efficiency and the effectiveness of the sales force simultaneously. For example, the primary purpose of a sales assistant is to improve efficiency by moving some selling tasks to a cheaper resource, yet a sales assistant can improve effectiveness as well. By focusing on certain tasks, a sales assistant may become more skilled than the salesperson at completing those tasks. In another example, the primary purpose of a skilled technical specialist is to increase effectiveness by bringing expertise to the customer. Yet a specialist can improve efficiency as well by using his or her skills to complete technical tasks more quickly. The following section organizes sales roles by their primary focus – either efficiency or effectiveness improvement. However, some ways that efficient sales roles can also improve effectiveness, and vice versa, are also noted.

Examples of Sales Roles that Focus on Efficiency Improvement

Sales roles that target efficiency focus on cost reduction. These roles are generally assigned to cover small or geographically disperse customers, sell easy-to-understand products, or perform routine selling tasks. Roles defined for efficiency do not necessarily lower effectiveness. Often, the

> ### Salespeople can be both efficient and effective
>
> The most successful salesperson at a financial services company that calls on banks, never visits his customers. He does all his selling over the telephone.

individual assigned to perform an efficient sales role is as effective as a face-to-face salesperson. The following section describes some of the roles companies use to improve efficiency.

Sales assistants

Sales assistants are hired to perform administrative selling tasks, thus freeing up a salesperson's time for high-value-added selling activities. Since sales assistants are typically paid less than salespeople, overall efficiency increases.

> ### Sales assistants can enhance sales force efficiency
>
> The salespeople at a major not-for-profit organization secure corporate support for their programs through direct contact with senior management at large corporations. Maximizing sales force productivity is very important. The company employs two sales assistants at headquarters that support the sales force. One of the assistants helps salespeople at the front end of the sales process, while the other helps at the back end. The front-end assistant is a prospect researcher. This individual reviews newspapers, journals, and trade publications, and scans the Internet, to identify potential leads and maintains a database of prospective corporate sponsors. Qualified leads are passed on to the appropriate salesperson for follow-up. The back-end sales assistant helps the sales force after a sale is closed by preparing monthly statements and bills. The two sales assistants also share additional sales support responsibilities such as creating promotional and selling materials, and assisting salespeople in obtaining services available only at headquarters. Because of the sales assistants, salespeople are freed up to spend more time selling.

Service consultant/Customer service specialist

Providing good after-sale service and support is critical for customer retention. Most salespeople spend between 12 and 30 percent of their time on service-related activities such as finding order status, answering questions about shipments, and resolving billing disputes. Many companies have successfully reduced this percentage by reassigning customer service responsibility to service consultants or customer service specialists. This enhances the effectiveness with which the task is done, and also enables the sales force to spend more time selling. A customer service specialist may be assigned to support several field salespeople. Often, a good deal of the service consultant's work can be done over the telephone.

Service specialists helps Giftcorp grow sales

Giftcorp, a provider of unique, creative, customized solutions for corporate gift giving, wanted its salespeople to visit more prospects and spend more time building long-term relationships with existing customers. To help the sales force achieve these goals, the company established an in-house service organization. Salespeople were stripped of all clerical duties. Instead of writing up orders, salespeople give customers a toll-free number which connects them to an in-house service representative. Company sales grew 30 percent in the first year that this new structure was implemented.

Not all customer service roles need to be filled by people. Many companies have created web sites that help customers obtain after-sale service and support. These sites enable work that was formerly done by the company to be transferred to the customer. This not only reduces the firm's costs, but can also increase responsiveness by being available 24 hours a day, 7 days a week.

Cisco customers use the Internet to check order status

In 1995, computer networking giant Cisco launched a system permitting customers to check the status of their shipments online. Prior to that time, customers would call salespeople to check on delivery. This forced salespeople to stay in the office trying to reach order administrators so they could report delivery status back to their customers. Delays returning calls or collecting information frustrated customers. By allowing customers to track their orders over the Internet on their own time, Cisco made customers happier and reduced the time that salespeople spent in the office.

Telechannels

Every company's sales strategy includes telephone contact. Telephone interactions can be as simple as scheduling appointments or as complex as negotiating a contract via teleconferencing. The telephone contact can be made by the salesperson him or herself, or by a telechannels group.

Telechannels refers to the use of salespeople who work primarily over the telephone, usually from a call center at a central location. Telechannels can include salespeople who initiate outbound customer calls, receive inbound customer calls, or do both. Some companies refer to the use of telechannels as *inside sales*, distinguishing it from *outside sales* that are made by salespeople working face-to-face with customers in the field. In addition to the telephone, inside salespeople often rely on other non-face-to-face channels such as direct mail, email, and the Internet to connect with customers.

Different terms are used to describe the use of telechannels by a seller at each stage of the selling process. Table 6.3 summarizes some of the most

TABLE 6.3 Telechannel roles at different stages of the sales process

	Pre-sales	Sales	Post-sales
Terms and definitions	**Telemarketing and Tele-prospecting** Using the telephone to generate and qualify new leads for another sales channel, such as a field sales force	**Telesales** Using the telephone to make sales. A telesalesperson asks the customer for a purchase order or a credit card **Tele-coverage** Using the telephone to maintain and nurture relationships with important customers, usually in addition to the efforts of a primary selling channel, such as a field sales force	**Tele-service** Using the telephone to provide non-technical customer assistance **Tele-technical support** Using the telephone to provide technical support to customers
Common activities	• Handle information requests • Generate and qualify leads for the field sales force • Schedule calls/make appointments for the field sales force	• Take and process orders • Handle orders for catalog sales • Sell peripheral equipment and supplies that are too small or unimportant for a field salesperson to handle • Cross-sell new products • Call on customers that are too small or unimportant for a field salesperson to handle • Call on geographically remote customers • Reactivate inactive accounts • Maintain dialog with key customers • Follow up on proposals submitted by the sales force • Check customer credit	• Contact dealers to sell promotions or to check inventory levels • Handle inbound customer service requests • Handle inbound technical support requests • Conduct satisfaction surveys
Examples	• An office products company uses an inside telemarketing group to identify good leads for the sales force • A software company routes all web prospects to its tele-prospecting group. The tele-prospecting group answers questions and pre-qualifies these leads	• A not-for-profit group uses telesalespeople to secure smaller corporate funding grants of $75,000 or less. Corporate grants over $75,000 are handled by an in-person sales force • A heating, ventilation, and air conditioning distributor added an outbound telesales group to call on small contractors that were not being reached by the face-to-face sales force	• Travelers can call an airline to check departure times after purchasing a ticket • The call center for a provider of tax preparation software receives over 1 million support calls every tax season

frequently used terms, and provides examples of selling activities that are commonly performed by telechannels at that stage of the selling process.

Telechannels are a personal but significantly less expensive way to reach customers than face-to-face contact. The average telesalesperson can make five times as many customer contacts per day as the average field

---

Telesales and field sales teams at Oracle

Oracle has invested heavily in the telechannel function. In the past, face-to-face sales-people outnumbered telesalespeople four to one. Currently the two groups are equal in size. Every face-to-face salesperson is teamed with a single telesalesperson. Together they share the same account list, execute a common sales strategy, and are paid commission based on the joint sales results.

---

salesperson. In addition, a telesalesperson usually costs the firm about half of what a field salesperson costs.

While cost reduction is typically the primary driver behind telechannel initiatives, using the telephone to reach customers can also help companies increase sales to both new and existing customers. New customers in geographically dispersed markets that have not been reached in person due to significant travel costs may be reached profitably through telesales. In addition because telesales has a lower cost per call than in-person sales, it becomes possible for the firm to sell to new, lower-potential customers profitably. Sales to existing customers can also increase through the use of telechannels. Telesales is frequently used to perform just some of the activities in the sales process. Pre-sales and post-sales functions are commonly assigned to telesales personnel. The additional contact with customers provides a way to improve customer retention and increase loyalty. Telechannels can facilitate faster customer service and more responsive technical support available 24 hours a day. By using the telephone, sellers

---

Some interesting facts about telesales

A 2001 survey of over 23,000 sales organizations in business-to-business markets revealed the following facts about telesales:

- Inside sales efforts (telesales, email, and direct mail) create 20 percent of all business-to-business sales; face-to-face selling creates 80 percent.
- 57 percent of customers contacted by telephone make a purchase; 62 percent of customers contacted in person make a purchase.
- The average sale made over the telephone is $17,894; the average sale made face-to-face is $82,741.
- On average, companies cover customers purchasing under $35,695 a year by using inside sales methods.
- Customers speak with an average of 4.6 different salespeople over the telephone each week; they meet face-to-face with an average of 1.8 different salespeople each week.

Source: Reed Research Group, *Evaluating the Cost of Sales Calls in Business-to-Business Markets*, January 2002, available at www.cahnerscarr.com.

---

can maintain higher frequency of customer contact after a sale, thus enhancing the firm's ability to build strong, ongoing customer relationships. When field salespeople work with inside salespeople on the same accounts, good coordination is essential for success.

Part-time salespeople

Companies sometimes employ salespeople to work less than a full-time schedule. Many retired people, as well as people caring for families and students, find part-time work attractive.

Often, part-time salespeople are cheaper to employ. They might (depending on local legislation) be paid an hourly rate which is less than the equivalent of their full-time counterparts. In addition, they are frequently not eligible for insurance benefits, pensions, or paid time off. If they do qualify to participate in the company's benefits programs, they might be asked to pay a larger share of their health insurance, while benefits such as life insurance, pensions, and payroll taxes that vary with salary will cost the employer less.

There are costs to employing salespeople part-time. A part-timer may require the same office space, car, and computer as a full-time person. The use of part-timers can be inconvenient for both customers and management, since part-time salespeople are not available during all regular work hours. Part-time salespeople can add complexity to the sales manager's job. The manager's span of control increases, part-time turnover rates are higher, and absenteeism is more unpredictable. Finally, numerous issues regarding the compensation of part-time employees can consume management time. For example, often the hours in sales jobs are open-ended, making it tricky to estimate how much to pay a part-timer. In addition,

---

Part-time sales roles help a book publisher cover remotely located stores

A book publisher had agreed with its major retail customers (book store and mass merchandiser chains) to provide in-store merchandising services. Salespeople visited individual store locations regularly to take inventories, organize shelves, and set up book displays. Covering the stores in sparsely populated areas was challenging. A small town might have only a handful of stores to be covered – not enough to keep a salesperson busy full-time – yet the next town was several hours drive away. The company solved its coverage problem by hiring part-time merchandisers in sparsely populated areas. The number of hours required for each part-timer varied depending on the number and size of stores within a reasonable driving distance from the salesperson's home. Part-time salespeople were cheaper to employ, since they were paid hourly and did not receive benefits. The company also hired temporary part-time help during busy promotional periods and during the holiday season.

Part-time sales roles increase sales force retention at Pfizer

A well run part-time program can help a sales force be more effective with customers through increased retention of experienced, talented salespeople. Pfizer has been consistently named the best pharmaceutical sales force by doctors in recent years. The company found that some of its high performing salespeople preferred to work part-time as they cared for family, pursued outside interests, or approached retirement. In 1999, Pfizer created a part-time sales force named Vista Rx, aimed at boosting sales in high-potential regions. Vista Rx positions were filled with Pfizer salespeople who had a strong track record with the company but preferred to work 60 percent of full-time with benefits. The program was a huge success. Sales in areas with Vista salespeople went up 1.5 to 4.5 percent over areas without Vista salespeople. Two years after the initial Vista launch, the number of salespeople in the program had more than doubled. The company's management believed that as many as 75 percent of these salespeople would have quit had they not been given the option to work part-time.

---

management must decide whether to compensate part-timers for company holidays, vacation days, and other time off.

Many part-time opportunities in sales are in lower-paying jobs such as call center telemarketers and customer service representatives. However, some companies have placed part-timers in significant roles.

Independent salespeople

Independent salespeople are not employees of the company. Instead, they work individually or for an independent selling organization (ISO) that is under contract to sell the company's products and services to customers. Manufacturers' representatives and independent contractors are examples of independents that work individually. ISOs include contract sales forces, distributors, agent organizations, and brokers. Independent salespeople often sell the products and services of more than one company. Typically, the company compensates them by paying a commission on sales. Some ISOs are very large – for example, large food brokers employ several hundred salespeople. Others are small, employing just a few salespeople to work in a defined geography.

The use of independent salespeople can help the firm gain efficiency. When an independent sells the products of several different companies, coverage costs can be shared. Thus the independent provides a cheaper way for the firm to get face-to-face customer coverage. Using ISOs can be the only way a company goes to market, or companies can use independents to serve some of their customers or geographic areas, such as small accounts or remotely located accounts. The use of independent salespeople also reduces risk for companies not ready or able to invest in their own sales force. For this reason, the use of independent salespeople is common when companies are launching a selling effort for the first time and they do not have market access or product line breadth to justify their own sales force.

Many companies use independent salespeople to sell products or to cover market segments that are of secondary importance to the firm's mission. That way, the firm's own sales force can be more effective by focusing on those products and markets that have the greatest strategic significance. This strategy is especially appropriate for sales forces that are responsible for many different products and markets and thus face bandwidth constraints.

The use of independent salespeople can also create effectiveness gains. Independent salespeople who have established connections and experience can be more effective at gaining entry into a new and unfamiliar market quickly. When a company's products have synergies with the other products that an independent sells, buyers that value the convenience of one-stop shopping may purchase more.

Independent salespeople help a Canadian sales force cover more geography

In a country as big as Canada, sales territories can be very large and geographically unmanageable. A Canadian specialty pharmaceutical company had its own sales force to cover major metropolitan areas, but with its limited product line it could not afford to cover rural areas. Thus, the company hired a contract sales force to cover sparsely populated areas. Since the contract sales force also sold products of other pharmaceutical manufacturers, costs could be shared and coverage was affordable. Eventually the company introduced several new products and added more of its own salespeople. With the additional headcount, sales territories became smaller and more workable. At this point, the company ended its relationship with the contractor and covered the entire geography with its own sales force.

The major downside of using independent sales organizations is that the firm gives up control of the quality of the salespeople, the selling process, and the customer relationship. In addition, when the independent sells the products of several different companies, the firm will not control the amount of selling time allocated to its products. The company must not only provide independent salespeople with good financial incentives to sell their products, but must also help them understand how the company's products can add value to the independent's customers.

Generalists

A generalist salesperson specializes only in the geography that he or she covers. A generalist selling organization would divide the country or the entire customer list into geographic sales territories that are assigned to each salesperson. Every salesperson would sell all products and perform all selling activities for all types of customers in his or her assigned territory.

Generalist sales roles are typically the most efficient way to cover customers for any fixed sales force size. There is less sales force travel and higher call activity because geographic sales territories can be constructed to be compact and contiguous. For this reason, companies seeking to reduce sales force costs often decrease the number of specialized sales roles and replace them with more generalist salespeople. More information and examples of generalist sales roles are provided in the Generalist sales roles section of Chapter 5 (Designing the Sales Force Structure).

Examples of Sales Roles that Focus on Effectiveness Improvement

Sales roles that enhance effectiveness focus on top-line impact. Effective sales roles generally focus on large customers, strategic products, and high-skill/high-value-added selling activities, where personal selling has the greatest influence. Successful firms strive to maximize effectiveness especially in those areas with high profit potential and significant strategic importance to the firm. The following section describes some of the roles companies use to improve effectiveness.

Product specialist

Product specialists focus on selling a particular product or product line. Because of their specialized knowledge, expertise and focus, product specialists can be more effective than generalists at selling their specific product line. One or more product specialists might call on customers independently, or they might assist a generalist account manager to provide a customer with product information, configuration assistance, training, or support. Account managers also leverage product specialists to help close sales. More information and examples of product specialists are provided in the Product-based specialization section of Chapter 5 (Designing the Sales Force Structure).

Technical specialist

Technical specialists concentrate on the technical aspects of the sale. Technical specialization allows tasks that are complex or that require in-depth knowledge to be performed more effectively by a salesperson who is specifically trained and experienced at performing those tasks. The role of the technical specialist typically goes beyond products. Applications

---

Sales roles that improve effectiveness: Customer trainer

Medical technology company SonoSite launched its initial product, the world's first all-digital, hand-carried ultrasound system, in 1999. The product was designed for use in private physicians' offices, hospitals, imaging centers, and radiology departments. SonoSite discovered that the most effective way to sell its product was with a team of professional salespeople. The company hired experienced sellers of capital equipment who were effective at selling customers on product benefits and successfully closing deals. Though salespeople were trained in the basics of ultrasound technology, most lacked the clinical background required to provide in-depth customer training and product support. To fill this void, SonoSite hired a team of nurses who were experienced users of ultrasound technology. The nurses filled the role of customer trainer, working together with salespeople to ensure the needs of each customer were met after a sale was made.

Sales roles that improve effectiveness: Application engineers

Fairchild Semiconductor is a large global supplier of products that help companies minimize, distribute, convert, and manage power. Recently, the company created six "Center of Excellence" design labs to provide customers quickly with custom designs for their specific applications. The centers are staffed with applications engineers who help the sales force develop and deliver the appropriate solution for each customer. The centers enable Fairchild to create and implement innovative, complete customer solutions more quickly.

---

specialists are quite common in industries, such as software and telecommunications, where technical products have multiple end uses. A generalist account manager often calls upon a technical specialist to provide customers with technical information, demonstration, consultation, training, or support, or to help close a sale.

More information and examples of technical specialists are provided in the Activity-based specialization section of Chapter 5 (Designing the Sales Force Structure).

Market specialist

Market specialists concentrate on selling to a particular customer or type of customer. Market specialists sometimes focus on selling to a particular industry. For example, Xerox salespeople who call on large accounts specialize in one of six industry sectors. Many firms have discovered the power of specialization by industry. Customers like to buy from salespeople who have empathy for and understanding of their unique circumstance and needs. This is particularly true in selling consulting services, where industry knowledge helps define how products are used, and is therefore just as important as product knowledge.

Other times, market specialists focus on a particular customer. Many Kraft salespeople are dedicated to selling to a single major customer, such as Wal-Mart or Kroger's. Market specialists become very knowledgeable about the customer or industry they serve, and thus are more valuable to customers and more effective at creating sales. More information and examples of market specialists are provided in the Market-based specialization section of Chapter 5 (Designing the Sales Force Structure).

Account manager

An account manager is a salesperson who has overall selling responsibility for an account. Account managers are typically generalists who have a broad knowledge of the firm's entire product line and selling process. Their depth of expertise is in understanding the customer's needs and decision criteria and process. Account managers are expected to develop and nurture relationships with important decision makers at their accounts. Account managers sometimes work alone, but since they often lack the depth of product or technical knowledge required by a customer, they frequently work with product, technical, or other specialists who can provide this knowledge.

Strategic account manager

Account managers for very large or strategically important accounts often have a special role. These account managers have been called strategic account manager (SAMs), key account managers (KAMs), national account managers (NAMs), or regional account managers (RAMs) depending on the size and scope of the accounts they handle. The more general term of strategic account manager (SAM) is used here when referring to these roles.

A SAM is typically dedicated to just one or a few major accounts. The SAM serves as the business manager of the firm's relationship with the customer, and is responsible for maintaining the business as well as finding any new opportunities within the account. Often, the SAM leads a strategic account team that is composed of multiple sales specialists working together to meet the often diverse and complex needs of the account. The SAM may also bring resources from other parts of a company to assist a customer.

An example of how one company established a strategic account management organization, in addition to its traditional account management organization, provides insight regarding the scope and responsibility of a SAM. A leading provider of business communication products and services had for many years maintained a generalist sales force model in which every account manager called on all types and sizes of customers and prospects. Accounts ranged from small, family-owned businesses to large national accounts with hundreds of locations. Increasingly, the firm's sales were becoming concentrated among a small number of large, national, key customers. A successful selling process with these large customers was very different from the process required for smaller accounts. Key customers usually had long, complex buying processes that included high-level decision makers from many different functions. Often, purchasing was done centrally for multiple locations. Buyers at these accounts expected specialized attention, such as customized warehousing solutions, and asked for price concessions. Smaller accounts did not have any of these needs.

In order to devote more significant and focused resources to these important customers, the firm redefined its sales roles. Two different account management roles were created – account managers and strategic account managers. Account managers (AMs) handled mid-sized accounts that required just one or a few of the firm's products and services. AMs also spent approximately half of their time prospecting for new customers. Strategic account managers (SAMs) covered large national and multi-national corporations that required integrated solutions consisting of many of the firm's products and services. Strategic account managers spent approximately 80 percent of their time maintaining and strengthening relationships with these most important customers, and spent only 20 percent of their time prospecting for new business. These new sales roles enabled the firm to establish valuable focus on its most important customers.

The new organization faced several challenges. Salespeople needed to be matched appropriately with the new roles. The skill set required for maintaining a consultative selling relationship with a large national account was substantially different from the skill set required for a typical AM whose main task was to drive growth by increasing market penetration. In addition, a communication process needed to be established so that pricing, compensation credit, distribution, and other needs could be coordinated between the SAMs and the various AMs who were responsible for working with the branch locations of national accounts.

Table 6.4 provides a summary comparison of the SAM and AM sales roles in terms of customer assignments and key responsibilities.

Table 6.5 summarizes some characteristics and skills possessed by successful and outstanding strategic account managers.

Global account manager

At many firms, implementing the strategic account management concept on a global level has become a competitive necessity. Many customers are

TABLE 6.4 Comparison of customer assignments and key responsibilities of strategic account managers (SAMs) and account managers (AMs)

	SAM role	AM role
Customer assignments	A small number of large multi-national corporations that require many of the firm's products and services within an integrated solution	A large number of mid-sized companies that require one or a few of the firm's products and services
Key responsibilities	• Assess and understand needs of multiple decision makers • Form cross-functional and cross-organizational teams as needed to meet customer needs • Consultatively sell multiple solutions or an entire program to senior executives and managers • Develop and execute a strategic plan to maximize profit opportunity with each customer • Coordinate sales efforts with AMs who call on local branch locations • Identify and assess opportunity to sell integrated solutions to strategically attractive prospects (20 percent of total time)	• Quickly assess and understand needs and identify application opportunities • Communicate firm's value proposition • Negotiate contract terms • Coordinate efforts with SAMs who call on headquarter locations • Identify and convert prospect accounts and competitor's customers to the firm's customers (50 percent of total time)

expanding their operations around the world as growth rates diminish in home markets, demand for products and services increases in emerging markets, technology advances erode communication and logistics barriers, and competitors expand global operations. More and more, customers expect companies to provide global solutions that reduce costs through

TABLE 6.5 Characteristics and skills of strategic account managers

A successful SAM:	An outstanding SAM:
Focuses on important customer events and processes	Also focuses on customer outcomes
Understands customer technology and systems	Also develops customer solutions
Thinks price and cost	Thinks value
Is close to company operations personnel and management	Is also close to company executives
Is reactive and responsive	Is also proactive
Understands customer's product and business needs	Is also politically astute
Utilizes resources judiciously	Achieves high ROI
Makes the company the preferred supplier at major accounts	Makes the company the dominant supplier at major accounts
Consistently achieves objectives	Consistently exceeds objectives

economies of scale, create value through collaboration, and enhance the customer's strategic advantage.

A global account manager (GAM) leads a sales team that provides a globally coordinated and integrated sales and service approach to important customers that have coordinated and integrated strategies worldwide. Most large, multinational companies have developed global teams – the Citibank team was described in Chapter 1.

A successful GAM excels by blending political, consultative, leader/managerial, and communications skills. Like traditional salespeople, GAMs must have excellent communication and selling skills as well as good product and market knowledge to be effective. However in addition to these skills, successful GAMs also possess an array of general management skills, including leadership and management abilities, business and financial acumen, and strategic vision and planning capabilities. Successful GAMs also have cultural empathy and a passion for international knowledge. Figure 6.4 provides a list of several of the more important GAM competency requirements.

Hunter and Farmer

Some companies have a sales role for the acquisition of new customers (hunters) and another role for the retention of current customers (farmers). Hunters are responsible for finding and bringing in business with new accounts. Once a sale is made, farmers cultivate and grow the relationship and generate repeat business within the account. Since most companies realize the majority of their revenue from current customers,

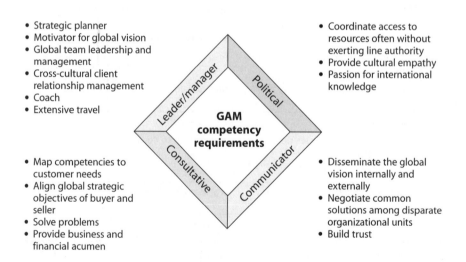

- Strategic planner
- Motivator for global vision
- Global team leadership and management
- Cross-cultural client relationship management
- Coach
- Extensive travel

- Coordinate access to resources often without exerting line authority
- Provide cultural empathy
- Passion for international knowledge

- Map competencies to customer needs
- Align global strategic objectives of buyer and seller
- Solve problems
- Provide business and financial acumen

- Disseminate the global vision internally and externally
- Negotiate common solutions among disparate organizational units
- Build trust

Leader/manager Political **GAM competency requirements** Consultative Communicator

FIGURE 6.4 GAM competency requirements

farmers play a critical role in protecting the firm's revenue stream. At the same time, the aggressive development of new accounts is encouraged, because hunters are dedicated to this pursuit. Firms need both active new account development and high current account retention rates to sustain optimal growth rates. Another benefit of this type of specialization is that the company can match a salesperson's personality and skills to the right job, thus increasing overall effectiveness.

Many fast-growth companies use hunter and farmer sales roles. Table 6.6 illustrates key selling responsibilities of hunters and farmers in the computer industry.

TABLE 6.6 Key responsibilities of hunters and farmers in the computer industry

Key responsibilities of an Account Executive – Acquisition (a "Hunter")
- Develop relationships with new customers and prospects
- Sell products, services, and solutions
- Acquire new accounts

Key responsibilities of an Account Executive (a "Farmer")
- Manage relationship between company and assigned client portfolio
- Conduct sales calls within assigned retention and development accounts in territory
- Communicate products, services, strategies to each client and sell the full portfolio of offerings available
- Manage internal communication of results among peers and cross-functional organizations
- Develop account plan and sales call strategy for each client
- Support and manage customer satisfaction issues when necessary
- Maintain and build revenue within assigned territory to reach and exceed quota
- Increase presence in assigned accounts

Service firm assigns hunting and farming responsibly based on salesperson experience

A provider of document services such as copying, printing, and databases to law firms has two levels of salespeople. Major account reps are senior salespeople who manage a few large accounts and spend a significant amount of time hunting for new accounts. Account reps are junior salespeople who manage many medium-sized accounts and spend very little time hunting.

Strike force/Launch force

A strike force is a sales force that is established temporarily to help a company respond to a particular need or take advantage of an opportunity. Strike forces have been used by companies to launch new products,

> **Examples of temporary strike forces**
>
> One pharmaceutical company has a new product task force whose mission is to get new products on the formularies, or lists of preferred drugs, of important medical insurance plans. Once their task is completed, the task force's mission changes. A medical device company with very low market share in the Denver area established a temporary three-person strike force there to improve performance. The strike force was given two years to achieve significant penetration of the market.

respond to competitive threats, or improve performance in a specific market.

Win-back specialist

A win-back specialist focuses on winning back customers that have switched to competitors. This type of specialist is common in industries with high customer defection rates, such as telecommunications. Win-back specialists can work either face-to-face or over the telephone. While success rates vary, this type of sales specialization has helped some companies win back 15 to 30 percent of their previously lost customers.

> **A job description at SBC Communications: Account Executive Win-back**
>
> The Account Executive Win-back is responsible for acquiring business that is with another service provider. The Account Executive (AE) will establish new network products and services...optimally using term contracts to retain these new revenue streams.
>
> For Mid-Market accounts:
>
> - The AE will work as an integrated member of assigned Mid-Market account teams.
> - The AE will establish 3 appointments per day and deliver 8–10 proposals a week.
> - The AE will meet or exceed net new revenue objectives of $4000–$6000 per month.
>
> For Small Market accounts:
>
> - The AE will be assigned to specific small market ZIP code territories.
> - The AE will establish up to 4 appointments per day and deliver 5 proposals a week.
> - The AE will meet or exceed net new revenue objectives of $4000–$6000 per month.

End-user specialist

The primary sales strategies of many companies focus sales force effort on members of the distribution channel that are not the ultimate users of the product or service. For example, P&G's sales force convinces major retailers to carry packaged goods that will ultimately be purchased by consumers. Selling to consumers is accomplished mainly through advertising and other types of promotion. Disney sells its theme park vacations to travel agents, that in turn influence the travel plans of families. An insurance company focuses its sales force effort on insurance brokers and consultants, who it hopes will recommend the company's products to small and medium-sized employers.

All companies that focus sales force effort on intermediaries in the distribution and purchase decision process are also challenged to create demand among end users. Some sales forces have developed specialized roles called end-user specialists for this purpose.

Medical device company creates patient advocate role to connect with end users

A seller of insulin pump therapy focuses its primary sales force effort on the doctors who treat diabetic patients. Doctors play the primary role in educating patients about the various treatment options and recommending a therapy approach. The sales force also has a role that works directly with the patients. Patient Advocates work primarily over the telephone answering patient questions, persuading patients to upgrade to newer model pumps, and providing patients with follow-up and support information.

The business-to-business sector frequently uses indirect selling organizations to connect with its customers. The indirect seller has the customer relationships and directly affects the business-to-business manufacturer's sales. A successful strategy for some manufacturers has been to use end-user specialists to go directly to large accounts and pull their products through the channel. This strategy works best when the manufacturer still credits the indirect seller with the sales to the large accounts.

Marketing liaison

Many companies struggle with integrating their marketing and sales functions smoothly. Marketing thinks that the sales force just wants to drop price to make the sale and is unwilling to implement the marketing strategy. The sales force thinks that marketing has never carried the bag and doesn't understand the customer. Recent research shows that, on average, companies feel that they are only getting 65 percent of the desired cooperation between these two vital functions.

Some companies have established marketing liaison positions to help sales and marketing work more effectively together. A marketing liaison typically reports to the firm's marketing department and can have either product line or geographic responsibility. He or she provides marketing support for salespeople through activities such as the creation of customized marketing materials and sales aids or assistance with pricing. Marketing liaisons can be located at headquarters, but work best if they are located in a field sales office. This position is common at companies with decentralized sales structures, where regional sales managers have profit and loss responsibility, in addition to sales responsibility.

Job sharing

One of the best ways for a sales force to improve its effectiveness is to reduce turnover of its most experienced and talented salespeople. To this end, more and more companies are allowing their best salespeople to work flexible work schedules, so that they can continue to sell while raising children, caring for aging parents, or even pursuing a hobby or second career. Options such as part-time work (see discussion earlier in this chapter) and job sharing can increase satisfaction and retention of high performing salespeople.

Can job sharing work in sales?

Many companies have successfully implemented job-sharing arrangements within the sales force, including Xerox, Condé Nast, and Abbott Laboratories. With job sharing, two salespeople work together to fill a full-time sales position. They share responsibility for a single sales territory or set of customers, splitting the compensation for the territory, including salary and incentive pay. The two salespeople typically work on different days, with at least one day per week of overlap. Job sharing is often preferred by customers over part-time work, because it allows everyday access to a salesperson. In fact, when two salespeople manage an account together and consistently back each other up, the customer relationship can be even stronger than it would be with a single account manager.

Successful job-sharing arrangements rely on extensive communication between the two partners. Presenting a unified front to colleagues, customers, and management is critical. Good job-sharing partners share the same work styles and goals, trust one another, have compatible personalities, and share a willingness to work off one another's ideas. In addition, flexibility and smart use of technology such as email and voice mail can enhance the success of a job sharing arrangement. The best job-sharing candidates are super-achievers who want to scale back their time in the office, but not their energy and enthusiasm for the job.

Sales Roles and Measurement

Firms need to find ways to measure the success of every sales role, whether the role focuses on increasing efficiency or improving effectiveness. Every sales role should have an objective and a metric for measuring the achievement of that objective. The success metrics typically used by selling organizations fall into the four categories displayed in Figure 6.5. The four categories are causally connected. The "People and culture" dimensions affect "Sales force activity", which in turn influences "Customer results," which has an impact on "Company results."

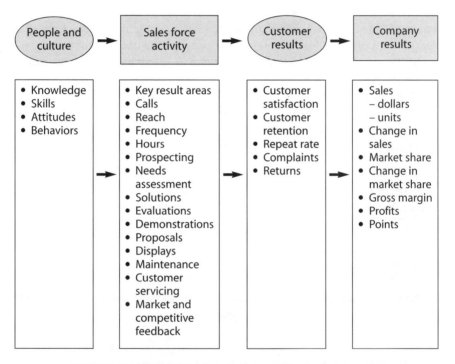

FIGURE 6.5 Examples of success metrics for sales roles

Different success metrics are appropriate for different roles. Many sales roles have a direct impact on company results. People in roles such as account manager or product or market specialist are responsible for meeting customer needs and generating sales for the firm. Thus, success in these roles is typically measured using customer and company results metrics. Other sales roles, such as lead generation or customer service, are linked to results, but more indirectly. Metrics that measure activity, such as the number of prospects contacted or customer service calls answered, are frequently used for measuring success in these roles.

> **Use of company results metrics is common**
>
> Over 95 percent of companies rely on company results metrics to some extent when evaluating their salespeople. Sales roles that are not linked to at least one company success measure typically do not last very long.

Some categories of success metrics are easier to measure than others. Company results measures such as sales and profits are usually the easiest to measure, while people and culture measures such as sales force knowledge, skills, attitudes, and behaviors are usually the hardest. In addition, some categories have a long-term impact while others are very short-term in nature. Managing people and culture or sales force activity tends to have a longer-term effect, while managing company results has a monthly or quarterly impact. Also, success metrics should be compatible with the firm's management style. A management team that embraces empowerment is likely to use company results metrics. On the other hand, a hands-on, control management will likely focus on activity measures.

Figure 6.6 describes some additional conditions of the selling environment that favor one set of metrics over another set.

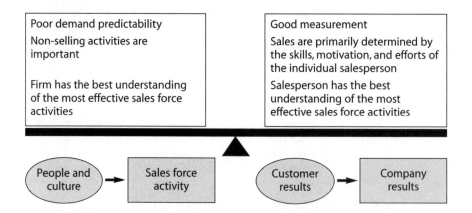

FIGURE 6.6 Success metrics should reflect the selling environment

Role of Sales Managers

First-line sales manager

First-line sales managers play a critical role in the sales organization. These are the managers to whom salespeople report directly. Typically, they are former successful salespeople. They know what it takes to succeed as a salesperson, and are therefore capable of earning the respect of those who report to them. However, a promoted salesperson benefits if he or she quickly discovers the significant role change that occurs with promotion to manager. The sales manager plays a vital and very different role in the sales organization than does the salesperson.

The salesperson's mission is to serve two constituencies: the customer and the company. A successful salesperson meets customer's needs and, at the same time, helps the company achieve its objectives. The sales manager's mission is to serve the customer, the company, and a third constituency: the sales team. Like the salesperson, a sales manager succeeds by meeting customer needs and achieving company goals. But the sales manager does not achieve these objectives entirely through his or her own initiative and activity. Managers achieve customer and company success when their salespeople are successful. Consequently, the existence of the third constituency – the salespeople – strongly differentiates the two roles. Managers are coaches, not players. They achieve their objectives through others.

Figure 6.7 shows the possible range of sales manager roles. In most instances, the sales manager achieves company goals by working through others. This "management" role can span the management of people and the management of resources. Most sales managers are primarily responsible for managing people. In some firms, they are also responsible for other resources. They may manage expenses and a local sales budget. They may manage physical assets such as an office and the equipment in it. They may also manage informational assets such as databases and insights into company strategy. On the "selling" branch of their responsibilities, they may

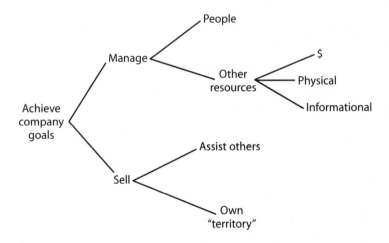

FIGURE 6.7 Possible scope of sales management responsibilities

assist others, for example with key accounts or challenging situations. In some companies, sales managers also have explicit sales responsibilities.

In a people management role, sales managers are responsible for selecting, building, leading, managing, and rewarding the team of salespeople. Table 6.7 illustrates the people-related activities that involve sales managers. First-line sales managers are likely to participate in all of these activities, but the ultimate responsibility for each activity varies across companies. Some decisions, such as recruiting and goal-setting, might be placed at a higher sales management level than first-line managers. This is done when the activity is best run centrally because of the skills required or the need for uniformity across the organization, or because it is just more efficient.

Regional and national sales manager

Large sales organizations often have several levels of sales management. For example, many organizations have regional managers that manage the first-line sales managers. The regional managers report to a national

---

TABLE 6.7 People management activities of sales managers

Select the team
- Recruit and screen applicants
- Hire and fire salespeople

Build the team
- Help salespeople develop skills, knowledge, and competencies
- Coach and counsel
- Set goals for salespeople, measure progress, and provide feedback

Lead the team
- Develop and share a vision
- Listen to and communicate with salespeople
- Grow personal knowledge
- Manage crises

Manage the team
- Delegate and empower while providing direction and advice
- Ensure that the sales strategy is implemented effectively
- Hold salespeople accountable for results
- Manage company assets, such as cars, computers, telephones, and office space
- Manage operating expenses, such as salaries, relocation, travel, entertainment, and training
- Be a good general manager, attending to a broad mix of marketing, finance, and human resource issues

Reward the team
- Provide extrinsic rewards, such as salary increases, bonuses, perks, trips, and promotions
- Provide intrinsic rewards, such as appreciation, recognition, security, and encouragement

sales manager or vice president of sales. With this multi-level organization, the salesperson is responsible for customers, first-line sales
managers are responsible for salespeople, regional or second-line sales
managers are responsible for first-line managers, and ultimately, the
national sales manager or vice president of sales is responsible for the
sales team as a whole. Higher levels of sales management are responsible for the programs and systems that drive sales performance. For
example, a vice president of sales has primary responsibility for sales
force success drivers such as team sizing, deployment, recruiting, training, targeting, compensation, and motivation. Figure 6.8 shows the
different levels of emphasis in the responsibilities of salespeople and the
sales leadership team.

	Drivers	Activities	Results
VP Sales	* * *		* * *
Sales Managers	* *	* *	* * *
Salespeople		* * *	* * *

FIGURE 6.8 Sales responsibilities

Should sales managers sell?

In addition to their managerial role, sales managers at a number of firms
play an important role in selling. The company's selling process can be
designed to include a role for the sales manager. He or she can bring product, market or activity specialization that is unmatched by others in the
sales force. Small start-up selling organizations usually need everyone to
sell – including the sales manager and even the CEO. In established selling organizations, sales managers may have responsibility for selling to the
firm's largest or key customers. In addition, they may assist salespeople on
difficult sales calls or with large accounts. Asking sales managers to play
a role in selling has both advantages and disadvantages.

On the positive side, sales managers are often promoted to their position
after proving themselves to be effective salespeople. By keeping a sales
manager involved with important customers, especially ones he or she
already has a good relationship with, the company continues to benefit
from their skills and experience. Companies frequently keep their sales
managers who are good at sales in a selling role for fear of losing sales
volume.

Some customers value having a manager involved in the sales process.
When a customer asks to speak with a person who has a higher level of
authority, a manager's involvement can be important to closing the sale.

When should sales managers have selling responsibility?

Consider limiting the selling responsibility of sales managers to the following situations:

- There is a real risk of losing an important customer unless the sales manager continues his or her involvement in the relationship.
- The customer perceives significant value to having someone in a position of power involved in the sales process.
- The manager is an exceptional salesperson whose skills and experience are unmatched by others in the sales force.
- There are key accounts that need special sales force attention, but there are not enough of them to dedicate a full-time key account salesperson.

Finally, many sales managers enjoy retaining some selling responsibility. It helps them stay connected to the marketplace and provides them with additional earnings opportunity.

The danger of giving sales managers selling responsibility is that they may spend too much time selling and not enough time coaching their team. Some firms find in necessary to limit the amount of selling in which their managers may engage.

Regardless of the company's decision about the selling responsibility of sales managers, role ambiguity must be avoided. Sales managers need to know what is expected of them, how they will be evaluated, and how they will be rewarded. Accountability is very difficult to engender when there is role ambiguity.

Sizing the Selling Organization

INTRODUCTION

Every sales force has a size, defined by the number of salespeople. That size changes over time as the company evolves its products and adapts to different market conditions. Companies use many different rules and approaches to determine the size of their sales force. Some of these rules and approaches often lead to poor decisions. Do any of these examples sound familiar?

- Avoid disruption and cost by keeping the sales force size the same as last year.
- Avoid risk by increasing sales force size only after the company has generated the sales to pay for the size increase.
- Split a territory when sales exceed a threshold.
- Reduce the sales force size by the extent of effectiveness increase expected from sales support investments.
- Contain sales force costs by maintaining a sales force size that keeps sales force costs at a constant percentage of sales.
- Launch a blockbuster new product by giving it to the same sales force that is promoting significant products now.

Companies routinely assume that last year's size is right for this year. For example, a vice president of sales is preparing his budget for the upcoming year. He reasons, "We had a sales force of 90 last year and we made our numbers. Next year's goal is a stretch. Why change anything? It's working!" The vice president is satisfied because by staying at the same size, he doesn't incur any reorganization costs. He also avoids disrupting customer relationships. However, the "same as last year" rule may have failed to consider that during the past year the economy had slowed down, the company canceled the launch of a new product, and major competitors decreased their sizes by 30 percent. All these changes suggest that perhaps last year's sales force size is too large for this year.

A second common approach is to use a "pay as you go" sizing strategy. For example, a small US pharmaceutical company entered into an agreement with a Japanese company to sell a new product in the US market. This product has the potential to be a blockbuster, but the company has only a small sales force to support it. Management decides to wait and see how the product sells before approving a proposal to add more salespeople. Later analysis reveals that if the company had added salespeople right away instead of pursuing this conservative strategy, sales would have been at least $300 million higher over a five-year period.

Another company that uses a "pay as you go" sales force sizing strategy uses a "$2 million territory rule" to determine when to add salespeople. As soon as a territory hits $2 million in sales, the company splits it and gives a part of it to a new salesperson. The veteran salesperson's "reward" for working hard to build business is to have his or her territory split in half. As a result, over time, too many salespeople are placed in geographies where salespeople were successful initially, and too few salespeople are placed in the other geographies. The company does not consider how much sales potential exists in the territory, or how much of that potential remains untapped.

Third, companies sometimes justify productivity enhancement costs by reducing the sales force. For example, a company installs a new CRM system and implements an expensive new training program. It argues, "These initiatives will increase sales force productivity by 10 percent. Therefore, our sales force can be reduced from 100 to 90. This head count reduction will actually pay for the initiatives." The company fails to recognize that its productivity enhancement initiatives actually reduce the firm's selling costs. A lower selling cost per call enables the company to call profitably on more accounts and prospects. Customers who were too expensive to call on before are now profitable to visit. Hence, expanding the sales force upon the implementation of the new productivity program may actually increase profitability.

Fourth, companies frequently do not allocate enough salespeople to support new product launches. For example, a company plans to launch an exciting new product in the coming year. Since the new product will be sold to many existing customers and requires similar selling skills to other company products sold by the sales force, the vice president of sales decides to add the new product to the sales force's portfolio. "This will be an exciting new challenge for the sales force and it gives us something new to talk about with our customers," she reasons. The vice president overlooks the importance of the fact that the new product will consume 50 to 60 percent of the sales force's time during the launch phase. This will drastically curtail the time available to sell other products. Therefore, assuming that existing products will retain their sales in the absence of sales force effort is dangerous. The new product launch will compromise the sales of existing products. Unfortunately, the full impact will not show up in the current year. Maintaining the current size will jeopardize company profits in the long term.

Finally, many companies hold sales force costs at a constant percent of sales. For example at an internal sales force productivity workshop, a country general manager asserts that he maximizes profits. When asked how, he responds that he "keeps sales force costs at 11 percent of sales." Since sales are down this year, he'll have to cut the sales force in order to contain costs. Such cost-containment approaches to sales force sizing are based on logic that is actually working backwards. They imply that sales should drive sales force effort. They overlook the fact that the causality is the other way around – sales force effort drives sales.

Even a well-respected CEO of a Fortune 50 firm ignored the fundamental marketing principle that sales force effort drives sales when he addressed his divisional vice presidents of sales. The CEO stated that last year he "cut the total company sales force size and sales went up." He did not allow any of the divisions to increase their sales forces and cut many of them. Will sales go up even further if he cuts the sales force again? What would have happened had he not cut the sales force? It is certain to say that his sales would have been even higher.

WHAT IS SALES FORCE SIZING?

The sales force sizing decision takes several forms. For example:

- How many salespeople are needed?
- How many should be generalists?
- How many should be specialists?
- How many sales managers are needed?
- How many telemarketing people are needed?
- How many support people are needed?
- How much should the company spend on the sales force?
- What percent of sales should be allocated to sales force expense?
- How will sales and profits vary with different sales force sizes?

A company's sales force size depends on its go-to-market strategy. A company using a direct sales force as its primary way to connect with customers requires more salespeople than one that relies heavily on other channels, such as distributors, resellers, partners, and telesales, to provide customer contact. The sales force size decision is also linked to sales force structure. For example, a different number of salespeople are required if a company uses a generalist sales force versus multiple specialty sales forces. Finally, the sales force size affects territory alignment. The number of salespeople a company chooses determines the size of each salesperson's territory and the number of customers he or she can see.

The remainder of this chapter is organized into three major sections. The first section discusses the link between sales force size and profitability of the firm. The second section begins with a discussion of the forces that cause sales forces to become too large or too small, then suggests five tests that you can perform to determine if your sales force is sized correctly. The final section of the chapter describes several analytical approaches that companies have used to successfully size their sales forces.

THE CRITICAL LINK BETWEEN SALES FORCE SIZE AND PROFITABILITY

A sales force is a powerful asset. It should be viewed by the company as an investment. The company invests money in its sales force. In return, the sales force provides customer and product coverage that in turn generates sales. Since the number of salespeople is strongly linked to both sales force costs and sales, the sales force size is an important determinant of a firm's profitability.

Sales Force Size Affects Customer Coverage and Product Effort

The size of a company's sales force drives customer coverage. It affects how many customers and prospects are called, how frequently they get visited, and how accessible the sales force is to customers needing assistance. Thus, sales force size is linked to customer satisfaction and retention.

Larger sales forces reach more customers and prospects. For example, the company represented in Table 7.1 and Figure 7.1 surveyed its sales force to determine the number of hours required to perform necessary selling activities for customers of various sizes. The company used this information to calculate the number of full-time salesperson equivalents (FTEs) required to cover accounts. It discovered that in order to cover the entire account universe, 504 salespeople would be needed. However, as the graph in Figure 7.1 shows, far fewer direct salespeople would be needed if some of the smaller account segments were covered with less expensive sales channels such as telesales.

Larger sales forces can spend more time with important customers. For example, the management of the company represented in Table 7.1 and Figure 7.1 decided to field a sales force of 161 salespeople to cover all the customers with over $50,000 of sales potential. All other accounts would be handled through telesales. But then another interesting trade-off emerged. Management wondered, "With 161 salespeople, would it be better to focus even more effort on the most important customers?" As Table 7.2 shows, with 161 salespeople it is possible to either cover all accounts over $50,000 of potential or spend 50 percent more time with accounts over $100,000 of potential while turning the $50,000–$100,000 accounts over to telesales. Management pondered, "Which strategy would be more profitable?"

Sales force size also affects product effort. When the sales force is bigger, more products can be sold and/or more time can be spent on each product. We have observed that profit maximizing strategies typically

TABLE 7.1 Link between sales force size and depth of customer reach

Sales potential of account	Average hours/week required to service accounts*	Number of accounts	Percentage of accounts visited	FTEs**
>$1,000,000	26.4	21	100	15.3
$500,000–1,000,000	8.7	76	100	18.3
$250,000–500,000	5.0	258	100	35.7
$100,000–250,000	3.1	443	100	38.0
$50,000–100,000	2.0	976	100	54.0
$25,000–50,000	1.8	3000	100	149.4
<$25,000	1.4	5000	100	193.6
Total				**504.3**

*   Based on results of sales force workload survey
** Full-time equivalent (FTE) capacity = 1,880 hours per salesperson per year

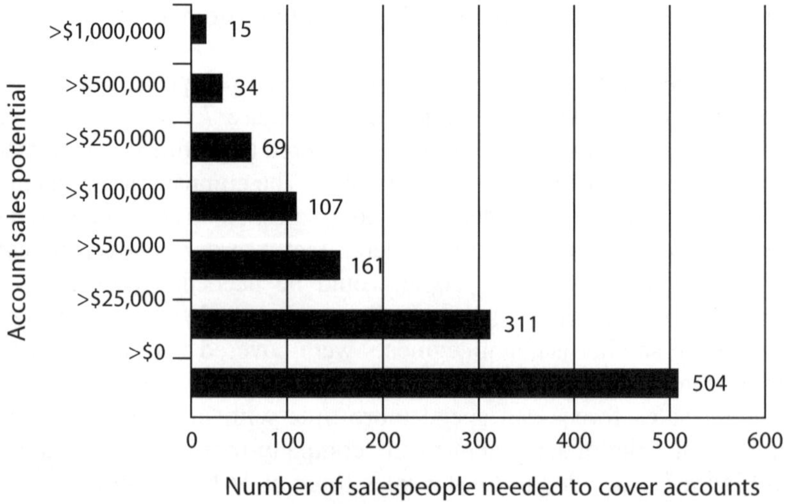

FIGURE 7.1 Number of salespeople needed for varying depths of account coverage

---

Focused product strategies dominate scattered strategies

One company's sales plan called for its 100 salespeople to spend time selling all of its 37 products. "Sell everything in the bag," is what sales managers believed. With this strategy, each product got on average 2.7 percent of the sales force's time, hardly enough to make a difference. Analysis revealed that it was far better to focus sales force effort on just eight key products, each receiving on average 12.5 percent of the sales force's time. With a more concentrated sales force effort, company sales and profits would increase.

TABLE 7.2 Alternative ways to cover customers with 161 salespeople

Sales potential of account	Average hours/ week required to service accounts*	Number of accounts	Coverage strategy A: reach all customers over $50K				Coverage strategy B: spend more time with customers over $100K		
			Actual hours/ week spent at accounts	Percent-age of accounts visited	FTEs**	Actual hours/ week spent at accounts	Percent-age of accounts visited	FTEs**
>$1,000,000	26.4	21	26.4	100	15.3	39.6	100	23.0
$500,000–1,000,000	8.7	76	8.7	100	18.3	13.1	100	27.4
$250,000–500,000	5.0	258	5.0	100	35.7	7.5	100	53.5
$100,000–250,000	3.1	443	3.1	100	38.0	4.7	100	57.0
$50,000–100,000	2.0	976	2.0	100	54.0	0.0	0	0.0
$25,000–50,000	1.8	3000	0.0	0	0	0.0	0	0.0
<$25,000	1.4	5000	0.0	0	0	0.0	0	0.0
Total					161.3			160.9

* Based on results of sales force workload survey
** Full-time equivalent (FTE) capacity = 1,880 hours per salesperson per year

focus the firm's resources on fewer products than marketing managers often recommend, and fewer customers than sales forces typically see.

Sales Force Effort Drives Sales

The sales force creates sales. A larger sales force can reach more customers, spend more time with key accounts, and promote more products than a smaller sales force. Therefore, a larger sales force will generate higher sales than a smaller sales force. Numerous data support this assertion. For example, the data in Figure 7.2 show sales performance for one product that is sold by a sales force with a broad product portfolio. Every salesperson determines individually how much time to spend selling each product in the portfolio. As the data show, some salespeople spend a lot of time selling this particular product while others allocate less time to it. Sales are positively correlated with effort. High levels of selling effort generate higher sales than lower levels of effort.

As the curve on the graph in Figure 7.2 shows, the relationship between sales and calls has diminishing returns. As the number of calls increase, sales increase also, but at a slower rate. This happens because experienced salespeople call on the easiest, most lucrative accounts first – those that produce the highest sales for the lowest levels of effort. Each subsequent call

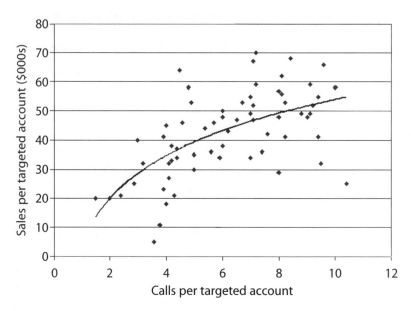

FIGURE 7.2 Sales–effort relationship

generates a little less in sales. Eventually, the sales curve flattens out when all accounts have been penetrated. At this point, there are no good accounts left to sell to, and additional calls yield very little incremental sales.

Sales executives intuitively accept the relationship between sales force effort and sales illustrated in Figure 7.2. Yet many frequently used sales force investment philosophies such as "pay as you go" and "maintain sales force investment as a constant percent of sales" ignore this relationship. A failure to recognize the critical link between sales force size and sales is the cause of many sales force sizing errors.

The impact of sales force effort on sales is not always immediate. Sales force effort affects sales this year and also in future years. Figure 7.3 illustrates this concept called carryover. There is strong evidence of

---

How much can you sell in a vacant sales territory?

What does it mean when a vacant sales territory produces higher sales than a territory that is fully staffed? This happens more frequently than you might expect. For example, at a consumer product company, a vacant territory ranked fourth highest out of 250 territories in sales for a full year.

Sales in vacant territories are attributed to the carryover generated by past selling effort. Customers may continue to purchase a company's products out of habit, because of long-term contracts, or because of high switching costs. Over time, sales in vacant territories will erode. Thus, sales managers place a high priority on filling territory vacancies quickly.

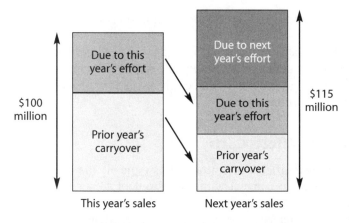

FIGURE 7.3 Illustration of carryover

carryover in most industries. For example, when sales occur in vacant sales territories, those sales are the result of carryover. Because of carryover, a change in sales force size has both a short-term and a long-term impact on the firm.

The importance of carryover varies significantly across industries and products. Some selling environments are conducive to high short-term impact, while others have significant carryover. Table 7.3 shows how various characteristics of the selling environment will usually affect how

TABLE 7.3 Characteristics of the selling environment that affect short-term sales impact and carryover

High short-term impact and low carryover	Low short-term impact and high carryover
Low customer switching costs	High customer switching costs
High levels of new incremental business	Low levels of new incremental business
Many new customers	Few new customers
Small purchase volumes	Large purchase volumes
Short selling cycles	Long selling cycles
No maintenance or service activity	Significant maintenance or service activity
New product	Mature product
High level of competitive noise	Low level of competitive noise
High market growth	Low or declining market growth
Products similar or nearly identical to competitive products	Highly differentiated products
Weak brand and/or company loyalty	Strong brand and/or company loyalty
Sales force is the only promotional vehicle	Many promotional vehicles in addition to the sales force
Weak existing customer relationships	Strong existing customer relationships
Sales contracts rarely exist	Sales contracts often exist

responsive sales are to sales force effort in the short-term and how much carryover exists.

Carryover must be considered when sizing a sales force. The full impact of size on sales is understated if only the first-year impact on sales is considered. The long-term impact can easily exceed the one-year impact in high carryover environments.

Sales Force Size Affects Costs

A sales force is a significant investment. It is typically the most expensive way for a company to connect with its customers. Other sales channels, such as telesales, the Internet, direct mail, and mass advertising, cost much less per contact than a sales force. Companies spend anywhere from 2 to 40 percent of sales on sales forces.

Sales Force Size Affects Profitability

Salespeople are the breadwinners for the company – they generate sales. At the same time, the sales force is a significant expense. Thus, sales force

---

Sales force costs

Recruiting and hiring costs – advertisements, recruiting fees, testing, reference checking, interview time, interview travel, training, employee relocation expense, legal expense for contracts.

Compensation costs – salaries, commissions, bonuses, FICA/FUTA, state and miscellaneous taxes, insurance and retirement benefits, Medicare, benefit maintenance, reporting and compliance.

Government requirement costs – state and local taxes and laws, workers compensation, licenses, required forms and filings.

On the job costs – travel and entertainment, auto expense, cell phone, laptop, and PDA expenses, customer promos, recurrent training, product training, accounting expense, dues and subscriptions, legal expense for HR responsibilities.

Facilities costs – rent, furniture and fixtures, computers and software, communications systems, administrative support, postage, office supplies, utilities, maintenance, business insurance.

Marketing costs – account forecasting, market share data, competitive awareness, sales meetings, product marketing materials.

Account investment costs – opening new markets and customers, new product development and introduction, routine distributor and customer training, interest on investment dollars.

Sales support costs – customer data, performance measurement, CRM systems.

Source: Adapted from *Outsourcing the Sales Function: The Real Cost of Field Sales* by Dr. Erin Anderson and Bob Trinkle

size has a major impact on the firm's profitability. A sales force that is too big produces high sales but costs the firm too much money. A sales force that is too small costs less but results in significant lost sales opportunity. A sales force that is the right size maximizes the long-term profitability of the firm.

Cost containment is not the same thing as profit maximization. Management is likely to undersize the sales force when it views the sales force as a cost rather than an investment. For example, many companies manage sales expense to a percentage of revenue. Thus, they constrain the size of the sales force to ensure that total costs do not exceed a preset percentage of sales. The US average is approximately 6.8 percent. While this is an effective method of controlling costs, it does not maximize profits. As illustrated in Table 7.4, when a sales force is undersized, a sales force cost that is a higher percentage of sales produces higher total profits than a sales force cost that is a lower percentage of sales.

TABLE 7.4 Example showing that cost containment is not profit maximizing

Financial projections for alternative sales force sizing plans
($ amounts are in thousands)

	Current plan	**Expansion**	**Reduction**
Number of salespeople	100	150	50
Sales	$100,000	$120,000	$70,000
Cost of goods sold (20%)	$20,000	$24,000	$14,000
Sales less COGS	$80,000	$96,000	$56,000
Sales force cost	$10,000	$15,000	$5,000
Other marketing cost	$5,000	$5,000	$5,000
Administrative costs	$5,000	$5,000	$5,000
Total marketing and admin. cost	$20,000	$25,000	$15,000
Pretax profit	$60,000	$71,000	$41,000
Sales force cost as percent of sales	10	13	7
Average sales per salesperson	$1,000	$800	$1,400

Companies with a short-term perspective undersize their sales forces

We conducted a study that analyzed sales force sizing data for 50 healthcare companies in six countries. The study found that companies who sized their sales forces to maximize first-year profitability sacrificed long-term profits. Because of carryover, the sales force should be viewed as a long-term investment. The sales force size that maximizes three-year discounted contribution in this study was 18 percent larger than the sales force size that maximizes first-year contribution alone.

IS YOUR SALES FORCE THE RIGHT SIZE?

The size of the sales force affects customers, salespeople, and the company. A sales force that is too small cannot serve the needs of customers effectively. Salespeople are overworked and the firm misses key sales opportunities. A sales force that is too large becomes an annoyance to customers. Salespeople are not challenged and the firm suffers from high costs and low productivity. A sales force that is the right size connects effectively with customers. Salespeople are stretched but not overworked. The firm enjoys high sales, reasonable costs, and strong profits.

How Does a Sales Force Become Too Small?

A vice president of sales wonders if his sales force is too small. Several years ago when the sales force was established, he decided that each salesperson could handle a $2 million sales territory. Today, sales have grown to over $3.5 million per territory. He wonders if the current size is constraining continued growth.

   Numerous external and internal change forces can cause a company's sales force to become too small. External forces include changes to the company's customers, its competitors, and its environment. Internal

---

PlaceWare expands sales force as web-conferencing market growths

The market for web-conferencing applications has grown dramatically in recent years, as more and more businesses embrace this technology and are comfortable using the Internet to conduct virtual meetings and conferences in real time. PlaceWare, a leading firm in this industry, increased its direct sales force by 58 percent during 2002 in order to take advantage of the tremendous opportunity in this high-growth market. The strategy paid off when PlaceWare was acquired by Microsoft in April of 2003.

AT&T expands its sales force to steal market share from competitors

In 2002, AT&T made an aggressive move to increase market share when its competitors faced challenges. Competitors including Global Crossing, Qwest, and WorldCom, were either facing bankruptcy or dealing with financial scandals. AT&T decided to take advantage of its prime position in the industry and steal market share away from struggling competitors. AT&T's sales force was undersized, so the company hired more than 600 salespeople from other telecom companies to start selling for its business sales unit. These salespeople were asked to contact every customer who was currently using products and services from the distressed telecom companies. The message the salespeople delivered emphasized AT&T's reliability, service quality, financial stability, and professionalism.

TABLE 7.5 Several change forces that can cause a sales force to become too small

External change forces

Customer change
- Market expands
- Customers ask more from the sales force
- Buying process changes so there are more purchase influencers
- Customer needs become more sophisticated
- Customers require global reach

Competitive change
- Competitors are expanding their sales forces
- New, larger, wealthier, smarter, more aggressive competitors
- Opportunity to take advantage of a competitor's weaknesses

Environmental change
- Better economic conditions
- Outlook for future sales is better than the company expected
- Industry deregulation
- Industry consolidation, strongest will survive
- Tight labor markets

Internal change forces

Company strategy change
- Start up sales force
- Launching new products
- Entering new markets
- Shifting to a product or market emphasis that requires more salespeople
- Selling process and go-to-market changes that require more salespeople
- Targeting more customers and prospects
- Switch from a cost to a revenue focus
- Size for market opportunity, not financial risk

Productivity enhancement initiative

Increased emphasis on:
- Increasing sales
- Increasing market share
- Increasing customer satisfaction
- Increasing new business development
- Increasing consultative, value-adding services
- Reducing workload and travel per salesperson because of large territories

forces include new company strategies and productivity enhancement initiatives. Table 7.5 lists different change forces that can create the need to expand a sales force.

How Does a Sales Force Get Too Big?

The president of a major division of a company suspects that his sales force has grown too large. Two years ago, business was so brisk that the attitude throughout the industry was that the sales force size should be bigger, always bigger. But now, in the midst of a persistently sluggish economy, the president feels pressure to cut costs, trim fat, and increase productivity per salesperson.

Many internal and external change forces can cause a company's sales force to become too large. Table 7.6 illustrates how different change forces create the need to downsize the sales force.

TABLE 7.6 Several change forces that cause a sales force to become too big

External change forces

Customer change	Competitive change	Environmental change
• Market contraction	• Fewer, weaker competitors	• Weak economy
• Buying process changes so there are fewer purchase influencers	• Competitors are downsizing their sales forces	• Financial success leading to overstaffing
• Customer consolidation	• Commodification, increased price pressure, margin erosion	• Outlook for future sales is less than the company had hoped
• Some customer segments prefer to buy via Internet or telesales		• New sales channels
• Customers need fewer services from salespeople		• New technology reduces a salesperson's work

Internal change forces

Corporate strategy change	Productivity enhancement initiative
• Mergers/acquisitions	Increased emphasis on:
• Shifting to a product or market emphasis that requires fewer salespeople	• Reducing costs
	• Increasing productivity per salesperson
• Selling process and go-to-market changes that require fewer salespeople	• Reducing calls to unprofitable accounts
• Targeting fewer customers	• Reassigning sales force tasks to less expensive personnel
• Selling fewer products	
• Pulling out of markets	
• Switch from a revenue to a cost focus	

Stockbrokers downsize in a weak economy

A bleak economic outlook frequently causes companies to downsize their sales forces. For example, with profits down 24 percent at NYSE-member firms in 2002, cost cutting was a major priority at most brokerages. One of the most significant cost-cutting measures used by the industry was to reduce the size of sales forces. Merrill Lynch cut 2400 brokers, Prudential Securities cut 1600, and Morgan Stanley cut 1100. Other cost-cutting techniques used by companies included: slashing expense allowances, paying smaller bonuses, eliminating incentive programs, increasing focus on variable versus fixed compensation, reducing benefits, freezing hiring, eliminating low producers, eliminating managers, reducing home office and support staff, and outsourcing. One brokerage firm, Advest Group, implemented several cost-cutting programs, but elected not to cut the sales force because, as stated by a company spokesperson, the salespeople "are the breadwinners."

RJR changes promotion strategy and reduces sales force size

Cigarette manufacturer R. J. Reynolds experienced a decline in volume coupled with lower margins in the highly competitive US market. In order to position the company for future profit growth, the company is targeting a $1 billion reduction in its cost structure by year-end 2005. Late in 2003, the company announced that it would refocus its sales effort on premium brands with high growth potential such as Camel and Salem, and reduce promotion substantially on other brands such as Doral and Winston. Significant sales force and other work force reductions are planned for 2004.

Five Quick Sales Force Sizing Tests

How do you know if your sales force is too large or too small? There are five tests that can help you determine if your company's sales force is the right size. These tests can be performed quickly and easily at most companies. The tests, which are described below, include a customer test, a sales force morale test, a selling activities test, a competitive position test, and a financial test.

Customer test

One of the ways to determine whether your sales force is the right size is to find out what customers think. Your sales force may be undersized if customers tell you "I'm not sure I know who my salesperson is," "I can't recall seeing my salesperson in a long time," or "I am considering switching to a supplier that gives me better service." On the other hand, if customers ask "Is all the attention I'm getting showing up in my price?" or "Can't I just get the information I need and place orders over the web?" the sales force may be too large.

Physicians are annoyed by too many pharmaceutical salespeople in 2003

Physicians report becoming increasingly annoyed by the number of pharmaceutical salespeople. Some doctors are visited by more than 20 different pharmaceutical salespeople every day. Many of these salespeople sell the same products and provide only one-way communication. Due to high profit margins and aggressive competition in the industry, pharmaceutical sales force sizes have increased beyond what customers say they want or need.

What customers say about your salespeople can provide important clues about the size of your sales force. Customer surveys can be used to measure the current customer point of view. Figure 7.4 depicts how customers may react across the spectrum of sales force sizes.

Sales force morale test

Sales force morale is linked to sales force size. When the sales force has either too many or too few salespeople, morale suffers. High sales force

---

What would customers say about your sales force?

◄---►

Too small	Right size	Too big
• My salesperson is not available to meet my needs	• My salesperson is available when I need him or her	• My salesperson is a pest
• I can't reach my salesperson when I need him or her	• I look forward to meeting with my salesperson	• I avoid meeting with my salesperson and I don't return his or her calls
• I am considering switching to a supplier that will give me better service	• My salesperson has a valuable role that complements other information vehicles, such as sales literature or a web site	• I prefer to get what I need through the company's literature, web site, or telesales group

FIGURE 7.4 Customer relationship spectrum

turnover can be a signal that a sales force is not sized correctly. Listen closely to the complaints of your good salespeople. In addition, find out why good salespeople leave the company. What you hear may provide some important clues about the size of your sales force.

When the sales force is too large, salespeople often complain about compensation. You may hear, "I can't make enough money in my territory," or "Opportunity is spread too thin." Complaints like this will be strongest in sales forces with compensation plans that have a large variable component tied to total sales. For example, a salesperson who is paid a straight commission on every sale will object strongly if the sales force is too large, because each salesperson will have too few customers and everyone will struggle to make good money. Another common complaint in sales forces that are too large, regardless of the compensation plan is, "I am no longer stimulated by my work."

When the sales force is too small, salespeople complain about workload. Of course, many employees exaggerate their workload whenever they speak to their boss, but if the sales force is under-sized, the frequency and strength of these complaints intensifies. You may hear, "I barely have enough time to take orders, let alone determine how customer needs might be changing or provide solutions to these needs," "I am overworked," or "I have too much travel and I'm never home." Too much work and travel is also a common cause of sales force turnover. One salesperson for a small sales force lived in a mobile home and did not even have a permanent address! While this worked in this instance, this kind of travel eventually leads to a salesperson quitting the job.

Too much sales force travel causes morale problems and turnover

The desire to increase productivity through lower salesperson travel led one company to expand its sales force. The company had a sales force of 28 people covering the entire US and significant travel variation existed across sales territories. This caused a great deal of stress in the sales force. Some territories covered massive geographies, encompassing several large states. The salespeople in these territories were almost never home. Other territories in major metropolitan areas were very small, requiring few or no overnight trips. The sales force had high turnover (40 percent per year) which the company attributed to the high travel requirements in many of the territories. Since the company's products were very complex and specialized, the cost to hire and train so many new salespeople every year was significant. The company decided to increase the number of salespeople to reduce the travel required for each individual salesperson. The expansion was funded in part by a decrease in hiring and training costs due to lower salesperson turnover. In addition, fewer sales were lost due to territory vacancies.

Sales compensation issues can also arise when the sales force is too small. Territory-level sales quotas can be quite high if company goals are based on market opportunity and the sales force is undersized. Salespeople will have difficulty achieving their goals, causing their compensation to suffer. Management will hear their complaints. Alternatively, salespeople can receive windfall incentive payments when their incentive compensation has a large variable component tied to total sales and the sales force is undersized. Since there are so many good accounts per salesperson, everyone looks successful. Management will find it difficult to tell who the good salespeople really are. Salespeople in this situation are likely to fight sales force expansion for fear of losing income.

Do your salespeople fight sales force expansion?

Have your salespeople resisted sales force expansion in the past, due to fear of lost opportunity? This happens often in sales forces with compensation plans that have a large variable component tied to total sales. For example, a salesperson who is paid a straight commission on every sale will object strongly to giving up customers to expansion territories. The salesperson knows that unless the market is growing very rapidly, he or she will struggle and need to work harder to make the same dollars in a smaller territory. When salespeople fight an expansion, management often backs down for fear of losing their best salespeople. For this reason, we have observed that sales force compensation plans with large variable components tied to total sales (rather than to a territory goal) often lead to an undersized sales force.

Selling activities test

A study of how salespeople spend their time provides many insights into sales force sizing. Too much time is frequently spent on non-critical selling activities in sales forces that are too large, including administrative tasks such as internal meetings and paperwork, or activities that should be performed by others within the company, such as handling customer service problems. In addition, salespeople in oversized sales forces frequently spend too much time with small, low-potential customers. For example in Figure 7.5, sales force effort is well matched to sales in customer segments A, B, C, and D. However, the sales force spends too much time with segment E, given the relatively low level of sales the segment generates. The company should consider downsizing its sales force, eliminating coverage of segment E, or, if practical, reaching this segment with a cheaper selling channel, such as telesales or the Internet.

Analysis of how salespeople spend their time can also show that the sales force is too small. Salespeople frequently do not spend enough time with important customers in undersized sales forces. They struggle just to keep up with basic tasks like order taking, and rarely have time to probe customers about their needs or to develop and propose complete solutions. In addition, they can be reluctant to prospect for new customers because they are already so busy serving current customers. In small sales forces that are undersized, sales territories can be very large and salespeople may spend too much time traveling. Figure 7.6 shows an analysis of how salespeople spend their time in one sales force

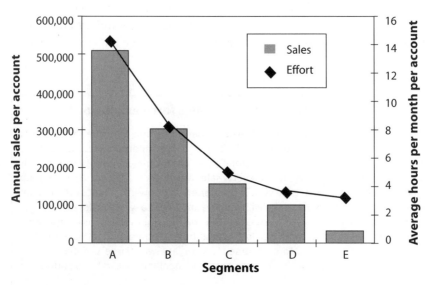

FIGURE 7.5 Sales and effort per account by customer segment

Hours by selling activity for a sales force that is too small

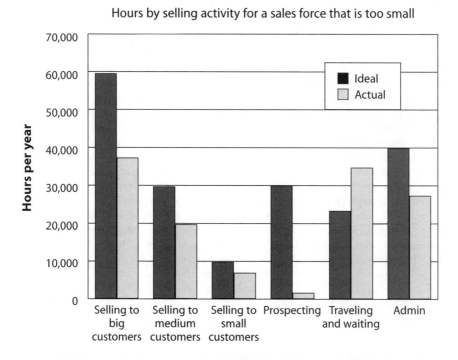

FIGURE 7.6 Ideal versus actual sales force hours by selling activity

that is undersized. The company estimated the ideal amount of time the sales force should spend on various activities and compared this with the actual amount of time spent. As the graph shows, too little time is spent on many critical activities, especially selling to big- and medium-sized customers and prospecting.

Competitive position test

It is important to compare your sales force investment with that of your competitors. Market share often depends more upon "share of voice" with customers than on the absolute amount of time the sales force spends with customers. If your major competitors are reducing their sales staffs, you may be able to downsize your sales force as well without losing market share. Your sales may decline if the entire market is declining, but you will maintain (grow) your competitive position by maintaining (growing) your share of voice. Similarly, if competitors are increasing staff, you will need to expand your sales force as well to maintain share of voice and thus preserve market share. The desire to maintain competitive parity can result in an entire industry adding salespeople beyond what is required to meet customer needs over time.

Why are there so many pharmaceutical salespeople?

The number of pharmaceutical salespeople doubled in the United States between 1997 and 2001. By 2001, industry leaders fielded mega sales forces of 5000+ salespeople. Many industry trends suggest that pharmaceutical sales forces actually should have been downsizing during this period. Competitive and price pressure from generic drugs and managed care was growing; public, media, and government scrutiny was intense; and other marketing instruments such as direct-to-consumer advertising were increasing in importance. In addition, partnerships and mergers and acquisitions among pharmaceutical companies continued as companies struggled to maintain high profits with fewer new drugs. Busy physicians were annoyed by the number of salespeople visiting them. Salespeople were frustrated by lack of access to physicians and felt limited accountability because several different sales forces often sold the same drugs to the same physicians. Calls per salesperson were down, sales force costs were up, and it was increasingly difficult to hire qualified salespeople.

Yet pharmaceutical sales forces continued to expand. High product margins meant that even low incremental sales brought in incremental profits. Pharmaceutical companies were engaged in a classic game of prisoner's dilemma. It was clear that the entire industry would benefit if everyone decreased their sales force size, yet the first mover would be at a disadvantage. No company was willing to sacrifice its share of voice in the short term.

How does your cost of sales compare with the industry average?

The average percentage of sales spent on the sales force varies widely across industries. You can get a sense for how your sales force size compares with other companies in your industry by comparing your cost of sales to the industry average as shown in Table 7.7. Keep in mind, significant variation within individual industries is expected when companies have very different sales force strategies. The figures given include the cost of sales compensation, benefits, and field expenses. They do not include the cost of sales management or overhead.

TABLE 7.7 Sales force cost as a percentage of total sales for various industries

Industry	Sales force cost as a percent of total sales*
Banking	0.9
Business services	10.5
Chemicals	3.4
Communications	9.9
Construction	7.1
Educational services	12.7
Electronics	12.6
Electronic components	4.9
Fabricated metals	7.2
Food products	2.7
Health services	13.4

TABLE 7.7 continued

Industry	Sales force cost as a percent of total sales*
Hotels and other lodging	1.9
Instruments	14.8
Machinery	11.3
Manufacturing	6.6
Office equipment	2.4
Paper and allied products	8.2
Pharmaceuticals	5.6
Printing and publishing	22.2
Real estate	2.8
Retail	15.3
Rubber and plastics	3.6
Transportation equipment	6.2
Wholesale consumer goods	11.2
Overall	**10.0**

* Includes cost of sales compensation, benefits, and field expenses. Does not include cost of sales management or overhead.

Source: reprinted with permission from *Dartnell's 30th Sales Force Compensation Survey: 1998–1999*, copyright 1999 by Dartnell Corporation. All rights reserved. http://www.dartnellcorp.com

Financial test

Financial performance can provide insights regarding the current sales force size. Having a sales force that is too large is good for sales, market share, and new business development. Yet it can be associated with high costs, low sales per salesperson, and low or declining profitability. On the other hand, a sales force that is too small will have high sales per salesperson and a low sales expense ratio. However, sales, market share, and new business development will not match what is possible with a larger sales force. Table 7.8 summarizes some of the financial implications of sales force sizing errors.

A breakeven analysis can help determine whether your sales force is too large, too small, or about the right size. The analysis requires the following five steps.

1. *Estimate the annual cost of a salesperson.* Include all costs that vary with the number of salespeople, such as salary, benefits, taxes, bonuses, automobiles, travel expenses, computers, call reporting, administrative support, and field support. For example:

    a. Total compensation, incl. salary and bonus: $75,000
    b. Value of benefits (30% total comp): $22,000
    c. Administrative and field support (15% total comp): $11,000

TABLE 7.8 Financial implications of sales force sizing errors

	Too small	Too big
Sales	Low, decreasing or not growing as quickly as hoped	High and growing
Market share	Low/losing customers to competitors	High/gaining from competition
Sales per salesperson	High	Low
Cost of sales	Under control and low relative to the industry	Out-of-control and high relative to industry
Profits	Would be better with a larger sales force	Would be better with a smaller sales force
New business development	Low	Medium

Should you celebrate when the sales per salesperson goes up?

Many companies use sales per salesperson as a performance metric. They reason that higher sales per salesperson imply greater sales force productivity. Be careful when using this measure. If sales per salesperson increase, it could mean that salespeople are in fact more productive. On the other hand, it could simply be a sign that the sales force has more business than it can handle. Keep in mind, the easiest way to maximize sales per salesperson is to fire all but one salesperson!

---

    d.   T&E, automobile, cell phones, computers, etc.: $10,000

    e.   Total cost of a salesperson: **$118,000**

2. *Estimate the gross contribution margin.* This is the percentage of sales that the company keeps as profit, after taking out variable product costs. Variable product costs include all costs that vary with how much of a product is sold, such as raw materials, manufacturing, royalties, freight to factory, and shipping to customers. Variable costs do not include allocations of fixed costs, such as factory overhead and R&D. Thus, variable product costs are less than cost of goods sold, which includes factory overhead. For example, if in one year the company sells $900 million of goods and spends $300 million on variable product costs, the company's gross contribution margin is ($900–$300)/$900 = 66.7 percent.

3. *Calculate break-even sales.* Divide the cost of a salesperson by the gross contribution margin. In the example, break-even sales is $118,000/.667 = $176,911. This is the amount a salesperson must sell in a year in order to cover his or her cost.

4. *Calculate the average annual sales per salesperson.* In the example, if the firm has 900 salespeople who sell $900 million in a year, the average annual sales per salesperson is $1.0 million.

TABLE 7.9 Implications of the average sales/break-even sales ratio and carryover on sales force size

Average sales/ break-even sales ratio	Carryover 10%	20%	30%	40%	50%	60%	70%	80%	90%
1.5	0.48	0.68	0.91	1.20	1.58	2.15	3.08	4.92	10.43
2	0.30	0.43	0.58	0.76	1.00	1.36	1.94	3.11	6.58
2.5	0.22	0.32	0.42	0.56	0.74	1.00	1.43	2.29	4.85
3	0.18	0.25	0.34	0.44	0.58	0.79	1.14	1.82	3.85
3.5	0.15	0.21	0.28	0.37	0.49	0.66	0.94	1.51	3.19
4	0.12	0.18	0.24	0.31	0.42	0.56	0.81	1.29	2.73
4.5	0.11	0.16	0.21	0.27	0.36	0.49	0.70	1.13	2.39
5	0.10	0.14	0.19	0.24	0.32	0.44	0.63	1.00	2.12
5.5	0.09	0.12	0.17	0.22	0.29	0.39	0.56	0.90	1.90
6	0.08	0.11	0.15	0.20	0.26	0.36	0.51	0.82	1.73
6.5	0.07	0.10	0.14	0.18	0.24	0.33	0.47	0.75	1.59
7	0.07	0.10	0.13	0.17	0.22	0.30	0.43	0.69	1.46
7.5	0.06	0.09	0.12	0.16	0.21	0.28	0.40	0.64	1.36
8	0.06	0.08	0.11	0.15	0.19	0.26	0.37	0.60	1.27
8.5	0.05	0.08	0.10	0.14	0.18	0.25	0.35	0.56	1.19
9	0.05	0.07	0.10	0.13	0.17	0.23	0.33	0.53	1.12
9.5	0.05	0.07	0.09	0.12	0.16	0.22	0.31	0.50	1.06
10	0.05	0.07	0.09	0.11	0.15	0.21	0.30	0.47	1.00

Matrix contains the years to break even. Most sales forces are sized so as to break even within 6–18 months.

☐	Sales force may be too small
☐	Sales force is the right size
▨	Sales force may be too large

5. *Compare break-even sales with the average sales per salesperson.* Compute the ratio. In the example, the ratio is $1,000,000/176,911 = 5.65. This means that, on average, each salesperson generates gross margin equal to 5.65 times his or her annual costs. Use Table 7.9 to find out what the ratio implies about sales force size. The meaning of the ratio varies depending upon the amount of carryover in the selling environment (see Figure 7.3 and Table 7.3 earlier in this chapter for more information about the carryover concept). A ratio of 5.65 implies that in a low carryover environment (60 percent or less), the sales force may be too small. In a moderate carryover environment (70–80 percent), the sales force is about the right size. In a high carryover environment (90 percent or more), the sales force may be too large.

HOW TO DETERMINE SALES FORCE SIZE

Several sales force sizing rules and approaches have been discussed earlier in this chapter. These rules and approaches along with their rationales include:

- Keeping the sales force size the same as last year in order to avoid disruption and additional costs.
- Maintaining a sales force size that keeps costs at a constant percentage of sales in order to contain sales force costs.
- Increasing sales force size only after the company has generated the sales to pay for the size increase in order to avoid risk.
- Matching the sales force sizing changes of major competitors in order to maintain share of voice.

All of the above rules and approaches have merit in certain situations. We have discovered, however, that the best sales force sizing approaches incorporate market dynamics and at the same time, recognize the needs of various stakeholders in the sizing decision. Accomplishing this typically involves two major initiatives. First, a good initial sales force sizing recommendation is developed using one or more of several data-driven and analytical market-based methodologies. Five such methodologies are described in this chapter – the activity-based method, the pipeline method, the target-return-per-call method, the sales response method, and the geographic concentration method. Second, a series of tests is performed to validate the sizing recommendation from the perspective of key stakeholders. This includes internal stakeholders such as people in the company's sales, marketing, and financial departments, as well as an important external stakeholder – the firm's customers.

Market-based recommendation	Stakeholder validation
Use an analytical, data-driven, market-based approach to develop an initial sales force size recommendation. • Activity-based method • Pipeline method • Target-return-per-call method • Sales response method • Geographic concentration method	Test and refine the initial recommendation from the perspective of key stakeholders. • Marketing: the competitive position test • Finance: the financial test • Sales management: the selling activities test • Salespeople: the sales force morale test • Customers: the customer test

FIGURE 7.7 A process for determining sales force size

Market-Based Recommendation

Market-based approaches to sales force sizing acknowledge the fact that sales force size determines customer coverage and product effort, and therefore drives company sales and profits. There are various market-based approaches to sales force sizing; five are described in this chapter. All of these methodologies combine analysis with management input to create good, data-driven initial sales force sizing recommendations.

Market-based approach overview

Figure 7.8 outlines four basic steps that are required in any market-based approach to sales force sizing. Market-based approaches always begin with focus on the customer. In Step 1, Customer understanding, the customer universe is identified and an understanding of the product, service, and support needs of customers is developed. In Step 2, Customer segmentation, customers with similar needs are clustered into market segments so that sales strategies can be tailored to the needs of each segment. In Step 3, Segment coverage strategy definition and segment value assessment, a sales force coverage plan is developed and the value that the sales force can generate by following that plan is estimated for each market segment. Finally in Step 4, Sales force sizing, the number of salespeople needed to implement the desired coverage plan is determined.

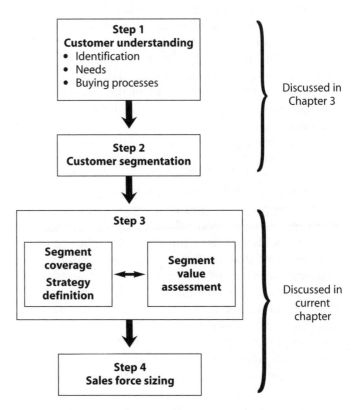

FIGURE 7.8 Four-step market-based process for sizing the sales force

The activities required for Steps 1 and 2 of the market-based process for sales force sizing are described in detail in Chapter 3 (Sales Strategy). The current chapter focuses on the last two steps of the process: Step 3, Segment coverage strategy definition and segment value assessment, and Step 4, Sales force sizing. An overview of these steps is provided first. Later in the chapter, more details and specific examples of how to complete the steps are provided within the descriptions of the five different market-based methodologies.

Overview of Step 3 – segment coverage strategy definition and segment value assessment. Step 3 of the market-based process for sizing the sales force involves determining the right sales force coverage plan for each market segment. The right coverage plan is linked to the value that each segment can generate for the company. Companies typically use financial measures such as sales, unit volume, and profits to determine a segment's value. Understanding this important link between coverage and value is critical to good sales force sizing decisions. Increasing sales force coverage of a customer segment results in higher sales but also higher costs. Determining the right level of coverage is critical to maximizing profits.

Measuring the link between segment coverage and segment value is not easy. Companies with the right data and analytical capabilities can measure the link directly; other companies rely on management input combined with diagnostic checks. The five market-based sales force sizing methodologies described in this chapter vary in terms of their sophistication in measuring the link between sales force coverage and the value it generates.

The coverage plan developed in Step 3 specifies the average workload required to cover each account in a segment. The word "average" is important. Some accounts within the segment will have heavier workloads, while others will have lighter workloads. In the end, salespeople determine the most appropriate sales coverage strategy for each of their accounts. However, average workload multiplied by the number of accounts in the segment yields the total effort planned for the segment.

A segment strategy that is based on measures of segment workload and value can be used to guide the selling effort of the sales force. Specifically, it helps the individual salesperson target better, it helps the training and marketing departments develop materials to describe, target, and sell to the customer, it helps the sales manager set account expectations and coach better, and it helps the company to create an equitable territory alignment.

Companies often discover through segment coverage analysis that not every customer segment is worthy of direct sales force coverage. For example, a direct sales force does typically not cover segments with the following characteristics.

- segments with low potential
- segments that are unresponsive to sales force effort
- segments for which other marketing activities (e.g. advertising, direct mail, Internet selling) are more effective at creating sales
- segments for which distributors, manufacturer's agents, a contract sales force, a part-time sales force, or a telemarketing sales force can reduce the cost of customer contact to an acceptable level compared with their reduced effectiveness.

Overview of Step 4 – sales force sizing. Step 4 of the market-based process for sizing the sales force involves determining the number of salespeople needed to implement the desired coverage plan. In order to do this, it is necessary to estimate the annual call capacity of a salesperson. This involves calculating the total number of working hours in a year and subtracting the time that salespeople are not available to call on customers. The time subtracted typically includes vacation days, sick days, and holidays, plus travel time as well as time spent in meetings and training, and completing administrative tasks.

Are your salespeople spending enough time with customers?

We see frequent examples of companies where the time a salesperson spends with customers erodes over years. Days in the field are whittled down by planning meetings, training sessions, and award trips, while selling hours in each day are reduced as administrative functions increase. A zero-based accounting of where the days and hours go, and a re-examination of what is truly valuable, can add between 10 and 25 percent to the capacity of many internally-focused sales forces.

Once the call capacity of a salesperson is known, the number of salespeople required to implement any coverage plan can be calculated.

Calculating the number of salespeople required to implement a coverage plan

Suppose a coverage plan calls for 120,000 hours with customers each year, and each salesperson has 1200 hours per year available for making calls. In this case, 100 salespeople are required to implement the coverage plan (120,000 total hours/1200 hours per salesperson = 100 salespeople).

General descriptions and examples of five effective market-based approaches for determining the coverage and value of each customer segment and the implied sales force size are provided below.

Approach 1: Activity-based method

The activity-based method involves developing a list of sales force activities required to cover the accounts in each customer segment, estimating the time it takes for a salesperson to complete these activities, then calculating the number of salespeople required to do the work. For example, the chemical company in Table 7.10 covers accounts in six major end-user market segments. The company's management estimated the percentage of accounts in each market segment that they want to reach with the sales force. Next, they listed the five major activities in the company's sales process – pre-call planning, technical calling, non-technical calling, post-call activities, and special situations – and estimated how long it would take a salesperson to complete each of these activities for the average customer reached in every market segment. Finally, management estimated that a salesperson has 1490 hours per year to spend calling on customers. Based on all this information, the company determined that it needs a total force of 24 salespeople. This calculation works as follows for the paint and coatings market segment:

TABLE 7.10 Activity-based sizing of a chemical sales force

End-user market segments	Paint & coatings	Paper	Carpet	Adhesives	Textiles	Non-wovens
Number of accounts	1600	900	330	650	850	100
Percentage reached	20	18	12	35	10	65
Task groups: (time in hours/year required)						
Precall planning	5.8	11.5	30.3	7.6	5.4	6.9
Calling: technical	7.2	9.4	18.4	9.4	9.5	6.0
Calling: non-technical	6.4	12.1	17.1	7.2	6.3	6.6
Postcall activities	6.6	11.0	36.9	6.8	5.7	6.3
Special situations	2.9	8.4	29.0	5.0	4.7	4.2
Total hours/year/account	28.9	52.4	131.7	36.0	31.6	30.0
Total accounts reached	320	162	39.6	227.5	85	65
Total hours/year	9248	8489	5215	8190	2686	1950
Rep task hours/year	1490	1490	1490	1490	1490	1490
Reps required	**6.2**	**5.7**	**3.5**	**5.5**	**1.8**	**1.3**

Total salespeople needed = 24

(1600 customers x 20 percent reach x 28.9 hours per customer per year) / 1490 hours per salesperson per year = 6.2 salespeople to cover the paint and coatings market

Coverage needs are summed across the six account segments to determine the total sales force size.

Companies that have a fairly consistent selling process across all calls, such as retail merchandisers or pharmaceutical detailers, may not require as much detail as the chemical company in their analysis of sales activities. For example, the consumer products sales force shown in Table 7.11 specified customer activities for each of its market segments in terms of frequency and duration of calls. The number of accounts in each segment is multiplied by the average number of calls per year (frequency) and by the average number of hours per call (duration) to estimate the total hours required for that segment. Total hours are then divided by the call capacity of a salesperson

TABLE 7.11 Activity-based sizing of a consumer sales force

Account/coverage description	Number of accounts	Calls per year	Hours per call	Total hours	Salesperson equivalents	% of effort
Service call–dept. store	841	12	1.0	10,092	7.6	11.7
Service call–other store	1279	4	1.0	5116	3.9	5.9
Group buyer	99	12	1.5	1782	1.4	2.1
Direct retail–over $25K	112	12	2.0	2688	2.0	3.1
Direct retail–$12–25K	784	6	2.0	9408	7.1	10.9
Direct retail–$5–12K	2543	4	2.0	20,344	15.4	23.6
Direct retail–under $5K	6559	3	1.0	19,677	14.9	22.8
Headqtrs/warehouse– over $25K	237	12	2.0	5688	4.3	6.6
Headqtrs/warehouse– $10–25K	85	12	1.5	1530	1.2	1.8
Headqtrs/warehouse– under $10K	128	12	1.0	1536	1.2	1.8
Key account–over $1000K	24	26	6.0	3744	2.8	4.3
Key account– $500–1000K	11	26	4.0	1144	0.9	1.3
Key account– $250–500K	16	26	3.0	1248	0.9	1.4
Key account– under $250K	31	26	2.0	1612	1.2	1.9
Telephone call	373	3	0.5	560	0.4	0.6
Total	13,122			86,169	65	100.0

Salespeople needed = 65

Note: Annual hours per salesperson = 1320

(in this case, 1320 hours) to determine the number of salespeople needed to cover each segment. By summing this information across all segments, the company estimates that it needs a total of 65 salespeople.

The data for developing activity-based size recommendations come from several sources. Salespeople and sales managers can articulate what has worked in the past and what they anticipate their customers will need in the future. Customers can tell the firm what they require from the selling organization. Other channel members, such as distributors and wholesalers, can supply yet another perspective. Finally, the firm can investigate how its competitors treat their customers and how sales forces in other industries organize their activities.

Companies can obtain activity information using face-to-face interviews, telephone interviews, focus groups, mail or Internet questionnaires, or group-judgment consensus approaches, such as Delphi techniques. Insights can also be gained by analyzing internal data sources such as salesperson logs, call reporting, or performance reviews.

The activity-based method of sales force sizing focuses on selling activities without directly acknowledging the link between those activities and the value they generate. The method presumes that the individuals who provide input for developing the coverage plan consider segment value when determining what level of activity is appropriate for each segment. Since the link between coverage and value is not explicitly measured, it is helpful to use data-based diagnostics to ensure that any coverage plan developed using the activity-based methodology is reasonable. For example, Figure 7.9 compares the cost of a coverage plan that was developed using the activity-based method to the historical contribution of accounts for each volume-based segment. The graph highlights two areas of possible concern. First, low-volume segments 7 through 9 did not generate

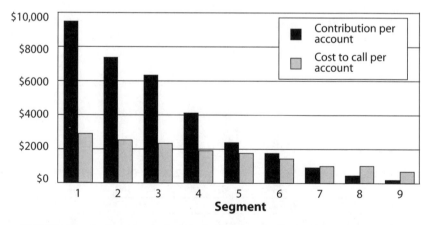

FIGURE 7.9 A diagnostic for evaluating an activity-based sales force coverage plan

enough business last year to pay for the cost of the proposed coverage. Second, segments 1 through 4 show historical contribution that is significantly greater than the cost of the proposed coverage. The company might consider shifting sales effort from segments 7 through 9 to segments 1 through 4 to increase effort on high-value accounts. However, this shift does not make sense in all situations. For example, if historical contribution from segments 7 through 9 is low only because the sales force has not covered these segments in the past, or if the segments are growing rapidly or are of special strategic importance to the company, then perhaps the coverage plan for these segments should not change. Similarly, if salespeople cannot access decision makers at the accounts in segments 1 through 4 more frequently than the coverage plan calls for, then perhaps the plan for these segments should remain as is. Diagnostic tools like this graph allow managers to assess the reasonableness of a proposed activity-based coverage plan.

Approach 2: Pipeline method

The pipeline method of sales force sizing builds upon the activity-based methodology. This approach leverages the sales process itself to determine coverage and thus sales force sizing needs. The pipeline method is especially good for sizing sales forces with complex or lengthy selling processes that consist of a series of milestones that advance the probability of a sale.

As shown in Figure 7.10, the pipeline method tracks sales force effort and results through the company's entire sales process. The model begins with a map of the major selling process stages, along with an estimate of the number of prospects entering the company's sales pipeline. The level of sales force effort required at each stage of the sales process is estimated based on the selling tasks required for that stage and the time needed to complete those tasks. In addition, the advance rate resulting from the sales force effort at each stage is estimated. Based on all of these inputs, the model calculates the number of salespeople required to carryout the company's selling process, along with the resulting sales, costs, profits, and return on investment (ROI).

Often, pipeline sales force sizing analysis is linked to the achievement of a sales goal. For example, the pipeline model shown in Figure 7.11 is for a sales force that has a goal of generating an incremental $50 million in sales from new customers. How many additional salespeople are needed to reach this goal? Suppose that historically 25 percent of the prospects contacted by the company request a proposal (RFP) and 50 percent of those receiving a proposal accept and become customers. The average deal size for the company is $50,000. The company expects these historical

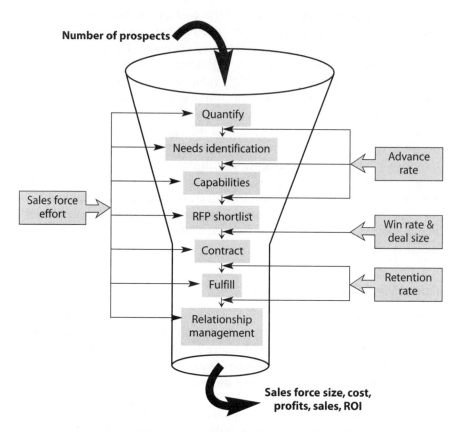

FIGURE 7.10 Pipeline method of sales force sizing

averages to continue in the foreseeable future. The number of prospects that need to enter the company's sales funnel in order to make the $50 million sales goal can be calculated:

$50 million sales goal / {(25% RFP rate) x (50% close rate) x ($50,000 per customer)}

= 8000 new prospects must be contacted

Analysis of the workload required at each step of the sales process can help the company determine how many additional salespeople are needed to reach 8000 additional new prospects, generate 2000 proposals (8000 prospects x 25% RFP rate), and close 1000 new deals (2000 prospects x 50%) creating $50 million in sales (1000 customers x $50,000 per deal).

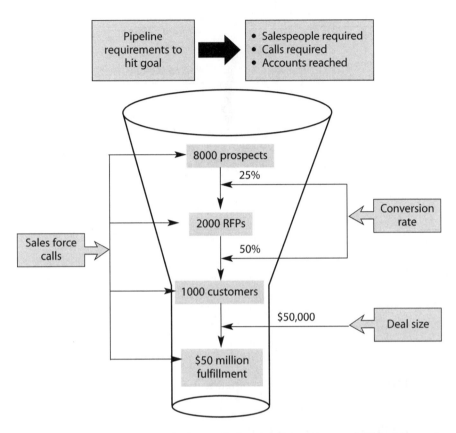

FIGURE 7.11   Pipeline analysis can link sales force size to achievement of a sales goal

The pipeline method example of sales force sizing in Figure 7.12 comes from a company that sells a small medical device to physicians. The company segments physician customers by usage history (users of the company's product, users of competitive products, and non-users who are new to this type of therapy), as well as by patient volume. Pipeline analysis is shown for one customer segment. Similar analyses are performed for all segments, and coverage needs are summed to determine total sales force size.

The company begins by mapping out its selling process for the customer segment. Four major selling process phases are identified. First, leads have to be generated and qualified. Second, qualified physicians have to be educated on the therapy method. Third, once a physician is sold on the therapy he/she must be convinced that the company has the best value proposition of all competitors. Finally, when the physician becomes a customer, ongoing service and support have to be provided.

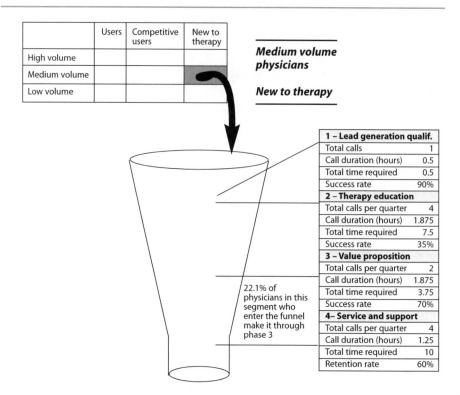

FIGURE 7.12 Example of the pipeline method of sales force sizing

Once the selling process is mapped out, the sales workload required and the success rate are estimated for each phase of the process. For example, the medical device maker estimates that lead generation and qualification can be completed fairly quickly (one half hour per account) and with a high success rate (90 percent of leads are qualified to go on to the next phase). The next phase, therapy education, requires more time per account (7.5 hours per quarter). This coverage is expected to generate a 35 percent success rate. Similar estimates in coverage and success rates are made for each phase of the selling process. All of this data is organized into a spreadsheet model. Additional inputs to the model include an estimate of the number of physicians that enter the sales pipeline, along with an estimate of a salesperson's workload capacity. From this data, the number of salespeople required to perform each phase of the sales process for each customer segment is calculated. Data for multiple segments are summed together to get a total sales force size estimate.

Sales pipeline models vary in their level of sophistication. Some models look statically at a single point in time, while others look dynamically

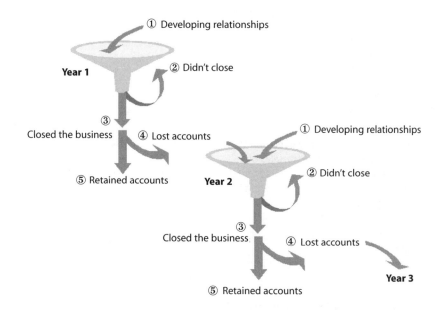

FIGURE 7.13 Multi-year pipeline method of sales force sizing

across several years. Figure 7.13 illustrates a multi-year model. Accounts that are lost this year can re-enter the sales funnel next year. The probability of closing the business with a previously lost account may be different than the probability of closing with an account that is a new developing relationship.

Constructed properly, pipeline models can provide several interesting insights in addition to sales force size. Table 7.12 summarizes some of these insights.

Using pipeline analysis to model selling strategies for current customers

Companies have successfully used pipeline analysis to model not only the customer acquisition process, but also customer retention and growth strategies. Companies have developed pipeline models based on the various stages of their relationship with current customers. For example, prospective customers first became aware of and try the company's products. Continued sales and service efforts against these customers convert them into regular users and ultimately loyalists, the most faithful customers. Pipeline analysis can model how different sales force strategies and investment levels are required to move customers from one stage of the relationship to the next.

TABLE 7.12 Insights provided by sales pipeline analysis

Effort allocation insights

How much time should we spend with each:

- customer segment?
- sales activity?
- product?
- selling channel?

Productivity insights

- What results are required at each stage of the sales process (advance rates, deal sizes, etc.) in order to achieve our sales objectives?
- Are any bottlenecks in the sales process limiting our performance?
- What is the value of better targeting?

Customer insights

- How will our base of existing customers likely evolve?
- What is the impact of a change in customer buying processes on sales resource needs?
- Where are prospects falling out in the selling process?

Approach 3: Target-return-per-call method

Most companies expect a certain rate of return on every investment, including the sales force. This target return on investment can be used as a guideline for determining which customer segments the sales force should cover, how much time should be spent with those segments, and thus how many salespeople are needed.

The steps of the target-return-per-call method are illustrated in Figure 7.14. The method involves estimating both the cost and the value of covering various market segments with the sales force, and then comparing cost and value to determine if the return on investment is attractive to the company. On the cost side, this involves developing an account coverage strategy and allocating sales force costs to accounts in each segment based on the time required to cover them. On the value side, this requires estimating sales and contribution due to sales force coverage for each customer segment. At a minimum, this involves developing a sales forecast for each market segment and subtracting variable product costs. Value estimation can be further enriched by accounting for carryover of effort from prior years as well as carryover of this year's effort to future years. Segments should receive sales force effort as long as the value the account produces is greater than or equal to the cost of that effort times the target rate of return. Once the appropriate level of sales force effort has been determined, the final step is to calculate the headcount required to carry out the coverage plan.

Table 7.13 shows how a large not-for-profit organization used the target-return-per-call method to size its sales force. The organization's

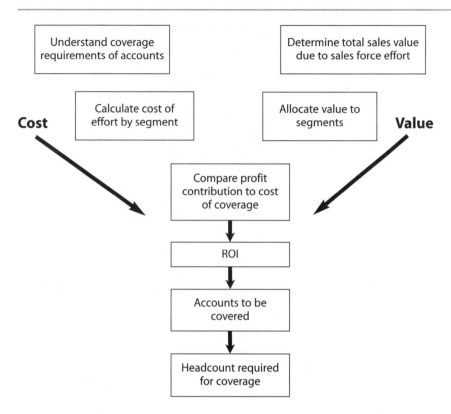

FIGURE 7.14 Target-return-per-call method of sales force sizing

salespeople call on corporations to generate sponsorship revenues. To estimate sales force size, the universe of customers was divided into three
major segments – existing accounts, former accounts, and prospective
accounts. Each of these major segments was further subdivided into seven
sub-segments, based on characteristics such as company size and contribution history. Next, the value of covering each customer sub-segment
with the sales force was estimated. Value estimates were based on analysis of sub-segment growth potential that incorporated historical trends,
primary market research, and sales management input. Next, the cost of
covering each sub-segment was estimated. Cost was determined by estimating the number of full-time equivalents (FTEs) required to complete
the major steps of the sales process for every sub-segment. Like the value
analysis, these estimates were based on data from a variety of sources,
including company historical data, primary market research, and sales
management input. FTE estimates were multiplied by the fully-loaded cost
of a salesperson (including benefits, salary, travel, computer, as well as
allocated costs for training, hiring, and other departmental and corporate
support) to determine the cost to cover each sub-segment. Finally, the

TABLE 7.13 Example of the target-return-per-call method of sales force sizing

Step 1 – Estimate value and cost of sales force coverage by sub-segment, then calculate profit and ROI. ➡ Step 2 – Rank sub-segments by ROI and determine desired depth of coverage and sales force size

Sub-segment	Value of coverage ($)	FTEs required	Cost to cover ($)	Profit ($)	ROI
Existing A	3,487,752	0.45	114,530	3,373,222	2945%
Existing B	25,801	0.29	73,808	-48,007	-65%
Existing C	1,382,440	0.34	86,534	1,295,906	1498%
Existing D	2,952,696	0.19	48,357	2,904,339	6006%
Existing E	6,889,883	0.50	127,256	6,762,628	5314%
Existing F	618,136	0.26	66,173	551,963	834%
Existing G	212,712	0.28	71,263	141,449	198%
Existing customers	15,569,420	2.31	587,920	14,981,500	2548%
Former A	475,128	0.44	111,985	363,143	324%
Former B	0	0.55	139,981	-139,981	0%
Former C	140,940	0.83	211,244	-70,304	-33%
Former D	1,013,292	0.51	129,801	883,491	681%
Former E	111,609	0.23	58,538	53,071	91%
Former F	731,208	0.21	53,447	677,761	1268%
Former G	285,740	0.06	15,271	270,469	1771%
Former customers	2,757,917	2.83	720,266	2,037,651	283%
Prospect A	12,353,643	4.15	1,056.221	11,297,422	1070%
Prospect B	1,986,658	1.28	325,774	1,660,884	510%
Prospect C	2,441,703	2.93	745,717	1,695,986	227%
Prospect D	416,311	0.76	193,428	222,883	115%
Prospect E	2,048,876	0.84	213,789	1,835,087	858%
Prospect F	253,340	0.19	48,357	204,983	424%
Prospect G	209.930	0.76	193,428	16,502	9%
Prospective customers	19,710,461	10.91	2.776,715	16.933,746	610%
Total	38,037,798	16.05	4,084,902	33,952,896	831%

Sub-segment	ROI	Cover?	FTEs required	Cum. FTEs
Existing D	6006%	Yes	0.19	0.19
Existing E	5314%	Yes	0.50	0.69
Existing A	2945%	Yes	0.45	1.14
Existing C	1498%	Yes	0.34	1.48
Former G	1771%	Yes	0.06	1.54
Former F	1268%	Yes	0.21	1.75
Prospect A	1070%	Yes	4.15	5.90
Prospect E	858%	Yes	0.84	6.74
Existing F	834%	Yes	0.26	7.00
Former D	681%	Yes	0.51	7.51
Prospect B	510%	Yes	1.28	8.79
Prospect F	424%	Yes	0.19	8.98
Former A	324%	Yes	0.44	9.42
Prospect C	227%	Yes	2.93	12.35
Existing G	198%	Yes	0.28	12.63
Prospect D	115%	No	0.76	13.39
Former E	91%	No	0.23	1362
Prospect G	9%	No	0.76	14.38
Former C	-33%	No	0.83	15.21
Existing B	-65%	No	0.29	15.50
Former B	0%	No	0.55	16.05

value of covering each sub-segment was compared with the cost of coverage by calculating the sub-segment profit and return on investment (ROI). Segments were ranked according to ROI, and the appropriate depth of coverage was determined. In this case, the company's management had set a target ROI of 200 percent. Thus, they decided that the sales force should cover the top 15 customer sub-segments, requiring a total of 13 full-time salespeople.

Approach 4: Sales response method

The sales response approach employs the "sales force drives sales" concept directly. If the relationship between sales force investment and company sales can be estimated, alternative sales force sizing scenarios can be assessed in terms of their short and long-term sales and profit consequences. A profit-maximizing sales force size can be determined by evaluating numerous alternative scenarios.

Natural variability in a sales force's call coverage can provide data for estimating the relationship between sales force effort and sales. In every sales force, some accounts receive high call frequencies; others receive low call frequencies. This may be due to something as subtle as misaligned sales territories (salespeople in large territories cannot cover all their accounts adequately), or as simple as a territory being vacant for part of a year. When accounts with similar sales potential have different call frequencies, it is possible to simulate the results of sales forces with different sizes. Sales at accounts receiving low coverage simulate what would happen with a small sales force since accounts will, on average, receive low coverage when the sales force is small. Similarly, accounts receiving high coverage simulate what would happen with a large sales force. This provides data for estimating the sales response relationship. A simple sales response relationship is presented in Figure 7.15.

To determine the right sales force investment in high-potential and low-potential accounts, compare the anticipated sales obtained under different call frequencies with the associated cost. Additional sales force effort against the high-potential accounts generates incrementally more sales, and consequently more gross margin, than similar investment in low-potential accounts. The recommended investment in high and low-potential accounts depends on the sales force costs. For example, assume all accounts are currently covered with low frequency. To decide whether or not to increase the frequency to each account segment, compare the cost of the additional salespeople needed to increase the coverage with the expected gross margin increase. For example, assume the additional sales force costs exceed the gross margin increase for low potential accounts, but are less than the gross margin increase for high potential accounts. In this case, the best sales force investment strategy is to increase to the call

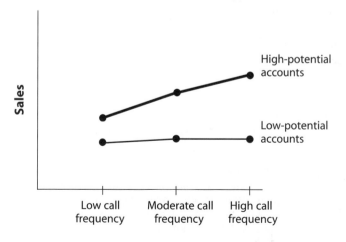

FIGURE 7.15 A simple sales response relationship

frequency on high-potential accounts and keep low call frequency on low-potential accounts.

By determining the best sales force investment strategy for each market segment, it is possible to determine the profit-maximizing sales force size. Using carryover estimates for each segment to forecast the three-year sales and discounted contribution associated with each sales force investment strategy enriches the analysis. Sales, one-year and three-year contribution curves can be established for each market segment using the sales-response approach. An example of these curves is shown in Figure 7.16.

The optimal sales force size for the segment is when the contribution is maximized. This is the point where the contribution graph peaks. Sizing the entire sales force is accomplished by summing the segment-level data for all market segments. This financial analysis can be accomplished using spreadsheet software.

Data for developing sales-response relationships usually comes from two sources: historical data and judgmental data. Cross-sectional and time-series historical data can be analyzed statistically. Examples of typical cross-sectional and time-series data that link sales force effort and sales results are displayed in Figure 7.17.

Both data sets show variation in call frequency. The cross-sectional data set shows variation in call frequency across different sales territories, while the time-series data shows variation over time. This variation can be exploited to forecast how responsive a market is to sales force effort.

Judgmental data can be used to complement historical sales and call data. Judgmental data can be collected by asking sales and marketing managers to forecast expected sales resulting from alternate sales force investment strategies. Questions such as the ones in Figure 7.18 can be used to develop sales-response estimates.

Judgmental data is best captured using an interactive, group consensus approach such as a Delphi forecasting exercise. Delphi sessions can use interactive computer networks to provide instantaneous feedback to participants, who can then revise their opinions in light of information other

---

Which is a better predictor of sales response – data or judgment?

The accuracy with which historical data and management judgment can predict sales response varies by market. Typically, forecasts based on historical data perform better when markets or products are stable. Judgmental data is preferred when markets are dynamic and changing or when products are new or competing in dynamic markets. The best forecasts integrate both judgment and the statistical analysis of historical data.

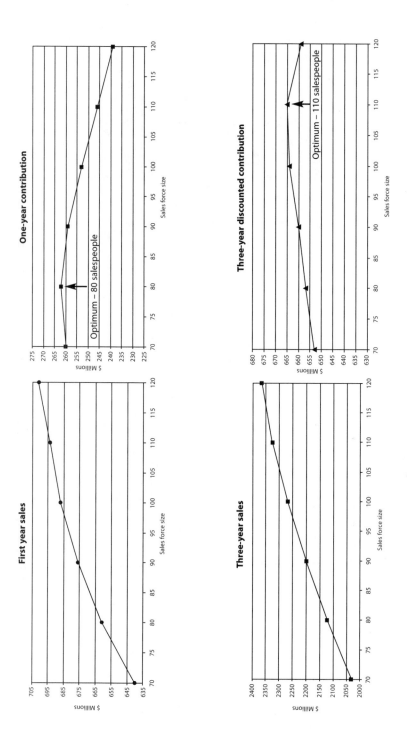

FIGURE 7.16 Sales and contribution for alternative sales force sizes

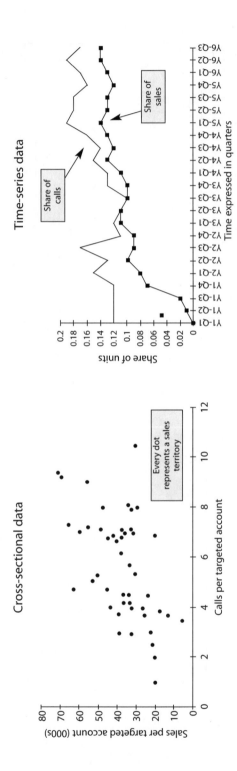

FIGURE 7.17 Historical data for developing sales response relationships

MARKET SEGMENT:
Estimate the expected sales arising from different sales force investment levels.

	Zero effort	50% current	Current effort	150% current	Twice current
Rep equivalents (REs)*	0	4	8	12	16
Sales estimate ($ millions)					

* One rep equivalent (RE) allocated to a market segment is the same as one full-time salesperson spending all of his or her time on that market segment. For example, three salespeople each spending one-third of their time selling to a market segment equals one rep equivalent.

FIGURE 7.18 Sample question for gathering judgmental data for sales response estimation

participants share with the group. Subsequently, useful sales-response estimates are derived.

Approach 5: Geographic concentration method

In some sales forces, travel time is a major part of each salesperson's workload. If salespeople are required to cover large geographies, the location of accounts can be a significant factor in determining the right customer coverage and thus the correct number of salespeople. The geographic concentration method for sales force sizing assumes that a sales force will not want to cover every account in person, due to the high travel cost. Thus, the computer-based model explicitly factors the impact of geography into the sales force sizing decision. With this method, a geographic optimization model builds sales territories by simulating the sales force coverage of accounts, based both on the sales potential of those accounts and on the travel time required to cover them. High-potential accounts take precedence over low-potential accounts. Accounts close to the geographic location of a salesperson take precedence over those that are far away from the salesperson.

One company used the geographic concentration method to determine how many salespeople to add to its US sales force of 57 salespeople. First, the company's sales force estimated the gross profit that could be generated by calling on each customer and prospect. This data was input to a coverage simulation model, along with the geographic location of each account and salesperson, as well as sales force workload capacity and cost data. Some of the outputs from the model are shown in Figure 7.19. The model identified 20 profitable new territory locations and prioritized them by projected returns. The model also estimated the sales, costs, and profits

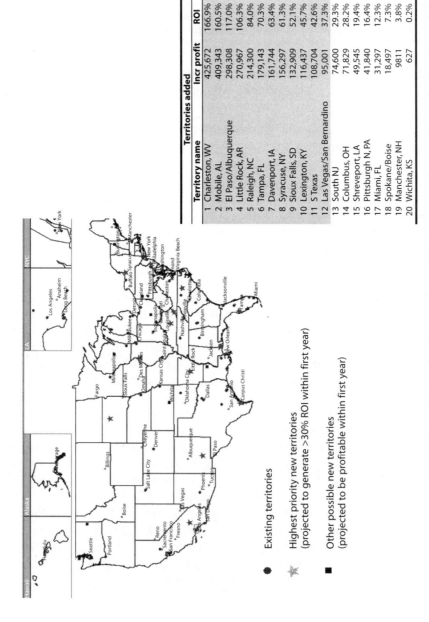

Territories added		
Territory name	Incr profit	ROI
1 Charleston, WV	425,672	166.9%
2 Mobile, AL	409,343	160.5%
3 El Paso/Albuquerque	298,308	117.0%
4 Little Rock, AR	270,967	106.3%
5 Raleigh, NC	214,300	84.0%
6 Tampa, FL	179,143	70.3%
7 Davenport, IA	161,744	63.4%
8 Syracuse, NY	156,297	61.3%
9 Sioux Falls, SD	132,909	52.1%
10 Lexington, KY	116,437	45.7%
11 S Texas	108,704	42.6%
12 Las Vegas/San Bernardino	95,001	37.3%
13 South NJ	74,600	29.3%
14 Columbus, OH	71,829	28.2%
15 Shreveport, LA	49,545	19.4%
16 Pittsburgh N, PA	41,840	16.4%
17 Miami, FL	31,297	12.3%
18 Spokane/Boise	18,497	7.3%
19 Manchester, NH	9811	3.8%
20 Wichita, KS	627	0.2%

● Existing territories

☆ Highest priority new territories
(projected to generate >30% ROI within first year)

■ Other possible new territories
(projected to be profitable within first year)

FIGURE 7.19 Example of the geographic concentration method of sales force sizing

associated with alternative sales force sizes and produced a list of which accounts could be covered with each sizing scenario.

Which market-based approach should you use?

Each of the five market-based approaches can provide a good initial estimate of sales force size. The specific method that works best for each sales force depends upon many situational factors. Often, combining analysis from several different methods creates the best approach. Here are some situations that we have found to be most conducive to using each of the five market-based sales force sizing methods.

When to use the activity-based method

The activity-based method of sales force sizing is often the easiest and cheapest method to implement. It is frequently used by companies that need an answer quickly, that have a strong sense for the range of appropriate answers, and that have limited resources to dedicate to a sales force sizing project. The activity-based method works extremely well for sales forces that perform well-defined and routine selling activities. Since the activity-based method does not directly link sales force effort to results, it is a good choice for sales forces that have difficulty measuring this relationship.

Example: sizing a retail merchandising force

A retail merchandising sales force in the consumer products industry is an ideal candidate for using the activity-based method of sales force sizing. This merchandising force performs routine tasks such as setting up displays and taking inventories at retail stores. Merchandisers affect sales at the store level only indirectly – account managers who have primary selling responsibility also cover stores. Thus, the link between merchandising activity and sales is very difficult to establish. Also, the time required for each merchandising activity is relatively easy to define. Time and motion studies can determine how long various merchandising tasks should take. In addition, merchandisers are required to visit each store with a specific frequency and perform a well-defined list of tasks on each visit. The activity-based approach is ideal for this sales force, since selling tasks are well defined and the linkage between effort and sales is unclear.

A word of caution about the activity-based method of sizing

Experienced managers often have good intuition about what sales force size is best. Activity-based analysis provides a useful way to confirm that intuition. However, the possibility exists for managers to "fudge the numbers" in order to get a desired result. We once worked with a sales vice president who, prior to seeing any analysis, had decided that he wanted to add 100 people to his sales force. The vice president was able to manipulate the spreadsheet containing the activity-based coverage model until the desired sales force size resulted. Since there was no mechanism for projecting how profitable an additional 100 salespeople would be relative to other sales force sizes, it was difficult to convince the vice president that adding 100 salespeople might in fact not be the best answer.

When to use the pipeline method

The pipeline method enriches activity-based sizing analysis for sales forces with lengthy, complex sales processes. By breaking down the sales process, greater insight can be gained regarding how salespeople should spend their time. The pipeline method also provides a blueprint and the metrics to track the progression of customers through the sales process over time. By focusing on the details and success rates of each individual selling activity, managers can provide better input regarding coverage needs. However like activity-based models, standard pipeline models do not require a direct linkage between effort and sales. Thus, they provide no mechanism for projecting the profitability of alternative sales force sizes.

Enhancing pipeline analysis with sales response modeling

State-of-the-art pipeline models incorporate sales response modeling. While traditional sales response models capture the overall relationship between sales effort and results, similar models can be developed which capture this relationship at each phase of the selling process. For example, sales response analysis can model the relationship between:

- time spent prospecting and the number of good leads that result
- time spent writing proposals and the number of proposals accepted
- time spent servicing customers and customer retention rates.

By combining pipeline analysis with sales response modeling, a sales force can project the sales and profit consequences of different sizing decisions. At the same time, the sales force learns the most profitable way to allocate time and resources to the various selling activities.

When to use the target-return-per-call method

The target-return-per-call method provides a fairly easy way for companies to link an activity-based plan with financial projections, thereby allowing managers to assess the reasonableness of a proposed coverage plan. Data for this method, including segment sales projections and coverage costs, is usually easy to obtain, and the analysis is fairly straightforward, making it a good choice for companies that need an answer quickly and at low cost. The analysis is especially useful for companies who want to determine what depth of coverage of the customer universe is affordable. For example, target-return-per-call analysis can help answer the question, "Given the firm's financial projections for next year, should the sales force visit every customer and prospect or should they focus on the largest accounts?"

A word of caution about the target-return-per-call method of sizing

Companies that use the target-return-per-call method often rely on sales projections that are developed independently of the sales force coverage plan. For example, a national goal is set, and then the firm's marketing department breaks the goal down by customer segment, assuming some level of sales force coverage. The model does not require that sales projections change when the coverage plan changes, and this is not realistic. In reality, more coverage leads to higher sales while less coverage leads to lower sales. Managers who use target-return-per-call models need to be aware that the analysis does not link effort and results directly. The link between coverage and financial data provides a reasonableness check, but it does not predict sales and profit consequences of alternative sizing decisions.

When to use the sales response method

Sales response modeling is theoretically the best way to determine sales force size. It is the only approach that directly links sales effort to results, allowing managers to predict the sales and profit consequences of alternative sizing decisions. For this reason, the approach has a high likelihood of producing a good answer. Sales response modeling, however, is not appropriate in all situations. It requires detailed sales and activity data. If these data do not exist, significant investment may be required to develop them. Even with good data, the method is typically the most difficult and expensive to implement because it requires statistics and complex modeling.

Case study: sizing pharmaceutical sales forces

We have developed hundreds of sales response models in the pharmaceutical industry. Pharmaceutical sales forces are ideal for sales response modeling for several reasons. First, the industry is rich with data. Prescription sales of a company's drugs as well as competitors' drugs are captured at a local level (or even at the physician level in some countries), and pharmaceutical companies can purchase this data for marketing analysis. Most pharmaceutical companies also invest in extensive call reporting systems that track every sales call. Sales forces are a significant investment for pharmaceutical companies and are typically the most important way that pharmaceutical products are marketed. Thus, pharmaceutical companies are willing to devote significant resources to ensure that sales forces are the right size.

Only companies willing to devote significant time and resources to a sales force sizing project should use the sales response method. Finally, sales response modeling is most useful in situations where the sales force is the primary creator of sales. If other marketing instruments such as advertising or alternate distribution channels contribute significantly to sales results, the method may not be appropriate.

When to use the geographic concentration method

The geographic concentration method is ideal for sales forces with territories that are geographically large. In the United States, this method has been most valuable to companies with national sales forces of 200 or fewer salespeople. The method helps the sales force significantly reduce travel time and costs by eliminating face-to-face coverage of geographically remote accounts. Since the approach is quite detailed and thorough, it has a high likelihood of providing a good answer. However, the approach requires extensive data including value and coverage information for each individual account (other approaches require value and coverage estimation only at the segment level). The use of geographic optimization models is an art, not a science. The software is highly customized, requiring the help of consultants.

> ### Are there other ways to consider geographic concentration?
>
> Companies unable to invest in the development of geographic concentration models can use simpler methods to consider the impact of geography on sales force size. Many software and mapping technologies exist that draw thematic maps based on a variety of business and demographic criteria. For example, a consumer products company used the thematic map in Figure 7.20 to examine population density as a surrogate for market potential. Accounts that fell in geographic areas of "low" and "very low" population density were eliminated from face-to-face coverage and were turned over to the firm's telemarketing group. Sales force size was determined based only on the coverage needs of the remaining accounts in more densely populated areas.

Scenario Analysis to Handle Uncertainty and Risk

Like most business decisions, sales force sizing choices are generally made in the face of uncertainty. For example, how will customers' priorities change next year? Will there be any new competitors? What will happen with the economy? Will the company's new blockbuster product be ready for launch? Many possibilities exist over which the sales force has no control. Good sales force sizing decisions must consider the risk and uncertainty inherent in the business environment. Risk management is an important part of the sales force sizing decision.

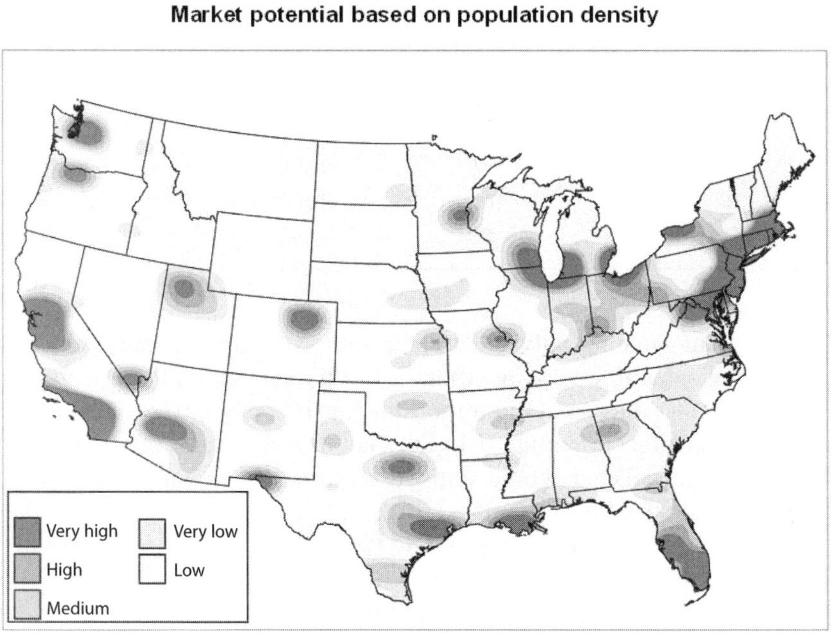

Market potential based on population density

Figure 7.20 Thematic maps can aid the sales force sizing decision

Risk management involves choosing among alternatives to reduce the effects of risk. This can be done with any of the five sales force sizing methodologies described above. For example, a company with three major new products under development is trying to determine the right sales force size. The new products are expected in the next one to two years, but the launch dates are tentative. The sales force needs to grow to support the new products, but timing of that growth is critical to profitability. If the sales force does not grow until the product launch dates are certain, there may not be enough time to hire and train new salespeople, thus jeopardizing the success of the new products. On the other hand, if the sales force grows too quickly before the new products are ready, the firm will incur high costs without sales from new products to help cover those costs.

The company completes a sales response analysis to determine the best sizing strategy for three different product launch date scenarios. The results of this analysis are summarized in Table 7.14. The pessimistic sizing scenario assumes that launch dates for all three products will be delayed by six months to a year. The optimistic sizing scenario assumes that all three product launches will occur six months to one year sooner than current projections. Finally, the realistic scenario assumes the most likely estimated launch dates of all three products.

TABLE 7.14 Sales force sizing recommendation for three alternative product launch scenarios

Launch date scenarios	Optimal team size	Estimated three-year contribution (in $million)
Optimistic	120	1026
Realistic	100	1002
Pessimistic	80	944

Risk management analysis can help this sales force decide which of these three sales force sizing strategies to pursue, given the uncertainly inherent in its situation. It is important for the company's management to understand the potential risk associated with pursuing each of the three strategies. What would happen to three-year contribution if the company pursues a particular sizing strategy and the launch date assumptions for that strategy prove to be incorrect? Table 7.15 provides some insight. For example, what if the sales force follows the pessimistic sizing plan and grows to just 80 salespeople, but the launch dates for the optimistic scenario actually happen? The company misses out on $54 million in contribution ($1026 – 972 million), because it has too few salespeople to fully support the product launches. A risk-averse management team may be willing to risk the possibility of lost sales in exchange for sustained profitability. On the other hand, what if the sales force follows the optimistic sizing plan and grows aggressively to 120 salespeople, but the launch dates for the pessimistic scenario actually occur? The company incurs high costs without the sales of new products to fund them and contribution is $62 million lower ($944 – $882 million). An aggressive management team may be willing to risk lower profitability in exchange for the possibility of high returns from aggressive product launches.

TABLE 7.15 Comparison of projected three-year contribution with alternative sales force sizing and launch date scenarios

Team size	Estimated three-year contribution (in $ million)		
	Pessimistic launch dates	Realistic launch dates	Optimistic launch dates
80	**944**	989	972
90	938	1001	997
100	923	**1002**	1014
110	905	996	1023
120	882	986	**1026**

Stakeholder Validation

The market-based approaches provide an estimate for the right sales force size. Once this estimate has been developed, a series of sales force sizing tests can be used to validate the recommendation from the perspective of key stakeholders. Four tests focus on the needs of internal stakeholders – marketing management, financial management, sales leadership, and the sales force. A fifth test validates the recommendation from the perspective of a very important external stakeholder – the firm's customers.

The stakeholder validation tests build upon the five quick sales force sizing tests described earlier in this chapter. These tests can help you gain acceptance for a sales force sizing change, not only from these stakeholders but also from top management. The tests can also uncover issues that need to be addressed for successful implementation.

Marketing validation: the competitive position test

Marketing managers are often concerned with the effect of a sales force size change on the company's position within the industry. To complete this test, compare the recommended level of sales force support for each major product to the support level of your competitors' products. This will help ensure that the sales force will not be out-shouted and that the company obtains the desired share of voice. A competitive position map, such as the one shown in Figure 7.21, is a useful tool for performing this analysis. On the map, the sales of and sales calls made by major competitors are compared. In general, companies with higher sales have larger sales forces and can thus make more sales calls. Companies with new products have high sales force investment levels in order to build their brand. The map shows what level of sales force investment is required if the company hopes to attain a certain sales goal. For example, the map reveals that successful high revenue products are supported by 200,000+

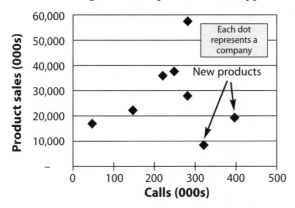

FIGURE 7.21 Competitive position map

> ## Validating sales force sizing changes for product management
>
> When a sales force sells a portfolio of products, the company's product managers are understandably concerned with the implications of any sales force size change on the selling time allocated to their product. Product managers will often ask to see a comparison of sales force time spent on their product versus other products in the portfolio or versus time spent last year. Assertive product managers will fight to ensure their products receive adequate sales force support.

calls and recent launches are supported by 300,000+ calls. If a company has a new product and hopes to become a major player in the industry, it needs to support its product with a sales force capable of delivering at least 300,000 calls to be competitive.

Financial validation: the financial test

At most companies, financial managers track the sales force cost-to-sales ratio. A quick check of this ratio will ensure that it is within historically established company and industry norms. Circumstances can justify a ratio that falls outside established norms temporarily. For example, if a company is expanding its sales force in anticipation of a new product launch, sales force costs will be temporarily high relative to sales until the new product becomes successful. However, it may be difficult to defend a higher than ideal cost-to-sales ratio to top financial management.

Often it is useful to break down the sales force cost-to-sales ratio by product, customer, or sales team to gain further insights about sales force size and costs. For example, the company in Figure 7.22 uses a measure

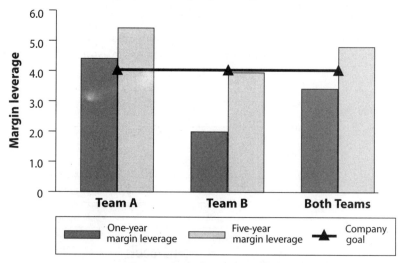

FIGURE 7.22 One- and five-year margin leverage by sales team

called margin leverage to track the financial performance of its sales forces. Margin leverage is calculated by multiplying sales times gross margin and dividing by sales force costs. The company has a goal that margin leverage should be 4.0 or higher. Thus, the sales force is asked to generate gross profits that are at least four times its costs. The graph compares the projected one-year and five-year margin leverage for each of the company's sales teams to this goal.

This company had just launched some new products and was investing in its sales force to help ensure their success. Sales team A was asked to focus on protecting sales of the company's older, established products, while team B focused on growing the company's newer products. Thus, team A was expected to generate "excess" margin leverage to help fund the company's investment in team B for the new products. Over time, team B was expected to increase their margin leverage as the new products became successful.

Sales leadership validation: the selling activities test

The sales leadership will be concerned about how the newly sized sales force will spend its time. Perform a selling activities check by asking the following questions:

- Does the coverage plan devote enough sales force time to the most critical selling activities?
- Do important accounts get enough attention?
- Do important products get enough attention?
- Will the sales force have enough time to prospect for new business?
- Is the amount of travel time reasonable?

Sales leadership will also want to ensure that the sales force is not out-shouted by other sales forces in the industry. Analysis comparing the

---

Smart resource allocation can be more important than smart sizing

One of the greatest benefits of using a market-based approach to size a sales force is that the analysis reveals ways to allocate sales force resources more effectively. Sales forces that allocate time appropriately to important customers, products, and selling tasks often outperform larger sales forces that have an average deployment of sales force effort. For example, our study of sales force sizing data for 50 healthcare companies in six countries revealed that on average, companies who use market-based sizing methods can improve 3-year profitability by 4.5 percent. Of this improvement, a change in sales force size accounts for 1.3 percent of the gain, while a change in deployment contributes 3.2 percent.

company's total sales force size with that of major competitors can answer this question.

Sales force validation: the sales force morale test

The sales force morale test validates a change in sales force size from the perspective of the sales force. Sales force acceptance of a sizing change is critical if the company hopes to keep its top performing salespeople. Ask the following questions:

- How will salespeople and sales managers be affected by the sizing change?
- Will there be an impact on earnings opportunities for salespeople? Does the compensation plan need to change to ensure that top performers can continue to earn good money?
- How will territory goals need to be adjusted?
- What impact will a size change have on sales force travel requirements?
- How much disruption to customer relationships and to sales force reporting relationships will be required to implement the size change? How can we help the sales force manage this disruption effectively?

Customer validation: the customer test

Finally, the customer test evaluates the impact of a sales force size change from the perspective of the customers. Customers will naturally be concerned about how a sales force size change affects them. Ask the following questions:

- How will customers in each market segment be affected by the sales force size change?
- If the sales force is downsizing, what is the customer reaction likely to be? How will we serve customers that will receive less attention from the sales force? How will we complete selling tasks that the sales force no longer performs? How can we reassure customers that they will continue to get good service?
- If the sales force is expanding, what is the customer reaction likely to be? Are some customers going to spend more time with our salespeople? Will multiple salespeople visit the same customer? How will they feel about this?
- How easy will it be to develop new accounts?
- How much disruption to customer relationships will be required to implement the size change? How can we help our customers manage this change in salesperson effectively?

Sales Territory Alignment

INTRODUCTION

Sales territory alignment is strongly connected to sales force performance. For example, consider two sales territories from the Midwest region of a large company. The Chicago territory leads the region in sales and as a result, the salesperson earns high commissions. The salesperson works hard and seems to be always on the road visiting customers. Yet many prospective customers from the territory have never been contacted and some existing customers complain that they are not getting sufficient service. Sales to existing customers have remained almost flat and sales to new customers are low.

The Indianapolis territory leads the region in market share. Customers and prospects are getting plenty of service; even the smallest accounts are seen with high frequency. Yet, no salesperson has successfully earned much commission in the territory and as a result, the territory has high salesperson turnover. The last salesperson who left complained that there weren't enough lucrative accounts in the territory to make a decent commission.

When sales managers evaluate territory performance, they frequently focus on characteristics of the salesperson working the territory. For example, the salesperson in Chicago is perhaps not generating new business because she lacks probing skills and doesn't spend enough time prospecting for new customers. The salesperson in Indianapolis who left the company perhaps was not earning high commissions because he did not work hard enough or spent too much time with small customers.

While these explanations are compelling, there may be another solution for improving sales performance in Chicago and Indianapolis – change the sales territory alignment. The Chicago territory is abundant with customers and potential. The salesperson doesn't have the time to cover it properly. She is earning high commissions just by skimming the business that is easy to get. The Indianapolis territory, on the other hand, does not have enough customers and prospects. The salesperson had penetrated all his accounts so deeply that there just wasn't much business left to get. He was forced to spend his time with marginal accounts, felt frustrated when he couldn't make the same money as other salespeople despite his hard work, and eventually left the company. The problem is the territory alignment. Adjusting account assignments might be the best way to improve everyone's effectiveness.

Territory alignment problems often masquerade as other problems, particularly when performance is involved. Sales managers can attribute poor performance to a salesperson's abilities, when in reality it should be attributed to a poor territory. Similarly, managers can view salespeople as successful when their success is mainly due to having the right territory.

Territory alignment is a significant sales force productivity area that is often overlooked. Our research has shown that most sales forces can significantly increase sales, productivity, and profits by improving their sales territory alignments. Good alignment allows sales force effort to be matched appropriately with customer needs, enhancing customer coverage. Good alignment fosters fair performance evaluation and reward systems, and is therefore closely linked to sales force motivation and morale. Finally, good alignment can help the company keep sales force travel time and costs under control.

WHAT IS SALES TERRITORY ALIGNMENT?

Salespeople have capacity to carry out selling activities. At the same time, customer accounts and prospective accounts have a need for these activities. The assignment of accounts and their associated selling activities to salespeople and teams is called sales territory alignment. Other names for this activity include sales territory assignment, realignment, deployment, districting, and design.

Not all selling organizations specify a territory alignment for each salesperson. For example, many salespeople in the office products, financial services, and insurance industries develop their own alignment in the course of selling business. They can sell to anyone with whom they develop a relationship, regardless of the type or geographic location of the customer. The same is true for many direct selling organizations, such as Avon or Amway. A large majority of sales forces, however, specify each salesperson's or sales team's account responsibility, activity mix, and accountability. Within a defined territory alignment, each customer sees a specific salesperson or sales team.

Sales territory alignments are defined within the context of the sales force structure. Companies with generalist structures often assign each salesperson to a specific geographic area, such as a set of postal codes, counties, or states. Companies with market-based structures typically define their sales territory alignments by specific accounts, in addition to geography. In these alignments, each salesperson covers all the accounts of a particular size, type, or industry within an assigned geographic area. Companies with product-based or activity-based structures define sales territory alignments by product or selling activity, in addition to account and/or geography. In these alignments, more than one salesperson is

---

Some alignments are very complex

An office products supplier assigns each account to up to five different salespeople: a telesales-person who generates and qualifies leads, a generalist salesperson who sells office supplies, a specialist salesperson who sells furniture, another specialist salesperson who sells computer supplies, and a customer service person who facilitates order fulfillment and provides ongoing support. For each account, a salesperson needs to know which activities and products he/she is responsible for. In addition, the salesperson needs to know which salespeople perform the other selling activities, since coordination between salespeople is important to success with an account.

assigned to cover each account, with each salesperson performing a different activity or selling a different product.

WHY IS GOOD TERRITORY ALIGNMENT IMPORTANT?

Sales territory alignment is a recurring sales force management concern. Developing good alignments can be time-consuming and difficult. Yet developing a good territory alignment is very important, since it leads to increased sales force productivity, revenue, and profits.

In this section you will learn how:

- good alignment matches sales force effort to customer needs, and thus enhances customer coverage and increases sales and profits
- good alignment fosters fair performance evaluation and reward systems, and is therefore closely linked to sales force motivation and morale
- good alignment helps keep travel time and costs under control.

Good Alignment Allows Better Coverage which Produces Higher Sales

Well-designed territories increase sales because customer and prospect coverage is improved. A salesperson in a territory with too much work cannot cover all the customers and prospects effectively. The salesperson's time is spent calling on easy accounts, leaving no time to cover other more challenging but potentially profitable accounts. As a result, the company misses out on important sales opportunities. At the same time, a salesperson in a territory with too little work will spend a disproportionate amount of time making non-productive calls, such as calls on low-potential customers. The sales generated from these low-potential customers are likely to be much less than what is possible from the accounts not covered in a heavy territory.

Figure 8.1 shows the extent to which customer coverage needs and sales force capacity is mismatched in a cosmetics company's sales force with 200 territories. This sales force performed merchandising duties at

---

Good alignment enhances sales force productivity

In many sales forces, some of the accounts that are not being covered in high-workload territories are significantly better than the accounts that are over covered in low-workload territories. By realigning territories, profitable accounts from high-workload territories can be reassigned to salespeople that have excess call capacity. The result is an increase in productivity that leads directly to higher sales and profits.

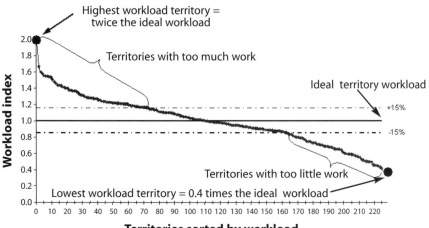

FIGURE 8.1 Mismatches in sales force capacity and customer coverage needs for a cosmetics sales force

retail stores including stocking shelves, setting up displays, and taking inventory. Based on the type and size of store, the company could fairly accurately estimate how long these tasks would take. It tried to create territories where store workloads matched the capacity of a full-time salesperson.

The actual store workload in each territory was calculated and indexed on the vertical axis. The territories are sorted from highest to lowest workload, and each territory is plotted as a point along the curved line on the graph. The "ideal territory workload" line on the graph represents the annual workload capacity of one full-time salesperson. Territories with indices that are significantly above 1.0 have too much work for one salesperson, while those that have indices significantly below 1.0 have insufficient work for one salesperson. By comparing the points along the curved line representing actual territory workload with the horizontal line representing ideal territory workload, it is possible to see the extent to which store needs and sales force capacity are mismatched.

No sales force can expect to have an alignment in which every salesperson has exactly the ideal workload. Due to geographic constraints, salesperson differences, trade area considerations, and data imperfections, some variation in workload across territories is inevitable. For this sales force, it was reasonable to expect almost all sales territories to fall within a range of plus or minus 15 percent from the ideal workload. In the case study shown in Figure 8.1, approximately 60 percent of the territories have workloads that deviate by more than 15 percent from the ideal.

Our research indicates that most companies have alignments in which many sales territories have either too much or too little work. Figure 8.2 summarizes territory workload data for a sample of over 4800 territories from 18 companies in four different industries. Well over half of the territories in this sample have a workload that is either too much for a salesperson to handle (too large) or too little to keep the salesperson busy (too small). Because of this, many accounts in high-workload territories are getting inadequate coverage. If some of these accounts are assigned to salespeople who have insufficient work, overall company sales will increase.

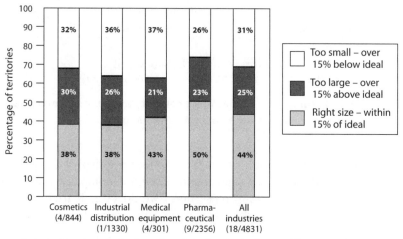

FIGURE 8.2 Mismatch in sales force capacity and customer coverage needs – comparison by industry

One company conducted an experiment to test the value of good alignment. A single sales region with 66 sales territories was selected as a test region. The test region used a rigorous, data-driven, technology-based approach to realign sales territories to match capacity with coverage needs. Regions in the rest of the country containing a total of over 600 sales territories continued to use traditional "seat-of-the-pants" approaches for

---

The cost of a poor alignment is significant

Our research reveals that poor coverage due to misalignment costs most sales forces between 2 and 7 percent of sales. For many companies, this means that millions of dollars are forfeited each year because sales territories do not allow customer opportunities to be matched appropriately with sales force capacity.

making territory boundary changes. One year later, sales results in the test region were compared with sales results for the rest of the country.

The results of the experiment are shown in Table 8.1. A sales growth to market growth ratio was used to measure sales success. A ratio over 1.0 percent means the company's sales are growing faster than the market, while a ratio below 1.0 percent means sales are growing slower than the market. The higher the ratio, the better the company is performing relative to the rest of the market.

The sales growth to market growth ratio in the test territories is compared with the same ratio for territories in the rest of the country (control territories). As the table shows, the test territories dramatically outperformed the control territories in the year following realignment. The company attributed much of this success to the better deployment of sales-people made possible by the structured alignment process that had been implemented in the test region. Better alignment allowed better coverage of customers, which translated into significantly higher sales growth.

TABLE 8.1 Territory alignment experiment results – sales growth to market growth ratios

	Control territories	Test territories
Before realignment*	0.9	1.0
After realignment**	1.1	2.1

* Before realignment data is for the 12 months prior to the test region realignment
** After realignment data is for the 12 months following the test region realignment

Good Alignment Allows Fair Rewards and Boosts Morale

There is high correlation between territory potential and territory sales. Across firms and industries, territory potential is often a better predictor of territory sales than is any characteristic related to the salesperson including experience, ability, or effort. Figure 8.3 shows the relationship between territory potential and sales for three companies in different industries: residential building products, insurance, and medical diagnostics.

Territories with high market potential often have high sales, regardless of sales force effort. In fact, in high carryover environments, a vacant sales territory with high sales potential will sometimes outperform a fully staffed territory with low sales potential. Similarly, territories with low potential tend to have low sales, but high market share.

Frequently, sales managers do not place enough emphasis on differences in territory potential when they evaluate, compensate and reward salespeople. When managers underestimate the importance of these differences and

Building products company – territory sales versus territory potential

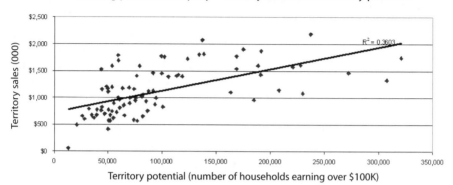

Insurance company – territory sales versus territory potential

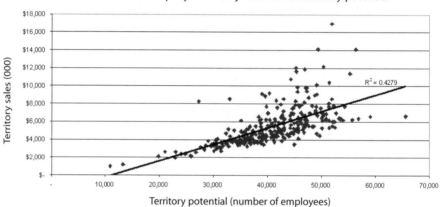

Medical diagnostics company – territory sales versus territory potential

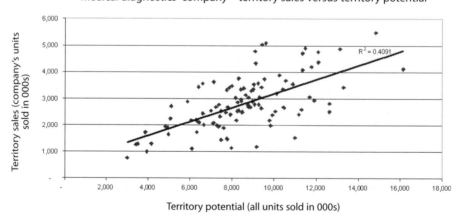

FIGURE 8.3 Relationships between territory potential and sales in three industries

treat salespeople as if their territories were identical, sales force morale suffers. Few salespeople will be content with what they consider to be inferior account assignments while their colleagues make more money and get more recognition with less effort because of superior territories. Territories with low potential, intense competition, or too many small accounts with a high quota are virtually guaranteed to lead to low job satisfaction and low motivation for salespeople. For this reason, unequal sales territories often lead to salesperson turnover.

> ### The importance of territory alignment in high incentive sales environments
>
> The link between territory alignment and sales force morale is especially strong when a large proportion of the pay and rewards for salespeople is tied to their level of sales. Sales forces with highly leveraged compensation plans, such as those that pay salespeople a commission on total sales, need to be especially careful that territory potential is equitably distributed. An equitable potential distribution is also very important in cases where non-monetary rewards, such as "President's Club," are tied to sales results. Differences in incentive payouts and rewards should reflect true variation in salesperson performance – not disparity in territory sales potential.

Companies sometimes misdiagnose territory alignment problems as incentive compensation plan problems. For example, the management at a medical devices company thought that something was wrong with its sales force compensation plan. The extremely wide range of incentive payouts

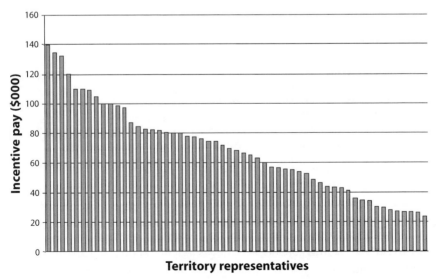

FIGURE 8.4 Range of incentive pay by salesperson

across the sales force did not accurately reflect true performance differ- ences. As the graph in Figure 8.4 shows, the "best" salesperson in the sales force received over six times as much incentive pay as the "worst" sales- person in the sales force. The top ten salespeople (who average $116,000 in incentive pay) earn four times as much incentive pay as the bottom ten salespeople (who average $28,500 in incentive pay). Our analysis revealed that nothing was wrong with the current compensation plan; instead, poor territory alignment was one of the major causes of the significant variation in incentive payout for this sales force.

Good Alignment Keeps Travel Time and Costs under Control

Many companies have successfully reduced sales force travel time through realignment. Travel reduction has a positive impact on sales force morale, especially when realignment distributes travel requirements fairly across salespeople. Less travel also reduces the firm's costs and allows more face time with customers.

Geography plays a role in determining territory difficulty

Two territories with equal sales potential can be inherently unfair if they vary greatly in the travel required to cover them. For example, contrast a downtown Boston territory with one in Montana. In the Boston territory, sales potential is concentrated in a very small geographic area. In fact, many accounts are located within the same high-rise building; travel between them is simply an elevator ride. In the Montana territory, sparse population density causes sales potential to be very spread out. The salesperson travels extensively to cover the accounts, and it is simply not prac- tical to call on every account very frequently. Due to the extreme travel differences, it is not fair to assume that the salesperson in Montana can sell as much as the one in downtown Boston, even though the two sales territories have equal sales potential.

Less travel allows more selling time for an industrial distribution sales force

The realignment of a large industrial distribution sales force resulted in a 13.7 percent reduction in salesperson travel time. This translated into an almost $1 million savings in travel expenses. In addition, the travel time reduction enabled the sales force to increase selling time by 2.7 percent. The company esti- mated that this increase in coverage would result in over $15 million in additional sales, and over $3 million in additional profits.

Companies can also reduce sales force travel time and costs by using less expensive selling channels such as telemarketing, direct mail, and Internet selling to reach low-potential, remotely located accounts or to perform some of the functions, such as prospecting, in the sales process.

Sales are often concentrated geographically

A consumer products firm decided to focus its field sales force efforts in the more densely populated areas, while using telesales to cover remotely located accounts. The field sales force was able to reach over 80 percent of the company's total sales volume by covering just 25 percent of the US geography.

These less expensive sales channels can be used either as a substitute for or as a supplement to reduced levels of sales force effort. While these approaches are not as effective as face-to-face selling, the benefits of travel time reduction often more than compensate for any lost sales.

WHEN IS SALES TERRITORY ALIGNMENT RELEVANT?

Ongoing Adjustments to Sales Territory Alignments

Sales territory alignment is an ongoing process. At some companies, the customer base changes frequently and alignment decisions are made daily. At other companies, the promotional cycle changes frequently and sales territory alignments are built around short-term promotional campaigns. Even at companies with a fairly stable customer base, promotional plan, and selling process, the ongoing course of business requires frequent minor adjustments to sales territory alignments. For example, if a "hunter" salesperson successfully generates business with a new account, the account shifts to a "farmer" salesperson who will service the account and

---

Alignment with a constantly changing customer base

At an office supply company, a dispatcher controls the constant assignment of new accounts to salespeople. The dispatcher is the keeper of the sales force alignment. Every time telemarketing qualifies a new lead, the dispatcher decides which sales-person has the right skills, is in the right location, and has enough time to follow up appropriately. Since this sales force is paid 100 percent on commission, the dispatcher has a very important and powerful position. In making each assignment, he must consider the needs of both the customers and the salespeople. From a customer perspective, the assignment should allow the new customer to meet with a qualified salesperson, and at the same time should ensure that the needs of other customers are not neglected. From a salesperson's perspective, all salespeople want more accounts so they can earn more money. The dispatcher wants to keep the good veteran salespeople happy; they are the major producers for the company. However, good veteran salespeople have accumulated many accounts already, and their repeat business may suffer if they are distracted with too many new accounts. New sales-people may not be as busy or as effective, yet if they are not given a fair chance to succeed, they will get frustrated and leave the company. The dispatcher has a difficult job, balancing the needs of the company, its customers, and the sales force.

---

cultivate the relationship. If a major account relocates its headquarters, the account may be reassigned to a salesperson who can cover it more conveniently. If a major account is lost to a competitor, adjustments to the alignment may be required so the salesperson who covered that account still has enough work to do.

Minor adjustments to sales territory alignments can also be driven by sales force personnel changes. For example, a sales manager may make a temporary reassignment of accounts when a salesperson goes on short-term leave. Similarly, when a salesperson leaves the company, another salesperson may be asked to cover major accounts in the vacant territory until a replacement is found. If an experienced salesperson leaves a territory and is replaced with a new salesperson, some accounts in that territory may be reassigned to other experienced salespeople, until the new salesperson's capability and capacity grow and she is able to effectively cover the accounts.

Alignment with frequently changing promotional cycles

A yellow page advertising sales force has promotional campaigns organized around the publication date of various yellow pages directories. Several months prior to a directory's publication, sales territories are established in the geographic area that the directory covers. Once the directory is published, the sales force moves on to a new geographic area covered by a different directory. In another example, a children's book publisher realigns part-time merchandising territories at the start of every six-week promotional campaign. Since the activities to be performed at various stores vary a great deal with each campaign, changing the alignment guarantees that no merchandiser has too much work or has to travel further than a specified distance from their home. Additional temporary salespeople are hired for the busiest campaigns, such as during the holiday shopping season.

Major Realignments

Major realignments occur every few years at many companies. Typically, major realignment is the result of an important sales force design change.

This section describes seven conditions that create the need for major realignment:

- when a company changes the structure of its sales force
- when a company increases the size of its sales force
- when a company decreases the size of its sales force
- when there are mergers or acquisitions
- when market conditions change
- when a new sales force is created
- when there are new products

When a company changes the structure of its sales force

When sales force structure changes, the reassignment of accounts to sales-people can be a major undertaking. For example, Figure 8.5 shows how changing from a product-based to a market-based sales force structure affects the alignment of customers and salespeople at a consumer products firm. Before the realignment (left-hand side of Figure 8.5), the entire sales organization was structured around products, just like the company's internal marketing department. After the realignment (right-hand side of Figure 8.5), the sales force was organized around key customers, with the goal of improving responsiveness to the needs of those customers.

This restructuring had a massive impact on the company's sales territory alignment. The company had over 2000 salespeople and merchandisers calling on approximately 90,000 retail stores, as well as the headquarter locations of major store chains. The life of virtually every salesperson and every customer was affected by the realignment. From a customer standpoint, the managers and buyers at retail stores and major account headquarters who were once served by salespeople from five separate product divisions now saw a single dedicated salesperson or team. From a sales force standpoint, salespeople and merchandisers who once visited a wide variety of stores including grocery, mass merchandise, club, drug, and

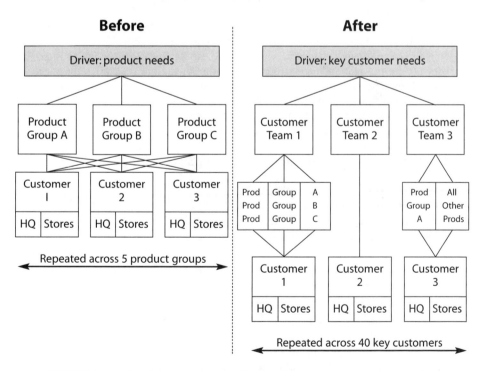

FIGURE 8.5 Sales force structure change at a consumer products firm

convenience stores, now focused on the stores of a single customer such as Kroger or Target. Many salespeople had to learn to sell additional products. In addition to affecting the alignment, a restructuring of this magnitude also has a major impact on other sales force programs and systems such as hiring, training, the role of managers, performance management and compensation, and sales systems.

In order to accomplish this major sales force restructure in just a few months, the company used a structured, data-driven realignment process. The project had strong organizational support at all management levels. All realignment recommendations were reviewed and approved by the company's sales management team. The company considered the realignment to be a success because it enhanced the company's relationship with its most important customers, increased responsiveness to customer needs, and at the same time reduced sales force costs.

Quality of implementation is critical in major sales force realignments

Major realignments often fail or succeed based upon the quality of their implementation. For example, implementation issues caused major problems for Xerox during its 1999 sales force restructure. The restructuring was designed to redirect Xerox's direct sales effort to its most important customers through the creation of industry-focused sales teams. In addition, smaller customers were realigned from the direct sales force to indirect channels. Unfortunately, the Xerox restructure was pushed down from the highest management levels without the full support of the sales force. There was confusion among salespeople, huge disruption of account relationships, and significant sales force turnover. Poor execution impeded what may ultimately prove to be a sound business strategy for the firm.

When a company increases the size of its sales force

Sales force expansion typically comes during exciting times at a company. The company's financial success, growing markets, or new products often drive expansion. Some of the key alignment decisions to be made during a sales force expansion are described below.

Which existing salespeople have too much to do? The customers assigned to these salespeople are likely not getting as much attention as they deserve. A good deployment of new salespeople relieves this workload and gives neglected customers the coverage they need.

What are the best locations for new salespeople? Recruiting new salespeople takes time. The sooner the right locations are identified for new

---

How do salespeople feel about sales force expansion?

Salespeople typically have mixed emotions about a sales force expansion. On the positive side, expansion is a sign that the company is doing well or has strong growth potential. More sales managers may be needed, creating more opportunity to get promoted. Sales territories will get smaller, meaning less travel and more nights at home for salespeople. On the negative side, however, smaller territories mean that most salespeople will be losing accounts and sales potential. In some cases, this means that a salesperson may have to work harder in a smaller territory to make the same money.

---

sales territories, the sooner the recruiting process can begin and the sooner the expansion territories become operational.

How can the alignment minimize disruption to existing salesperson– customer relationships? Existing salespeople have worked hard to develop strong relationships with their customers. Account reassignments should be done in a manner that minimizes any potential negative impact to both the salesperson and customer. This issue is particularly salient for companies planning multi-phased sales force expansions that require continuous realignment.

Minimizing disruption can be tricky with multi-phased expansions

At one company that was continually expanding its sales force many customers were assigned to three different account managers in a period of just over six months. A few customers were even reassigned to a new account manager, only to be realigned back to their original account manager six months later. The sales force became frustrated because assignments were constantly changing. Several top performers left the company. In addition, many customers were unhappy because they felt that all the change showed that the company did not value their business.

Do we need new sales districts or regions? How will this affect sales reporting relationships? Sales force expansions often create the need for more sales managers to supervise the additional salespeople. Companies like to identify the best locations for new sales managers quickly, so that promotions can be offered to qualified candidates within the company and/or recruiting of new sales managers from outside the company can begin. In addition, if the sales force has district or regional offices, time is needed to find a suitable location and recruit office staff. Sales reporting relationships can be affected as well, so that many existing salespeople may report to a different manager. Changing bosses can affect a salesperson's life significantly, and is usually a major cause of sales force anxiety during realignments, although sometimes it can help as well.

What impact will a sales force expansion have on the earnings opportunities, and therefore motivation, for the best salespeople? The impact may be significant when the sales force compensation plan has a large variable component tied to total sales, rather than to a territory-specific goal. For example, a salesperson who is paid a straight commission rate on every sale she makes will object strongly to having her territory cut. Unless the market is growing very rapidly, she will struggle to make the same dollars in a smaller territory as she did in a larger territory. For this reason, sales forces that compensate using commission plans may need to implement a transitional compensation plan during expansions. We frequently find undersized sales forces in such situations because highly paid salespeople in commission environments can be vehement in their opposition to sales force expansions.

When a company decreases the size of its sales force

Downsizing a sales force is a painful process that can be brought on by poor financial performance, loss of a product line, or a change in market needs. Companies that downsize typically face intense pressure to act quickly to reduce costs. The inherent uncertainty causes intense anxiety among salespeople and managers. Realigning sales territories during downsizing is often a stressful and emotionally draining experience.

The major challenge when downsizing a sales force is deciding *"Who stays and who leaves?"* Clearly, it is in the company's best interest to both keep its best salespeople and to assign them to the best possible territories for serving market needs. But implementing this can be difficult.

When making downsizing decisions, companies must look separately at the needs of the market and the individual salespeople. Management's primary goal is to position the company for success in the marketplace. To this end, management must identify the right locations for salespeople and managers, so that the sales force can continue to meet the needs of customers. On the people side, there is a need to determine which salespeople are the strongest and which are weakest. Historical sales data, recent personnel evaluations, and sales management judgment are useful inputs to the people evaluation process.

How do salespeople feel about downsizing the sales force?

Downsizing the sales force is traumatic for both the exiting and remaining salespeople. The exiting salespeople enter the ranks of the unemployed. Remaining salespeople may feel relieved to have "made the cut", but typically also feel uncertain about their future and distrustful of management. Productivity may suffer during this time. Top performers often begin looking for new positions outside the firm during a downsizing, and recruiters tend to target companies in turmoil and transition.

> ### Matching the best salespeople with the best locations
>
> Matching the best salespeople to the best locations is one of the most difficult tasks of downsizing. To the extent that the company's best salespeople and managers are working in the right locations, the decisions are fairly straightforward. However, there will be some good salespeople and managers working in locations that are no longer needed, and weaker salespeople and managers working in locations that are needed. When possible, it is better to relocate a good salesperson or manager into the right location, rather than keeping an average performer or keeping a weak territory. The matching process can be further complicated when sales management positions are eliminated. In these situations, there may be sales managers who should be given the option of taking a demotion to salesperson, rather than being let go. Companies need to be careful that the process they use to match salespeople with territories during downsizing is rational and objective so that it is fair and legally defensible. For this reason, it is best to establish specific rules about which salespeople should be given priority when redundancies occur.

Minimizing the disruption of customer–salesperson relationships is very important when a sales force downsizes. Downsizing is filled with uncertainly for both salespeople and their customers. When customers who may already be concerned about the financial health of the selling company learn that their salesperson is changing, they may feel compelled to consider a competitor's offering. Attention to maintaining key customer relationships is especially important when a sales force downsizes.

When a company downsizes, the average sales territory gets larger. This means that most salespeople will gain accounts and prospects. Sales managers can help to motivate salespeople who survive a downsizing by emphasizing that with a larger territory, salespeople have the opportunity to maintain and hopefully increase sales volume and perhaps personal income as well.

When there are mergers or acquisitions

Sales territory realignment can be especially challenging when a company acquires or merges with another company. If both companies already have a sales force in place, there are often redundancies in coverage and downsizing is likely. In addition to facing all the alignment challenges and uncertainties inherent in any downsizing situation, in a merger there is the

---

> ### Helping salespeople learn how to work a larger territory
>
> A salesperson who survives a downsizing may need help prioritizing how to spend their time in a larger sales territory. For example when Carbis Inc., a company which sells capital equipment to oil refineries and chemical companies, reduced its sales force by 25 percent, salespeople were asked to refocus their efforts only on those customers who were interested in buying immediately.

added difficulty of integrating two sales forces that likely have very different skills, experiences, and cultures. Salespeople may be required to learn to sell different products to different customer segments or to perform different selling tasks as the sales processes of the two companies are merged and redefined. In addition, the merged company is often operating under severe time and cost constraints. Sales executives may feel pressured to paste together a merged sales organization as quickly and as cost-effectively as possible. Having a structured realignment process is especially critical if the company hopes to quickly create a new and improved merged sales organization.

Disruption is inevitable when two sales forces merge

Even with a structured process, realignment during mergers is frequently disruptive. For example, consider the following sales force relocation statistics from the merger of two large sales forces with a pre-merger combined total of approximately 7400 salespeople. Following the merger, 1500 sales positions were eliminated. Approximately 700 of these salespeople voluntarily accepted a severance package, another 700 were terminated, and 100 were transferred to different positions within the company. Of the 5900 salespeople remaining, only 200 were asked to relocate. The company minimized the number of relocations by creating approximately 100 holding territories in major metropolitan areas. Displaced salespeople that the company wanted to keep could work temporarily in a holding territory until a permanent territory opened up near their home. After the merger, the holding territories were maintained as training territories for new salespeople.

When market conditions change

Major changes in market conditions, such as an increase or decrease in competition, a shift in customer needs, and a change in customer buying habits, frequently drive companies to change the overall size or structure of their sales force, thus necessitating realignment. Subtle changes in market conditions can make it necessary to realign as well, even if sales force size and structure do not change.

Demographic shifts affect territory alignments. For example, the US Bureau of Labor Statistics projects that the US population aged 65 and over will grow by 30 percent in the next 15 years. However, the growth varies by region. The southern and western regions of the country will grow by over 40 percent, while the northeast will grow only 14 percent. For firms whose end users are mainly in this age group (that is, health care and leisure travel), this population trend will dramatically affect the right geographic deployment of the sales force. Failure to react to demographic shifts like these can result in missed opportunities.

Medtronic Physio-Control adjusts sales force alignments in Houston

A change in status of a major account had a significant alignment impact in the Houston area for Medtronic Physio-Control, a leading developer and manufacturer of defibrillators and other life-saving medical devices. Physio-Control had a market-based sales force structure in Houston. One group of salespeople sold to the pre-hospital market, which includes police, fire, and EMT units. Another group sold to hospitals. A third group sold a device that can be used by lay people with minimal training. This device was sold to commercial enterprises where people gather, such as large corporations, stadiums, and health clubs. When Physio-Control signed a major contract to supply the entire Houston police force with its defibrillators, the workload for pre-hospital salespeople in the Houston area was substantially reduced. Once this major account was sold, pre-hospital salespeople did not have enough other accounts to keep fully busy. The cost for Physio-Control to dedicate pre-hospital salespeople in Houston was no longer justified by the potential return, since the market was saturated. Thus, the company eliminated several pre-hospital sales positions in Houston, and asked the remaining pre-hospital salespeople in the area to expand their scope of responsibility, selling both to the commercial market and to the small number of pre-hospital accounts that were not part of the major contract. This shift effectively increased the number of commercial salespeople in Houston and decreased the number of pre-hospital salespeople. By adapting the alignment when market conditions changed, Physio-Control allowed the remaining salespeople in Houston to remain productive and successful.

When a new sales force is created

When a company creates a new sales force, an alignment must be established. Three principles for creating effective new sales force alignments are outlined below.

Do it right the first time. When a new sales force is created, the company has a unique opportunity to design a sales territory alignment from scratch, based solely on market needs and company goals. The alignment criteria will be very clear in this situation. Alignment decisions are not constrained by the locations of existing salespeople, legacy account situations, or other historical baggage. There is no need to avoid disrupting established customer and sales force relationships. Companies should take advantage of this unique opportunity by

> ### Successful sales forces respond to demographic shifts
>
> According to the US Bureau of the Census, the mean population center of the United States shifts to the southwest every year. In 1800, the population center was located in Maryland. By 1900, the center had shifted to Indiana and by1950 it was in Illinois. According to the last major census in 2000, the mean population center of the United States is in Phelps County, Missouri.

investing the time to do the alignment right the first time. Once the sales force is in place, the alignment cannot be changed again without resistance from a customer, a salesperson, or a sales manager.

Create the alignment before hiring salespeople. When a company forms a new sales force, recruiting new salespeople is one of the most important and time-consuming tasks. Frequently companies are anxious to start recruiting and begin to hire salespeople before an alignment is established. This is a mistake. Once salespeople are hired, the alignment is constrained by the locations of those people and it may no longer be possible to create the best possible alignment. Companies can begin the recruiting process before alignment is completed, but should wait to make final hiring decisions until the alignment is known. That way, the company knows that it is hiring the best people in the best locations. Recruiting is easier as well, since it is possible to tell prospective candidates exactly what their territory assignment will be if they join the company.

Hiring a salesperson in the wrong location is costly

A startup medical products company was eager to get started hiring 40 salespeople for its new US sales force. Company recruiters were told "hire the best salespeople you can find" in major locations around the United States. One of the top recruits lived in Boise, Idaho, and the company promptly hired him. Unfortunately once the alignment was created it became evident that Boise was a poor choice for a territory location for a medical products sales force with only 40 salespeople. The area was sparsely populated and the salesperson had to travel extensively. The Boise territory had less than half the ideal account workload and potential. If the company had redeployed this resource elsewhere, the returns would have been much greater. More than half of the Boise salesperson's time was wasted because he was located in the wrong place.

Develop a future alignment blueprint if continued sales force expansion is planned. Often when companies add a new sales force, they also plan for future expansion. For example, a new sales force starts with 60 salespeople and assuming success, plans to add an additional 10 salespeople every six months for two years to a final size of 100. When future expansion is planned, the company should lay out a long-term alignment plan, prioritizing the most profitable locations for each wave of expansion. For example, initially identify the best locations for 100 salespeople, and then prioritize the top 60, the next 10, and so forth. By having a forward-looking plan, the company ensures that the alignment for every phase of expansion is consistent with its long-term plan. As a result, less disruption will be required with each expansion wave. In addition, forward planning allows the company to hire opportunistically. For example, if an excellent candidate becomes available in a territory that is slated to become active in six months, the company can consider adding the territory right away, to avoid losing the candidate.

Continuous sales force expansion is often met with resistance by salespeople, especially in sales forces that tie a large variable component of sales compensation to total sales. With each expansion wave, the sales account base per salesperson decreases, making it more difficult for a salesperson to earn the same money as before the expansion. Sales forces in this situation need to plan to change the sales compensation plan as they expand if they hope to keep their best performers.

When there are new products

New products are often the driving force behind sales territory realignments. In some cases, an entirely new sales force is established to sell a new product. New products can also be added to the portfolio of an existing sales force. Often in these cases, the size of the sales force is increased. Thus, each salesperson gives up some accounts to expansion territories, freeing up time for every salesperson to sell the new product. Three principles for incorporating new products into an alignment are outlined below.

The best locations for expansion territories should be based on the combined workload and potential for the existing products and the new product. It cannot be assumed that the number of expansion territories should be uniformly distributed across existing sales regions, especially if the new product will be sold to a different market than existing products. For example, if a sales force of 100 people organized into 10 sales regions, expands by 10 percent, one strategy is to give each sales region one expansion territory. However, this strategy will almost assuredly not lead to the best alignment. If the workload or sales potential for the new product is more concentrated in some regions, it might be better to give those regions two or more expansion territories and others none. Expansion decisions should be driven by data, not by equity for existing sales managers.

Timing of a sales force expansion in anticipation of a new product launch is important. Sales forces should implement a newly expanded alignment well ahead of the product launch date, thus giving salespeople plenty of time to complete training, to become familiar with their territories, and to perform pre-launch activities for the new product. Then when the launch date hits, salespeople already know their customers and can focus on making the new product a success. Timing of an expansion can be tricky when the new product launch date is not certain. It may be necessary to have a contingency plan covering what the sales force will do if the launch is delayed. There are two risks to balance, a product to launch without salespeople in place or salespeople with nothing to sell.

Alignment is affected whenever a sales force's product portfolio changes, even if the size of the sales force does not change. Product portfolio changes affect the distribution of workload and sales potential across various sales territories. Companies stand to lose significant sales and profits if they do not reexamine sales territories alignments when their product portfolio changes significantly.

The impact of product portfolio changes on alignment in pharmaceuticals

At a pharmaceutical company, the patent for a blockbuster drug expired. As a result, the sales force began to spend dramatically less time selling that drug and more time selling other, newer drugs. The alignment of the sales force had been historically based on workload and sales potential for the blockbuster drug. Our analysis revealed that the workload and sales potential of the new product portfolio was not distributed equally across the existing sales territories. With the existing alignment, more than a third of the company's salespeople had a workload of less than 80 percent of their capacity. At the same time, other salespeople would miss opportunities to make profitable calls because they had too much work in their territory. The cost of these missed opportunities was estimated at $32 million in sales annually.

IMPLEMENTING A SUCCESSFUL ALIGNMENT

Sales forces must overcome several obstacles to create and maintain good territory alignments. Yet, the benefits of good alignment are significant.

This section describes six rules for successful realignment:

- Select the right alignment criteria.
- Manage disruption.
- Manage incentive compensation issues.
- Use a structured alignment process.
- Utilize the power of alignment software.
- Audit alignments annually.

Alignment Rule 1: Select the Right Alignment Criteria

Defining alignment objectives

A sales force must begin any realignment effort by defining alignment objectives that are consistent with its sales force strategy. The degree to which the alignment accomplishes these objectives affects customers, salespeople, and company results. Four common alignment objectives are described below.

Alignment objective no. 1: Equalize marginal returns. Equalizing marginal returns is the objective preferred by economists. Economic theory states that when a company allocates a scare resource like sales force effort, profit maximization occurs when there are equal marginal returns to each input. In this case, sales force effort is the input. The theory builds on the law of diminishing returns. Each salesperson has a limited amount of time and wants to spend that time as productively as possible. Thus, a salesperson calls first on the customer that yields the highest marginal return, next on the customer that yields the next highest return, and so on. A territory alignment that allows the last call made by each salesperson to generate the same addition to total revenue will maximize the firm's profits. When this happens, it is not possible to improve total company sales by reassigning any single account from one territory to another.

Recent data and modeling advances make it possible for companies in some industries to measure marginal returns to sales force effort at the account level. When these data are available, it is possible to design territories based on marginal profitability. However, creating this data and using these models is difficult, often requiring the help of an expert. Thus, instead of equalizing marginal returns, most companies use a combination of alignment objectives numbers 2, 3, and 4 below, which are practical alternatives.

Alignment objective no. 2: Match territory workload to salesperson capacity. Having the right workload distribution across the sales force improves responsiveness to customers, ensures that salespeople are challenged but not overworked, and improves sales force morale. In cases where all salespeople are equally effective, the best strategy is to balance workload equally across territories. However, if there is wide variation in salesperson effectiveness, it may be better to give more work to salespeople with greater experience and ability. Some companies have training territories with a lighter workload specifically designed for new salespeople.

Alignment objective no. 3: Distribute sales potential fairly to salespeople. Equitable distribution of potential to salespeople improves sales results and sales force morale. In cases where the sales compensation plan has a large variable component tied to total sales, rather than to a territory-specific goal, the right distribution of sales potential is critical in order to provide all salespeople with a fair opportunity to earn money. Some companies give their most experienced salespeople territories with above-average sales potential. New salespeople have to prove themselves in a smaller territory before they are trusted with more lucrative accounts. Management needs to be careful when using this approach. If a talented new salesperson is not given a territory large enough to allow him or her to succeed, that salesperson may become frustrated and leave the company. To avoid this problem, a company can establish rules that define an acceptable range of territory potential. For example, no territory's potential should deviate by more than 15 percent from the average territory in the sales force.

Alignment objective no. 4: Develop compact, travel-efficient territories. Territories that are geographically compact and travel efficient facilitate responsiveness to customer needs. Compact territories also give salespeople fewer overnight trips and keep travel costs down.

Creative alignment solution leads to equitable distribution of sales force travel in Canada

Canadian sales forces face travel challenges. Canada is the second largest country in the world in area (after Russia), yet it is one of the most sparsely populated. Ninety percent of the Canadian population lives within 200 miles (320 km) of the US border. One sales force wanted to distribute travel time equitably among its Canadian salespeople, so that everyone would share equally in overnight travel. Each salesperson was given two sales territories – an urban territory and a rural territory. A salesperson's urban territory was located in a populous area close to home, while his or her rural territory consisted of smaller towns requiring overnight travel to reach. Some of the most remote rural territories, such as those in the northern territories, could only be reached by small airplane. Each month, salespeople spent three weeks at home calling on urban customers, followed by one week on the road seeing rural customers.

Unfortunately, the different alignment objectives cannot always be achieved simultaneously. For example, it may be necessary to build territories with lighter workload or potential in sparsely populated areas, in order to make them geographically compact. Often it is not even possible to achieve equitable workload and potential distribution simultaneously. While workload and potential are closely correlated, territories with a greater proportion of large accounts will have a higher potential-to-workload ratio, while those with a greater proportion of small accounts will have a lower potential-to-workload ratio.

The extent to which each alignment objective is important depends upon the mission of the sales force, the compensation plan, and the nature of the sales force's relationship with customers.

A comparison of alignment objectives	
Part-time merchandising sales force	**High-commission chemicals sales force**
The primary alignment objective for a part-time merchandising organization in the consumer products industry was to build compact territories with manageable workloads. This would enable salespeople to perform their required duties at stores (stocking shelves, setting up displays, taking inventories) without exceeding the weekly hours limit for part-time personnel.	The primary alignment objective for a highly commissioned chemical sales force was to distribute sales potential fairly. An equitable distribution of potential across sales territories allowed fair earnings opportunities for the salespeople. In addition, minimizing disruption of account–salesperson relationships was very important for this sales force (see alignment rule 2 later in the chapter) because the sales process was complex and customer knowledge was a significant source of competitive advantage.

Alignment objectives need to be defined and agreed to up front, typically by top sales and marketing management. It is also helpful to get input from selected field sales managers. Field input can ensure that "real world" issues are addressed and can also enhance sales force buy-in.

Measuring alignment criteria

Once the objectives of the realignment have been agreed to, the next step is to build a database that can be used to measure the alignment against the objectives. Accurate and complete data is important for a realignment process to be transparent and measurable. If field sales managers do not have confidence in the data, they will not embrace the realignment. A company should plan to spend time creating, evaluating, and verifying any data that drives alignment decisions. Since territories are an aggregation of accounts or geographic areas, even though account-level data may be estimated or derived, the territory-level aggregation can be very accurate.

The best alignment databases include a mix of company internal and external data sources. Internal sources, including customer lists and sales history, reflect the company's experience with its customers. Internal sources also enhance acceptance by the sales force, especially when salespeople are familiar with the data and play a role in creating it. External sources, including market and demographic information, provide an outside perspective, and help prevent biases that can exist in internally created databases. Having more than one data source can also help protect against biases in any single alignment database.

Most companies will develop alignment databases that contain data from two to five separate sources, with multiple attributes from each source. Attributes are the measures that reflect the workload and potential for the sales force. Table 8.2 provides an example of the types of attributes used by companies in multiple industries.

Alignment Rule 2: Manage Disruption

Salespeople depend upon relationships. They have relationships with their customers, with their managers, and with other salespeople on their team. One of the biggest obstacles to overcome when realigning territories is the resistance to disrupting these relationships. Controlling disruption is especially important when a salesperson's customer knowledge is a significant source of competitive advantage. This is generally true in selling environments that are largely relationship-based rather than transaction-based. However, not all disruption is bad. By changing the alignment of the right accounts, companies can improve sales force motivation and increase sales.

TABLE 8.2 Samples of alignment attributes by industry

General

Actual and/or projected sales
• by product
• by type of customer
Market sales
Salesperson home locations
Number of accounts
Population demographics

Pharmaceuticals

Physician specialty counts
Patient volumes
Epidemiological data
Influential physicians
Teaching institutions
Managed care/Buying affiliations
Surgical procedures
Hospital beds

Health and beauty aids

Retail outlet type (mass merchandiser,
  drugstore, grocery store)
Store all commodity volume (total store
  sales of all products)
Call activity requirements

Office products

Number of white-collar workers
Office and distribution locations
Headquarter locations
Number of accounts
Customer types

Newspaper advertising

Classified and retail advertising
Account size
Merchandise types
Advertising potential
Consumer spending

Diagnostic equipment

Testing volume
Installed machines
Contract information

Building materials

Housing starts
Number of architects, builders, contractors
Projected population growth

Disruption from the sales force's perspective

The stress caused by change makes realignments unattractive to many salespeople and managers. Salespeople must give up existing, comfortable customer relationships and establish new ones. Often, the realignment of a single account between territories is seen by one salesperson as losing the best account and by the other salesperson as gaining the worst. Salespeople may feel that time spent cultivating customer relationships is not appreciated by management and was in vain.

In some cases, realignment requires the relocation of salespeople and managers. Salespeople rarely welcome relocation. Uprooting leads to a new social environment, possibly new schools for children, and potentially a new job for the spouse.

Relocation is expensive for the company and is often a major component of a realignment budget. For example, if the sales force shown in Figure 8.6 wants to deploy sales force effort appropriately against market opportunities, 11 salespeople must relocate from the Northeast, Mid-Atlantic, and Central regions into the South and West regions. There may be additional relocations within regions. With the cost of relocating a home-owning employee averaging $60,000, this company could pay $660,000 out-of-pocket. When there are major inequities across regions, entire district or regional offices may need to relocate.

Realignment can also lead to changes in reporting relationships and selling team assignments. Strong established working relationships might be severed, leading to further uncertainty and stress in the sales force.

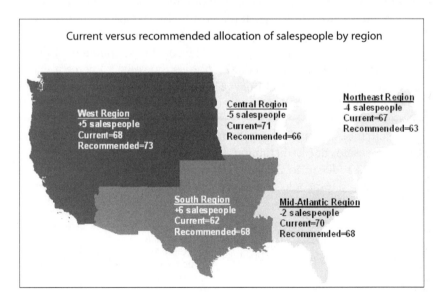

FIGURE 8.6 Realignment can force relocation of salespeople

One of the best ways to enhance the quality of an alignment and to ensure sales force buy-in to the inevitable change that accompanies any realignment is to involve the sales force in the realignment process. Carefully selected sales managers can be part of the core realignment team. In addition, the structured realignment process described below allows all sales managers to be involved in the final design of the areas they will manage. Throughout the realignment process, communication with the sales force is extremely important. As soon as it is appropriate, management should share the realignment objectives and criteria with the sales management team and in some cases, the entire sales force. Often it makes sense to do this even before details of specific changes are shared, so that salespeople understand that the realignment process will be fair and objective.

Disruption from the customers' perspective

In many industries, salespeople need in-depth customer knowledge to be effective. When an account is reassigned to a new salesperson, customer knowledge may be lost. The cost of this effectiveness loss for the following year can be estimated using the formula shown in Figure 8.7. Suppose an account that buys $100,000 a year is realigned to a new salesperson. In this sales force, any salesperson (old or new) can affect only 20 percent of the sales volume, meaning that the account would purchase $80,000 anyway, due to carryover from the prior years' effort. For example, the account may have a long-term contract or buyers may continue to purchase out of habit regardless of sales force effort. Now suppose that because the new salesperson has less customer knowledge, he or she will be 30 percent less effective than the old salesperson. The cost to the company of disrupting the account will be the $100,000 in sales times the 20 percent that can be affected by a salesperson times a 30 percent loss due to new salesperson coverage. Thus, the first-year cost to the company of disrupting this account is $6000.

A well thought-out, comprehensive relationship transition program reduces lost sales due to disruption. For example, each customer transferred should be introduced to the new salesperson by the exiting salesperson. Together, the salespeople coordinate the transition. A compensation plan

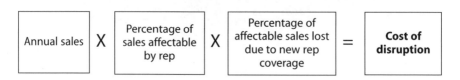

FIGURE 8.7 Measuring the cost of disruption

Can some disruption be good?

There is much anecdotal evidence suggesting that when accounts are reassigned, sales are not always lost. In fact, a new salesperson can actually increase sales with some customers. The best salespeople are not necessarily those who have long-standing, personal relationships with customers. When sales calls become social calls because of the high degree of familiarity, the selling process suffers. Bringing a new salesperson with a fresh perspective into a territory can have a positive impact. The new salesperson may discover ways to increase sales that the old salesperson over-looked. Also, a new salesperson can often make a difference to reluctant prospects and can eliminate some of the "no see" accounts. Realignment provides new challenges for salespeople and extends each salesperson's experience set. It can create the excitement needed to motivate a sales force that has become complacent. This effectiveness gain may offset some of the effectiveness loss due to disruption. In fact, some firms have a policy of routinely reassigning accounts that are not generating the sales that the firm expects.

rewarding smooth transitions encourages teamwork between the new and exiting salespeople and helps maintain customer-company relationships. For example, a salesperson might be paid based on sales performance at both his or her old accounts and his or her new accounts for a period following realignment.

Evidence from an industrial distribution sales force supports the need for a well thought-out, comprehensive account transition program following realignment. This sales force tracked monthly sales prior to and following a major realignment. Two groups of accounts were identified. The "test" group consisted of accounts that were assigned to a different salesperson as a result of the realignment. The "control" group consisted of accounts that were not impacted by the realignment; these accounts maintained a relationship with the same salesperson throughout the period of the study. Accounts within each group were segmented based on their annual purchases into three segments based on sales: small to medium sized, large, and extra-large volume purchasers. Average monthly sales to test and control accounts in each volume segment were tracked over a 13-month pre-alignment period and a 7-month post-alignment period.

During the pre-alignment period, the monthly sales trend for test accounts was similar to the trend for control accounts. During the post-alignment period, however, some differences between the test and control groups emerged. Specifically, large accounts ($50,000–100,000 in annual purchases) in the test group purchased significantly less than those in the control group. On average, sales to these large volume purchasers were 20 percent lower at accounts where the salesperson relationship had changed. For small- and medium-volume purchasers (under $50,000 per year), there was no significant difference in sales between control and test accounts in the post-alignment period. There was also no significant difference in sales between control and test accounts for the extra-large accounts (those with over $100,000 in annual sales) in the post-alignment period. A summary of these findings is presented in Table 8.3.

TABLE 8.3 Disruption impact study – results summary

	Small and medium volume accounts	Large volume accounts	Extra large volume accounts
Annual purchasing volume ($000)	$2–50	$50–100	$100+
Purchasing impacted by change in salesperson relationship?	No	Yes	No
Did strong salesperson relationships exist before realignment?	No	Yes	Yes
Was relationship transition program implemented?	No	Somewhat	Yes

Table 8.3 also provides information regarding the nature of the salesperson's relationships with accounts in each segment. This information provides a possible explanation for the results. Salespeople did not have strong relationships with accounts purchasing under $50,000 prior to the realignment. A change in relationship, therefore, had little or no impact on sales to these accounts. At accounts purchasing over $50,000, salesperson relationships before the realignment were much stronger. A change in relationship therefore had a significant impact. At the very largest accounts (purchasers of over $100,000), relationship transition was taken very seriously. Due to the special attention that test group accounts in this segment received, no sales loss occurred. As this case illustrates, careful planning for relationship transition is often an important part of a successful realignment.

How much disruption?

Significant alignment improvement is often possible without high levels of disruption. For example, an evaluation of a major US pharmaceutical sales force's alignment revealed that in order to achieve the best possible distribution of workload across sales territories, the company should realign over one-third of its accounts. The company's management felt that this was too disruptive. Thus, it considered alternative alignment scenarios which required fewer account reassignments. The company ultimately chose an alignment that reassigned less than 5 percent of the accounts, yet still improved workload distribution significantly. The company projected that the better workload distribution resulting from the reassignment of just 5 percent of the accounts would generate almost $100 million in incremental revenues over time.

Alignment Rule 3: Manage Incentive Compensation Issues

Sales force incentive compensation plans often create major obstacles when implementing a new alignment. Incentive compensation plans influence sales force behavior. Unfortunately, this behavior is not always consistent with what is best for the organization as a whole. For example, incentive plans based on sales volume encourage salespeople to want more accounts than they can cover effectively. More accounts mean more opportunities to build sales. Incentive plans based on market share encourage salespeople to want fewer accounts than they could manage. With fewer accounts, salespeople can penetrate their accounts more deeply and drive out the competition, thereby increasing market share. Finally, growth-oriented incentive plans encourage salespeople to want territories with large numbers of accounts with untapped potential.

Salespeople do not want to give up income. A salesperson whose territory is targeted to be realigned may fight to keep it with the following argument: "I have done a good job for you. I built this territory. It is unfair that my 'reward' is to have my territory split." If management receives complaints from their best performers it may relent in the realignment effort. We have observed that many sales forces that have compensation plans with large variable components are significantly undersized because their salespeople fight giving up accounts so vehemently.

The resistance to realigning sales territories increases as the proportion of pay based on incentive (as opposed to salary) increases. This is because the higher the incentive component of compensation, the more likely a change in territory boundaries will affect a salesperson's income. The table in Figure 8.8 compares the percent of territories that are properly sized before and after realignment. The study is based on data from approximately 2800 territories at eight randomly selected companies, five of which pay mostly salary and three of which pay mostly incentive. As the data show, the percentage of properly sized territories improved significantly after realignment for both the "salary" and the "incentive" territories. However, a higher percentage of "salary" territories were the right size both before and after the realignment. Fear of the potential impact on salespeople's earnings prevented the management of the companies with "incentive" territories from achieving better alignment.

The type of incentive plan also influences the degree to which a sales force is likely to resistance realignment. As Table 8.4 shows, resistance is typically low to moderate in sales forces that have quota-bonus incentive plans. This is because territory quotas typically change when the territory alignment changes, so salespeople are more likely to feel that their income potential will be similar before and after realignment. However with

	Pre-alignment	**Post-alignment**
Incentive	38%	64%
Salary	53%	84%

Numbers shown above represent the percentage
of territories that are properly sized before and
after alignment

**FIGURE 8.8 Comparison of territory alignment quality: mostly incentive
versus mostly salary territories**

commission plans based on total sales, resistance is typically much higher. A change in a salesperson's territory directly affects his or her ability to earn money.

Firms that expect to grow the sales organization continuously may need to think about having an expansion-friendly incentive plan such as a quota-bonus plan, as opposed to a commission plan. Then, if a salesperson's territory changes, the quota can change as well. Concerns over the potential reduction of a salesperson income due to realignment can also be addressed by phasing in compensation changes over time. A transitional compensation plan may cost more money in the short term. However, through better alignment most companies realize a long-term benefit of 2 to 7 percent higher sales. These incremental sales can be used in part to fund the temporary cost of the transitional compensation plan.

TABLE 8.4 Resistance to realignment varies with different incentive plans

Type of plan	Salary	Quota-bonus		Commission on total sales	
		Less than	Over	Less than	Over
% at risk	0%	15%	30%	30%	50%
Resistance to realignment	Low	Low	Moderate	High	Very high

How to implement a transitional compensation plan

There are many ways to design a transitional compensation plan. Suppose a company estimates that the business a salesperson loses when his or her territory is split will replace itself in three years. During that time the company can devise a plan to pay salespeople a portion of what they earned before a split, as long as they meet or exceed a performance standard. For example, in his or her first year with a new territory, a salesperson might be guaranteed 100 percent of last year's pay, then 75 percent the second year, and 50 percent the third. Making the guarantee contingent upon meeting a performance standard is important, to prevent salespeople from becoming complacent. Another approach is to continue to give each salesperson some fraction of commission on accounts he or she loses through realignment for a period of time. This fraction can diminish over time. This approach provides incentive for the old salesperson and new salesperson to work together to ensure a smooth account transition.

Alignment Rule 4: Use a Structured Alignment Process

Sales force realignment should be viewed by the company as a significant change management effort. If it is to be successful, realignment must be handled carefully and intentionally using a well-thought-out process.

The costs and benefits of delegating the alignment task to first-line sales managers

When faced with a major realignment, many companies delegate the work to the first-line sales managers who manage the salespeople directly. The company feels that these managers have the best knowledge of local conditions and are therefore most qualified to determine where territories should be realigned. In addition, delegating alignment decisions forces first-line managers to take responsibility for the changes. That way they can manage any dissonance that arises from salespeople. Also, delegating the alignment task to first-line sales managers gets many people involved so the work is shared and gets done quickly.

While delegating alignment has many advantages, there is one major disadvantage. Even if first-line managers develop a good alignment within their area of responsibility, major inequities may exist across the country. Because of the different experiences, personalities, and viewpoints of field sales managers, cross-regional personnel allocations are often based on inconsistent criteria. These regional headcount misallocations contribute to national territory misalignment even in cases where sales managers develop good local alignments.

> ### Management judgment regarding alignment decisions can be inconsistent
>
> A sales organization operating under a decentralized regional structure gave regional managers the authority to determine the appropriate sales headcount for their region. To provide a basis for comparison, a national model was created which allocated headcount to regions based upon the percentage of national market potential in each region. One regional manager, whose background was in sales, requested a significantly larger number of salespeople than the national model suggested. Coming from a sales background, this manager knew that "more people mean more sales." In contrast, another regional manager, whose background was in finance, requested significantly fewer people than the national model suggested. Coming from a finance background, this manager knew that "more people imply higher costs." In addition, more people mean more management and more work, which some managers want to avoid.

A process that works: central alignments with local adjustment

The best way to accomplish successful realignment is to have a central alignment that acts as a benchmark, with local adjustments. The central benchmark alignment should be created by an objective party, and should be based on objective business criteria. It should use consistent logic for determining staffing needs across the country. It provides quantifiable criteria against which all alignments can be judged. Local adjustments to this central benchmark can then ensure that local conditions are taken into account. The process of incorporating local input also facilitates acceptance of the realignment by the entire sales organization.

Figure 8.9 illustrates a seven-step process for realignment that integrates central benchmarking and local adjustment. In Step 1, alignment criteria such as "maximize profits," "distribute workload equitably," and "minimize disruption" are determined. In Step 2, a database is developed. The database usually includes customer and prospect locations, travel time data, and alignment attributes such as market potential, sales, and workload. In Step 3, proposed sales territory headquarter locations are determined centrally, based on business needs. A headquarter location is the city or area out of which the territory will be based. This is also called the territory center. For larger sales forces with several management levels, centers for sales regions or districts are determined as well.

This analysis defines where each member of the sales force should be located in order to cover the market effectively. It is important to determine the best sales force locations first, before creating territories. It is impossible to create good territories if salespeople are located in the wrong places. Preliminary personnel assignments are made at this time. This gives management a preview of where to start hiring salespeople and managers (if an expansion is planned), who stays with the sales force (if a downsizing is anticipated), or who needs to relocate (if several sales forces merge and are integrated).

In Step 4, the sales management team audits and adjusts the sales territory centers and personnel assignments. In small sales forces, the leader of the sales force performs this task, while in larger sales forces an audit group takes on the task. The audit group should include multiple management levels, such as regional or divisional sales directors and district managers. In Step 5, optimal territory alignments are developed centrally. Territories are grouped into regions or districts to create the sales management structure if required. Also, the proposed personnel assignments are adjusted once again, since the specific geography and account assignments for each territory are now known.

In Step 6, the alignments and personnel assignments are audited and finalized once again with the help of the sales management team. The input of first-line sales managers is critical at this point in the process. Since these managers oversee the salespeople directly, they are intimately familiar with the needs of local markets and sales personnel. Their input facilitates a smooth implementation of the new alignment in Step 7 of the process.

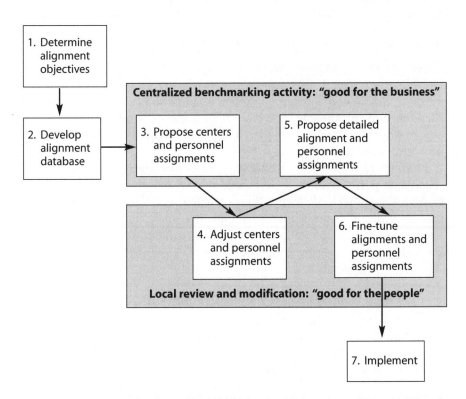

FIGURE 8.9 A process for realignment – central benchmarking with local review

The process illustrated in Figure 8.9 facilitates successful implementation of alignment changes. The process builds an alignment that is "good for the business" because the central benchmarking activity defines consistent, objective alignment criteria that support the company's strategic goals for the sales force. The central benchmark also ensures that salesperson resources are distributed appropriately across the nation. At the same time, the process builds an alignment that is "good for the people" because the input of local management is a fundamental part of the process.

The value of sales force buy-in during realignment

The human resources director at a large pharmaceutical firm summarized the value of sales force buy-in during realignment: "A lot of people don't realize this, but after an alignment, most of the dirty work ends up in my office. After we aligned poorly five years ago, I received almost 1000 complaints from the field force. We did it right two years ago. I received only two complaints. We had a minimum of disruption, relocations, and turnover." Another quotation from a district sales manager: "My input was taken into account. Management didn't just give me an alignment and say 'go work it.'"

Alignment Rule 5: Utilize the Power of Alignment Software

There are many different ways to assign accounts to salespeople. In fact, there are over 1000 ways to assign just ten accounts to two salespeople. Since the problem grows exponentially with additional accounts and salespeople, one can imagine the enormity of the task for any reasonably sized sales force. For large, complex sales forces, the problem is immense.

Fortunately with today's technology, sales managers no longer have to spend days poring over maps and account-level reports to perform realignments. Computerized technologies, when coupled with structured processes like the one shown in Figure 8.9, make it possible for sales managers to create good alignments quickly without frustration and without losing significant time in the field.

Alignment software handles alignment complexity

The consumer products firm that restructured from a product-based to a market-based structure (see Figure 8.5) had 2000 salespeople and merchandisers, 40 vertical teams focusing on important accounts, plus a generalist team for smaller and rural accounts. There were five different types of salespeople selling five categories of products to over 90,000 accounts. To facilitate teamwork among different types of salespeople, many territories had to overlay geographically. Developing a good alignment for this sales force would be virtually impossible without the aid of computers.

Three types of software are available to enhance the territory realignment process. Territory optimization software uses algorithms that evaluate millions of potential alignments to find one that best meets specified criteria regarding territory profitability, workload, sales potential, size, travel, and/or disruption. Territory alignment evaluation software allows sales managers to create their own "what if" alignment scenarios using computerized maps and worksheets. Finally, personnel matching software helps companies assign salespeople to territories based on criteria that are consistent, objective, and fair. All of these types of software are available on personal computers. Territory alignment evaluation capabilities are also available over the Internet.

Territory optimization software

Territory alignment optimization software harnesses the computational capabilities of computers to create alignments. To use this software, a company's territory alignment objectives are formulated as a mathematical problem for a computer to solve. For example, the computer model can be instructed to maximize sales or profits while matching territory workload or sales potential to each salesperson's capacity. Constraints on territory travel time, maximum allowable disruption, or the integrity of geographic trade areas can be included as well.

We have developed algorithms to find optimal sales territory alignments and use them in our consulting practice at ZS Associates. Because optimizers can generate multiple alignment scenarios quickly, they are especially valuable to companies that want to compare several alignment alternatives. For example, one company used an optimizer to compare alignments for several alternative sales force sizes. Another used an optimizer to assess the trade-off between achieving an ideal sales territory workload distribution and minimizing the disruption of existing relationships. Still another company used an optimizer to assess how alternative territory radius limits would affect customer coverage. Finally, companies

---

Sample statistics produced by alignment optimization software

- The number of profitable calls the sales force can make, after considering salesperson capacity and territory travel requirements.
- The number of missed opportunities (the number of profitable calls that will not get made because salespeople are too busy).
- The capacity utilization of salespeople (the extent to which a salesperson's time is utilized effectively with profitable calls).
- A measure of territory compactness, such an average territory radius.
- The amount of sales force disruption (the number of accounts reassigned to a different salesperson).

have used optimizers to create multi-year alignments for sales forces experiencing multi-phased expansion or contraction.

The summary statistics provided by territory alignment optimizers make it possible to easily compare different alignment options. Alignment optimization outputs can include maps, graphs, and spreadsheets, as shown in Figure 8.10.

The most sophisticated territory optimization models mimic the behavior of smart salespeople. The models trade off the sales potential of a customer against the workload required for that customer. High-potential customers take precedence over low-potential customers. Customers geographically close to the home location or territory office of a salesperson take precedence over those that are far away from the salesperson's location. Thus, the model provides a realistic simulation of what is likely to happen if the alignment were implemented.

While alignment optimization is very powerful, it is typically not enough. For a successful alignment implementation, it is critical to obtain input directly from sales management. It is impossible for a computer to represent the full complexity of a sales environment or understand the local nuances of salespeople, customers, and prospects. Optimization algorithms are based on data and rules, and data are not perfect and rules have exceptions. The only time a company can expect to implement an alignment created by optimization software without changes, in our experience, is when a new sales force is created from scratch.

Territory alignment evaluation software

Territory alignment evaluation software, typified by the ZS Associates MAPS® software, applies computer power to a data intensive and complicated task. A typical MAPS® application combines a computerized map of territories with workload, market, and sales data for the accounts or geographic units that make up the territories. A first-line manager working on either a personal computer or over the Internet can adjust territories to see how sales and potential would be redistributed in the revised alignment.

Using MAPS® greatly simplifies the alignment task. For example, every account is shown with a symbol on a map on the screen. The account is colored to indicate which sales territory it "belongs to." It is also possible to see any numerical data associated with the account, such as sales of a particular product. With one click of a mouse, an account can be moved from one sales territory to another. A report is instantly available listing accounts by territory, including totals of any data included in the database. For large alignments, this type of software saves a great deal of time and money.

Proposed alignment for the Albany, New York Sales District

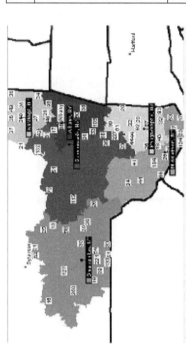

Territory Location	Possible Calls	Achievable Calls	Missed Calls	Capacity Utilization
Saratoga, NY	1512	1502	10	93%
Albany, NY	1786	1586	200	99%
Schenectady, NY	1597	1597	0	99%
Binghamton, NY	1797	1610	187	100%
Poughkeepsie, NY	1584	1584	0	98%
Middletown, NY	1659	1610	49	100%
White Plains, NY	1580	1465	115	91%
Yonkers, NY	1670	1515	155	94%
	13185	12469	716	97%

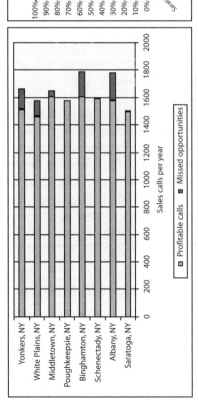

FIGURE 8.10 Sample output from a territory alignment optimizer

---

Features of territory alignment evaluation software

- Is interactive, easy to use, and menu driven.
- Integrates any data needed to align with geographic data.
- Provides on screen maps showing roads, geographic boundaries, and individual account locations.
- Supports easy access to the data attributes associated with individual accounts and higher level geographic units.
- Compares attributes across territories, districts, and regions and computes area totals.
- Models multiple types of sales forces and supports various hierarchy schemes.
- Allows several alignment scenarios to be saved and compared.

Personnel matching software

Personnel matching software helps streamline the difficult task of assigning salespeople to territories after realignment. Even with the best of intentions, it is often hard for managers and decision makers to remove personal bias and make decisions that are truly best for the whole company. Companies that want to be fair and avoid lawsuits should use criteria that are consistent and objective when making personnel assignments. Software that aids in this task has proved to be especially useful in situations requiring major realignment and reassignment of personnel, such as the merging of multiple sales forces, significant downsizing of a sales force, or other major sales force restructuring.

Personnel matching software recommends an assignment of salespeople to territories based on an objective set of decision rules. These rules can be customized and prioritized appropriately for each situation. Sales management controls the hierarchy and weighing of the rules. For example, the assignment rules might be as in Table 8.5.

The preliminary assignments suggested by the software can be adjusted, based on management input. The software aids in this process by tracking changes, providing status reports for matched/unmatched personnel and staffed/vacant districts and territories, and generating disruption summaries.

Alignment Rule 6: Audit Alignments Annually

We have has worked with companies that have not analyzed their territory alignment in five to ten years or longer. Alignments that have been neglected for long periods of time are usually seriously out of sync with current market needs. These companies are leaving millions of dollars on the table, as many valuable customers are not getting the attention they deserve and many talented salespeople are not being fully utilized. Every alignment should be examined annually to ensure that it keeps pace with ongoing market and product-line change.

TABLE 8.5 Sample assignment rules for personnel matching software

A salesperson who ...	Gets priority over a salesperson who ...
Lives close to the territory center	Lives far from the territory center
Lives within the territory	Does not live within the territory
Currently covers many of the accounts in the territory	Currently covers only a few or none of the accounts in the territory
Currently sells the same products or performs the same selling tasks	Does not currently sell the same products or perform the same selling tasks
Has an "exceptional" performance rating	Has an "average" performance rating
Has been with the company a long time	Was recently hired by the company

Territory alignment audit questions

- How has the market changed? Has a change in competition triggered the need for additional sales force effort?
- How has the company's product portfolio changed? Does the alignment reflect the new product priorities specified in the marketing plan?
- How has the selling process changed? Is the same amount of effort required to close a sale? Are salespeople required to perform additional sales activities?
- How has the target customer profile changed? Are the right prospects included in the existing territory alignment?
- Which territories or regions are growing and which are declining? What are the reasons behind these changes?
- Are there better data sources available for consumer and market information?
- Are the internal data sources up-to-date and as accurate as can be?
- Is the sales force highly motivated and excited about prospects at the company?
- Does the sales force appear to be over or under worked?
- Do the sales territories match sales force efforts with customer needs?

Managing territory vacancies

Salesperson turnover creates opportunities to re-deploy sales effort without relocating salespeople. A vacant territory in a low potential area can be closed down, and a new person can be hired in another location with greater opportunity. One national sales manager keeps a sales force location map in his file cabinet. The map is the future blueprint for his sales organization. On the map, each territory is represented with a dot in one of three colors. Green dots are existing territories with good future potential, black dots are existing territories with poor future potential, and yellow dots are proposed new territory locations. Each time a territory is vacated, the manager checks the map. If a vacancy occurs in a black dot territory, the territory is closed and a new territory is opened up in a yellow dot location. Through proactive attrition management, the sales organization maintains a good alignment without relocating salespeople.

Sustaining the Successful Selling Organization

INTRODUCTION

This book has focused on sales force design. Sales force redesign is a major decision for most companies. It usually takes a significant event for a company to initiate a redesign. Earlier chapters described the types of triggers – the five forces – that spur resizing or restructuring of a selling organization. A company that has not achieved its forecast for several years because the sales force is not delivering sales will redesign. Market dynamics, such as customer consolidation and commoditization, will render a current structure obsolete. Companies will create a new sales force as they enter new markets with new products. An aggressive competitor can re-energize an entire industry by expanding its sales forces. Very rarely do companies redesign when productivity improvement is the only benefit for the change. The disruptive nature and the potential risks associated with change usually make companies defer the redesign decision until a significant event actually requires that change occur.

Best-in-class sales forces do not wait until they absolutely need to restructure to increase performance. Sales leadership in these firms is constantly dissatisfied and continuously seeks ways to improve and get better. The intense competition that exists in most markets today compels companies to continuously improve their sales processes while at the same time reducing selling costs. Continuous improvement within the sales force can happen in many different ways. A salesperson uses travel and waiting time to connect with customers on the telephone. An overly aggressive agenda for an internal sales force meeting reduces the meeting's duration and allows salespeople to spend more time in the field. The expense approval process is streamlined to reduce administrative time. An on-demand computer-based training module reduces travel and enhances impact. A contest focuses attention on a competitive product launch. Goal-setting is improved with new territory-level data on sales potential. Marketing people who understand customer and salesperson needs increase the time they spend in the field to 40 percent, enhancing salesperson effectiveness.

The continuous vigilance of a strong sales management team also enhances a sales force's ability to evolve and adapt when faced with significant new external or internal challenges. Changing the sales force design is just one way that companies respond to change pressures. Frequently, an effective response is possible without redesigning the sales force, by adjusting the systems and processes that affect the sales force. A new hiring profile may be needed. Sales training programs may need an update. Sales support systems may need enhancement. The incentive plan may need adjustment or a completely new look. The performance management system may need to be upgraded to reflect the needs of a new environment. Sales effort may need to be redeployed to different products or customers with greater profit potential. Whatever adjustments are made, the new systems and processes must align well with the current sales force design in order for a firm to serve the needs of its customers effectively and at the same time achieve its goals.

This chapter describes the sales force components and systems that are needed to make any sales force design work well, and it also discusses how a sales force can sustain its effectiveness over time. The chapter begins by providing two frameworks for thinking about the sales force: a Sales Force Monitor for constantly assessing the sales organization and a Sales Force

---

Rapid Coat tightens up sales management on multiple fronts

Rapid Coat is a small manufacturer of powders for powder coating. Being focused most on production, it added salespeople in an ad hoc manner over several years, and the mandate was simple:"Go get orders." Orders came in, products were shipped, but collections lagged and Rapid Coat was in dire straits with a severe cash crunch. There had been low control on the quality of orders and insufficient attention paid to the ability of the customers to pay promptly. Rapid Coat focused more on the technical quality of the product and the logistics of delivery. The ten salespeople all worked for the founder.

Just having salespeople in a particular configuration was clearly not enough. Other systems needed to be improved and aligned. In 1999, in a revamp of its sales function, a professional sales manager was hired. The company segmented its customers into three groups – small job coaters, medium-sized coaters, and large OEMs and multinational users. A segment-specific and sometimes customer-specific product, sales process, pricing, placement, and credit policy was implemented. The company became customer-focused, agile, and prompt in reacting to their needs. An ISO 9001:2000 system was installed in 2001 for continually improving customer satisfaction and other quality objectives. A performance management system and various training and coaching programs for salespeople were put in place. These actions not only brought the company out of the red but also set it on a healthy growth path.

Productivity Framework for understanding sales force dynamics and diagnosing problems. Following the frameworks, the chapter describes four ways that sales leaders identify and address sales force issues, concerns, challenges, and opportunities. Specific examples of analytical tools that the firm can use to identify ways the sales force can improve continuously are also provided. Following this is a discussion about the successes and failures of companies who have instituted cross-country and cross-division sales force effectiveness programs.

A THINKING FRAMEWORK FOR SALES FORCE EFFECTIVENESS

Sales forces are complex. Their effectiveness depends upon hundreds of factors. It is virtually impossible for everything to be going right in a sales force. Consequently, successful sales leaders can never be complacent with the status quo. They must constantly assess and evaluate the selling organization, looking for improvements and adapting when necessary.

Figure 9.1 presents a thinking framework – the Sales Force Monitor – that can be used on an ongoing basis to examine and improve the selling organization. The framework is very general and organic. It is likely that most selling organizations are already using a similar thinking framework.

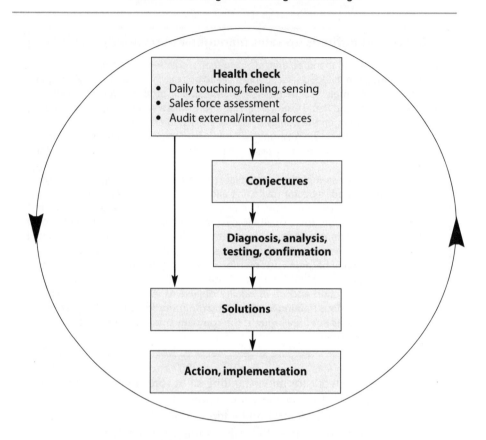

FIGURE 9.1 Sales Force Monitor

What will be unique to this approach will be the models and analytics that enhance various steps within the framework.

The Sales Force Monitor begins with a Health check. The firm's sales leadership team is constantly in touch with the selling organization. It is feeling and sensing its needs and its effectiveness. It sees the issues, challenges, and opportunities that arise regularly. It can anticipate significant external and internal events that might disrupt the current selling process. Dedicated leaders are consumed by this activity.

Sometimes leaders see solutions to their sales force concerns very quickly. A new product launch requires a change in the selling process. Sales leadership decides to upgrade the training program by offering an online module to quickly educate the field on the new requirements. An incentive compensation plan is not paying for performance. Goals were set too low and the field is getting unjustifiable windfall gains. Sales leadership decides to quickly adjust its goal-setting paradigm and its incentive plan payout structure.

Other times, solutions for sales force issues and challenges are not obvious. The sales force is relying on existing accounts and not developing enough new business – Why? Our salespeople are not as good as the competitor's salespeople – Why? Conjectures are needed to try to get to the heart of the problem. Through diagnosis, analysis, and testing, each conjecture is either accepted or rejected. Solutions to the conjectures provide the foundation for good remedies.

Solutions need to be implemented, tracked, and adjusted when necessary. The process continues, over and over, as the sales force improves with each iteration.

A SALES FORCE PRODUCTIVITY FRAMEWORK

Figure 9.2 shows a Sales Force Productivity Framework with five components. The framework is a causal model in that the components affect one another in a sequential fashion. For example, sales force activity affects customer results and customer results have an impact on company results. Meanwhile, the skills, capabilities, values, and motivation of the salespeople drive their behavior and activities. Finally, there is a set of fundamental decisions that every selling organization needs to make that affects the salespeople, the activity, customer results, and company results. These fundamental decisions are called the Sales Force Drivers.

Each of the five components of the Sales Force Productivity Framework is described below, moving from right to left in the framework. Sales, profits and market share are outputs of the sales force system. They are also the metrics that the company uses to evaluate its performance. A well-honed selling organization helps the company achieve its financial objectives.

Company results can be measured in terms of absolute levels, percent of goal attainment, or growth over last year. It is useful to evaluate these statistics from both a short-term and a long-term perspective, because sales force decisions affect both time frames.

Customer results drive company results. Customers buy consistently from

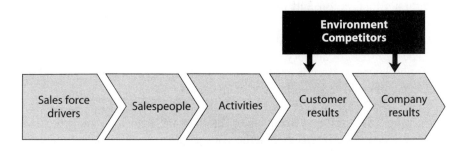

FIGURE 9.2 A Sales Force Productivity Framework

companies they trust. Sales forces that have high customer satisfaction ratings and high retention and repeat rates will usually have higher sales, profits and market share.

Sales force activity creates customer results. Salespeople bring life to the sales process by executing activities such as lead generation, needs analysis, solution development, proposal presentation, negotiation, installation, customer service, and account maintenance and expansion.

Salespeople determine sales force activity. Competent, motivated people working in a "success" culture demonstrate the right behaviors and engage in the right activities.

The *sales force drivers* represent the final component of the sales force system. They are at the root of the causal model. They are the basic decisions sales leaders make and the processes they use that directly determine the composition, personality, and behavior of the selling team. These decisions ultimately affect all components of the sales force system. The sales force productivity drivers fall into five categories. These categories are developed in Figure 9.3.

The *Definer* category contains all of the decisions that determine the organization and the role of the salesperson, such as job definition and territory definition. Decisions specifying the best go-to-market strategy, size, and structure of the sales force, and territory alignment are included in this category. This book focuses on these decisions.

The *Shaper* category consists of all of the processes that create the team that works in the organization. These decisions affect the skills, capabilities, and values of the salespeople. They include strategies for culture formation, and processes for hiring, training, and coaching salespeople, as well as the processes that hire and develop the management team.

The *Enlightener* category is comprised of processes that help the sales force understand the marketplace, prioritize opportunities, solve customer problems, and use their time more effectively. Customer research, targeting, product prioritization, sales process design, CRM, and account planning are programs that fall into this category.

The *Exciter* category of decisions and programs impact the selling organization's inspiration and motivation. How leaders inspire, the fulfilling nature of the work, together with decisions on incentive compensation and general motivation fall into this category.

The *Controller* category includes systems that manage performance by defining success, setting expectations, tracking performance, and linking with the other drivers to enhance performance.

The sales force drivers are the core set of decisions and processes that determine sales force performance. They are the decisions and processes that, if done correctly, ensure that the salespeople are of top quality and work within a success culture, establish the right activity to satisfy customers, and

Sales force drivers   **Impact**

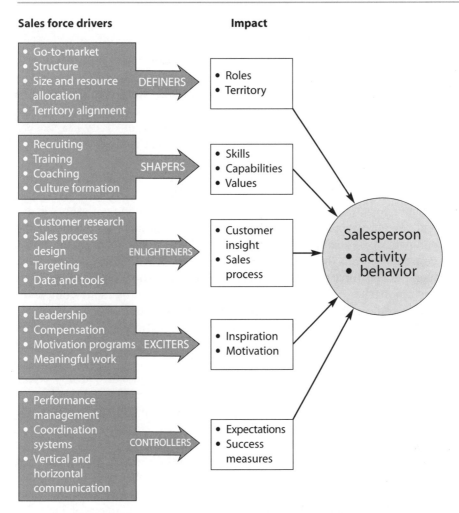

FIGURE 9.3 Categories of sales force drivers and their impact

achieve company financial objectives. They are presented here in categories with clean lines of causality, but in reality the influence of each driver may cut across categories. For example, coaching has been placed in the shaper category, but it also has an element of control. Similarly, communication has been placed in the control category, but it also can enlighten a salesperson.

IDENTIFYING AND ADDRESSING SALES FORCE ISSUES, CONCERNS, CHALLENGES, AND OPPORTUNITIES

Effective sales leaders constantly look for improvement opportunities. There are at least four ways that the leadership team thinks about the issues, concerns, challenges, and opportunities that affect the sales force. The four approaches are described below, followed by detailed descriptions of analytical approaches that the sales management team can use to gain insights with each approach.

First, sales leadership can identify sales force issues and opportunities by listening to the constant signals from customers, salespeople, sales managers, and other executives. The Sales Force Productivity Framework provides an organized way to identify, gather, and address the important sales force issues that are identified through these signals.

Second, sales management may be concerned that something is not working or an opportunity has been lost. Examples include "We don't seem to be getting the best people," "Are we over paying our sales force?" and "We need to double our effort in our key product area because the competition is distracted by a merger." The leadership team intuits its concern and feels that action needs to be taken. Usually these concerns fall into the sales force driver component of the framework. Data-based analytical approaches, called quick checks, have been used by many companies to assess the extent of the concern that the leadership team may face.

Third, the leadership team may just be dissatisfied. It feels that things could be better. The team is not quite sure where improvement is needed but it knows that improvement is possible. Comparisons with competition, past performance, or suggestions by management gurus frequently create the dissonance. The Sales Force Performance Scorecard and the Performance Frontier approaches are designed to help the leadership team achieve sales force improvement.

Finally, the effective sales leadership team has its eye out for any major company, market, competitive, or environmental shift. The five forces that were described earlier in the book provide a list of the types of shifts that all companies experience every so often. These shifts may require a sales force redesign and certainly will require a renewal of many of the sales force drivers. Three examples of shifts and several strategies for how a sales force can adapt without redesign are presented later.

Analyzing Sales Force Signals through the Sales Force Productivity Framework

The Sales Force Productivity Framework provides a basis for organizing sales force information and developing good improvement strategies. Every sales force issue, challenge, concern, or opportunity falls within one of the five components of the framework in Figure 9.2. "Not opening enough new accounts" is a company result. "Low awareness among competitive accounts" is a customer result. "Not spending enough time on developing new accounts" is an activity. "Sales force complacency and lack of account development skills" reflects on the sales force. "A hiring process that recruits only farmers and a training program that does not develop new business development skills" are both sales force driver issues.

Some sales force issues are obvious, but many are not. Often, a significant issue or opportunity gets lost because no one thinks of it. For example, one sales force struggled for several years with a non-accountable sales force culture. The sales force blamed its performance problems on external events and on the marketing group. Sales leadership did not acknowledge that they were propagating a "victim" culture.

An alert leadership team will work hard to uncover sales force issues. For example, one VP of Sales recently observed that a best practice selling process was not consistently implemented across the sales force. Underperforming salespeople were not engaging in the right activities. The Sales Force Productivity Framework provides a list of places to look to identify non-obvious issues and opportunities. Sales leadership needs to investigate how the sales force is performing relative to each of the five components. Figure 9.4 provides examples of the types of questions that need to be asked every year.

The causality implied in the Sales Force Productivity Framework means that every sales force issue, concern, challenge, or opportunity can be

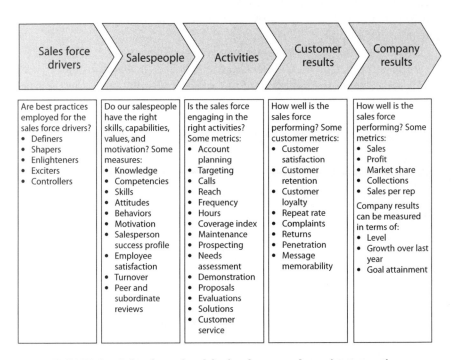

Sales force drivers	Salespeople	Activities	Customer results	Company results
Are best practices employed for the sales force drivers? • Definers • Shapers • Enlighteners • Exciters • Controllers	Do our salespeople have the right skills, capabilities, values, and motivation? Some measures: • Knowledge • Competencies • Skills • Attitudes • Behaviors • Motivation • Salesperson success profile • Employee satisfaction • Turnover • Peer and subordinate reviews	Is the sales force engaging in the right activities? Some metrics: • Account planning • Targeting • Calls • Reach • Frequency • Hours • Coverage index • Maintenance • Prospecting • Needs assessment • Demonstration • Proposals • Evaluations • Solutions • Customer service	How well is the sales force performing? Some customer metrics: • Customer satisfaction • Customer retention • Customer loyalty • Repeat rate • Complaints • Returns • Penetration • Message memorability	How well is the sales force performing? Some metrics: • Sales • Profit • Market share • Collections • Sales per rep Company results can be measured in terms of: • Level • Growth over last year • Goal attainment

FIGURE 9.4 Sales force health check – sample review questions

addressed by some sales force driver change. For example, not converting enough new business can be addressed by developing a training module to help people open new accounts, by changing the hiring profile to include hunter qualities, by changing the incentive compensation plan to include higher incentives for opening new accounts, or by restructuring the selling organization so that some salespeople specialize in new account development.

Figure 9.5 provides a specific example of how the causality implied within the Sales Force Productivity Framework can be used to resolve a sales force issue. Figure 9.5 demonstrates that while the causal relationships go from left to right, diagnosis is usually from right to left. In this example, sales are below expectations. Asking "why" leads to the conclusion that there need to be more sales from new accounts. Asking "why" again shows that salespeople are spending too much time with friendly customers, and not enough energy with the more challenging new accounts. "Why?" Spending time with salespeople as they perform their normal activities reveals that salespeople are comfortable with their current success, and are also not sure how to deal with accounts where there are strong, entrenched competitors. The sales force drivers chosen to influence this chain of events are: (1) train salespeople on competitive flanking strategies that enable them to discover customer needs that are minimally met by strong competitors and help them develop a value-added customer offering, and (2) provide expanded marketing support for new business development.

The Figure 9.5 example shows one way the framework can be used for issue resolution. The "why" questions are traced upstream to the drivers. In fact, the diagnosis can begin at any of the five components in the sales

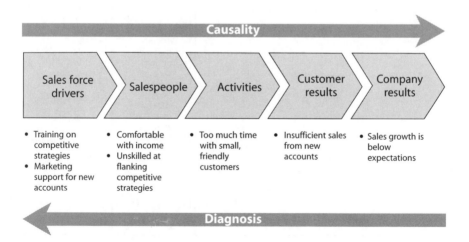

FIGURE 9.5 Diagnosis – flowchart and illustration

force productivity chain. Alternatively, insightful sales leaders can go directly to the sales force driver component if they feel certain that they have identified a troublesome driver.

Sometimes, too many issues or opportunity conjectures create a large list of driver improvement candidates. In these cases, firms are typically most successful if they prioritize the drivers and focus their improvement efforts on a small number of the most important ones first.

CRM system enhances sales approach at the AlliedSignal

During the mid-1990s, airplane parts supplier AlliedSignal Aerospace heard a consistent complaint from its customers: "You're too hard to do business with." The company had four separate business units and sold 40 different product lines. Many different AlliedSignal salespeople called on the same major airline customers, and there was no way for those salespeople to share information about sales opportunities, the status of maintenance requests, or the products customers had on their aircrafts. Several AlliedSignal salespeople might visit the same customer in the same week or day without knowing they were doing so. Large customers had as many as 50 different points of contact with the company. The lack of coordination frustrated customers, many of whom began turning to lower-cost suppliers for airplane parts.

In order to address its customers' concerns, AlliedSignal management realized that significant improvements were needed in one of its sales force drivers: specifically, the data and tools that enlightened salespeople about each customer's situation and needs. In 1998, the firm began working with Siebel Systems to implement a customer relationship management (CRM) system that would improve customer information access across the sales force. The project continued as the firm merged with Honeywell in 1999. By 2002 a single common customer information system was in place for sales reps, field service engineers, product-line personnel, and response center agents across Honeywell Aerospace's three main business units.

The new system, called Atlas, enabled Honeywell to replace its old product-centric sales approach with a new customer-centric approach. Salespeople and service engineers from across Honeywell began working together in customer teams, coordinating their activities through Atlas. For some customers, a single salesperson was assigned to lead the customer team, serving as the primary point of contact, regardless of the product or service the customer wanted to buy. Thus, if a customer had a problem, it had one point of contact with Honeywell, not one for every Honeywell part on its airplane. Atlas also allowed quicker sales force access to information, thus improving productivity and increasing time available for customer contact and selling.

Going to the gemba with the Sales Force Productivity Framework

One of the principles of kaizen, or "constant improvement by all people at all times" is to address problems by going to the "gemba" first. The Japanese word "gemba" refers to the "real place" or the place where the action takes place. In sales, the action takes place at the interface between the company and the customer. By looking at the "gemba" one can begin to understand what the problems and opportunities are. For example, salespeople are spending a lot of time waiting. Salespeople are hesitant in their knowledge of certain products. Customers like to hear about what is happening in their industry. Salespeople have to keep going back to headquarters to check about delivery dates. Observing such problems and opportunities, and repeatedly asking "why" can lead back upstream to the sales force drivers. Figure 9.6 shows how the Sales Force Productivity Framework can be used to go to the "gemba". That is, to study how the interaction between the company and the customer can be enhanced through sales process improvements.

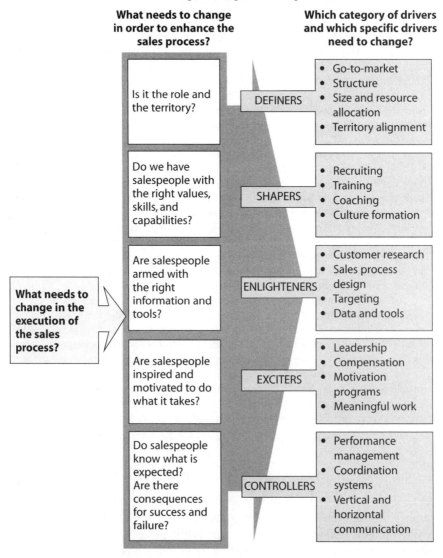

FIGURE 9.6 Diagnosis for sales process change

In this framework, spotting an opportunity in the sales process leads to the quest for causes. Is it the sales role or territory, a *definer*? Is it the people, who are influenced by the *shapers*? Is it customer knowledge, an *enlightener*? Is it in motivation, an *exciter*? Or is it in communication, a *controller*?

Strategies for achieving sales force goals and the Sales Force Productivity Framework

Sometimes, a company sets out to use the sales force to improve a particular result. For example, a company might launch a sales campaign to get market share from a certain competitor, improve performance in a particular sales district or region, or increase sales to new customers. Different sales force drivers are important to the achievement of each of these goals. In such situations, the Sales Force Productivity Framework can be used to identify the focal points of change. Figure 9.7 provides an example of how sales force drivers link to the attainment of specific sales force goals. In this example, the goal of improving under-performing territories is mapped to activities, which is eventually linked to the drivers that need enhancement.

Sales force goals can be established for any of the five productivity components – company results, customer results, salesperson activity, salesperson skills, or the sales force drivers themselves. The goals determine which sales force drivers need attention. For example, if a company has a goal of increasing retention of its top employees, the drivers that are most closely linked to this goal include meaningful work and compensation (exciters), performance management (a controller), and culture (a shaper).

Addressing Specific Concerns with Quick Checks

Sales leaders frequently raise questions concerning their sales force drivers. "Do we need to improve our hiring?" and "Is the incentive compensation plan motivating enough?" are two examples. They conjecture that best practices are not being implemented.

Quick checks can help a company determine whether or not an improvement can be made to a specific sales force driver. These tests provide insights through data-based analysis. Quick checks can be performed fairly rapidly and easily at most companies. Earlier chapters in this book have provided examples of quick checks for the sales force design drivers (structure, size, and alignment).

Quick checks usually use cross-sectional territory level data. They contrast how different salespeople are performing. Companies do not need to benchmark against other companies to determine best practices. They have

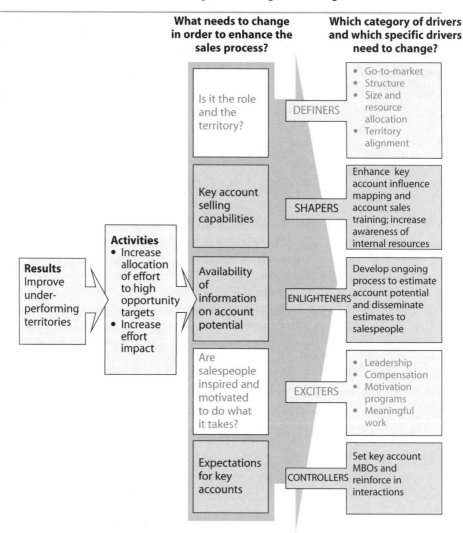

FIGURE 9.7 Example of linking goal to drivers

experiments going on all the time within their own sales forces. Each sales-person is an experiment. His or her activities and successes provide valuable information on the effectiveness of the sales force productivity drivers.

Quick checks can be either one- or two-dimensional. One-dimensional quick checks examine the pattern of a specific sales force measure to see if it is within normal limits. For some measures, the normal limits imply that the measure should be very similar across the sales force. An example is the hours that each salesperson needs to work to cover his or her terri-tory. Other measures, such as incentive pay, are typically better when they differentiate among salespeople.

The *New York Times* upgrades sales force incentive compensation plan

Management at the *New York Times* felt the incentive compensation plan used by its advertising sales department did not fairly reward effort against results. The sales force worked in teams, which were organized by market. Some teams worked in more stable markets where revenue was easier to predict, but many of the smaller teams worked in volatile markets where accurate prediction was difficult. As a result, members of small teams often received windfall gains or losses in incentive pay due to serendipitous events external to their selling effort. The firm wanted a new compensation plan that was more fair and motivational to all participants. A new plan was developed that explicitly addressed the issue of market volatility. Salespeople working in volatile industries could start receiving incentive pay when they achieved just a portion of their sales goal, for example 80 percent attainment. Teams in the more stable markets had to come closer to their goal, for example within 95 percent of attainment, before receiving incentive pay. The sales force embraced the new incentive plan. The gap between minimum and maximum payouts, which was mainly caused by market volatility, decreased by 60 percent.

Two-dimensional quick checks examine the relationship between two measures. Either the presence or absence of a relationship between the two measures can point to a problem or opportunity, depending on what the measures are. For example, a high positive correlation is expected if one plots sales against a known predictor of sales such as territory opportunity or potential. The presence of outliers signals problems or opportunities. On the other hand, suppose one looks at the relationship between territory potential and the bonus of salespeople operating in a quota-bonus plan. If a negative relationship exists (salespeople with high potential earn less), this suggests that the plan is favoring those with lower territory potential and potential was inadequately accounted for in the goal setting process.

Figure 9.8 shows a general example of a two-dimensional quick check. The measure on the horizontal axis is a known predictor of the measure on the vertical axis. For example, a good predictor of sales should be territory sales potential, the salesperson's competency, or the salesperson's effort level. The specific measures chosen depend upon the sales force driver that the firm wants to evaluate. When each territory is plotted according to the two measures, patterns across territories typically emerge. Many territories fall within an expected range of performance, but there will also be outliers. By studying the behavior and characteristics of the salespeople that are the outliers, interesting insights frequently emerge. For example, salespeople in the upper left-hand quadrant of Figure 9.8 are generating results that are better than expectation. By understanding the external and internal forces that contribute to this success, insights can be gained that may benefit the entire sales force. Similarly, salespeople in the lower right-hand quadrant

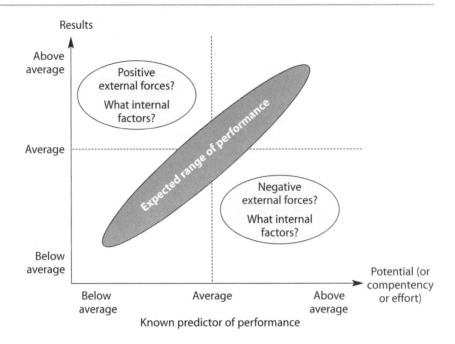

FIGURE 9.8 A generalized quick check template

have results that are below expectation. Again, insights regarding the external and internal forces that explain this performance deviation often lead to performance enhancement opportunities.

Some examples can help to illustrate the concept of a quick check. Figure 9.9 shows a two-dimensional quick check to evaluate the effectiveness of an incentive compensation plan. Recent performance evaluation ratings were plotted against the earnings percentile for each salesperson. By studying the relationship between the performance ratings and incentive payout, the company gained insight about the effectiveness of its incentive compensation plan. For the most part, salespeople with higher performance ratings earned the most money. However, some salespeople appeared to be paid more or less relative to their performance ratings. Based on this information, the company tried to find out if the anomalies were because of internal factors such as poor goal setting, external market factors or the people themselves. Too many people in the underpaid and overpaid quadrants usually imply an incentive compensation problem.

Another example of a two-dimensional quick check shows a way to evaluate the effectiveness of one of the inputs into a sales force recruitment process. Figure 9.10 examines the relationship between the ratings given to salespeople when they were candidates in the recruiting process and the performance of those salespeople two to three years later. Not all salespeople

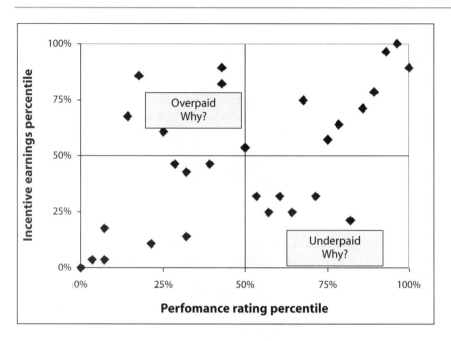

FIGURE 9.9 A quick check of a sales incentive plan

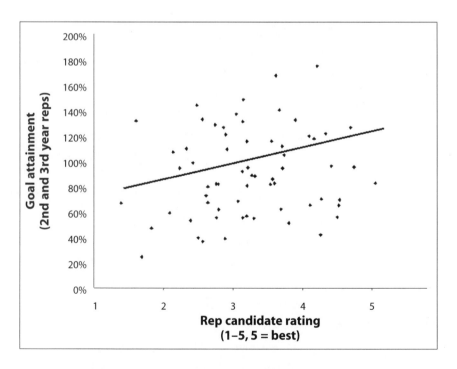

FIGURE 9.10 A quick check of sales force recruiting

with high recruitment ratings turned out to be stars. By studying the outliers, one can discover specific skills and personal characteristics that are being under- and over-emphasized during the recruiting process.

Figure 9.11 shows a one-dimensional example of a quick check that a company used to evaluate the effectiveness of its sales managers. The company did a survey to determine how sales managers spent their time. Data like this can help a company determine whether first line sales managers are spending enough time on important activities such as developing and coaching their salespeople and leading the sales team. If too much time is being wasted on non-critical activities, such as administration and internal meetings, adjustments to the sales manager's job may be needed.

Addressing General Concerns with the Sales Force Performance Scorecard and Performance Frontier Analysis

Sometimes, sales leadership feels that the selling organization needs to perform better, but is not sure exactly how to make the greatest impact. There may be numerous reasons behind their dissatisfaction. "Several

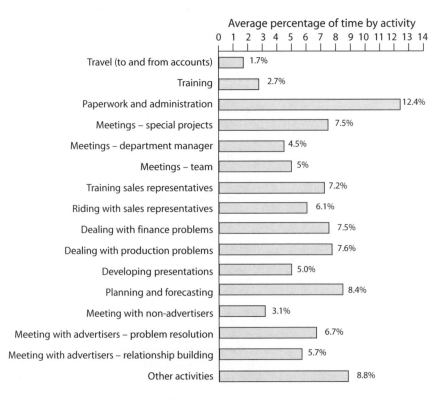

FIGURE 9.11 A quick check of sales managers

How to address sales force complacency?

A company with a small engineering sales force has never offered the sales force incentives, choosing to be a 100 percent salary environment. Very few people leave. Management is concerned that the sales force may be too complacent. The sales force seems content to call on existing accounts and is not sufficiently motivated to convert important new business. How can changes to the sales force drivers help to solve this problem?

---

sales force performance metrics are disappointing," "The environment requires more efficiency," and "New products are late and our margins are eroding" are just a few.

Sales leadership needs a place to look for improvement and a process by which to proceed. The Sales Performance Scorecard and the Performance Frontier analysis are tools used by some firms to launch their productivity programs.

The Sales Force Performance Scorecard

The Sales Force Productivity Framework suggests that a sales force is only as effective as its sales force drivers. The best sales forces execute all the drivers well. The decisions and processes that define, shape, enlighten, excite, and control the sales force are best-in-class. The Sales Force Performance Scorecard provides sales leadership with a view of how its productivity drivers are faring and identifies those drivers that need improvement.

The scorecard profiles each driver in terms of two measures: competency and impact. Each driver is first evaluated in terms of how good or how competent the selling organization is at that driver. Next, each driver is evaluated in terms of the impact the driver has on the selling organization's ability to succeed. The Sales Force Performance Scorecard is developed based upon these two measures. The Scorecard uses each measure as an axis. An example is presented in Figure 9.12.

The scorecard provides a valuable tool to assess the current status of the sales force productivity drivers. The position of each driver on the scorecard suggests a specific action. For example, a productivity driver with low impact but high competency, such as sales force size in the example, can be maintained at current levels for the time being. Productivity drivers with high impact and high competency, such as motivation in the example, need to be monitored closely to ensure that their performance stays high. Those with low impact and low competency, such as indirect marketing support in the example, can be monitored in case the impact of the driver increases over time. Top priority for management attention goes to productivity drivers with low competency and high impact, such as sales manager

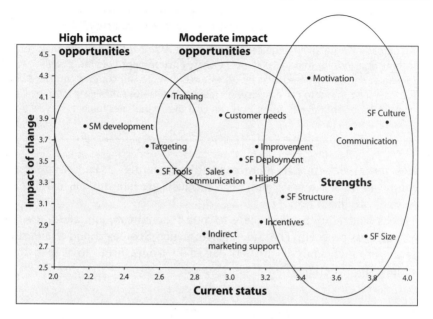

FIGURE 9.12 A Sales Force Performance Scorecard

development, targeting, and training in the example. These areas present the greatest opportunity for productivity gains.

In order to create a scorecard, a firm must measure both the impact and the current competency of the relevant sales force productivity drivers. Many companies rely on management judgment to derive competency and impact scores. Some companies have begun to use the quick checks to derive competency scores.

Performance Frontier Analysis

The Performance Frontier approach attempts to derive improved selling strategies by analyzing top performing salespeople to discover factors that contribute to their success. Performance Frontier analysis consists of two parts. First, the company must identify the salespeople who are and who are not doing well. The salespeople who have attained the highest levels of performance define the firm's Performance Frontier. Recent performance rankings and evaluations can be used to identify these people, but quantitative criteria such as market share and quota attainment can be useful as well. Second, the company needs to understand the reasons for performance differences. The answers are sometimes evident in the numbers. A high performer may work more days, make more calls, or allocate effort in a smarter way than an average performer.

However, the reasons for performance differences frequently lie in qualitative or non-quantified factors. For example, a high performer may be more motivated, have stronger selling skills, or engage in certain behaviors that are particularly effective with customers. Observation and synthesis are required to discover what these desirable characteristics, skills and behaviors are.

Performance of sales forces is enhanced significantly by moving salespeople towards the performance frontier. The Sales Force Productivity Framework provides a list of productivity drivers that may need attention in order to bridge the gap between the best and the average salespeople, thus raising the performance level of the entire selling organization. Drivers in each of the definer, shaper, enlightener, exciter, and controller categories have been selected when companies have used this analysis.

Marriott Vacation Club pursues sales growth goals

Marriott Vacation Club (MVCI), a seller of time-share vacation ownerships, set out in 1995 to achieve and exceed aggressive sales growth goals. As part of this effort, the company overhauled its entire sales operation, particularly the sales force. While the company had a great product and a good sales process in place, it needed the right drivers to shape and motivate the people to make it happen. To start, the company revamped its hiring process. A study was made of 125 of the company's top performing salespeople to reveal unique themes and traits that lead to sales success at the company. A new selection process resulted which became an integral part of MVCI's hiring strategy. In addition, an improved training program was implemented. New hires receive extensive training compared with that offered by other firms in the industry. In addition, ongoing training is offered to salespeople throughout their careers and frequent roundtable discussions encourage salespeople to share best practices. Innovative recognition programs for salespeople were also established. Diverse sales contents, incentives, and reward programs allow salespeople to accrue performance points, which lead to professional advancement. Peer recognition programs were established to further increase sales force motivation. In 2003, the sales force was won an American Business Award for best sales organization in the United States.

A non-obvious challenge for most companies is how to determine the best performers. Most sales managers think they can identify their best salespeople. They attribute territory success to the individual. Evidence suggests, however, that exceptional results are often due more to territory factors (such as high potential) than to salesperson factors (such as ability or hard work). Correlations between territory potential and sales dominate correlations between any salesperson characteristic and sales. It is important to control for the impact of factors such as territory potential and size when determining the Performance Frontier salespeople.

Two analytical approaches for establishing the set of Productivity Frontier salespeople have been developed: the control for territory potential approach and the multiple measures approach.

The control for territory potential approach for defining the set of high performing salespeople. Figure 9.13 plots all sales territories for a packaging company. The two dimensions in the plot are territory potential and territory sales. Territory potential is based on a combination of account-specific estimates provided by salespeople and business demographic data, and is measured in relative terms where 100 represents the average territory. Each dot represents a different sales territory and is labeled with a territory number.

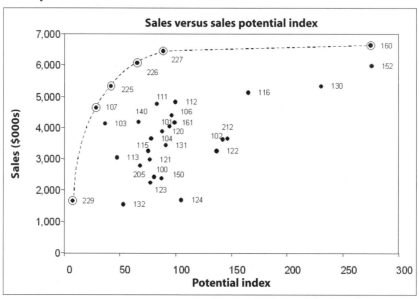

FIGURE 9.13 The Performance Frontier for a packaging manufacturer

The dotted curve connecting the territories at the top of the plot represents the Performance Frontier. The Performance Frontier predicts the sales that are possible for every level of territory sales potential. Why? Because someone in the sales force has demonstrated that it is possible to achieve this level of performance. For example, by looking at the range of sales between territories 225 and 226 (between $5.2 and $6 million), it is possible to forecast how much a salesperson with similar territory potential (45 percent of average to 70 percent of average) should be able to sell. Performance Frontier salespeople are those who are in the neighborhood of the Performance Frontier curve. Many companies use a range, such as 10 percent, to define this group.

The multiple measures approach for defining the set of high performing salespeople. The multiple measures approach suggests that truly outstanding salespeople will excel on multiple performance measures. The approach defines the Performance Frontier salespeople as those that score highly on the most important sales force measures available to the firm. Figure 9.14 shows an example in which the salespeople were measured on the market share of a growth product (Product A) and the market share of a new product (Product B). In this case Performance Frontier candidates

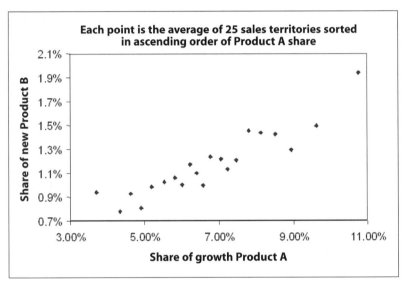

FIGURE 9.14 Identifying high performers: an illustration

The Novartis Group brings focus and skills to the sales process

The Novartis Group is a leading, multi-national manufacturer of pharmaceutical products. In 2001, the firm embarked on a global sales effectiveness initiative. In the first phase of this effort, Novartis Pharmaceuticals Corporation in the United States concentrated sales activity on approximately 35 percent of the total physician universe. This paid immediate dividends for the firm. In the second phase, "performance frontier representatives" or salespeople who were high performers were studied, and their behaviors compared with those who were not high performers. A set of performance markers was identified, and incorporated into a training program for the sales organization. At a presentation to analysts in September 2003, the company showcased the fact that Novartis salespeople who had been trained on the behaviors of performance frontier representatives were chosen by physicians as the best salesperson they see 46 percent of the time, compared to only 22 percent of the time for Novartis salespeople who did not have the performance frontier training. This preference was also linked to better results. The Novartis Group continues to roll out this program globally, even as new phases of the sales effectiveness initiative are under way to build on the successes so far.

were selected from salespeople who performed well on both products, and also had consistently high performance ratings.

Responding to Major External and Internal Changes without Sales Force Redesign

An effective sales leadership team keeps its eye out for any major company, market, competitive, or environmental shift. Earlier chapters of this book describe how a sales force redesign can enable a sales force to be more competitive and effective when faced with a major shift. Not all change pressures require sales force design change however. The power of the sales force comes from its ability to react and adapt. Effective response to change is possible by examining the other sales force drivers – the people, systems, and processes that support the design and make it work. Three examples are provided in this section. In each case, the Sales Force Productivity Framework is used to demonstrate how focal points are identified when a company faces an opportunity or challenge.

In each of these examples, a few targeted drivers are selected for focus. Too many simultaneous sales force enhancement initiatives clog the system and jeopardize the sales force improvement program. Particularly when initiatives cut across multiple functions and groups, successful sales organizations typically focus on a small number.

New product launch

New products require adjustment to the sales force drivers. Sometimes, sales force size needs to increase to provide adequate selling effort to both the new and existing products. Other times, the sales force structure needs to change in order to provide the focus and expertise needed to sell the new

TABLE 9.1 Illustration of prioritized issues to address prior to and during a new product launch

Sales force driver	Example of new product launch issues
Shapers – training	Provide new product training on customer needs, product characteristics, value proposition, and sales process.
Enlighteners – targeting	Provide information about who to call on, how frequently, and with what value proposition.
Exciters – compensation	Revise the incentive plan to direct salespeople to balance their energy appropriately between existing products and the new product.
Controllers – performance management	Set activity and results goals for the new and existing products to evaluate performance and provide feedback to the sales force.

Cisco adapts training processes for frequent new product launches

During the height of the Internet boom, computer networking giant Cisco Systems acquired a new company on average about every three weeks. This meant almost non-stop addition of new products to the portfolio of Cisco's sales force – a difficult task in a complex industry where hundreds of new products are introduced every year. Cisco prided itself on having a well-trained sales force, but flying salespeople to a central location for training every time a new product was introduced had become impractical. The firm needed a new training strategy if it hoped to quickly and successfully expand the bandwidth of its salespeople, allowing them to assimilate newly acquired products quickly. The firm developed an internal online learning portal called Field E-Learning Connection. The portal provided salespeople access to thousands of different training modules which could be viewed on screen, downloaded to a computer, or printed in magazine format. Salespeople could quickly familiarize themselves with new products without losing valuable time in the field. The system cut training-associated travel by 60 percent.

---

product effectively. However, even if a sales force has enough people and has the right structure in place to accommodate a new product, several sales force processes and systems need attention and adaptation. Table 9.1 shows an example of how the list of sales force drivers can be used to identify the focal points of attention during a new product launch.

Environmental challenge or opportunity

Successful companies adjust sales force drivers in response to changes in their industry and country environment. Environmental changes include new sales channels such as the Internet, changes in economic conditions, industry deregulation, and technological advances. Table 9.2 shows how a firm facing a weakening economy that affects its customers' ability to buy can use the Sales Force Productivity Framework to identify needed sales

TABLE 9.2 Illustration of issues to address eroding customer demand

Sales force driver	Examples of activities
Definers – resource allocation	Increase effort with current customers on products with the strongest economic benefit to customers, and on new targeted accounts.
Enlighteners – customer research	Refine knowledge of customer market strength and evolving decision-making criteria; develop insights into needs and value proposition from new customers.
Exciters – compensation and motivation programs	Make sure that the high performing salespeople are paid competitively for their performance so they stay with the company. Establish recognition programs that signal that the sales force is appreciated for everything that it is doing.

Sales force programs at Lucent Technologies help to position the firm for the future

Telecommunications company Lucent Technologies enjoyed tremendous success and an outstanding reputation during the late 1990s. But when the telecommunications industry slumped in 2000, the firm was hit hard. The stock price fell from $57 per share in December 1999 to under $1 per share in September 2002. Significant cuts were made to the number of employees including the sales force.

Three key sales force programs were established during 2003 in order to refocus and motivate the sales force. First, recognition programs that had been suspended to save money during hard times were reinstated. The company also added some low-cost but powerful recognition programs, such as personal thank you letters from senior management to top performers. Second, the company doubled the amount spent on sales force training. This showed the sales force that the company was investing in them. Salespeople felt more valued and as a result became a harder working and more dedicated group. Third, the sales compensation plan was revised, offering higher payout opportunity for top salespeople. These programs helped to create a more aggressive and sales-oriented culture at Lucent Technologies.

---

force driver adjustments. Some firms in this situation will increase the amount of "hunting" or effort allocated against new opportunities. Other firms facing this situation, as in the example given, will focus on customer retention while reducing the effort on targeting new customers.

Customer challenge or opportunity

Customer change is a major driver of sales force change. Customer changes can include buying process changes, market consolidation, the emergence of new markets, and increases in customer sophistication or global reach. Sales forces can also adjust the sales force drivers in order to exploit opportunities with customers. Table 9.3 shows how a company

TABLE 9.3 Illustration of issues to address to enhance cross-selling

Sales force driver	Examples of activities
Shapers – training	Train salespeople on how to spot opportunities for other divisions, and on how to work in a "project and team" environment.
Enlighteners – targeting	Include cross-selling targets in the territory plan.
Exciters – compensation	Set up cross-selling incentives.
Controllers – performance management	Establish cross-selling activity and result goals and insert them into the performance management system.

Making cross-selling work at Brenton Banks

Iowa-based Brenton Banks wanted to facilitate the cross-selling of its banking and brokerage products. The banking department of Brenton sold deposits, loans, and trust services and the brokerage department sold investment products. The two departments operated as "silos." A strong referral culture did not exist, and bankers and brokers preferred to keep their customers to themselves. Brenton management recognized that more proactive sharing of leads and cross-selling could generate significant growth, yet the desire for salespeople to protect their turf was so intense that ordinary incentives to share leads did not work. To break down the sales barriers, Brenton reorganized its bankers and brokers to promote a team selling approach. Bankers and brokers were given a single net income goal that was not broken down according to the old organization chart. Bankers and brokers met twice a week, first to discuss their plans for the week and later to share their best client names. Joint sales calls crossing the traditional banking and brokerage boundaries were common. Bankers could receive commissions for broker product sales and brokers could receive commissions for bank product sales. The new approach encouraged the entire sales force to be much more sales-oriented and proactive about developing leads and cross-selling.

---

with multiple divisions assembled through acquisitions can use the Sales Force Productivity Framework to identify adjustments to sales force drivers that will facilitate the cross-selling of products and services by multiple sales forces within the company.

MULTI-DIVISION AND MULTI-COUNTRY SALES EFFECTIVENESS INITIATIVES

Many companies with large sales forces have initiated cross-divisional and worldwide programs to enhance sales performance. Numerous large multi-national companies have had global programs for many non-sales functions for some time. For example, research, product development, and manufacturing are often centralized, with a corporate-wide view and system that determines where and how these functions will be performed. Sales is the current frontier for globalization. Many firms believe that much can be done across countries, and not just within a country, to improve sales

Global Programs Can Enhance Sales Force Performance

A large, multi-national pharmaceutical company had historically relied on new product introductions to achieve earnings growth. But the firm was facing a short-term research pipeline gap. In order to increase productivity and fuel earnings growth, the company developed internal effectiveness and efficiency programs. A global initiative was launched to increase the productivity of the firm's sales forces around the world.

effectiveness. For firms with multiple divisions in a single country, the opportunity lies in sharing knowledge and insights across divisions.

Thus far, multi-division and multi-country sales force effectiveness initiatives have not been uniformly successful. In these early efforts, failures are as common as successes. But successes, where they exist, have had dramatic impact. Table 9.4 lists some common signs of success and marks of failure for cross-organizational initiatives.

TABLE 9.4 Signs of success and marks of failure for cross-organizational sales force effectiveness initiatives

Signs of success	Marks of failure
It's Year 1, and improvements can already be seen	It's Year 2, and the planning, measuring, and diagnosing continues
People managing the enhancement program are sought after by their customers, the management teams of the operating units	People managing the program are avoided by the management teams
Enhancement initiatives are seamlessly integrated into the ongoing management processes and timelines	Enhancement initiatives make unplanned demands on people's time, and are driven more from outside the operating units
The program survives even as productivity enhancement teams change	The program dies when the team changes
People from countries or divisions have formed informal or formal groups around issues of interest such as CRM, incentives, and sales manager development, to share ideas and best practices	Most of the work appears to be controlled by gatekeepers
Participation is driven by the conviction that performance will improve	Participation is driven by the position power of the program sponsors

Sharable and Unique Sales Force Components

In order to understand why some cross-organizational initiatives (either across countries or divisions) are successful and others are not, it is important to understand the sales function across operating units. Of the many processes and systems that support sales, some are unique to the country or division while others are much the same across countries or divisions.

The go-to-market strategy and the sales force design decisions need to be local decisions. Different environments require different selling strategies. For example, a company may have a single generalist sales force in Japan, use a local partner in Germany, and have account managers supported by product specialists in the United States. It would be naive to dictate the same go-to-market strategy and sales force design for every country. The implication for global and multi-division initiatives is that for sales force productivity drivers that need to be customized locally to be effective, a common answer cannot work. Different approaches are required in each country or division.

At the same time, a number of productivity drivers can use generalized, best-in-class approaches or processes. Product training programs have strong similarities across countries. A good training program can be developed centrally and then customized locally. Conceptual frameworks have

---

Cross-country sales force initiatives help Linde Gas Therapeutics move from commodity to therapeutic gases

Linde Gas Therapeutics is a leading provider of gases and services to the healthcare market including hospitals, institutions, and homes. Most of the products such as oxygen and nitrous oxide are mature and exposed to commoditization. Recent scientific developments have shown that certain gases have important roles as biological messenger molecules, and that well-known gases and new gas premixes have unexplored beneficial effects which can lead to extended uses. As a result, Linde Gas Therapeutics has decided to refocus its business and to combine gas and pharmaceutical technologies to satisfy unmet medical needs. This has been achieved by investing in the development of innovative gas-based therapies. A first and major milestone was achieved in December 1999 when the FDA approved INOmax for the treatment of hypoxic respiratory failure (HRF) in the newborn. The firm's refocus involves a significant transformation in its traditional hospital and institutional business.

The repositioning of the hospital and institutional business around "gas therapies" (how to use gases effectively) and "gas solutions" (value-added services) has been a significant sales force challenge. The Linde Gas Therapeutics organizations in different countries were once very independent, and the company operated in a very decentralized way. In the hospital market, the traditional focus of the company has been on manufacturing and logistics – salespeople are more versed on how to pipe the gas to the various parts of the hospital than on the protocols for using the gas. How can Linde Gas Therapeutics create a new global business strategy and bring the sales forces in the various countries into this strategy?

Linde Gas Therapeutics is using a three-pronged multi-year approach on the sales force front. First, multi-country teams have developed a common way to segment their customers by size and what they value (price, value-added services, or research-support). Countries are adapting this global model and providing local texture to each of its elements.

Second, for each type of customer a sales process supported by a CRM system is being put in place. The objective of this step is to bring more focus on the value-adding components of Linde Gas Therapeutics' offerings, and not just on price and technical issues. In the value-seeking customer segment, decision influence also shifts to pharmacists and physicians, so the sales process has been adapted to include them.

Since the sales team also has to upgrade, the third component is a revamped training program that focuses on the value-adding elements and the new sales and sales management process. Contrary to the past when sales training was largely the result of autonomous local activities, this new initiative is designed and led as a group-wide local and global co-operative effort.

been developed for targeting, hiring, performance management, incentives, and other drivers that are transferable across countries. Local market, business, and cultural factors will drive the decisions, but common frameworks can bring discipline to the process of finding a good answer. The key to any effectiveness initiative is not to propagate common answers, but to help a country or divisional organization find an answer that will meet its needs.

When working across divisions, the nature of the industry frequently drives the differences or commonalities. Consider a company such as 3M, whose business includes products for healthcare, consumers, graphics applications, communications, and transportation. Some products are sold directly, others go through distribution. Some sales organizations are driven by a small set of key accounts, others cater to thousands of customers. The demand of some products is driven by advertising and distribution, for others, it is driven by design collaboration with customers. Sales force driver decisions need to be customized for every division, but there are many insights and sales force principles that can be shared and leveraged across these diverse groups. Examples include: How to hire? How to motivate? How to manage complex key accounts?

Dos & Don'ts for Cross-Divisional and Multi-Country Sales Effectiveness Initiatives

Table 9.5 shares some insights on what works and what does not work when implementing cross-organizational sales force effectiveness initiatives.

TABLE 9.5 What to do and what to avoid with cross-organizational sales force effectiveness initiatives

Issue	What to do	What to avoid
Objectives	Focus on a specific goal such as enhancing a particular product's sales performance, or improving a small set of sales force productivity drivers such as targeting and incentives.	Avoid trying to improve too many drivers without a clear business objective. With too many initiatives, there is no focus, and the expertise needed to succeed is difficult to assemble.
Scope	Is it a sales force issue? Sometimes, the significant payoff lies in coordinating sales with other departments such as marketing. If trying to enhance product success, look across company functions. If trying to enhance a specific driver such as hiring, focus within a function.	Avoid a scope that is not linked to the business goal. Business goals come first; scope and process can only follow, not lead.
People resources	Use local and global experts from within or outside the company. With internal resources, plan a career path so that expertise does not exit just as it is developed. With external help, either plan for a burst of effort, or forge a partnership with a clear working relationship.	Avoid using resources, internal or external, that bring energy but little expertise. Smart people without relevant experience frequently come up with an intuitive, but wrong answer. Use wise people to guide smart ones.
Measures and dashboards	Use relevant and useful measures at all levels. Match the granularity of the information on the dashboard to the person who sees it, and who can act on the information.	Avoid comparative measures which have no cross-country or cross-division comparison value, such as sales per rep or percent of incentive at risk. Also avoid too much granularity on global dashboards, as they only invite headquarters people to second-guess country or division actions and initiatives.
Forcing versus facilitating	Empower country (division) organizations to seek the best ideas from other countries (divisions), and provide mechanisms to disseminate good ideas.	Do not enforce adherence to productivity enhancement rules across countries (divisions). No one answer fits all situations, and only solutions that a country (division) believes in will be implemented with success.
Multi-country and cross-divisional forums	Use global or regional forums on difficult but focused issues of broad interest, such as how to launch new products while growing current products.	Avoid broad forums on broad issues. These lead to complaints of low value, and significant distraction from productive activities. Process-heavy and outcome-light initiatives drain organizational energy and motivation.
Sales effectiveness czar	Done well, this is a success factor. Treat countries and divisions as customers, and create an environment where they want your assistance.	Done poorly, this can be a key cause of disaster. Do not act as if country (division) personnel are resources that you control.
Global sales effectiveness initiatives	Begin with great care and learn from others' successes and failures.	Do not jump in with untested preconceptions. Over 70 percent of such initiatives are value-draining and not value-adding, and a majority of them peter out as well.

Managing Change

INTRODUCTION

For every company, there are dozens of good sales force designs but millions of bad ones. Once a company discovers one of the good designs, there are hundreds of ways to make it work, but millions of ways to make it fail. A good design cannot work effectively without good implementation. This chapter discusses how a sales force can make the transition successfully from one sales force design to another.

Why Is It Important To Focus On Implementation When Changing Sales Force Design?

Even the best sales force design ideas will fail if they are not implemented effectively. Careful attention to transition strategies during any sales force redesign effort is important for several reasons. First, any change to sales force design affects customers. Customers may see more or fewer of the company's salespeople as a result of a redesign. They may have to use new channels to perform some of their buying activities. They may need to establish relationships with different salespeople from the company. An effective transition from one sales force design to another enhances the company's relationship with its customers and adds customer value. An ineffective transition, on the other hand, can reduce service levels for the customer, disrupt important relationships, and result in lost sales and market share for the company.

What Xerox customers said about the firm's reorganization

Xerox realigned its sales organization twice during 1999, in an effort to shift more direct selling effort towards the largest, global customers while creating industry-specific selling teams. The restructuring effort was not initially successful, as performance fell well short of goal and many Xerox salespeople left the company. Customers complained of neglect by Xerox salespeople after the restructure and a lack of willingness to negotiate price even as the sale was being lost. One commercial printing customer, whose long-time Xerox service rep was reassigned through the restructure, reported seeing 11 different service reps over a five-month period – none of whom knew how to service his machines. As a result, the customer replaced his Xerox machines with those of a competitor.

Any change to sales force design also affects salespeople. When done right, sales force morale and motivation improve, or at least do not decline. Problems are anticipated and dealt with effectively. Poor implementation of a new sales force design is demotivating to the sales force. Salespeople do not work at peak performance and spend too much time on non-productive tasks. Good salespeople leave the company.

Salespeople are naturally anxious about any change in their responsibilities. A salesperson taking on a new role feels uncertain about his capability to perform the new job effectively. A salesperson changing account assignments is upset about losing old customer relationships and anxious about establishing new ones. A salesperson who is asked to relocate feels stress about disrupting family and establishing roots in a new community. A salesperson reporting to a different manager wonders about the new boss's expectations and work style. A salesperson who has to use new skills and behaviors may find the situation daunting or challenging.

A sales force design change is also stressful for sales managers. Managers often play a key role in communicating specific changes to their salespeople. This might include telling a veteran salesperson that her job has been eliminated, or informing another that he will have to relocate. These conversations can be extremely stressful. In addition, managers may be concerned about the security of their own jobs. They may worry about losing control or power through the reorganization or they may fear that the reorganization will create more work for them. Sales force reorganizations create stress for employees that support the sales force as well, including people in the human resources, systems, and training departments.

While change creates anxiety, it also creates excitement. With reorganization come new opportunities for the sales force. A star performer picks up a major new account with big earnings potential. A salesperson is reassigned

---

Cisco is challenged by sales force redesign implementation

During the height of the Internet boom, computer networking giant Cisco Systems was well known for its ability to acquire and effectively integrate new companies quickly. Using a well-defined process of assimilating new employees into the Cisco culture, Cisco successfully acquired over 60 companies between 1993 and 1999. This meant almost non-stop integration of sales forces – a difficult task in a complex industry where hundreds of new products are introduced every year. Extensive online training systems were critical to the successful assimilation of newly acquired sales forces. These systems enabled new salespeople to quickly become familiar with Cisco's objectives and expectations. At the same time, the systems helped existing salespeople become familiar with new products, without losing valuable time in the field.

Many of the companies that Cisco acquired were small start-up companies, with just a handful of customers and salespeople. But the acquisition of two larger, more established companies proved to be especially challenging for Cisco's sales force. When Cisco acquired switch maker StrataCom Inc. in 1996, the company decided to integrate the 200 StrataCom salespeople into the existing Cisco sales force structure of 1800 salespeople. The integration did not go smoothly. Roughly a third of the StrataCom salespeople quit within a few months because they lost accounts to Cisco salespeople and because of changes in their commission plan. In addition, Cisco salespeople were reluctant to sell StrataCom's lower-priced switches because they netted a significantly lower commission than the more expensive Cisco routers.

When Cisco acquired fiber optics equipment maker Cerent in 1999, the 100-person Cerent sales force was maintained as an independent sales force. Cerent salespeople kept their accounts, even if a Cisco salesperson already called on the same customer. Cerent salespeople also received pay boosts averaging 15 to 20 percent to make their compensation more comparable to that of Cisco salespeople. (The authors suspect that integrating the Cerent salespeople into Cisco's existing structure would have been a better long-term strategy, but Cisco was not willing to risk the implementation challenges it had experienced with StrataCom.)

to a new industry team, providing a great opportunity to learn and expand her experience. A district sales manager must hire several new salespeople, providing a chance to upgrade the existing skill set in the district and build his own sales team. Successful sales force change initiatives stress the positive aspects of change, leverage the excitement it creates, and use it to build new and revitalized energy within the sales force.

Focusing on implementation during a sales force redesign is also important because numerous internal processes and systems are affected. When sales roles change, new training programs must be developed. Sometimes, a new recruiting profile is needed. Information needs change, necessitating new and redesigned sales reporting systems. Sales force incentive programs must be developed or updated. Systems and processes throughout the company must adapt to new and different ways of doing business. Sometimes this is challenging. For example, when a large pharmaceutical company split its sales force, the company needed to maintain two separate computers for a time until their systems could be updated to handle two sales forces.

When design changes are significant, implementation is perhaps the most difficult part of sales force design. Many good sales force designs fail because they are not implemented effectively.

A SALES FORCE CHANGE PROCESS FRAMEWORK

Figure 10.1 provides a framework for understanding the process of implementing successful sales force change. The impetus for sales force change can come from outside or inside the company. Causes include the firm's customers, its competitors, the environment, as well as company strategy changes and initiatives to continuously improve. The change process involves three major activities: design the plan, mobilize the resources to make it happen, and implement. Guiding principles define the firm's goals and specify important rules for decision making throughout the various change process stages. In addition, good change processes acknowledge the outlook of the people who are affected by the change. This includes appealing to both the rational (why are we doing this?) and the emotional (how does this affect me?) needs of the various customers, salespeople, and other stakeholders involved.

Guiding Principles

Guiding principles answer the question "Why are we doing this?" These principles define the rules of the game and provide an objective way to resolve any dilemmas that arise during the change process. Guiding principles are tied to company goals and are typically statements of strategy.

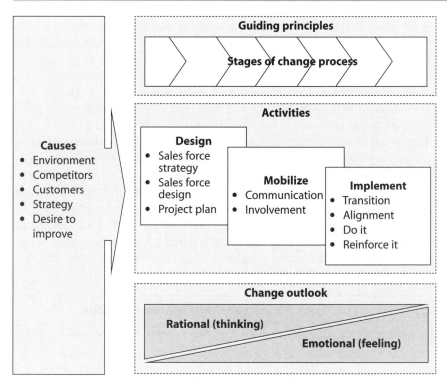

FIGURE 10.1 A sales force change process framework

For example, "We want to put the best possible person in each job," "We want to get closer to our customers," or "We want to increase sales and reduce costs."

Guiding principles become rules for decision making throughout the change process. For example, suppose a company is splitting its generalist sales force to achieve product specialization. A high-performing salesperson wants to be assigned to Team A, but has been most successful in the past selling the products of Team B. The firm looks to the guiding principles to make a decision about the best possible placement for the salesperson. If the primary guiding principle is "increase product expertise," then the salesperson is assigned to Team B. On the other hand, if the primary guiding principle is "do what it takes to retain good salespeople," then the salesperson is assigned to Team A.

Activities: Design–Mobilize–Implement

The change process involves three major activities: design, mobilize, and implement. These activities facilitate discovery of a good sales force design and at the same time, assure successful implementation.

Design activities include making many of the decisions that have been discussed throughout this book. Sales strategy and go-to-market strategy must be formulated, the role of the sales force in executing these strategies needs to be defined, and sales force size, structure, and alignment need to be specified. In addition, an implementation plan needs to be developed.

Mobilization activities focus on getting the organization ready with the understanding, motivation, and resources to make the change when it comes. These activities build consensus and create the confidence that the redesign can really happen. Sales leadership needs to get behind the redesign initiative. They need to participate in the decision making and should be informed on the progress of the change initiative. Communication is also important. Key members of the sales force should know what is going on so that they can provide suggestions and help roll out the changes as they are announced. Involvement creates more support for the change effort because when people have input into defining the changes that affect their work, they are more likely to take ownership of the results.

The "Four P's" of transition communications

Good organizational communication during times of transition incorporates the four "P's":

- The *purpose*: Why is the company doing this?
- The *picture*: What will the organization look and feel like when we reach our goal?
- The *plan*: Step-by-step, how will the organization get there?
- The *part*: What can and must you do to help the plan move forward?

Implementation activities focus on making the design a reality. A transition plan is put into action. Every person within the sales force learns what his or her new assignment will be. New salespeople and managers are hired, as necessary. In addition, the company's systems and processes are aligned with the new design. New hiring profiles are adopted, training programs are developed, compensation plans are designed, sales reporting systems are updated, customer target lists are developed, and account plans are specified. At the same time, performance management systems are implemented to guide and reinforce the new strategies and philosophies.

Redesign initiative fails due to lack of stakeholder buy-in

The CEO and three top management heads of a large company wanted to implement a new sales structure in the company. One day before the decision was to be announced, all the sales directors threatened to quit as a group if the new strategy was implemented. As a consequence, the project had to be dropped.

Figure 10.2 illustrates the timing of the three sales force change activities. Companies that implement change successfully typically do not wait until design is complete to begin mobilizing and planning for implementation. In fact when teams that have been responsible for implementing organizational change are asked what they would do differently on their next project, most say they would begin their mobilization and implementation planning activities earlier, instead of viewing them as add-ons or afterthoughts. For example if key stakeholders are consulted during the design stage, the design will be better and there will be greater organizational support. In addition, if implementation issues are anticipated up front, downstream problems will be anticipated early while there is plenty of time to avoid them or solve them, and implementation will be easier.

Change Outlook

Successful change efforts acknowledge the thoughts and feelings of the people who are affected by the change and deal with their outlook on both rational and emotional levels. Early on in a redesign effort, most people react to news of change rationally. They focus on broad issues of strategy and customer and product impact. As the redesign progresses, however, people begin to focus on specific personal issues. Often, emotions take over. People wonder, "How much of my life is going to change?" They get nostalgic about "the good old days" and worry about how the new design might impact them negatively. Companies that deal with these emotions directly can avoid trouble down the road.

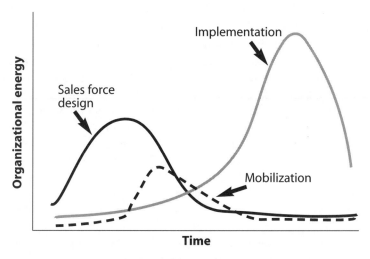

FIGURE 10.2 Organizational energy throughout the sales force change process

> ### Early mobilization efforts lead to more acceptable solutions
>
> A pharmaceutical company with three divisions was to launch three new products. The most logical sales force design was to give two of the new products to one division because of product portfolio synergies, and to give the third product to another division. But management discovered through its early efforts to socialize the new plan that all three divisions felt strongly that they deserved to launch at least one new product. The sentiments were so strong that management changed its design and let all three divisions launch one product each.

Effective communication both from management and with peers can help people understand and accept change. Often, communications from the leadership team are most appropriate for helping people comprehend change on a rational level, while discussions with peers have the biggest impact on an emotional level. Both levels of communication are essential to symbiotically cover the rational and emotional needs of people.

WHAT TO PAY ATTENTION TO

Customers

Attention to customers is absolutely critical when sales force design is changing. Customers will become anxious when they hear that change is imminent. How will the new sales force design affect them? Will they need to educate a new salesperson about their needs? Will all the experience and knowledge be lost in the transition? Will they have to change the way they do business with the firm? Will it cost them time and money to deal with a new person? Astute competitors often take advantage of this anxiety in the marketplace by using sales messages that further increase customer uncertainty. Even the best customers may reason that since things are changing anyway, perhaps the time is right to consider competitive offerings.

While attention to all customers is important during times of transition, firms must pay special attention to their most important accounts. According to the Pareto Principle, this is the 20 percent or so of customers that account for 80 percent or more of the business. These are the customers that the firm cannot afford to lose – and the ones that competitors may be most interested in poaching. Additionally, companies with long selling processes must pay particular attention to prospective major sales in the pipeline. A prospect may find a change of salesperson or selling team midway through the sales process to be particularly disruptive. Prospective sales to accounts that are also evaluating competitive offerings are especially vulnerable.

New salesperson is unfamiliar with customers and their history and needs

A large investment management firm used by one of the authors had two reorganizations within a year in its account management function. When the second new account manager was appointed, he called to introduce himself, and one of his questions was, "How long have we had your account?"

Communication with customers is critical during times of transition. Customers need to understand how the change benefits them, perhaps through greater sales force expertise, more channel options, better service, or simply by assuring the viability of the supplier through a lower cost structure. They also need to see that the firm has an effective transition process in place. For example, suppose Salesperson A is currently working with an account on a prospective major deal, but Salesperson A will be losing that account to Salesperson B once the new design is implemented. Salesperson A could begin working together with Salesperson B to close the deal. That way, the customer has confidence that the knowledge gained by Salesperson A during the sales process is not lost. Salesperson B is fully informed about the customer's needs and has gained the customer's confidence by the time the transition is complete. The two salespeople might also share any commission or bonus earned from the sale.

Sales Team

It is also important for the firm to focus on the needs of its sales team when the sales force design changes. Salespeople and sales managers can have several reasons to become anxious during times of transition. They may fear that change will threaten their job security, increase their workload, reduce their earnings potential, or make the work less important or more difficult to do. Other sales forces may take advantage of this anxiety by attempting to hire away the firm's top people. Sales force recruiters often

---

Agere focuses on customers during transition

When semiconductor company Agere expanded its direct sales force and reduced its dependence on manufacturer representatives, smooth customer transition was a top priority. The 65 new salespeople that took over accounts that were previously managed by manufacturer reps worked closely with customers during the transition to ensure that customers accepted the change and that their requests were not lost in the shuffle. Successful implementation of the new go-to-market strategy allowed Agere to better understand and respond to the demands of its customers, and encouraged the development of stronger long-term relationships.

---

target people at firms that are going through transition. Ambitious sales personnel may reason that given all the uncertainty, perhaps the time is right to consider a job change.

Salespeople

Salespeople who are opposed to a sales force design change can react in one of several ways. They may openly oppose the change by complaining or even slowing down their work. They may quietly oppose the change through diminished loyalty and decreased motivation. Finally, they may leave the company and take their accounts with them.

Firms must pay special attention to their top-producing salespeople during times of transition. These are the salespeople that the firm cannot afford to lose – and the ones that other sales forces will pursue most aggressively. Additionally, companies with long selling processes must protect salespeople that have major prospects in the pipeline. For example, a transition compensation program can be implemented that encourages a salesperson to stay involved with a sales process that she has started, even if she will no longer be responsible for the customer after the reorganization. Such programs also encourage effective transitions from a customer standpoint.

As shown in Figure 10.3, salespeople may resist change for many different reasons. The firm must address this resistance with an appropriate response.

Sometimes, salespeople express fear, anxiety, and doubt about the prospect of change because they cannot control and predict it, or they do not understand it. Communication from management and involvement of the people who will be affected by the change in the implementation process can help a firm deal with this type of resistance. Moving quickly also helps to minimize the impact of sales force anxiety on the transition to the new organization.

Salespeople may also resist change because they feel that they are already working at full capacity and they know that implementing change will take a lot more work. The old way of doing business has worked in the past, so why not make things easy and just maintain the status quo? To deal with this objection, the firm can provide additional resources to help during the transition. Many firms hire consultants to help with major sales force changes, not only to improve the quality of the answer and its implementation, but also to ease the transition workload for internal staff.

Salespeople also resist change because they fear that they do not have the capability to take on new roles or they are afraid that their responsibility and earnings opportunity will decline. Appropriate responses for a company dealing with these concerns are shown in Figure 10.4. The sales force

Why salespeople resist change		How to deal with this
Can't control and predict it Don't understand it Have fear, anxiety, and doubt	→	Communication and involvement Do it quickly
No time to do it	→	Provide resources
No capability to do it	→	Provide training
Responsibility and earning potential will decline	→	Apply empathy and integrity Provide short-term compensation protection

FIGURE 10.3 Why people resist change

changes that are easiest to implement are those that place most of the company's current salespeople in the "winner" corner. Salespeople will be happy and excited to take on new roles that provide good opportunity and where they are capable of doing well. Sales force changes that place too many current salespeople in the "no oxygen" corner will fail. If a salesperson is asked to assume a role with unfavorable opportunity that he or she is not qualified to perform, he or she will likely leave the firm. Sales force changes that place many current salespeople in the "role/compensation" and "training/coaching" corners can work, but they may require significant transition effort on the part of the company to succeed. A salesperson who is asked to take on a new role that has less opportunity but that he or she has the

---

Integration advocacy group enhances success of a pharmaceutical merger

When pharmaceutical giants Astra and Zeneca merged in 2001, combining the two worldwide sales organizations was a major undertaking. To encourage the project's success, top management wanted the sales force to be informed and involved throughout the process. An integration advocacy group was formed consisting of a people from a variety of sales roles at both companies, including various types of salespeople, district sales managers, regional sales managers, as well as sales training and operations specialists. The group acted as a customer focus group for management, providing advice and feedback on the various sales force decisions that had to be made. Members of the group acted as advocates for their peers. The group helped the company make better decisions and achieve better acceptance of those decisions by the sales force. In addition, communication with the entire sales force was emphasized throughout the merger process. Routine teleconferences, question-and-answer sessions, and newsletters tracked the project's progress and kept everyone informed about new decisions. A priority throughout the project was to move fast. As stated by the firm's vice president of sales, "We knew we could not do it perfectly in six or nine months, but we could get it 90 percent correct and avoid unnecessary impacts on employees by not agonizing over the last 10 percent."

capability to perform may require role enhancements or additional monetary compensation. On the other hand, a salesperson who lacks the capability or confidence to perform a new role that has good opportunity, will require coaching and training in order to develop the skills necessary for success.

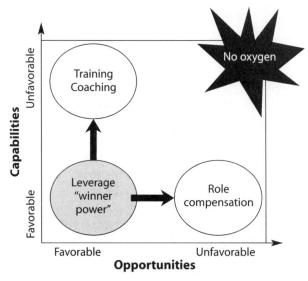

FIGURE 10.4 Company response to changes in salesperson capabilities and opportunities following a sales force redesign

Sales managers and other personnel in the firm

Besides the salespeople, there are many other people within the company that will be affected by a sales force redesign. Sales managers, marketing personnel, human resources, systems, and other departments that interact with the sales force will all need to adapt to the new ways of doing business. Change leaders within the company must assess who else within the firm needs to be engaged in the change process, how they influence others within the organization, and how they are likely to view the changes taking place.

The "allies map" shown in Figure 10.5 provides a good framework for thinking through this assessment. Within the firm, there will be stakeholders that support and those that oppose the change effort. Some will be very active in expressing their views and getting involved, while others will be more passive. Where each stakeholder falls on the allies map determines how that person should be approached about and involved in the change effort. Strong, visible, and effective sponsorship is a major factor in any project's success. The more active supporters a project has (top right "engaged" corner of the allies map), the easier the change will be to implement. Change leaders within the company need to recruit as many active

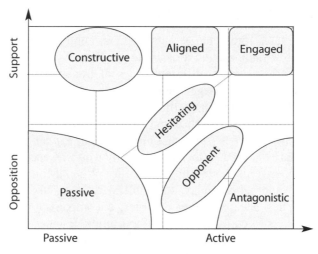

FIGURE 10.5 Allies map

supporters as possible, and expand the group by energizing the "aligned" or "constructive" segments. To do this, they must generate excitement among passive supporters by communicating a compelling vision and strategy. Time spent with those actively opposed to the change effort (bottom right "antagonistic" corner of the allies map) is usually time wasted. The goal with this segment is to diminish the negative impact that their active opposition to the changes might have on the rest of the group.

Processes and Systems

The firm must also pay close attention to the impact of a sales force redesign on the many important processes and systems that support the sales force. The hiring profile for sales and sales management positions may need to change. Sales force training needs, performance evaluation systems, career paths, and compensation plans may be affected. Sales force redesign can also have a major impact on sales information and support systems. Redesigning these systems and processes can be a major undertaking for the firm, and significant time and resources may be required to keep these systems aligned with the new sales force design. Chapter 9 provides a framework to view the processes and systems that need to change.

Incentive compensation plans rewarding smooth transitions are often a good way to encourage the successful implementation of sales force redesign. For example, if salespeople are paid based on sales performance at both their old accounts and their new accounts for a period following a transition, teamwork between new and exiting salespeople is encouraged and strong customer–company relationships are maintained.

EXAMPLES OF TRANSITIONS

The forces of sales force change – customers, competitors, the environment, corporate strategies, and a desire to get better – cause sales organizations to experience many different types of transitions. For example, when customers become larger, more complex, or more demanding, a company might *restructure* its selling organization into industry focused teams to provide greater expertise and value to customers. When a major competitor grows its sales force, a company might *expand* its sales force to maintain share of voice. When the economy weakens, a company might *downsize* its sales force to sustain profitability. When a company *acquires* or *merges* with another company, a new blended selling organization must be created. When a new market emerges, a company might *create* an entirely new sales force to exploit the opportunity. Each of these different types of transitions – restructuring, expansion, downsizing, mergers and acquisitions, and new sales force creation – has its own issues and challenges.

Chapter 9 introduced a sales force productivity framework. At the root of this framework are *sales force drivers*, or the basic decisions sales managers make and the processes they use that determine the composition and personality of the selling team. Five major categories of drivers or decisions, as shown in Figure 10.6, affect the activities and behaviors of salespeople.

Whenever a sales force experiences redesign, the sales force drivers must be reevaluated. The company's specific situation and the nature of the transition determine which drivers will need the most attention. For example, when a company expands its sales force, the sales force drivers in the *shapers* category have primary importance. New salespeople must be recruited and trained and new sales managers must be selected. On the other hand, when a company downsizes its sales force, drivers in the *exciters* category need the most management attention. The challenge is to provide leadership that inspires the team during difficult times and to maintain sales force motivation. Table 10.1 provides a summary of the major issues and sales force drivers that are relevant in different transition situations. The specific issues that emerge with each type of transition is provided in the section that follows.

Expansion

Sales force expansion can be driven by a company's financial success, growing markets, or new products. During a sales force expansion, significant management attention focuses on the shaper category of sales force drivers – specifically, the recruiting and training of new salespeople and sales managers. Often, significant effort is required to hire people in

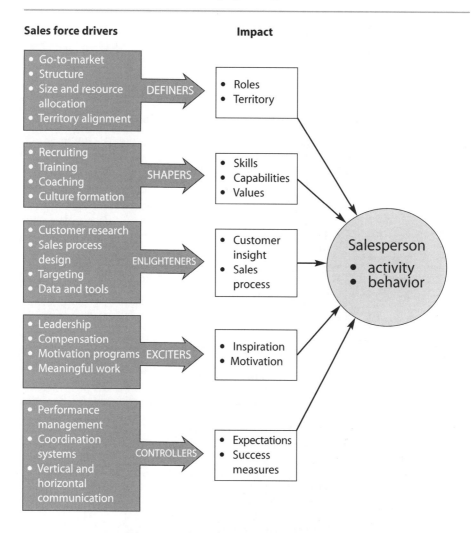

Sales force drivers   **Impact**

FIGURE 10.6 Sales force drivers and their impact

various locations across the country. Once hired, the new salespeople must learn the company's culture and be trained on the products, markets, and sales approach – often in a very short timeframe. Also when the number of salespeople increases, the number of sales managers may need to increase as well, creating additional recruiting and training challenges.

Salespeople typically have mixed emotions about sales force expansion. On the positive side, expansion signals that the company is doing well and has strong growth potential. Additional salespeople can share the workload, making each salesperson's job more manageable and reducing travel requirements. Expansion also creates promotion opportunities. On the negative side, however, sales force expansion usually

TABLE 10.1 Major issues and sales force drivers during transitions

Type of transition	Major issues	Definers	Shapers	Enlighteners	Exciters	Controllers
Expansion	• Placing new people geographically, realignment of existing people • Recruiting and training of new salespeople • Selecting the best sales managers • Maintaining earnings potential for top existing salespeople • Having flexible support systems that adapt with continued growth	√ √	√ √	√	√	
Downsizing	• Keeping strong sales leadership • Protecting strengths – keeping the best salespeople and customers • Deciding who to let go • Minimizing the pain to the organization		√	√	√ √	√
Creation	For a new sales force in an established environment: • Building on known best practices • Executing well For a new sales force in a new and uncertain environment: • Developing the best sales strategy • Adapting as the organization learns For all new sales forces: • Selecting the best sales leader • Balancing the need to plan with the desire to act	√ √	√ √	√ √	√ √	√ √
Merger	• Blending two different cultures and building on the best aspects of each • Protecting strengths – keeping the best salespeople and customers • Moving quickly but effectively	√ √	√ √	√ √	√ √	√ √
Acquisition	• Assimilating the acquired sales force into the dominant culture • Training salespeople to sell new products or to new markets	√	√	√	√	√
Restructuring	• Redesigning sales processes and systems that provide salespeople with customer insight • Hiring or retraining salespeople for new responsibilities	√ √	√ √	√ √	√	√

means that existing salespeople will lose accounts and sales potential. This can have a significant effect on the earnings opportunity, and therefore motivation, of existing salespeople. The impact is particularly significant when the sales force compensation plan has a large variable component that is larger if the sales volume in a territory is larger. For example, unless the market is growing very rapidly, a salesperson who is paid a straight commission rate on every sale will struggle to make the same money after his or her territory is reduced. Sales forces where salespeople have strong customer linkages, and incentive plans are commission-oriented, often implement transitional compensation plans following a sales force expansion so that top salespeople can maintain their current income level. Firms sometimes use compensation guarantees for a year or less. In some unusual circumstances, firms even resort to a "territory-buyback" in which a salesperson continues to earn commission on accounts transferred to another salesperson for a transition period.

Companies with future sales force expansion plans should consider establishing "expansion-friendly" compensation plans upfront. For example, a plan that pays salespeople based on their achievement of a territory goal or quota allows salespeople to maintain earnings after expansion because each territory's goal can be adjusted when the territory changes.

A company can also help salespeople maintain earnings after a sales force expansion by providing additional customer targeting information to each salesperson. With smaller sales territories, salespeople will have time to go deeper down the list of targeted accounts and make calls on some of the smaller prospects that they previously did not have time to see. By providing each salesperson with information about possible new leads within his or her territory, the company helps the sales force achieve deeper market penetration more quickly.

Companies that plan to expand their sales force continuously over several years must have flexible support systems that can grow and adapt, as the sales force gets bigger. A particular challenge for companies planning multi-phased sales force expansions is to manage the ongoing

---

Transition compensation at Coloplast

Healthcare products company Coloplast used a formal compensation wind-down program when it expanded its sales force. The firm's average closing cycle is six to nine months. So when the sales force expanded many salespeople had to give up accounts that were in the pipeline. To recognize the past efforts of the salespeople losing the accounts, the company continued to pay them 25 percent of the commission on sales made to these accounts for a couple of months after the expansion. This also provided incentive for the old salesperson to work with the new salesperson to facilitate an effective transition and help close the sale.

disruption that occurs to existing salesperson/customer relationships. Disruption is inevitable with sales force expansion. Yet account reassignments, particularly for important accounts, should be considered carefully and implemented in a manner that minimizes any potential negative impact to either the salesperson or the customer.

Sales force expansion at Initiate Systems

Hoping to accelerate growth, data integration software company Initiate Systems expanded its services in 2003 from a healthcare focus into three additional vertical markets: finance, hospitality, and government. The sales organization had to grow to support these new markets.

Several factors contributed to the successful expansion of the Initiate Systems sales force. First, the company hired a very experienced director of sales to lead the initiative. This individual had many customer contacts in the new market areas, enabling him to jump-start the selling process. Next, the company hired four experienced salespeople, all located near its Chicago headquarters. Locating all salespeople together allowed them to work with each other and share ideas, and to easily tap into corporate resources. To attract the best possible people, the company guaranteed salespeople a commission draw for two quarters. The first quarter draw was given clear and free, while the second quarter draw was recoverable, netting out of real commissions earned. Since the salespeople were all very experienced, no formal training program was required. Instead, the director of sales traveled with each salesperson to provide guidance. Salespeople moved up the learning curve quickly and started earning real commissions within six months.

Downsizing

Downsizing a sales force is a difficult process. Companies that downsize typically face pressure to act quickly to reduce costs. The inherent uncertainty causes intense anxiety among salespeople and managers. Redesigning a sales force during downsizing is often a stressful and emotionally draining experience.

Strong sales leadership is essential during downsizing. In order to minimize the pain to the organization, survivors need to know as quickly as possible that they have a job – these are the people the company cannot afford to lose. Those that are asked to leave should be told with sensitivity and offered appropriate help with career placement. Throughout the downsizing process, timely and straightforward communication from management is crucial for maintaining sales force morale and motivation. Truth is much more important than trying to put an artificial positive spin on events.

A major challenge in any downsizing situation is addressing the question of "*Who stays and who leaves?*" Ideally, the company creates the best

---

Multiple waves of downsizing and its effect on motivation

During the downsizing of a sales force for a telecommunication company, managers attended a one-day workshop on how to fire salespeople. Since this was the third (and they knew not the last) downsizing at the firm, managers wondered, "I wonder if someone is being trained on how to fire me." Morale and motivation were at new lows, and had not hit bottom yet.

---

possible design for its new smaller sales organization and then places the best performing salespeople into roles within that organization. Average and weak performers are asked to leave, and the overall performance level of the sales force improves. Unfortunately, this scenario is often difficult to achieve. To the extent that the company's best salespeople and managers are located in the right places and have the right skills to fill new roles, the decisions are fairly straightforward. However, there will be some good salespeople and managers who have skills or work in locations that are no longer needed. At the same time, weaker salespeople and managers may have some skills or work in locations that are needed. Companies that want to be fair and avoid lawsuits should use criteria that are consistent and objective when making decisions about who stays and who leaves in a downsizing. Specific rules should be established about which salespeople should be given priority when redundancies occur. Factors such as tenure with the company and historical performance ratings, as well as a candidate's current job assignment and home location, need to be considered and applied fairly and consistently across the sales force.

The salespeople who survive a downsizing have to work larger sales territories. They may need help with prioritizing how to spend their time most productively. The company can provide guidance through training, as well as information on account histories or revised target lists that refocus sales force attention on the most important accounts. Performance expectations of salespeople may need revision as well.

Focusing on key customers is very important when a sales force downsizes. Downsizing creates uncertainty for customers. A customer may be concerned about the financial health of the selling company or may fear that the job of the salesperson assigned to his or her account will be eliminated. These fears can compel customers to consider competitive offerings. Thus, attention to maintaining key customer relationships is especially important when a sales force downsizes.

Sales Force Creation

Companies in many different situations can have a need to create a new sales force. A start-up company may decide to establish a new sales force

---

Elf Lubricants downsizes while shifting workload to telesales

The leading player in the French lubricants market, Elf Lubricants, faced a significant decline in sales during the late 1990s, as European cars became more efficient, engine technology improved, and the intervals between oil changes increased. In an effort to improve its market position and control costs, management decided to downsize the company, while it focused on key growth sectors. The sales force was reduced significantly, and each remaining salesperson was responsible for handling a larger number of accounts. To help salespeople manage this increased workload, Elf set up a call center to handle customer orders and complaints. This shift returned the company to profitability while meeting customer needs. Telephone orders cost the company 10 percent of what it had cost to take an order in person at the customer site. Customers supported the change since the highly trained telesales representatives serviced their needs quickly.

to launch its first product. A company that sells through distributors may establish its own sales force to gain better control of the sales process. A company with an existing sales force may create a new sales force to sell a new product if existing salespeople lack the time or expertise needed for success. Table 10.2 summarizes several reasons why companies establish new sales forces to support both new and existing markets and products.

Customer relationship transition and sales force downsizing

Careful planning for customer relationship transition is an important part of a successful downsizing effort. When an industrial distributor downsized its sales force, account transition and retention was taken very seriously at the firm's largest customers. Each large customer that was transferred to a different salesperson was introduced to the new salesperson by another salesperson or sales manager who was already familiar with the account. The team worked together to ensure a smooth transition. As a result, no loss in sales occurred at these large accounts. However, at medium-sized accounts, relationship transition was not emphasized. Many of these accounts were not transitioned effectively to a different salesperson and sales to this customer segment decreased by 20 percent.

Creating a new sales force is exciting. The company has a unique opportunity to create an organization from scratch, based solely on market needs and company goals. Decisions are not constrained by the desires or shortcomings of existing salespeople, established account relationships, or other historical baggage. Companies can take advantage of this unique opportunity by investing the time to design the best sales force the first time. Once the sales force is in place, almost every change will be met with some resistance from a customer, a salesperson, a sales manager, or a stakeholder in another company department.

Most sales leaders are action-oriented. When told to create a new sales force, their first reaction is to start hiring salespeople immediately. This is a mistake. If a newly created sales force is to succeed, careful upfront planning and design are essential. The drivers in the definer category – including all the sales force design issues discussed in Chapters 2 through 8 of this book – should be addressed before any hiring, beyond the very highest levels within the sales organization, takes place. The definer drivers include the sales strategy and the go-to-market strategy, as well as sales force structure and role definition, size, and deployment. By addressing the definer drivers first, the firm avoids many hiring mistakes, such as hiring a salesperson with the wrong skills in the wrong location. In addition, having an overall design in place up front encourages compatibility and

TABLE 10.2 Need for sales force creation

		Product	
		Existing	**New**
Market	**Existing**	May need to create a new sales force if: • No sales force exists currently • Markets change radically • New selling processes are required • Specialty field forces are necessary • Distributors are ineffective • Distribution terms are unfavorable • Distributor results are untraceable • A merger or acquisition occurs	May need to create a new sales force if: • No sales force exists currently • Current salespeople or distributors lack requisite new skills • Distribution terms are unfavorable • Distributor results are untraceable • Product expertise resulting from specialization is essential for success • Substantial sales and profits are anticipated • Introduction of other new products is expected to leverage the new sales force
	New	May need to create a new sales force if: • No sales force exists currently • Current salespeople or distributors lack necessary contacts • Distribution terms are unfavorable • Distributor results are untraceable • Market expertise resulting from specialization is essential for success • Substantial sales and profits are anticipated • Entry into other new markets is expected to leverage the new sales force	May need to create a new sales force if: • No sales force exists currently • Current salespeople or distributors lack new skills or contacts • Distribution terms are unfavorable • Distributor results are untraceable • Sales specialization is essential for success • Substantial sales and profits are anticipated • Introduction of other new products is expected to leverage the new sales force • Entry into other new markets is expected to leverage the new sales force

alignment of the various processes and systems that shape, enlighten, excite, and control the sales force.

Table 10.3 provides a suggested timing of activities for creating a new sales force and marketing organization. Initial planning should begin approximately 18 to 24 months before the new sales force is to be in place.

Creating new sales forces in known and unknown environments

The keys to successful sales force creation vary depending upon whether the new sales force will sell in an established or a new selling environment. Creating a sales force in a known environment is typically much easier. For example, a start-up biotechnology company launching its first sales force to sell a new drug can build upon established best practices in the biopharmaceutical industry. Success strategies might include studying the design of other sales forces, hiring people with industry experience, and figuring out how to execute more effectively. Creating a sales force in an unknown environment, on the other hand, is much harder, and requires the ability to adapt as the vision changes while on the learning curve. For example, when the Internet first emerged as a viable business channel, many start-up dot-com companies struggled to figure out the best way to sell their services in an entirely new environment. There were no existing paradigms to build upon; designing a sales force required creativity and vision. Successful companies spent a lot of time addressing questions of sales strategy (who to call on, what to sell, how to sell it) and remained flexible to change that strategy as they learned through experience.

Sales force creation at Iron Mountain Inc.

In 2000, Boston-based records management firm Iron Mountain Inc. wanted to create a sales force to launch its new document shredding service. The principals who sold the firm's traditional services, such as corporate records storage and off-site data protection, were skilled at consultative selling and long-term customer relationship management. The new service, however, required a totally different kind of sales force, one oriented towards high-volume, transaction-based selling.

Management began the sales force creation process by focusing on sales strategy. They addressed questions such as: Who is the customer? How do they want to buy the service? What sales process is needed for success? A well-thought-out sales strategy provided the basis for the development of a hiring profile. Candidates with backgrounds in high-volume sales (for example, sellers of copier equipment or telecommunications services to small and medium-size businesses), were recruited and hired to fill 22 sales positions.

Measuring the performance of salespeople in the new sales force was tricky. Management did not know what the success rate for the new service would be. So rather than rewarding salespeople based on sales results, the sales force was initially evaluated based on effort metrics such as the number of calls made or proposals generated.

TABLE 10.3 Suggested sales force creation activity timing

Time frame (months pre-formation)

24–18	18–12	12–9
Hire sales/marketing vice president	**Determine resource needs**	**Establish distribution channels****
• Determine job profile	• Identify activity requirements	**Define sales force vision**
• Identify candidates	• Design H.O. management team	• Determine desired culture
• Screen candidates	• Define roles and responsibilities	• Establish sales force objectives
• Select best candidate	• Develop job descriptions	• Identify best practices
Identify target customers	**Hire director of marketing***	**Acquire and integrate information/data**
• Estimate overall market opportunity	• Determine job profile	• Determine information needs
• Segment overall market	• Identify candidates	• Identify data sources
• Value market segments	• Screen candidates	• Select data vendors
• Determine target customer segments	• Select best candidate	• Build databases
• Profile target customers	**Hire director of sales***	**Determine sales force design**
• Understand target customer needs	* If a director-level split is required	• Identify indispensable activities
• Estimate competitive spending		• Define sales force channels and roles
		• Design organizational structure
		• Determine optimal sales force size
		** If distribution coverage is required to complement direct sales force:
		• Analyze distribution needs and identify partners
		• Negotiate distribution terms
		• Select channel partners and build relationships
		• Design incentive system and measurement system
		• Develop distributor quotas

Time frame (months pre-formation)

9-6	6-3	3-1
Determine deployment strategy	**Hire sales managers**	**Initiate training program**
• Create workload/market potential index	• Identify activity requirements	**Design measurement program**
• Identify preliminary regional deployment	• Define roles and responsibilities	• Determine sales performance goals
• Design geographic sales territories	• Develop job descriptions	• Establish measurement criteria
Design sales support program	**Design training program**	• Develop management systems
Design compensation program	• Determine training needs	• Develop performance review process
• Determine compensation objectives	• Define course modules	**Design automation program**
• Establish compensation criteria	• Identify trainers/training vendors	• Determine automation needs
• Determine base salary levels	• Select trainers/training vendors	• Identify automation vendors
• Design incentive compensation plan	**Hire sales representatives**	• Select automation vendor
• Develop quotas	• Identify activity requirements	**Visit key customers**
	• Define roles and responsibilities	• Announce sales force launch
	• Develop job descriptions	• Understand key customers' needs
		• Identify service expectations
		• Negotiate purchase agreements

> ## Sales force creation at CV Therapeutics
>
> In 2003, biopharmaceutical company CV Therapeutics submitted its first new drug application to the FDA for approval of Ranexa™, a novel cardiovascular drug that treats angina. As the company awaits FDA approval (expected in 2004), management is working feverishly to lay the foundation for a sales organization that can successfully launch the new product. The company plans to hire, train, and deploy a cardiology specialist sales force as quickly as possible after receiving FDA approval. For this to happen successfully, a great deal of upfront planning is necessary.
>
> The company has hired a VP of Sales with extensive experience leading biotechnology and cardiovascular sales forces to lead the effort of building a sales and marketing infrastructure at the firm. Already, a comprehensive plan for hiring and training the national sales force has been developed. Recruiting agencies and contractors have been screened and selected. In addition, an employee referral program has been initiated. A compensation plan has also been created including benefits, salary ranges, and incentive pay. Hiring can begin as soon as FDA approval is received. As soon as hiring is completed, the company plans to bring the new sales force together as a team within one week to begin training.

Mergers and Acquisitions

The implementation of a sales force redesign can be especially challenging when a company acquires or merges with another company. Mergers almost always imply change. If both companies already have sales forces in place, there are usually redundancies in coverage, management demands cost reductions, and downsizing is likely. In addition to facing all the challenges of downsizing, mergers add the complexity of combining two sales forces that may have very different skills, experiences, and cultures. When two companies of roughly equal size merge, the integration process can be extremely difficult as the merged company strives to blend the two different cultures and build on the best aspects of each. When a larger company acquires a smaller company, the integration is typically somewhat easier, but is still challenging. The acquired sales force must assimilate successfully into the dominant culture. In either case, the company is challenged to protect its strengths by holding onto its best salespeople and customers while completing the transition.

> ## Computer Associates encourages acquired company's sales force to stay
>
> Attrition is often high during corporate acquisitions. When Computer Associates acquired Legent Corporation in 1995, the company was fearful that many good Legent salespeople would leave due to the uncertainty created by the merger. In order to increase retention of Legent salespeople, Computer Associates doubled the commissions of the Legent sales force for the next year.

Typically during a merger, sales leaders feel pressure to create a merged sales organization as quickly and as cheaply as possible. The longer the integration takes, the longer salespeople will wait, anticipate, worry and therefore be internally focused rather than focusing on their customers. In the meantime, aggressive competitors will take advantage of the situation by stealing the company's best customers and salespeople. Speed of implementation also enhances sales force acceptance of change. There is a short window of opportunity following a merger announcement when change is anticipated and expected by the sales force. Over time, the implementation of further change becomes more difficult because salespeople will expect greater stability in their jobs.

The intense pressure to cut costs quickly following a merger or acquisition can lead to three common sales force design mistakes. First, there is a tendency to downsize too much. Companies frequently believe that every department throughout the company should "share the pain" equally. However since the sales force drives the top line, excessive downsizing leads to both immediate and long-term sales loss. Second, there is frequently a "conquer" mentality on the part of the stronger company, which is usually the larger company. Instead of blending the best of both sales force systems, the stronger company takes over, even though there may be much to learn and maintain from the processes and systems of the smaller player. Third, the pressure to move quickly causes insufficient effort to be devoted to the design of the new sales organization.

Despite the intense time and cost pressure, companies should not overlook the fact that a merger provides a unique opportunity to draw on the best practices of two different sales organizations and build a new and superior organization that blends the best of both, or to fix things that have been broken for a long time. By following an organized sales force redesign process, it is possible for a company to proactively create a new and better merged organization and at the same time, do it quickly.

Restructuring

A sales force restructure has the potential to affect the life of virtually every salesperson and every customer of a company. For example, Table 10.4 highlights the salesperson and customer impact of sales force restructures that occurred at CIBA Vision and Xerox. More detail on both of these restructures is provided in Chapter 1 of this book.

When a sales force restructures, significant management attention is directed toward the definer category of sales force drivers. Major sales force structure changes can have an incredible positive impact on a firm, but they are also risky. The disruption of a restructure has the potential to jeopardize customer relationships, hinder the achievement of a revenue

368   Sales Force Design for Strategic Advantage

Merging the Hewlett Packard and Compaq Computers sales forces

The 2002 merger of Hewlett Packard (HP) and Compaq Computers was the largest in computer industry history and created an organization of 140,000 people. HP and Compaq had been rivals for years, selling against one another at the same accounts. Bringing together the consensus-building team-focused HP organization with the fast paced aggressive sales culture of Compaq was a challenge.

Joint teams working on the integration effort, dubbed clean room, had access to confidential and sensitive materials from both companies.

The go-to-market integration team was faced with the task of integrating two large, diverse sales organizations. The companies both had large sales forces consisting of generalists (account managers) supported by specialists (product line experts). However, the two companies had very different field operations approaches. HP was a centralized organization with a strong headquarters group that made most field force decisions including defining market segments, deciding upon the number of salespeople for each area, and determining the ratio of sales force generalists to sales force specialists. Compaq, on the other hand, had a decentralized organization. The integration team determined that the new company should operate with a balance between the efficiencies of centralized sales deployment definitions and guidelines, and the agility and flexibility of making decisions as close to the customer as possible.

The company organized its go-to-market efforts along four customer segments: Corporate Accounts, Enterprise Accounts, Small & Medium Businesses, and Consumers. Throughout countries and regions around the world, the sales force is organized around these customer segments. Four customer-facing generalist sales forces are the primary customer contact, one for each of the customer segments. Over ten specialty sales forces that provide specific expertise in areas such as storage, software, servers, outsourcing, consulting, services, workstations, personal computers, printers, and supplies support them. The sales forces in each segment are also complemented and supplemented by additional sales channels such as indirect channels of distribution, call centers, and web based selling.

In many situations, HP and Compaq salespeople were calling on the same accounts. Prior to the merger, the integration team defined which salesperson (HP or Compaq) would retain each account. Customer input was used to make this decision for large accounts. For smaller accounts, the integration team analyzed data and solicited sales force input to make decisions. One goal of the integration was to increase the coverage and reach of the sales force. Many salespeople that lost accounts were given accounts that were not previously covered by either company.

Extensive planning, good communication, and swift implementation helped HP avoid losing many customers after the merger. The day the merger closed, HP released detailed product road maps that could be communicated immediately to customers. Also, a new management structure was announced including defined account teams for the top 100 customers. The entire sales force received clear instructions on how to operate initially within the new company.

Six months following the merger, the sales force integration was nearly complete. All members of the sales organization knew their assignments and had received all required cross-product training. Those being laid-off had been notified and a unified sales compensation plan for those remaining had been launched. The entire 6000-person sales organization attended a four-day meeting in Las Vegas that was focused on creating "Passion for customers". The meeting helped begin to define the new sales culture and also served to bring the organization together, especially during the surprise 70-minute concert by John Cougar Mellencamp.

goal, or trigger excessive sales force turnover. For these reasons, companies never take major sales force structure changes lightly. They are typically willing to invest significant time and resources to developing the best possible sales force design. Companies often create task forces for this purpose. A sales force redesign task force can include key personnel from within the company, as well as members from outside the company such as customers, distribution partners, or consultants.

When a sales force restructures, significant management attention is also directed toward the shaper and enlightener categories of sales force drivers. Salespeople need to be hired or retrained to take on new roles and responsibilities. For example, at Xerox a salesperson who sold copiers before the 1985 restructure had to be trained in how to sell the firm's entire product and service portfolio, including information processing systems, printing systems, office systems, and sales engineering. The company implemented an extensive multi-year training program in order to accomplish this massive retraining effort. At CIBA Vision, 45 new salespeople had to be hired and trained quickly to fill positions in the new sales force structure. A well-structured, intensive hiring and training process enabled the company to get the new salespeople hired, trained, and out into the field in just over two months.

New data and tools are also required after a restructure to enlighten salespeople about their new responsibilities. For example at Xerox, new information systems were installed in district sales offices to provide salespeople with quick access to up-to-date customer, product, and competitive data. Major sales force restructures frequently also affect performance management and compensation systems.

FIVE CHANGE IMPLEMENTATION INSIGHTS

Where is the Money?

Successful companies ensure that their strengths are protected whenever a change is made to the sales force. Understand where most of the money is currently coming from. Who is selling what to whom? During a sales force transition, keen attention to the salespeople and customers who are responsible for much of the sales almost always pays off. Which customers are the most important, and what impact will the change have on them? How

TABLE 10.4 Examples of the salesperson and customer impact of sales force restructuring

CIBA Vision 2003 – restructuring from generalists to product specialists

	Sales force structure	Salesperson perspective	Customer perspective
Before	Single generalist sales force sells contact lenses and solutions to eye care practitioners	Sell all company product lines Have total responsibility for meeting all customer needs Work a smaller geographic sales territory	Work with one salesperson who sells the company's full product line
After	Two product-specialty sales forces – one sells lenses and one sells solutions to eye care practitioners	Sell just one product line Share customer responsibility with a salesperson in another product division Work a larger geographic sales territory	Work with two salespeople, each with specialized expertise in a particular product line

Xerox 1985 – restructuring from product specialists to market specialists

	Sales force structure	Salesperson perspective	Customer perspective
Before	Five product specialty sales forces. Each sells a specific Xerox product line to customers of all sizes and types	Sell a specific company product line Sell to a variety of customer types and sizes Share customer responsibility with salespeople in four other product divisions	Work with five separate sales teams, each with specialized expertise in a particular product line
After	Five market-specialty sales forces. Each sells all Xerox product lines to a specific size and type of customer	Sell all company product lines Focus on a specific type or size of customer Have total responsibility for meeting all customer needs	Work with one sales team that sells the company's full product line and has expertise in working with businesses of similar size and type

---

Key success factors during any sales force transition

Effective implementation of significant sales force change during any type of transition is typically enhanced through the following:

- Focus on customers and the use of customer impact as a primary guiding principle.
- Use of task forces to create better and more widely accepted answers.
- Rapid transition to reduce uncertainty and to shift focus quickly away from internal changes and toward customers.
- Best practice orientation for developing outstanding people, processes, and systems.
- Extensive communication from top management that encourages spirit of cooperation and collaboration and minimizes unproductive rumors and speculation.
- Targeted third-party involvement to minimize internally focused agendas, avoid conflict between departments, and enhance speed of implementation.

---

will the firm take care of these customers during the transition? The impact of a sales force change should also be evaluated from the perspective of the firm's top salespeople. What orders are in the pipeline? Which salespeople are responsible for the sales and how will you take care of them? "Taking care of" top salespeople might include assuring that they continue to get paid fairly, providing encouragement and recognition, involving them in the change process, and communicating with them to remove their uncertainty.

The Biggest Single Reason that Sales Force Design Change Efforts Fail is Because the Impact on Salespeople is Not Managed Effectively

People will naturally resist changes that threaten their security, opportunity, or self-esteem. Salespeople, like others, want to be successful. Any change that is perceived as a threat to success will be met with resistance. At the same time, salespeople know that they have customer power. They may be the customer's most important and sometimes only connection with the company. When sales force change is not managed effectively, salespeople can use this customer power as a source of leverage to get what they want. For example, a good salesperson whose territory is reduced during a sales force expansion may threaten to go work for a competitor and take his or her best customers along, unless his or her compensation is protected. Successful change plans often include a person-by-person assessment of how the change will affect each person in the sales force in terms of their responsibilities, role, and earnings opportunity.

The Probability of Success Diminishes as the Complexity of the Sales Force Design Change Increases

Complex sales force design changes can severely disrupt customers, salespeople, sales managers, support structures, and internal processes and systems. It is very challenging to keep a business going while such changes are taking place. Complex changes are also, to some extent, a "leap into the unknown" for most companies. While there are many contingencies the firm can plan for, the number of unanticipated situations grows significantly as change complexity increases. For these reasons, the more complex a sales force design change is, the more difficult it will be to implement successfully.

Implementation Begins at Design

Sales force design and implementation begin at the same time. A sales force redesign effort can only be successful if the process of determining the right sales force structure and size is closely linked to the plan for transitioning the organization to that structure and size. For example, if major changes are anticipated, involving all the stakeholders in the design assures a better answer, and makes the transition easier.

Most sales force design efforts begin with a reasonable idea of the general type of solution that will emerge. For example, during a merger, companies often have a size reduction in mind. During a transformation from product to customer focus, the creation of customer teams is an almost certain outcome. During the launch of several new products, a sales force expansion and restructure is likely. In each of these cases, it is possible and useful to identify the helping factors and the barriers up-front. Then, processes that leverage the helping factors and address barriers and fears can be created.

Successful implementation plans specify the communication channels that will be used throughout the sales force redesign process. In the earliest stages of any sales force redesign effort, it is important to identify which stakeholders including customers, salespeople, sales managers, need to be involved in clarifying the issues, coming up with the solution, challenging the solution, and implementing the solution. For each stakeholder, appropriate communication channels such as meetings, events, and training can be planned.

Change is About Changing Oneself

Most people, particularly those in leadership positions in companies, frequently view change as something that is needed of others. "In the new structure, I want my people to spend more time with customers and less time doing administrative work," says a sales vice president. Yet in order to make this happen, is the VP willing to stop asking questions of the sales force and triggering initiatives that create the administrative work? "We need more teamwork," asserts another sales leader. Yet does this leader demonstrate teamwork by showing respect for her counterparts in marketing, service, technical support, and logistics? Change efforts are often about leaders changing their behaviors so that others are inspired to follow in their footsteps.